Applications and Strategic Implementation of AI in Policing

Eric Halford
https://orcid.org/0000-0002-3913-1679
Rabdan Academy, UAE

IGI Global
Scientific Publishing
Publishing Tomorrow's Research Today

Vice President of Editorial	Melissa Wagner
Director of Acquisitions	Mikaela Felty
Director of Book Development	Jocelynn Hessler
Production Manager	Mike Brehm
Cover Design	Jose Rosado

Published in the United States of America by
IGI Global Scientific Publishing
701 East Chocolate Avenue
Hershey, PA, 17033, USA
Tel: 717-533-8845 | Fax: 717-533-7115
Website: https://www.igi-global.com E-mail: cust@igi-global.com

Library of Congress Cataloging-in-Publication Data

LCCN: 2025043917 (CIP Data Pending)
ISBN13: 9798337352282
Isbn13Softcover: 9798337352299
EISBN13: 9798337352305
British Cataloguing in Publication Data
A Cataloguing in Publication record for this book is available from the British Library.

Table of Contents

Detailed Table of Contents

UK policing is being gainfully encouraged to adopt new technologies as a requirement to become more productive with limited resources, but also to reflect the society it polices. The extent to which AI systems, tools, and algorithms are being adopted, and the pace of adoption, is overplayed. The field has a natural and historic affinity with Complexity Theory, which it is argued is a compelling framework for public service administration in the age of AI augmentation. Epistemology and methodology are explored, using hypernetwork theory as a mathematical tool for prioritising data maturity functions that represent police organisations within operating model design. The argument is made that the application of AI will not be successful, or be accepted by the public, without an effective data foundation strategy. An example is provided of a data strategy for a UK metropolitan police force, adapted from Carruthers and Jackson (2022), as applied to organisational priorities reflective of the hypernetworks modelled.

The chapter examines the application of Artificial Intelligence (AI) in policing in Himachal Pradesh, India, and its implications for privacy, governance, and ethical accountability. It analyses AI-enabled initiatives such as predictive analytics, facial recognition, smart traffic surveillance, and cyber-crime intelligence within the legal framework of Section 69 of the Information Technology Act, 2000 and the landmark

K.S. Puttaswamy v. Union of India (2017) judgment on the right to privacy. Using reliable secondary data, the study adopts an exploratory and descriptive research design to assess institutional collaborations, capacity-building initiatives, and technological deployments by the Himachal Pradesh Police. The findings highlight concerns related to algorithmic bias, data retention, transparency, and accountability. The paper proposes policy measures to align AI-based policing with constitutional principles through judicial oversight, ethical audits, data minimisation, and citizen-centric governance.

Artificial Intelligence (AI) is gradually shaping the future of modern investigative policing with enhanced operational effectiveness, predictive capability, and evidence analysis. This chapter examines the strategic application of AI in law enforcement, focusing on its applications, benefits, limitations, and guidelines for ethical and responsible implementation. While AI offers powerful technologies for crime prediction, digital forensic analysis, and monitoring, it also poses phenomenal risks with regard to privacy, bias, and transparency. Effective deployment depends on a multi-stakeholder strategy that incorporates technical readiness, cultural sensitivity, legal safeguards, and co-design through user participation. Drawing on examinations of world models of governance, sectoral cases, and evolving AI threats such as deepfakes and self-operating machines, this book stresses the importance of proactive governance and continuous monitoring.

This chapter presents a governance sensitive architecture for AI integrated police education that treats officer formation as ontological reconstitution rather than technical retrofit. It integrates andragogy, experiential and situated cognition, diffusion and sociotechnical adoption theory, and competency-based engineering to build simulation intensive, adaptive, analytically instrumented curricula. The chapter details cyber-physical simulation, algorithmic personalization, multimodal assessment, and stackable micro credentials across the career arc, and specifies an operating model that synchronizes curriculum, incentives, oversight, and financing with mitigations for culture, infrastructure, privacy, and budgets. Polycentric governance, fairness by design, and public dashboards convert learning into civic

Accurate crime scene documentation is critical for investigations. Traditional methods are labor-intensive, error-prone, and fail to capture 3D data. LiDAR and Deep Learning (DL) offer solutions: LiDAR provides precise 3D point clouds, while DL automates analysis. Models like PointNet, PointNet++, and DGCNN enable object detection, segmentation, and classification. Challenges include high computational demands and sensitivity to sparse data. Integrating LiDAR and DL improves reconstruction, semantic understanding, and evidence documentation. Low-cost LiDAR and efficient DL models offer practical opportunities for low-resource settings. This review (2015–2025) highlights gaps and potential in LiDAR–DL fusion for crime scene investigations.

The machines gain increasing computational capacity in deep learning algorithms results in generation of highly realistic videos, termed as deepfake videos. These videos are especially face-swapped deepfakes and are very risky because they may be employed for some malevolent intentions. This proposal concerns the differentiation between a real and a deepfake using a novel hybrid approach in deep learning through a Res-Next Convolutional Neural Network that followed the architecture of Long Short-Term Memory based Recurrent Neural Network. Its frame-level feature extraction was performed through a Res-Next Convolutional Neural Network that performs both replacement and recreation of deepfakes videos.

Preface

INTRODUCTION

As Editor of *Applications and Strategic Implementation of AI in Policing*, I am pleased to present this timely and forward-looking volume that examines one of the most consequential transformations in contemporary law enforcement. Artificial Intelligence (AI) is no longer a speculative or emerging concept; it is an active and rapidly evolving force reshaping policing, intelligence, and security practices across the globe.

This edited collection brings together a diverse group of scholars, practitioners, and subject-matter experts who collectively explore the opportunities, challenges, and implications of AI in policing. Their contributions reflect both the promise and the complexity of integrating advanced technologies into systems that are inherently human-centered, legally constrained, and socially accountable.

The book is structured around three interconnected dimensions that define the current and future landscape of AI in policing.

First, strategic implementation addresses perhaps the most critical question: how AI can be responsibly and effectively embedded within law enforcement organizations. Beyond technological capability, successful adoption depends on governance frameworks, ethical oversight, legal compliance, workforce readiness, and organizational change management. Contributors in this section offer practical models and evaluative approaches that can guide agencies in navigating these complexities while maintaining public trust and accountability.

Second, criminal application examines how offenders are increasingly leveraging AI to facilitate, enhance, and conceal criminal activities. From automated phishing campaigns to deepfake-enabled fraud and adaptive cyberattacks, AI is transforming the modus operandi of criminal actors. Understanding these developments is essential for anticipating emerging threats and building resilient countermeasures.

Third, law enforcement use cases highlight how agencies worldwide are adopting AI-driven tools to enhance operational efficiency and effectiveness. These applications span predictive analytics, digital forensics, surveillance augmentation, resource allocation, and administrative optimization. The chapters in this section provide insight into both the capabilities and the limitations of current systems, grounded in real-world deployments and case studies.

This volume is intended for a broad audience, including policing and intelligence professionals, security practitioners, government policymakers, and scholars and students. It aims not only to inform but also to provoke thoughtful consideration of how AI should be designed, deployed, and governed within the unique context of law enforcement.

As Editor, I hope this work contributes meaningfully to ongoing dialogue and decision-making in this critical domain. The integration of AI into policing is not simply a technical evolution; it is a strategic and societal shift that demands careful reflection, interdisciplinary collaboration, and responsible leadership.

ORGANIZATION OF THE BOOK

In **Chapter 1**, Philip Davies offers a grounded and critical perspective on the current state of AI adoption within United Kingdom policing, challenging prevailing narratives that overstate both the pace and maturity of technological integration. Drawing on Complexity Theory and hypernetwork modelling, the chapter emphasizes that successful AI deployment is fundamentally contingent on robust data foundations and organizational readiness. Davies compellingly argues that without strategic data maturity and coherent operating models, AI initiatives risk failure both operationally and in terms of public legitimacy, providing a practical framework through a metropolitan police data strategy.

Chapter 2 by Kundesh Sharma shifts the focus to governance, presenting a nuanced examination of algorithmic policing in Himachal Pradesh, India. The chapter situates AI deployment within constitutional and legal frameworks, particularly the right to privacy, and highlights the tensions between technological innovation and civil liberties. Through an analysis of real-world implementations, Sharma underscores critical concerns such as algorithmic bias, transparency, and accountability, ultimately advancing policy recommendations that align AI-driven policing with democratic and constitutional safeguards.

In **Chapter 3**, Muhammad Usman Tariq explores the strategic integration of AI into investigative policing, offering a comprehensive overview of operational use cases alongside governance challenges. The chapter highlights the transformative potential of AI in predictive analytics and digital forensics, while simultaneously addressing risks related to bias, privacy, and transparency. Importantly, it advocates for a multi-stakeholder, co-designed approach to implementation, emphasizing that sustainable adoption requires not only technical capability but also cultural, legal, and ethical alignment.

Chapter 4, authored by Ashraf Alam, advances the discussion into the domain of police education, proposing a forward-looking, governance-sensitive architecture for AI-integrated learning. Rather than viewing AI as a mere technical enhancement, Alam conceptualizes it as a catalyst for the ontological transformation of policing professionals. The chapter outlines an innovative model incorporating simulation-based learning, adaptive curricula, and polycentric governance, while maintaining a strong emphasis on ethical safeguards, public accountability, and institutional legitimacy.

In **Chapter 5**, Petros Violakis provides a critical examination of the criminal application of AI, exploring how offenders exploit advanced technologies to enhance and conceal illicit activities. Grounded in established criminological theories, the chapter introduces a structured offender classification framework and presents empirical insights into AI misuse patterns. Violakis not only highlights the evolving threat landscape but also offers targeted policy recommendations aimed at strengthening detection capabilities and mitigating the risks associated with dual-use technologies.

Chapter 6, authored by Angelo Brown presents a case study of AI-driven policing in the United States, offering a balanced assessment of its promises and pitfalls. Through comparative analysis and city-level case studies, the chapter reveals persistent challenges in oversight, transparency, and effectiveness. By contrasting the fragmented U.S. regulatory environment with more centralized European approaches, Brown provides valuable insights into governance models and concludes with pragmatic recommendations for ensuring accountability and public trust in AI-enabled policing.

In **Chapter 7**, Afshan Razzaq critically examines the use of facial recognition technologies in UK policing through a human rights lens. The chapter argues that, in the absence of AI-specific legislation, current practices risk undermining fundamental rights. By synthesizing existing literature, Razzaq calls for proactive legal and regulatory intervention, emphasizing the need to address ethical and civil liberties concerns before they become entrenched within policing systems.

Chapter 8, by Apiwe Macingwane and Omowunmi Isafiade, introduces a technically robust approach to crime hotspot detection using streaming data analytics. By integrating multi-factor weighting mechanisms with clustering algorithms such as DenStream and CluStream, the chapter demonstrates how real-time data processing can enhance resource allocation and operational decision-making. The authors provide a compelling case for the practical deployment of these models, particularly in contexts requiring timely and data-driven policing responses.

In **Chapter 9**, Mfundo Maneli, Omowunmi Isafiade, and Oluwasola Adedayo explore the integration of LiDAR and deep learning technologies for 3D crime scene reconstruction. The chapter highlights the limitations of traditional documentation methods and presents a forward-looking review of technological advancements that enable more accurate and semantically rich representations of crime scenes. It also addresses practical challenges and opportunities, particularly for low-resource environments, positioning LiDAR–DL fusion as a transformative tool for investigative practice.

Chapter 10 presents a focused exploration of deepfake detection, where Ganesh Kumar K and colleagues propose a hybrid deep learning framework combining ResNeXt and LSTM architectures. The chapter addresses the growing threat of synthetic media in criminal contexts and demonstrates how advanced neural network models can be leveraged to distinguish between authentic and manipulated video content. This contribution underscores the importance of developing countermeasures to emerging AI-enabled threats.

Finally, **Chapter 11**, by Nikhil Kumar Goyal examines the evolving intersection of AI and cybercrime, with particular attention to ransomware and advanced persistent threats. The chapter highlights how AI enhances the sophistication, scale, and persistence of cyberattacks, while also complicating law enforcement responses due to jurisdictional and attribution challenges. Goyal's analysis reinforces the dual-use nature of AI and calls for strengthened legal and institutional frameworks to address these emerging threats.

Together, these chapters reflect the breadth and depth of contemporary scholarship and practice in AI-enabled policing. They collectively reinforce a central theme of this volume: that while AI offers transformative potential, its successful application depends on thoughtful governance, ethical integrity, and strategic implementation.

CONCLUSION

As this volume draws to a close, it is evident that Artificial Intelligence stands at a turning point in the evolution of policing, one that is as transformative as it is complex. The contributions brought together in this collection collectively affirm that AI is neither a panacea nor a peril in isolation; rather, it is a powerful socio-technical force whose impact will ultimately be shaped by the choices of those who design, govern, and deploy it.

Across the chapters, several unifying insights emerge. First, the successful integration of AI in policing is fundamentally dependent on strong institutional foundations, particularly in relation to data quality, organizational readiness, and professional capability. Second, the governance of AI must remain central to its adoption. Issues of accountability, transparency, fairness, and legality are not peripheral concerns but core determinants of legitimacy and public trust. Third, the dual-use nature of AI, its capacity to both prevent and facilitate crime, demands that law enforcement agencies remain adaptive, forward-looking, and collaborative in their approach.

Importantly, this volume also highlights that technological innovation must not outpace ethical reflection or democratic oversight. The future of AI in policing will not be defined solely by advances in algorithms or computational power, but by the extent to which these tools are aligned with the principles of justice, proportionality, and human rights. In this regard, the role of policymakers, practitioners, and scholars is both shared and continuous.

It is my hope that this collection serves not only as a reference point for current practice and research, but also as a catalyst for ongoing dialogue and critical inquiry. The path forward requires interdisciplinary collaboration, sustained investment in governance frameworks, and a commitment to ensuring that innovation enhances—rather than undermines—the social contract between law enforcement institutions and the communities they serve.

In closing, the strategic implementation of AI in policing is not simply a question of capability, but of responsibility. The decisions made today will shape the contours of policing for generations to come. It is therefore incumbent upon us to proceed with both ambition and caution, guided by evidence, ethics, and an unwavering commitment to the public good.

Eric Halford
Rabdan Academy, UAE

Acknowledgement

This edited volume has benefited from the time, expertise, and intellectual generosity of a diverse and highly knowledgeable group of contributors. Bringing together scholars, practitioners, and subject-matter experts from different jurisdictions and professional backgrounds, the book reflects the breadth and complexity of contemporary debate surrounding artificial intelligence in policing. The chapters collectively span strategic implementation, criminal application, and operational use cases, offering perspectives that are critical, applied, and forward-looking. In this respect, I am sincerely grateful to all chapter authors for their commitment, professionalism, and willingness to contribute to a volume addressing such a timely and consequential area of policing scholarship and practice.

This volume has also been strengthened by its international reach. With contributions addressing policing and AI across multiple national and institutional contexts, the book benefits from a genuinely comparative perspective. This breadth has been essential in ensuring that the discussion does not remain confined to a single system or jurisdiction, but instead reflects the shared opportunities, risks, and governance challenges that accompany the growing use of AI in law enforcement globally. I am particularly appreciative of the contributors' willingness to engage constructively with editorial feedback and to help shape a coherent volume around issues of governance, legitimacy, ethics, crime, and innovation.

I would also like to acknowledge all those involved in the review process, whose time and careful engagement helped make this volume possible and contributed significantly to the quality of the chapters. In addition, I offer my gratitude to the leadership at Rabdan Academy, whose trust and confidence in my work continue to provide an environment in which ambitious and practice-oriented scholarship can be developed. That support has been invaluable in enabling the sustained effort required to bring together and edit a collection of this nature.

Finally, I wish to thank my family for their patience, understanding, and continued support throughout the process of editing this volume. As with all major academic projects, the work has extended well beyond ordinary hours, and their support through the many evenings and weekends devoted to this book has made its completion possible.

Section 1

Strategic Implementation of Artificial Intelligence in Law Enforcement and Policing

Chapter 1
The Development of Organisational Artificial Intelligence Applications in Policing:
Getting United Kingdom Policing "Match Fit" Before We Start the Game

Philip Davies
http://orcid.org/0000-0001-8655-313X
Greater Manchester Police, UK

ABSTRACT

UK policing is being gainfully encouraged to adopt new technologies as a requirement to become more productive with limited resources, but also to reflect the society it polices. The extent to which AI systems, tools, and algorithms are being adopted, and the pace of adoption, is overplayed. The field has a natural and historic affinity with Complexity Theory, which it is argued is a compelling framework for public service administration in the age of AI augmentation. Epistemology and methodology are explored, using hypernetwork theory as a mathematical tool for prioritising data maturity functions that represent police organisations within operating model design. The argument is made that the application of AI will not be successful, or be accepted by the public, without an effective data foundation strategy. An example is provided of a data strategy for a UK metropolitan police force, adapted from Carruthers and Jackson (2022), as applied to organisational priorities reflective of the hypernetworks modelled.

DOI: 10.4018/979-8-3373-5228-2.ch001

INTRODUCTION

Artificial Intelligence (AI) has been with us for a while, but recent popularised advances in certain tools have brought the application of AI into greater focus along with a publication sprint of legislation, policy, and governance in its use, particularly aimed at public services. To get 'match fit', UK policing first needs to understand the rules of the game, ensure the best preparation with a service-wide uplift in data foundation activity, and, as with all successful teams, establish winning strategies and tactics before crossing the white line onto the field of play. This chapter, written by a serving UK senior police officer and the police lead for the National Data Integration & Exploitation Service, sets out the current legislative, political and operational backcloth to the adoption of AI technologies in UK policing.

Initially, this chapter will provide a brief exploration of how the different types of AI, and the latest legislation and policy, have or potentially will have implications for application in policing. The first point to make, which perhaps is an obvious one but not prominently recognised by many police leaders, is that AI is not a singular noun, and has no single agreed-upon definition as a concept. There are basically three types of AI (Johnson *et al.*, 2025), early logic or symbolic programming, primarily used in research and the development of programming languages; neural networks that allow computers to 'learn' and are behind such technologies as facial recognition; and natural language processing, which more recently led to innovations in translation, search engine and content creation responses. There is no General Artificial Intelligence (yet), and there is certainly little chance of this enslaving humanity any time soon, as some social media platforms would have you believe (ironically powered by AI search tools). Julian Togelius, a prominent figure in the intersection of artificial intelligence and video games describes current application as *"narrow AI"* (Togelius, 2024, p.3), that being the enhancement of machines to do a particular job (or connected tasks) very well, be that *"AI systems, AI tools, or AI algorithms"*. Some of the current applications on the market use AI methods that have been in existence for a long time such as symbolic AI (colloquially referred to as "Good Old-Fashioned AI" (GOFAI) (Togelius, 2024, p.84)), and neural network AI. It is the newer generative AI that is getting all the attention right now, and with this growing interest, there is a need for policing to have an informed position, and with that, the need to navigate the legal and regulatory framework the police service is bound by, to develop a strategic mechanism for getting the best out of AI, whilst balancing operational delivery with the privacy rights of UK citizens. To stretch the sporting analogy even further, this is about 'putting a foot on the ball'.

THE LANDSCAPE OF POLICE AND AI APPLICATION

The European Union AI Act 2024 recently provided a set of principles and a legal framework that is relatable to the ethics of police use of AI (Future of Life Institute, 2025). The purpose of the Act is to ensure AI systems in the EU are safe, transparent, ethical, and respect fundamental rights, and applies to any organisation developing, deploying, or distributing AI systems in the EU, even if based outside the EU. The Act requires developers to maintain technical records and summaries of training data, including transparency of training data sources and usage; compliance with EU copyright laws; and adherence to safety testing, structured, adversarial testing methods, and post-deployment monitoring.

Of pertinency to policing is the risk levels categorised in the Act, which describe law enforcement as a critical sector and therefore of high risk if mishandled or abused. In parallel, UK policing, via the National Police Chiefs' Council (NPCC) of England and Wales published both an AI strategy and a toolkit in early 2025 to advise forces on technology development. (For the purposes of brevity, in this context UK policing is in reference to policing within the 43 forces making up England and Wales; Scotland and Northern Ireland having their own devolved governance arrangements.) The NPCC brings together senior police leaders across the UK to set national direction, coordinate operational policing, and drive improvements for the public. Its remit is strategic, collaborative, and focused on ensuring consistency and progress across all police forces (www.npcc.police.uk).

The NPCC strategy overtly aligns itself to a published set of ethical principles ("the Code of Ethics") and the core mission of policing, that of preventing and detecting crime and keeping people safe, alongside operational efficiency. Ambitiously, the NPCC set the objective of UK policing becoming a global leader in responsible adoption of AI, and to do so whilst maintaining public trust in the ability of policing to deploy technology effectively and transparently. Integrating AI into the public sector demands a determined and planned course of action (Krishna *et al.*, 2023).

The newly published NPCC AI Strategy (2025) has a well-structured set of strategic priorities to support the development of effective technology innovation:

(i) Enhance productivity
(ii) Using AI to tackle crime and harm
(iii) Countering the criminal threat from AI

This is bolstered by the new Data (Use and Access) Act 2025, having just received royal assent, which lifts certain restrictions on some automated decision-making, and opening up further potential for real-time access across public service IT systems (UKAuthority News, 2025). This has been recognised at a policy level. The

NPCC now has a dedicated committee for AI to deliver on this strategy, chaired by a Chief Officer, in addition to the more established Digital, Data and Technology Board, and its subsidiary Police National Data and Analytics Board, both chaired by Chief Constables.

Police reform, as would be expected, is a politically driven agenda. A Home Office white paper entitled '*From local to national: a new model for policing*', published in January 2026 sets an ambitious agenda aimed at modernising policing, rebuilding public trust, and improving performance across the service, with a clear mantra of technology, productivity, and regaining public trust. Data will have its own development strand through the newly formed National Data Integration and Exploitation Service (NDIES), for which this author is the police lead. The Home Office agenda has been influenced by the Police Foundation (2023) publication *Police Productivity Review*, which featured technology heavily. The latest round of the police inspectorate's PEEL regime reflects the need for effective organisational management and efficient resource use. Police Effectiveness, Efficiency, and Legitimacy (PEEL) is also a respectful nod to Sir Robert Peel who was instrumental in the development of the British Policing Model in 1829.

At the time of writing, details of the mechanics of this reform are still unclear, although a review team has recently been established to begin the work. What is clear is that data will play a significant role, and this resource is the raw material for AI applications UK policing will utilise in responding to this reform, and for achieving the NPCC AI Strategy. The AI Strategy also sets the ambition over the next 3 years for the development of a national AI lab to test and evaluate AI tools; guidance for local forces on building and assessing tools; and a national governance framework with an emphasis on public accountability, expert input, and continuous evaluation. The accompanying NPCC AI Toolkit (2025) provides practical guidance and a deliberate signpost to ethics, but reflects a tendency to focus on tactical applications (such as facial recognition) rather than strategic applications (such as organisational simulation). This betrays a hidden dynamic in UK policing culture – that of purse-holders and policymakers being heavily influenced by technology suppliers on what is in the marketplace. Senior practitioners in policing need to become more intelligent customers through digital literacy, which presently does not have a bespoke training programme via the national lead for occupational competence, the College of Policing. The training programme for Chief Officers (The Executive Leadership Programme) (College of Policing, 2025) has at time of writing, less than two days within a 12-week programme dedicated to Data, Digital and Technology (DDaT), and is still in its infancy, having only been introduced three years ago; the implication is that a generation of Chief Officers still in post have had to learn the hard way. Greater engagement with the academic community would also be of benefit. Wirtz *et al.* (2019) identified that public sector specific AI research is still in its infancy and so far, *"...fails to provide an integrated view of AI applications and challenges for the public sector"* (2019, p.608).

From the experience of this author, as a senior practitioner and digital lead in UK policing, there are several inhibitors to achieving these objectives. First and foremost, there is an inherent localism, which some may argue fosters innovation, but in reality, creates short-term focus on tactical technology initiatives rather than long-term more expensive strategic developments with slower benefits realisation, particularly for national data assets. In recent history there has been some very public large-scale IT programmes that have not delivered to expectations, or worse failed to deliver on launch, creating nervousness for the Chief Officers of each autonomous force. Secondly the marketplace is weak and uncoordinated, although the Police Digital Service (PDS), formed in 2015, is making progress in representing UK policing as a customer. Currently technology providers can pitch 43 times for their products, and multiple force customers find themselves in a development group that moves at the pace of the lowest common denominator. Thirdly, digital leadership is not seen as a core skillset for Chief Officers. Add to that the police reform agenda which is fuelling Chief Officer and politician advocacy of widespread change, and the technology agenda is at risk of being pushed further down the agenda than it already is. However, the proposed National Policing Service, and the absorption of the National Data Analytics Office within it are promising opportunities (Gargan, 2025). It could also be argued that cultural resistance to change is a contributing phenomenon, but the position of this author is that this is much less pronounced than in the past. Traditional and popular sociological views on policing culture, such as Reiner (2010) would argue that cultural resistance to technology change is a barrier, but there is significant contemporary evidence that this is more an issue of investment and leadership than culture. The last published Police digital experience survey, conducted by Policing Insight (2025) and supported by the Home Office, NPCC, PFEW, and Police Digital Service, indicate frustrations over issues of poor technology, rather than the speed of change. The results have not yet been fully published at time of writing, but headline findings were released in early 2026, with 6,678 officers and staff responding, indicate frustrations over issues of poor technology, rather than the speed of change, and the most recent nationally reported findings from the HMICFRS (2025) State of Policing 2024–25 assessment, highlights widespread dissatisfaction among officers with outdated systems, poor digital tools, and inconsistent investment across forces.

The policing model in the UK has consent at its core, even if contested and opposed by some at inception, and much more recently questioned again due to a series of events that have damaged its reputation. Reiner (2000, p.15) describes how the English model quickly became an 'unequivocally beneficent institution'. Public consent was borne of the Peelian principles laid out in the formation of England's first professional police service in 1829 and remains true, even internally revered, as a philosophy. Torrible (2022) demonstrates the ongoing police occupational culture reinforcing its importance at a tactical level. UK policing has a long-established *Code of Ethics* with its current edition published in 2024. This code directly informs the College of Policing *Data Ethics Principles*, (College of Policing, 2025) – the ink still wet on guidance that one could argue should have been around when data first became a core resource for policing decades ago, but is probably more recently influenced by the significant interest in AI. There has been guidance before, it must be stressed, but this was largely connected to Management of Police Information (MOPI) compliance, (College of Policing, 2014), which is the service response to Data Protection Act 1998 responsibilities (legislation which was updated by the 2018 Act). The Data Ethics Principles are robust:

(i) Public Good – Data use must enhance public safety and wellbeing.
(ii) Respect and Dignity – Uphold the highest standards of respect for individuals and communities.
(iii) Fairness and Impartiality – Avoid discrimination, especially against vulnerable groups.
(iv) Transparency and Proportionality – Be open about data use and ensure it's proportionate to the policing task.
(v) Robust Evidence – Base decisions on reliable, bias-aware data.
(vi) Evaluation – Assess risks before and after data use.
(vii) Human Decisions Supported by Technology – Technology should assist, not replace, human judgment

These are reflected heavily in the NPCC AI Strategy (2025), and terms such as 'robustness', 'transparency' and 'explainability' will (or should) weigh heavy on the mind of AI developers seeking to supply policing. Tools using neural networks can produce outcomes where the journey to reach that outcome is opaque. Large Language Models (LLM) were not initially created for accuracy and are influenced by the biases that exist in large open-source volumes of text (Togelius, 2024:112). They were built for prediction of the next word, not factual or ethical completeness. Such problems are being worked through now the technology has developed further with its potential being recognised. Sohail & Zhang (2025) suggest LLMs now significantly shape working practices across a variety of fields.

The real barrier to expansion of AI application in policing may not be one of politics, aptitude or ethics, but one of finance. The police funding formula is a system used by the Home Office to divide a fixed national policing budget between the 43 police forces in England and Wales. It does not calculate absolute need, but instead shares money based on relative need, using indicators such as population, crime levels, density, and local costs. While the total funding has increased, many forces argue that it remains insufficient to meet operational demands and inflationary pressures. Several Chief Constables have been vocal in the press about the austerity they are facing, for example NPCC Chair Chief Constable Gavin Stevens, reported in The Independent (2025) newspaper, called the most recent Government Spending Review a 'huge blow' for policing; and NPCC Finance Lead Chief Constable Paul Sanford, in the same press coverage highlighted that forces are increasingly relying on borrowing to balance budgets, with debt costs expected to rise by nearly 50%. A recent UNISON report suggests that across England and Wales, a projected budget shortfall of around £1 billion may be experienced by 2027 within the latest Government Spending Review.

It is therefore more important than ever that UK policing is an intelligent customer when it comes to AI application investment and it needs a sophisticated understanding of the dynamics of the organisation, and its data as a raw material before investing. This is not a new debate. The National Audit Office (2015) has called for more robust understanding by police leaders of their service demand and cost drivers, and without better data and strategic planning, forces may struggle to maintain levels of service. His Majesty's Inspectorate of Constabulary and Fire and Rescue Services (HMICFRS) have required all forces to produce Force Management Statements to demonstrate this since 2018. The NPCC AI Toolkit (2025), and the NPCC AI Playbook for Policing (2025), indicates in this author's view that policing is more interested in tactical applications rather than address this strategic shortfall in thinking and application.

UPTAKE OF AI IN POLICING

The extent to which UK policing has adopted AI to date has perhaps been overstated in terms of the current level of investment and evidence-based impact of such investment. We are 'dipping our toes in the water' as a service, although the service rhetoric recognises that modern policing needs to respond to law enforcement requirements in an era of data and technology proliferation. The international literature on AI within policing indicates the primary application investments are in are crime pattern predictive analytics (AI algorithms) (Hung & Yen, 2021), child safeguarding data analysis (Wilson *et al.* 2020), facial recognition (AI tools utilising neural network methods) (Matulionyte & Zalnieriute, 2024) and digital forensic investigation (Dusin *et al.,* 2024) with mixed results reported by all these sources. Raji and Sholademi (2024) comprehensively explore the use of AI algorithms in US policing as a predictive analysis tool but raise concerns over its effectiveness and potential biases. Forecasting criminal activity requires analysis of historic datasets, which are only as good as the data models and field design, data entry, and ongoing data quality governance processes.

In addition to this, one may also consider the proliferation of Large Language Model (LLM) and Natural Language Processing (NLP) tools being developed, currently on the back of the dramatic uptake in use of such applications by the general public since the launch of Chat-GPT, Copilot, and Gemini amongst other noteworthy entries. Obvious applications would include auto-generation of police statements and other reports, although recent experiments in the UK indicate some applications are not ready for widespread use. Walley & Glasspoole-Bird (2025) evaluated one such pilot exploring auto-generated statements from victim accounts and found that although the readability of AI statements was acceptable, the AI was poor at writing the statements with a clear context and narrative about the specific incidents. Readability was low but just about acceptable. The AI used words not normally used by witnesses. Statements were mainly academic in style and contained small errors and omissions, partly hallucinated by the AI. Experienced officers produced better work.

Wirtz *et al.* (2019) produced a literature review summary of public sector AI applications, which is a useful generic descriptor, but is already a little out-of-date with the recent explosion of generative AI tools. Using one of these tools (Copilot) provided a cohesive summary of the current landscape of UK police AI application when asked, but drew heavily from the NPCC AI Playbook (2025) in a response to such a query with the following summary of examples, which had gaps due to its reliance on open source information, and gave the impression to the reader such deployments are routine, which they are not – a small but pertinent example of the argument for better data and reduced bias. The list was subsequently 'augmented' by the author's own knowledge:

(i) Predictive Policing: AI algorithms analyse historical crime data, social media activity, and environmental factors to predict where crimes are likely to occur. This helps forces allocate resources more effectively (Kent Constabulary).

(ii) Facial Recognition Technology (FRT): Used to identify individuals in real-time by comparing live footage with databases of known persons (Metropolitan Police). Copilot did not recall or mention the issues with Human Rights legal challenge on this, such as *Bridges v South Wales Police 2020.* Although this was for retrospective searching, not live recognition.

(iii) AI in Call Handling: AI supports call handlers by transcribing conversations, conducting risk assessments, and retrieving background information (Humberside Constabulary).

(iv) Natural Language Processing (NLP): AI analyses large volumes of text to identify threats, patterns or specifics on law and policy (no example given by CoPilot, but the College of Policing have a prototype called 'CoPPA').
(v) Automated Detection: AI-powered cameras detect mobile phone use or lack of seatbelt use while driving (Devon and Cornwall Constabulary).
(vi) AI Drones: Used in search and rescue operations, especially for missing or vulnerable individuals (Police Scotland).
(vii) Redaction and Translation Tools: AI assistance in redacting sensitive information and translating documents, streamlining case preparation and evidence handling (no example given but Greater Manchester Police have deployed some of this, as have several other forces – and one could argue the software is not AI -enabled based on some definitions).
(viii) Statement and Report Generation: Not mentioned at all by Copilot but as previously mentioned, deployed and under review within Hertfordshire Constabulary.

The recent survey by The Police Foundation (Muir & O'Connell, 2025) asked England and Wales forces what areas they were either currently using or considering for AI technologies. Not one mentioned strategic-level application (unless 'back office' or 'business support' functions count in this regard - one could argue not, or that it very much depends on the detail of these requirements.)

COMPLEXITY SCIENCE AND AI: A CALL FOR A NEW ORGANISATIONAL STRATEGY AND GOOD DATA FOUNDATIONS BEFORE APPLYING AI ENHANCEMENTS

Why are these applications not focussed on strategic organisational problems? Johnson *et al.* (2025) provides a potential answer in observing that the generalisation of AI tasks

> *"... to more complex real-world problems requires detailed, accurate models of the targeted world. But getting machines to build models of messy complex real-world situations is an unresolved scientific challenge and currently a major limitation of AI."*

With policing, there is the added ethical dimension of 'explainability'. Models of real-world scenarios have been accomplished by humans with the support of computers within the discipline of complexity science, although there are limited examples in UK policing (Davies, 2024). At an organisational level, AI systems, tools and algorithms have the potential to analyse complex datasets to uncover hidden correlations, simulate various scenarios, and offer real-time recommendations.

This would empower policing to make data-driven decisions that are informed by a nuanced understanding of the complex systems in which they operate (Qudrat-Ullah, 2025: 12). In other words, policy and operating model design that is evidence-based and capable of being simulated before being enacted.

Johnson and Cook (2014) propose that policy design should be treated as a distinct scholarly field. They argue that policymaking requires clarifying what is needed, creating systems capable of meeting those needs, and developing solutions that balance the interests of multiple stakeholders. Building on this, Johnson et al. (2017) advocate the use of policy informatics as a means of supporting such work. Contemporary tools—particularly computer-based simulations, data-driven approaches, and interactive visualisation—naturally align with this agenda.

Ghorbani *et al.* (2014) reinforce this perspective, noting that Agent-Based Modelling (ABM) offers a powerful way to represent individual actors whose behaviours collectively shape how populations respond to top-down policy interventions. A review of recent contributions in *The Journal of Artificial Societies and Social Simulation* highlights ongoing interest in the intersection of ABM and policy design (Davies, 2024). Mitcham (2023) observes that ABMs have been applied in criminology since the mid-2000s and are especially valuable when empirical data are missing, inconsistent, or contradictory, or when policymakers require rapid insight. Gilbert et al. (2018) similarly contend that computational modelling can inform both the development and the assessment of policy.

Artificial Intelligence has been associated with Complexity Science, at least conceptually and methodologically, since the first embryonic branches of both disciplines grew from the study into cybernetics in the 1940s. However, whilst AI primarily focussed on the building of intelligent machines, Complexity Science, or Complexity Theory as it is also known, studies nonlinear systems in general that displayed emergent behaviour, initially from within the natural sciences, but rapidly developing into diverse disciplines such as economics and the social sciences. Both AI and Complexity Science evolution can be correlated to the development in power of computing (Gershenson, 2025) (Mainzer, 2025). A central argument of this paper is to recognise that relationship, and particularly from a strategic or conceptual position, adopt the 'worldview' of Complexity Theory (Davies, 2024) in building a lasting framework for AI application that moves beyond the tactical deployment of solutions to strategic applications (Kolt *et al.* 2025).

Perhaps the reason that AI applications in policing have been focussed on the tactical is that Forces have yet to achieve a level of maturity at a strategic level to recognise practical applications for organisational AI tools, such as digital twinning to test new policies virtually before engaging with reality. This is due to a lack of exploration into not only how organisations look or are designed to look (operating models), but also how they behave. Complexity Theory provides ontological and epistemological frameworks that can help with this. Davies (2024 p.27) explores Complexity Theory origins *"in mid-twentieth century thinking on artificial intelligence, cybernetics, cellular automata, and system dynamics and general systems thinking"*. There is no unified theory of complexity but a recent synthesis of more frequently referenced properties states:

> *"A complex system is an open system made of many heterogenous parts in a state that can move far from equilibrium. It is sensitive to initial conditions and when subsequently exposed to non-linearity and feedback from the interaction of the parts with the dynamics of the system and others that interact with it, self-organization and adaption can occur, resulting in the emergence of new system states."*
>
> (Davies 2024, p.28)

The literature on Complexity Theory is vast, and beyond the scope of this paper to explore deeply. There are examples in more recent literature of how Complexity Theory has influenced research into policy, management and the study of organisations and institutions (Mathews *et al.*, 1999) and has propagated from this into management consultancy (e.g. Diamond, 2008), (Snowden & Boone, 2007), although a search of prevalent journals on public management found very few practical applications of complexity in research and application in the public sector. There are numerous examples of where Complexity Theory and AI research have interacted. A philosophical difference is in the concept of emergence. Complexity theorists recognise the relevance of emergent properties in a system in the development of new system states. The Artificial Intelligence community, it could be argued, is either dismissive of emergence (Gershenson, 2024, p.8), or perhaps nervous of the concept as the sophisticated artificial systems being built need to be consistent to be useful (and sellable). From a regulatory standpoint, the UK Government's guidelines for AI procurement warn of avoiding *"Black-Box Algorithms"* (2020, p8), which highlights a wider consideration of being able to have an explainable approach to AI development outcomes. An advisory note reflected this in the NPCC AI toolkit for police leaders. Gershenson (2024) explains that for both Complexity Science and Artificial Intelligence both have in common the cycle of the generation of great expectations and disappointments, and neither can be considered a mature scientific discipline. In the field of policing, which is very adept at risk-management processes, this should be reflected on. AI not a field with widespread public support for operational experimentation, particularly in an era where public trust and confidence in policing has diminished. At a tactical level, there is literature to support the use of Complexity Theory to develop tools for modelling and evaluating AI systems (López-Ruiz, 2025).

From a geo-political position, Ilcic *et al.* (2025 p.1) argue that Complexity Science *"offers a valuable framework for navigating AI's integration into global governance systems"*. The same argument can be made for policing. The potential for AI to be both transformative for effective decision-making, but also disruptive by introducing the risks of data bias, inequality exacerbation, and reduced governance oversight due to a lack of will or understanding creates the potential for unpredictable outcomes of investment by public services. Ilcic *et al.* recognise the valuable role of Complexity Science in navigating the unpredictability and complexity of AI integration into society (2025 p.4):

> *"As AI systems grow in capability, their interconnections with other technologies can generate effects that are opaque and challenging to disentangle in real-world contexts. This complexity calls for a revaluation of our problem-solving and decision-making frameworks, necessitating the adoption of new methodologies that can accommodate the dynamic, often non-linear nature of AI driven systems."*

Their proffered solution is a governance framework that supports AI governance within institutions that are resilient under uncertainty, and that this *"requires a multifaceted approach that draws on Complexity Science"* (2025, p12). As with most complexity research, this involves and nurtures interdisciplinary collaboration. UK policing will need to adapt its traditional governance structures (which tend to be linear and rigid) to accommodate such a dynamic, which Ilcic *et al.* position as one of decentralised, modular, and adaptive institutions to respond to a rapidly evolving technological landscape. This philosophy of adaption is central to Complexity Theory.

A prominent philosophy in UK policing currently is that the core role of policing is a simple one. Answer calls for help, get there quickly and do a good job, bring criminals to justice and support victims, and identify opportunities to prevent future occurrences. The current popular mantra of getting 'back to basics' and 'getting a grip' (which was even the title of an HMICFRS report by the Chief Inspector of Constabulary in 2023) should also reflect that whilst the core role of policing may be simple, our organisations and operating environments are complex. The intricacies of decision-making for policing extend far beyond simple linear models and intuitive judgments. As Qudrat-Ullah (2025, p.35) argues, when linking AI-driven decision-making processes to a complexity science framework, *"Understanding the theoretical foundations of complexity is paramount for navigating the multifaceted challenges that decision-makers face."* AI has potential to manage this complexity, once both the complexity and the tools are understood. To achieve such understanding, as humans we often turn to modelling – the simplification of the real messy world into something we can engage with.

MODELLING, DATA FOUNDATIONS, AND THE FORMATION OF A DATA STRATEGY IN A POLICE FORCE

The problem Complexity Theory has had historically is communicating its ideas to a wider audience. Davies (2024, p.6) explores extensively the literature with regards to modelling social systems and argues that *"computer simulation is clearly one of the principal vehicles for complexity research and that any move from the theoretical to the empirical would benefit from application of Agent-Based Modelling (ABM)"*. Gilbert and Troitzsch (2011, p.1), cited by Davies (2024) describe simulation as being *"increasingly ... used to assist in developing, implementing and evaluating public policy"*, based on the concept of emergence of complex behaviour from relatively simple activities. Davies also provides a brief explanation of these applications and how they can be adapted for police operating model design.

> *"ABMs are computer models where inputs in the form of agent behaviours and values, along with an environmental setting are allowed to interact based on these rules, with the outputs being the behaviour of the model over time. This is an important departure from more established statistical methods for analysing social systems, as these are almost all based on the assumption of a linear relationship between variables."*
>
> (Davies 2024, p. 4)

Add AI into the equation (if you will pardon the pun) and you have the potential of making these simulations more sophisticated and worthy of the 'digital twin' label. It is argued that such tools must be grounded in an evidence-based representation of the organisation, that absorbs qualitative as well as quantitative measurements on how the organisation behaves.

To address this grounding of data in ways that captures the most important aspects of an organisation's operating model, a mathematical method for bridging between the quantitative and qualitative data, and the coding of an ABM can be utilised – that of hypernetwork theory (Atkin, 1974, 1981; Johnson, 2013). The important aspects of an operating model (and their relevant data sources) can be identified as vertices with relationships to each other. Davies (2024, p. 57) summarises the mathematics from Atkin & Johnson in terms that allows for the development of recognisable dynamics in police operating models (Figure 1).

> *"A 'vertex' is a point or a node, which when connected to other vertices becomes a 'simplex' if the vertices have a relational connection. Where the relations between each connected vertex are explicit and important that simplex is referred to as a 'hypersimplex'. Hypersimplices linked together form a 'hypernetwork' ... This can provide algebraic content to aid the modelling process. The aspects of human systems can be represented as a 'backcloth' (structure) of hypersimplices, with activity in the system represented as 'traffic' along it. If the traffic*

or backcloth changes, the other is impacted. A hypersimplex is a higher level of representation of an assembly of relations that has ready application in a complexity framework."
(Davies 2024, p. 57)

Figure 1. Hypersimplices of human networks

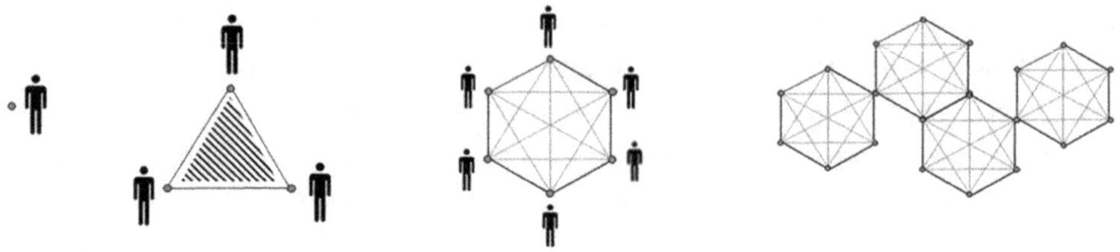

Adapted from Johnson (2013)

In Complexity Science connections matter (complexity comes from the Latin *plexus*, meaning "entwined"), and a compelling example in the social world is provided in the book *Linked* (Barabási, 2014), as an introduction to networks. Understanding the relationship between things improves the likelihood to successfully model the behaviour of the system; or least recognise what is left out of such simplifications (all models being simplified reality).

Greater sophistication of modelling can be explored by using qualitative data as a source as well as quantitative. Davies (2024) developed an ABM of a neighbourhood policing model where the emotional response to new policy by Police Community Support Officers (PCSOs) was simulated over time, allowing the stress-testing of impacts on recognisable policy decisions such as supervisor ratios and geographic allocation of beats. Such experiments could be greatly enhanced with AI tools and operationalised in a wider presentation of the organisation at multiple levels, from individual, team, and function, up to a metalevel of the whole organisation (and even beyond to partner agencies).

This modelling process can also be used to map out and prioritise an organisation's current data landscape for maturity to a level where AI applications can support organisational decision-making. This can only be achieved and systemised with a revolution in data strategy and management investment by the police service, in which the whole system is catered for, in an interconnected way. An example of such a data strategy (one of the few published in the UK police service at the time of writing) will be described later in reference the programme of work Greater Manchester Police (GMP) has embarked on.

The formalism of representing the meta-level relationship between core functions of a police force at an organisational level using hypersimplices can be demonstrated with the example of the work undertaken by GMP to map priorities for their data strategy. Through a fieldwork exercise interviewing business and technical leads, reviewing performance data of functions, and alignment to the vision of the organisation, six functions were identified in most need of investment in data maturity, not just individually, but relationally as well. Identifying the strength of those interdependencies provides opportunities for multiplying the benefits. The six core functions within the data landscape were:

1. Human Resources, Training and Development, particularly the suite of datasets used to manage recruitment, deployment, retention, progression, skills oversight, and performance management of employees [H].
2. Public Contact, particularly primary data entry issues and the proliferation of channel shift facilities being developed that could exacerbate the issue [C].
3. Operational Records (crime, safeguarding, covert assets, intelligence and performance analytics) [O].
4. Evidential & Criminal Justice data, particularly opportunities to streamline and augment administration through to the Crown Prosecution Service and make best use of data available from other agencies [E].
5. Business data, particularly the suite of datasets used to support business activity, including finance, fleet, and equipment [B].
6. Diversity, Equality & Inclusion (DEI) data, in particular the management of datasets and requirements of accurately recording protected characteristics (as required by the Equality Act 2010), and to deliver the national Police Race Action Plan thematics [D].

Each has a relationship with the other in a complex system, but this relationship is not reflected in the connectivity of the data. For example, public contact data strongly represents the inputs into the policing system, the operational data tracks the work being done to investigate crime and safeguard the public, and the criminal justice data represents the outputs of the work, but none directly connect to the Human Resources data representing the capacity and capability to do the work. Add into that the disconnect with the finances and resources to equip staff to do the work, and the dynamics of how the staff represent the community they police, and how they police in those communities, and the ability to represent productivity is immature. All six priority areas are demonstrably connected, and it should be the ambition of the police service to connect the data that informs these relationships, and as a consequence increase the value of the data in providing connected insights.

Hypernetwork theory would represent the above dynamic as follows. For a set of six nodes <H, C, O, E, B, D>, there is an indivisible 6-ary relation, in 5-dimensional space. This creates 63 (2^6) possible combinations of relationships, including solo node combinations, but excluding the null value (i.e. non present < >). In a real sense, these relationships have their own strengths, influences, and consequential feedback loops, and understanding the dynamics of these provided a more sophisticated method for prioritisation and benefit of outcomes.

Figure 2. The hypersimplex of GMP data priorities

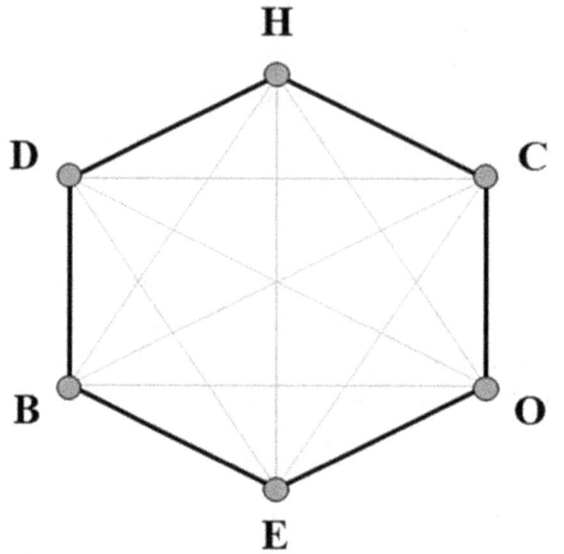

The more nodes in the combination, the more complex it is to establish processes to connect the data within a warehouse, with all the data quality issues and field mapping work that would go with it. Some relationships more closely align to organisational needs than others, which provides context for prioritisation. This is also a reflection of national needs, as the police reform agenda pushes for greater efficiency and productivity. Currently GMP wants to mature its position on productivity measurements and demonstrable outputs. In one sense, that means putting the right people in the right place at the right time, with the right skills to progress investigations quickly and deliver better justice outcomes for victims of crime, as an example. The relationship could be expressed as:

<H, O, E>, where H = Human Resources, O = Operations, and E = Evidence & CJ

Figure 3. A priority hypersimplex of data priorities

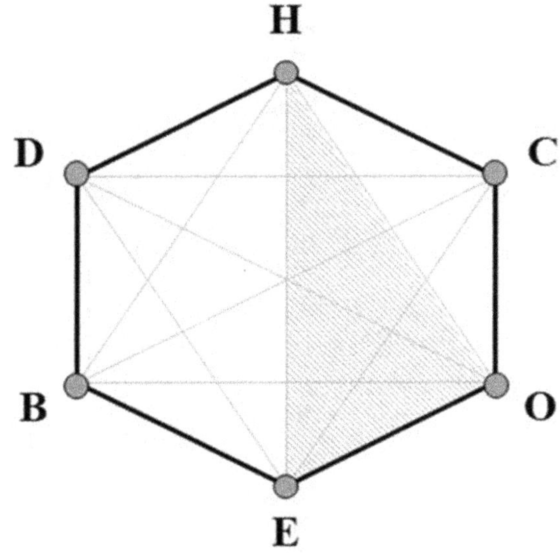

Currently, this is probably a higher priority than ensuring the fleet manager has mature insight into the long-term requirements of patrol vehicles to match calls for service by location:

<B, C>, where B = Business data and C = Public Contact

Figure 4. A hypersimplex representation of fleet management

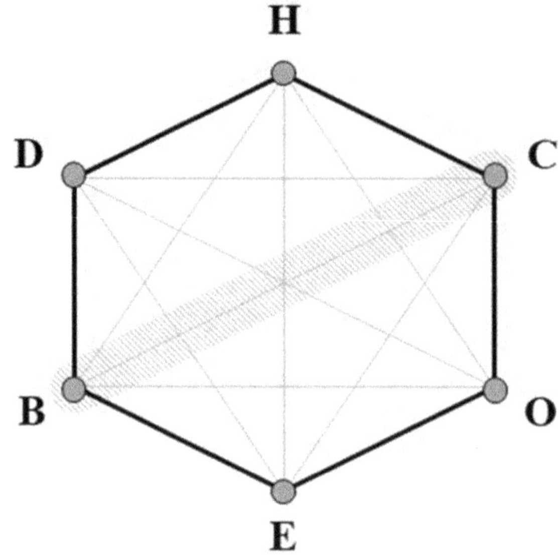

So, an ordinal scale of importance can be developed. This second example highlights another aspect to support the modelling process. That of levels – systems of systems. The fleet management process is a lower meso-level property of <B>. This could be represented in hypernetwork theory as <B-1>, the structure of the system a level below with its own collection of node relationships. At a micro level you may have the data reflecting the dynamics of the vehicle workshop <B-2>, the structure two levels below. The micro-, meso- and macro- level relationships also interact with each other. Something at a micro-level could potentially impact the whole system if it is sensitive to it. This is an important dynamic in Complexity Theory, and one which AI tools can support in terms of analysis and the speculation of possible futures for a system by computing the reaction of multilevel relationships to change. Policing is an open system, in that many levels of it interact with the environment and are impacted by it. The problem arises in traditional modelling and analysis techniques in that they do not account for many subsystems being affected (even co-evolving) with their environment (Johnson, 2006). The result is what many a police leader has felt – being blindsided on a Tuesday afternoon by a growing risk to policing business or the public that was not in your central oversight and was not a problem (you thought) yesterday. Whilst it could be argued that theoretically everything is connected to everything else, strong connections are identifiable and can be used to define a system with enough representation of the real messy world that we can apply the power of AI tools to help, particularly tools that make use of neural network methods.

Each of the nodes identified above represents a variety of activities either recorded on core systems, or (more commonly) floating around SharePoint on local Excel spreadsheets and other artifacts, often duplicated several times as different people work on versions of the same document. To become 'data mature' these assets need to be mapped, reviewed for usefulness against a clear business requirement, and set on a pathway to becoming connectable and well-managed in the future through the support of technology. Effective data discovery, mapping, and quality management can also support police requirements for ethical and transparent processes in embracing AI systems, tools, and algorithms. This position is well recognised by those that influence the UK Government, such as the think tank 'The Police Foundation', who's recent paper on policing and AI reflected the struggle policing has with making the full use of its data, despite at its heart being a "complex information business" (2025, p.1), and by an independent review commissioned by the Centre for Data Ethics and Innovation (CDEI) in which the Royal United Services Institute for Defence and Security Studies (RUSI) found *"... widespread concern across the UK law enforcement community regarding the lack of official national guidance for the use of algorithms in policing"* (Babuta, A., & Oswald, M., 2020, p.8). The report highlighted inconsistent data practices, limited analytical maturity, and poor organisational readiness. This is good evidence that UK policing is not maximising its data.

In order to become data-mature, the NPCC are currently developing a 'Data Readiness' tool for UK forces to assist with future AI applications. This is likely to be governed through the newly formed National Data and Analytics Office (NDAO) through to the Digital, Data and Technology (DDaT) Committee. A sub-committee of DDAT, the National Police Data and Analytics Board (of which this author has membership) leads on data foundations. Without investment in understanding and prioritising data relationships at a force level, the task of complying with these frameworks magnifies. GMP's development of a data strategy seeks to recognise these interconnected data ecosystems and ultimately has within it an ambition of a 'digital twin' of the organisation.

TOWARDS A DIGITAL TWIN

What would an organisational-level application of AI look like? In essence the ambition is to develop a digital twin of GMP, not in a sense that the term is used in industry, but as a recognition of the power AI could bring to human system representation in the form of a simulation of the operating model of the force.

Digital twinning is not a new concept within some industries. (Vohra, 2023) describes *"a digital twin basically meaning a replicated model of any object or product in digital form"*, usually remaining *"connected with the original object or product it is replicating and receiving real-time data"*. Issues, errors and inhibitors to performance that could be encountered can be forecast before they happen which can assist avoidance and major losses which otherwise might have been incurred. In human systems this is more complex, and a range of possible futures to test whether a particular policy will work is a more likely outcome of creating such simulations (Davies, 2024).

Kumar *et al.* in Vohra (2023) explore the role of Digital Twin technology in the medical sector. They state the two main characteristics of digital twin technology are:

(i) "each description stresses the relationship between the physical model and its simulated equivalent; and
(ii) sensors are used to produce real-time data, which is used to create the relation."

The more complex the system, the more sensors are required to model it effectively, and the more likely the application of AI tools would be useful, deployed under the framework of Complexity Theory, modelled using hypernetworks. Ruijer *et al.* (2021), recognising that the study of complex systems in public administration is growing in interest, suggests a method of 'probing' these systems with 'living labs' producing policy interventions that can be interacted with by the researcher or policymaker. They recognise that making sense of such systems is not *"a uniform and harmonious process since processes of change entail conflicting perspectives and interests"* (2021, p.8). That is perhaps another way of saying that some of the policy interventions did not work, or the policymaker got a result they were not expecting (Davies, 2024). In policing it could be said that policy is often experimental (based on professional experience and policing philosophy), but doubtfully openly admitted to as such, so providing a platform to engage the senior policing practitioner with complexity theory via the use of an ABM 'Digital Twin' in testing policy impacting the public is arguably a safer vehicle for exposure than Ruijer *et al.*'s proposition of using a Police Force as a Petri dish.

John Casti, prominent Sante Fe Institute faculty member, promoted the prospect of computers creating *"silicone surrogate"* worlds (Casti, 1997b, p 35) to allow controlled experiments on complex systems that could be repeatable with the processing power available at the time. The Sante Fe Institute (founded in 1984) being the first research centre dedicated to the study of complex systems, as a multi-disciplinary environment. Heath *et al.* (2009) highlighted in their survey of ABM gaining popularity from the 1990s onwards as a departure from classical simulation approaches. Epstein (2008) highlighted the discipline of policy dialogue as an alternative to simple prediction as a use for modelling, which could be translated into evidence-based decision-making at an organisational level without too much of a stretch, as demonstrated with the example of Neighbourhood Policing policy in the predictive computer simulations developed by Davies (2024) previously referenced.

Herbert Simon—widely regarded as a foundational figure in early AI research during the 1950s and 1960s—argued in *The Sciences of the Artificial* (1969; 1981; 1996) that understanding complex phenomena can be advanced through the construction and study of simulations. In this work, he presents simulation both as a tool for supporting decision-making and as a means of generating new forms of knowledge. Simon maintained that uncertainty does not prevent intelligent action, but it does require approaches that are flexible and resilient, rather than optimisation strategies that only function effectively in narrowly defined and perfectly understood conditions. Building on this logic, Johnson (2006, p. 37) suggests that the value of simulation lies not in forecasting exact outcomes but in exploring the range of possible system states and understanding how those states are distributed. Epstein (1999) similarly contends that agent-based modelling introduces a distinctive "generative" mode of inquiry within the social sciences—one that differs from both inductive and deductive traditions. Although Jones (2008) does not provide concrete policing examples in his discussion of complexity frameworks, he does acknowledge that the interconnected and dynamic nature of policing means that future developments are inherently unpredictable.

Across the social-science literature, simulation is therefore typically framed as a method for deepening understanding rather than as a predictive instrument. Its strength lies in enabling the examination of potential futures and in enhancing insight into the system through the very process of designing and experimenting with the model. The same could be said for 'digital twinning'.

Such a concept has its challenges. Lyytinen *et al.* (2024) explore the notion of a digital twin for organisations and concludes that in order to be successful, the more obvious 'twinning' of things (resources) and business processes, must also be accompanied by the inevitable outcome of large human systems – that of *"agency, conflict, and emergence"* (2024, p.77). They conclude that this is not currently possible, but such models are useful all the same for real-time multi-dimensional analysis of organisational design. The application of hypernetwork theory provides a tool for exploring the relationships within human systems to progress this by at least providing a framework of priority and discovery in developing a data strategy. For example, as previously referenced, Davies (2024) explored this by modelling the relationship between Police Community Support Officers and their behavioural reaction to policy change in their working environment. The hypersimplicies developed from thematic coding of interviews with officers became the foundation for computer simulation of prospective policy outcomes.

The testing of possible futures is only part of the benefit of having an organisational digital twin for a Police Force. Real time information on how the organisation is performing, how it is managing incoming demand with the resources it has at its disposal, and where the productivity risks lie, all point towards a more mature organisational management process that is becoming an increasing expectation of the UK police service, to the point of it being a core inspection topic by the HMICFRS PEEL framework 2025-27. This can only be achieved if the Force invests in the delivery of a data strategy.

A WIDER DATA STRATEGY REQUIREMENT FOR POLICING

The work involved to understand and model the organisation to prioritise investment will falter unless supported by a data strategy led from the top of the force. For UK policing, there is also a legislative and regulatory requirement to get data right before embarking on AI development. Policing has a legal requirement to discharge duties under the Data Protection Act 2018, and General Data Protection Regulations (GDPR) (Regulation (EU) 2016/679, 2016), central to public expectations on legitimacy. Codes of practice are set out in Section 124(5) of the Anti-social Behaviour, Crime and Policing Act 2014 under the principles for police information and records management, reflected in the College of Policing Authorised Professional Practice for Management of Police Information (MOPI). Under the Investigatory Powers Act 2016, the Investigatory Powers Commissioners Office may sanction a Force if it fails to demonstrate effect control over surveillance data, subject to audit and inspection (Sections 229-245 of the Act).

The NPCC has published numerous vision and strategy documents over recent years promoting the need for Digital, Data and Technology (DDaT) progress, most notably the 2020-2030 National Policing Digital Strategy, and the newly released 2025-2030 update. This acknowledges external influences such as the COVID-19 pandemic and the cost-of-living crisis, which have shaped policing priorities. It introduces new initiatives like the National Data and Analytics Office, expanded cyber capabilities, and the Police Science and Technology Strategy to ensure consistent decision-making. While the 2020-2030 strategy laid the groundwork for digital transformation, the 2025-2030 refresh adapts to emerging challenges and refines priorities to better align with current policing needs. Data features more heavily on the revised strategy also, particularly the requirement for core 'pan-policing' datasets and has its own 'enabling pillar' for the strategy (2025, p.28).

HMICFRS inspection now reviews how high-quality data, and analysis informs strategic planning and decision-making. This carries through to the new 2025-2027 PEEL assessment framework (Question 1) which will assess that *"...the force can show how it continues to improve productivity through digital, data and technology solutions."*. The NDAO has indicated future thematic inspection on data maturity, building on the Data Maturity Assessments already carried out by the Police Digital Service on behalf of the NDAO. This will inform police reform work and the development of national data and performance capabilities.

Whilst few examples of a published data strategy have been retrieved from a literature review, those that were available (MPS, West Yorkshire, Police Scotland) evidence the benefits of an effective data strategy. In response, GMP have recently developed its first comprehensive and standalone data strategy aligned to its objectives of becoming more productive for its communities. This strategy has been endorsed by the Senior Command Team, and the subsequent programme of work will report directly to the Chief Resourcing Officer. This will address entries on the organisation's risk register common to most Forces in relation to data management, and an NPCC (DDaT) endorsed assessment process that scored GMP with relatively low maturity in late 2023 (common across the UK according to the National Data and Analytics Office); a score that would be mirrored in a draft NPCC AI Data Readiness toolkit GMP gained early access to. This assessment will be potentially revisited as part of a future HMICFRS thematic inspection programme. The headline strategy objectives were developed using the Carruthers and Jackson (2023) data model, adopted by the NPCC National Police Data Board to set a standard for data maturity, which was used in the 2023 national self-assessment initiative. Through a series of workshops with internal stakeholders, business leads, and practitioners ten interconnected themes were developed, aligned to the context and priorities of the organisation (Figure 5). The overall objective was set as *"Enabling outstanding policing through effective use of our data assets to improve productivity and keep people safe."*. This was an important gateway statement to draw in both the operational 'public service motivation' context, and the wider business context of the current political and financial framework UK policing is experiencing.

Figure 5. A summary diagram of the GMP Data Strategy

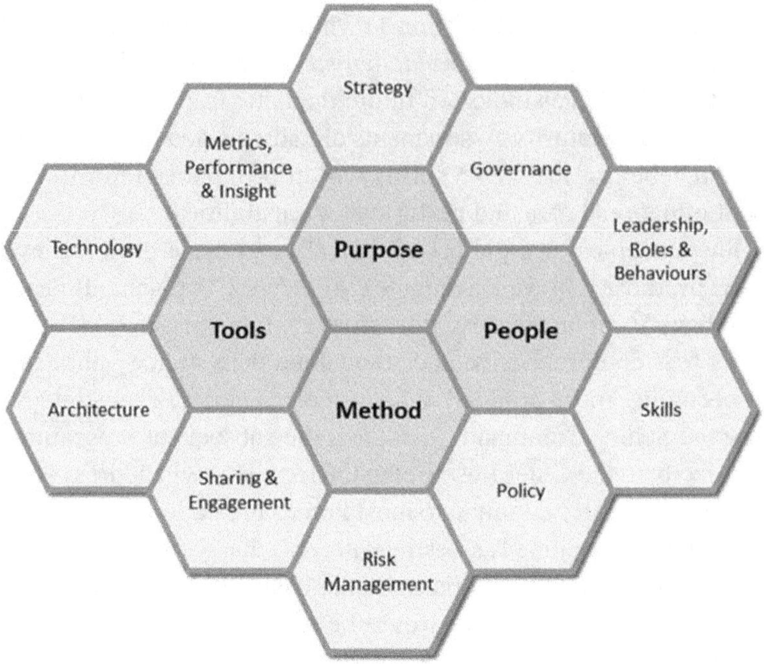

Adapted from Carruthers and Jackson (2023)

The above illustration is deliberately representative of a series of strategy objectives that are interconnected. It is intended as a starting point for a living document that matures through engagement with the business. There is significant alignment with these objectives and those of the newly published NPCC National Policing Digital Strategy (2025-2030) roadmap. In summary, the context for each theme was agreed as follows, which is being taken forward to a formalised programme of work:

Strategy: Develop a strategy that prioritises and delivers enablers for GMP's Plan-on-a-Page, Digital Policing Programme, and wider alignment to policing reform. It is imperative to map our assets and ensure there is a robust 'return on investment' ethos to all business cases relating to these assets from requirements developed with Information Asset Owners (IAOs).

Governance: Establish a Data Board at Chief Officer level to oversee the strategy, and improve corporate data governance, ownership, and processes of innovation to comply with ethical, legislative and regulatory requirements for operational and organisational use.

Leadership, Roles & Behaviours: Establish a fully engaged business owner network for the development of requirements for data quality and utilisation. Raise awareness and effectiveness of IAO's responsibilities towards GMP's data strategy.

Improve data literacy within our leadership. Reduce organisational behaviours that impact data quality.

Skills: Develop comprehensive training programmes to enhance data literacy among police personnel. Focus on building skills in data analysis, data science, and IT among staff. Control the proliferation of localised product development. Improve retention of skills police staff within the public sector.

Policy: Establish a process for all new policy development to engage with data governance on development and evolve and enhance adherence monitoring processes for all data regulatory requirements through the Strategic Information Risk Board (SIRB). Reduce the 'cottage industry' of local data products.

Risk Management: Undertake a risk review and prioritisation exercise and develop a robust mitigation plan for the overarching data quality risk within the force risk register, championing personal responsibility in managing our data.

Sharing & Engagement: Explore opportunities for connectivity with the wider GM data landscape for the benefit of our communities. Create public-facing dashboards to share crime statistics, legitimate use of powers, and police performance metrics with the community.

Architecture: Align current and future IT architecture to a roadmap of improvement in data quality, connectivity, and productivity. Develop a programme of work that improves data maturity as recognised and reflected in HMICFRS inspection themes and NPCC (DDaT) assessments.

Technology: Establish an uncontested position of current data inputs and their accuracy, and future technology requirements with prioritisation for automation and exploitation of AI. Develop effective migration strategies for legacy applications that minimises operational risk. Reduce 'cottage industry' product development within the organisation.

Metrics, Performance & Insight: Identify and deliver a suite of interoperable and predictive analytics that enable effective operational and organisational governance assurance with minimum manual effort and maximum leverage of self-service tools. Align development of products to requirements of outstanding PEEL and Force Management Statement (FMS) categories and have a tracking process for requests.

This strategy establishes a framework for the organisation to get 'match fit' on the raw materials to fully embrace AI. It is put forward as a model of good practice for other forces to emulate and will provide a platform for AI opportunities and further exploration of digital twin modelling concepts. The programme of work is being designed so that the functions most important to a model representing the business of policing are prioritised to create momentum for organisational level application, as well as the tactical applications growing in popularity in policing. The prioritisation is aligned to the wider programme of change in the organisation to deliver the overall plan of service deliver and hence has both the endorsement and ongoing oversight of the Senior Command Team. As with all organisational strategies, one comes up against the very real human problem of sustained delivery of change and adopting of new ways of working, but an exploration of this is not the subject of this short paper.

CONCLUSIONS

The UK police service is being gainfully encouraged to adopt new technologies as a requirement to become more productive with limited resources, but also to reflect the society it polices. Legislation, policy, and guidance is currently navigating the duel-edged sword of progress with ethical deployment of technology. However, the extent to which AI systems, tools and algorithms are being adopted, and the pace of adoption, is being overplayed. There is understandable caution, and the connection has not yet been strongly made with the possibilities such applications could offer, and that relationship with having good foundations of the basics in the data AI tools will rely upon. Across the service in the UK, the level of data maturity to fully enable applications is not at the required level. There is also a focus on the tactical level of applications to respond to productivity challenges, when a more ambitious strategic level of application could perhaps be more fruitful in the long term. AI systems, tools and algorithms are developed to enhance and augment human endeavour to deal with the complex. The field has a natural and historic affinity with Complexity Theory, which is also, it is argued, a compelling framework for public service administration in this new age of AI augmentation. A complexity epistemology and methodology provide tools to achieve a level of maturity in data management that will ultimately feed policy design and operating model analysis supported by AI. At the very least it provides an effective way of prioritising data management and improvement directly relatable to the productivity of the organisation and provides a more transparent and safer environment to pilot AI systems, tools and algorithms. It can potentially provide a bridge between the operational and the technical through the exploration of defined system levels, which it is recommended is used in addressing the issue of strategic data literacy in senior police officers, by providing operational context, and preparing police leadership to 'play the game – and win'.

Note from Publisher

Correction Notice: A correction to this manuscript has been published
Reason: Poor Quality Images

Author inquired about the poor quality of their images and sent us new files. We have replaced the images, so they are better represented.

Correction Date: 8th May 2026

REFERENCES

Atkin, R. (1974). *Mathematical Structure in Human Affairs*. Heinemann Educational Books.

Atkin, R. (1981). *Multidimensional Man: Can Man Live in 3-Dimensional Space?* Penguin Books.

Babuta, A., & Oswald, M. (2020). *Data analytics and algorithms in policing in England and Wales: Towards a new policy framework*. Royal United Services Institute. rusi_pub_165_2020_01_algorithmic_policing_babuta_final_web_copy.pdf.

Barabasi, A.-L. (2014). *Linked*. Basic Books.

Behaviour, A.-S. Crime and Policing Act (2014), c. 11 (UK). https://www.legislation.gov.uk/ukpga/2014/12/contents

Carruthers & Jackson. (2023). *Data Model*. https://carruthersandjackson.com/data-maturity/

Casti, J. L. (1997b). *Would-be Worlds: How Simulation is Changing the Frontiers of Science*. John Wiley & Sons, Inc.

College of Policing. (2014). *Authorised Professional Practice for Management of Police Information (MOPI)*. https://www.college.police.uk/app/information-management/management-police-information

College of Policing. (2024). *Code of Ethics*. https://www.college.police.uk/ethics/code-of-ethics

College of Policing. (2025). *Data Ethics Principles*. https://www.college.police.uk/app/data-ethics/data-ethics-principles

College of Policing. (2025). *Executive Leadership Programme* https://www.college.police.uk/career-learning/courses/executive-leaders-programme-elp

Data Protection Act. (2018).

Davies, P. (2024) *Applications of Complexity Theory in an English Metropolitan Police Force*. [Doctoral dissertation, Open University]. Centre of Policing Research & Learning.

Diamond, L. (2008). *Twelve Simple Rules of Systems Thinking for Complex Systems*. https://icasc.ca/twelve-simple-rules-of-systems-thinking-for-complex-global-issues/

. Epstein, J. (2008). *Why Model?* Journal of Artificial Societies and Social Simulation. 2008-10, Vol.11 (4).

Epstein, J. M. (1999). Agent-Based Computational Models and Generative Social Science. *Complexity*, *4*(5), 41–60. DOI: 10.1002/(SICI)1099-0526(199905/06)4:5<41::AID-CPLX9>3.0.CO;2-F

Future of Life Institute. (2025). *High-level summary of the AI Act.* https://artificialintelligenceact.eu/high-level-summary/

Gargan, N. (2025). *Learning from the inside out.* [Conference Presentation] Staffordshire Police Leadership Team (08/07/25).

Gershenson, C. (2024) *Complexity, Artificial Life, and Artificial Intelligence*. Artificial Life 1-15. Massachusetts Institute of Technology.

Gershenson, C. (2025). Complexity, artificial life, and artificial intelligence. *Artificial Life*, *31*(3), 289–303. DOI: 10.1162/artl_a_00462 PMID: 39576152

Ghorbani, A., Dechesne, F., Dignum, V., & Jonker, C. (2014). Enhancing ABM into an Inevitable Tool for Policy Analysis. *Policy and Complex Systems*, *1*(1), 61–76. DOI: 10.18278/jpcs.1.1.3

Gilbert, N., & Troitzsch, K. (2011). *Simulation for the Social Scientist* (2nd ed.). Open University Press.

Heath, B., Hill, R., & Ciarallo, F. (2009). *A survey of agent-based modeling practices* (January 1998 to July 2008). *Journal of Artificial Societies and Social Simulation*, *12*, 9.

Home Office. (2024). *Home Secretary announces major policing reforms*. https://www.gov.uk/government/news/home-secretary-announces-major-policing-reforms

Home Office. (2024). *Police Grant Report: 2025 to 2026.* https://www.gov.uk/government/publications/provisional-police-grant-report-2025-to-2026

Home Office. (2026). *From Local to National: A New Model for Policing*. https://www.gov.uk/government/publications/from-local-to-national-a-new-model-for-policing

Hung, T., & Yen, C. (2021). On the person-based predictive policing of AI. *Ethics and Information Technology*, *23*(3), 165–176. DOI: 10.1007/s10676-020-09539-x

Ilcic, A., Fuentes, M., & Lawler, D. (2025). Artificial intelligence, complexity, and systemic resilience in global governance. *Frontiers in Artificial Intelligence*, *8*, 1562095. DOI: 10.3389/frai.2025.1562095 PMID: 40529642

Independent, The. *Spending review a 'huge blow' for police and 'will hamper efforts to recruit 13,000 neighbourhood police officers' (*https://www.independent.co.uk/news/uk/crime/police-spending-review-npcc-reeves-b2768233.html

Insight, P. (2025). *UK Police Digital Experience Survey 2025: Headline Findings.* Policing Insight. https://policinginsight.com

Investigatory Powers Act. (2016).

Johnson, J. (2006, October). Can Complexity Help Us Better Understand Risk? *Risk Management, 8*(4), 227–267. DOI: 10.1057/palgrave.rm.8250023

Johnson, J. (2013). *Hypernetworks in the Science of Complex Systems.* World Scientific.

Johnson, J., & Cook, M. (2014). Policy Design: A New Area of Design Research and Practice. In Aiguier, M., Boulanger, F., Krob, D., & Marchal, C. (Eds.), *Complex Systems Design & Management* (pp. 51–62). Springer International Publishing. DOI: 10.1007/978-3-319-02812-5_4

Johnson, J., Denning, P., Odlysko, A., Walker, M., Delic, K., Yaffe, P., & Picton, P. (2025) *Foundational Technologies of Artificial Intelligence. Ubiquity Symposium, an Association for Computing Machinery publication.*

Johnson, J., Nowak, A., Ormerod, P., Rosewell, B., & Zhang, Y.-C. (2017). *Non-Equilibrium Social Science and Policy.* Springer Open. DOI: 10.1007/978-3-319-42424-8

Jones, M. (2008). A Complexity Science View of Modern Police Administration. *Public Administration Quarterly, 32*, 433–457.

Kolt, N., Shur-Ofry, M., & Cohen, R. (2025). *Lessons from complexity theory for AI governance.* arXiv. .DOI: 10.1016/j.patter.2025.101341

Krishna, S., Aljohani, N., Mishra, D., Garg, N., Verma, V., & Malathy, V. (2023). Applications of Artificial Intelligence in Public Sector and its Challenges. *4th International Conference on Computation, Automation and Knowledge Management.* DOI: 10.1109/ICCAKM58659.2023.10449594

López-Ruiz, R. (2025). *AI and Statistical Complexity.* Complex Systems with Artificial Intelligence – IntechOpen.

Lyytinen, K., Weber, B., Becker, M., & Pentland, B. (2024). Digital Twins of Organization: Implications for Organization Design. *Journal of Organization Design, 13*(3), 77–93. DOI: 10.1007/s41469-023-00151-z

Mainzer, K. (2025). Complex systems and the evolution of artificial intelligence. In *Thinking in Complexity* (pp. 171–252). Springer.

Mathews, K. M., White, M., & Long, R. (1999). Why Study the Complexity Sciences in the Social Sciences? *Human Relations*, *52*(4), 439–462. DOI: 10.1177/001872679905200402

Matulionyte, R., & Zalnieriute, M. (2024). *The Cambridge Handbook of Facial Recognition in the Modern State*. Cambridge University Press. DOI: 10.1017/9781009321211

Mitcham, J. (2023). Agent-Based Simulation of Policy Funding Tradeoffs Through the Lens of Legitimacy and Hardship. *Journal of Artificial Societies and Social Simulation*, *26*(3), 12. DOI: 10.18564/jasss.5169

Muir, R., & O'Connell, F. (2025). *Policing and Artificial Intelligence*. The Police Foundation.

National Audit Office. (2015). *Financial Sustainability of Police Forces in England and Wales*. https://www.nao.org.uk/reports/financial-sustainability-of-police-forces-in-england-and-wales/

. National Police Chiefs Council (NPCC) (2024). *AI Strategy.*

National Police Chiefs Council (NPCC). (2025). *About Us*. https://www.npcc.police.uk/About-Us/about-us/

National Police Chiefs Council (NPCC) (2025). *National Policing Digital Strategy 2025-2030.*

National Police Chiefs Council (NPCC). (2025). *Artificial Intelligence (AI) Playbook for Policing*. https://library.college.police.uk/docs/NPCC/Artificial-intelligence-playbook-policing-2025.pdf

Nespeca, V., Comes, T., & Brazier, F. (2023). A Methodology to Develop Agent-Based Models for Policy Support Via Qualitative Inquiry. *Journal of Artificial Societies and Social Simulation*, *26*(1), 10. DOI: 10.18564/jasss.5014

Qudrat-Ullah, H. (2025). *Navigating Complexity: AI and Systems Thinking for Smarter Decisions*. Springer. DOI: 10.1007/978-3-031-82742-6

Raji, I., & Sholademi, D. (2024). Predictive Policing: The Role of AI in Crime Prevention. *International Journal of Computer Applications Technology and Research*, *13*(10), 66–78.

Regulation (EU) 2016/679 (2016) *General Data Protection Regulations (GDPR).*

Reiner, R. (2010). *The Politics of the Police* (4th ed.). Oxford University Press. DOI: 10.1093/he/9780199283392.001.0001

Ruijer, E., Dingelstad, J., & Meijer, A. (2021). Studying complex systems through design interventions Probing open government data ecosystems in the Netherlands. *Public Management Review*, •••, 1–21.

Simon, H. (1996). *The Sciences of the Artificial.* MIT Press.

Snowden, D. J., & Boone, M. E. (2007). A leader's framework for decision making. *Harvard Business Review*, *85*, 68. PMID: 18159787

Sohail, A., & Zhang, L. (2025). Using large language models to facilitate academic work in the psychological sciences. *Current Psychology (New Brunswick, N.J.)*, *44*(9), 7910–7918. DOI: 10.1007/s12144-025-07438-2 PMID: 40438548

Togelius, J. (2024). *Artificial General Intelligence*. MIT Press. DOI: 10.7551/mitpress/15378.001.0001

Torrible, C. N. (2022). Trust in the police and policing by consent in turbulent times. *Safer Communities*, *21-3*(3), 171–183. DOI: 10.1108/SC-08-2021-0036

UKAuthority News. (2025). *New Data Act for UK receives Royal assent.* https://www.ukauthority.com/articles/new-data-act-for-uk-receives-royal-assent

UNISON. (2025). *Police Force Shortfalls 2025/26.* https://www.unison.org.uk/at-work/police-and-justice-staff/key-issues/police-force-shortfalls-2025-26/

Vohra, M. (2023). *Digital Twin Technology: Fundamentals and Applications.* Wiley-Scrivener publishers.

Walley, P., & Glasspoole-Bird, H. (2025). *An Evaluation of the Pilot Application of Artificial Intelligence to Witness Statement and Report Generation at Hertfordshire Constabulary*. Open University Centre for Policing Research & Learning Publication.

Wilson, C., Dalins, J., & Rolan, G. (2020) *Effective, Explainable and Ethical: AI for Law Enforcement and Community Safety.* 2020 IEEE / ITU International Conference on Artificial Intelligence for Good (AI4G), 2020, p.186-191 DOI: 10.1109/AI4G50087.2020.9311021

Wirtz, B., Wyerer, J., & Geyer, C. (2019). Artificial Intelligence and the Public Sector – Applications and Challenges. *International Journal of Public Administration*, *42*(7), 595–615. DOI: 10.1080/01900692.2018.1498103

Chapter 2
Governing Algorithmic Policing in Himachal Pradesh:
Artificial Intelligence, Privacy, and Constitutional Accountability

Kundesh Sharma
http://orcid.org/0009-0005-7485-4169
Lovely Professional University, India

ABSTRACT

The chapter examines the application of Artificial Intelligence (AI) in policing in Himachal Pradesh, India, and its implications for privacy, governance, and ethical accountability. It analyses AI-enabled initiatives such as predictive analytics, facial recognition, smart traffic surveillance, and cyber-crime intelligence within the legal framework of Section 69 of the Information Technology Act, 2000 and the landmark K.S. Puttaswamy v. Union of India (2017) judgment on the right to privacy. Using reliable secondary data, the study adopts an exploratory and descriptive research design to assess institutional collaborations, capacity-building initiatives, and technological deployments by the Himachal Pradesh Police. The findings highlight concerns related to algorithmic bias, data retention, transparency, and accountability. The paper proposes policy measures to align AI-based policing with constitutional principles through judicial oversight, ethical audits, data minimisation, and citizen-centric governance.

DOI: 10.4018/979-8-3373-5228-2.ch002

INTRODUCTION

In India, artificial intelligence (AI) is rapidly transforming governance and public administration, particularly in areas that require constant surveillance, prompt decision-making, and the processing of large volumes of data. One of the most significantly transformed fields is policing, where applications now extend beyond algorithmic monitoring and predictive analytics to include automated traffic monitoring and cyber-intelligence technologies. In Himalayan states, including Himachal Pradesh, this technological shift has added significance because of the region's complex topography, inter-state boundaries, ecologically sensitive zones, fluctuating tourist numbers, and increasing cyber vulnerabilities. Together, these factors create a distinct security context that requires enhanced technological support (Himachal Pradesh Police, 2024).

Over the last decade, the Himachal Pradesh Police (HPP) has undertaken several initiatives aimed at modernisation, including the deployment of smart traffic cameras, predictive patrol mapping, cybercrime reporting systems, and partnerships with institutions such as IIT Mandi. Prominent developments include the Northern Region Police Coordination Committee Meeting held in Shimla in 2024, the HPP–IIT Mandi technology partnership (2020–2025), the *AI for Good Governance* workshop in 2025, and iCAST-based cyber-security capacity-building initiatives (Ministry of Electronics and Information Technology [MeitY], 2025). These efforts align with national-level programmes such as the National Cybercrime Reporting Portal, the Indian Cybercrime Coordination Centre (I4C), and digital capacity-building initiatives under the Digital India programme (Ministry of Home Affairs, 2023).

Nevertheless, AI-based policing also raises significant legal, constitutional, and ethical concerns. The landmark Supreme Court judgment in *K.S. Puttaswamy v. Union of India* (2017) recognised privacy as a fundamental right under Article 21 and established the tests of legality, legitimate aim, proportionality, and minimal intrusion as essential safeguards governing state surveillance. At the same time, Section 69 of the Information Technology Act, 2000 permits the state to intercept and monitor communications, although it requires procedural safeguards and accountability (Government of India, 2000). Because AI systems often rely on opaque algorithms and may influence high-stakes decisions, these constitutional principles are crucial in preventing abuse, bias, and unnecessary intrusions.

In India, AI has already been applied across a wide range of policing functions, as outlined in Table 1. As a result, civil society organisations such as the Internet Freedom Foundation (2021) and the Centre for Internet and Society (2022) have raised concerns about algorithmic policing tools, including facial recognition, automated number-plate recognition, predictive heat maps, and deep-learning surveillance systems. These studies identify several associated risks, including false positives, demographic bias, indefinite data retention, and inadequate statutory oversight. Comparable concerns have also emerged internationally. For example, in *R (Bridges) v. Chief Constable of South Wales Police* (2020), the UK Court of Appeal held that the use of live facial recognition lacked sufficient legal and procedural safeguards to protect privacy. Similarly, criticism of algorithmic risk assessment tools in the United States has drawn attention to bias in predictive systems, with studies such as Angwin et al. (2016) highlighting the discriminatory effects that can arise in algorithmic decision-making. Concerns relating to transparency, algorithmic auditing, and proportionality in high-risk AI applications have also been emphasised in the European Union's Artificial Intelligence Act (European Commission, 2021).

Table 1. AI adoption and digital policing initiatives in India

State/Agency	AI / Digital Policing Initiative	Purpose / Key Features
Delhi Police	Crime Mapping Analytics & Predictive System (CMAPS)	Predictive policing, hotspot identification
Himachal Pradesh Police	Him Pragati Portal & e-FIR System	Digital case registration, citizen-centric policing
Telangana Police	AI-based Facial Recognition (Darpan)	Identify suspects, match criminal photographs
Maharashtra Police	Automated Multi-Modal Biometric Identification System (AMBIS)	Fingerprint & facial biometrics integration
Punjab Police	PAIS (Punjab AI System for Crime Analytics)	Crime pattern detection, database integration
National Level	Crime and Criminal Tracking Network & Systems (CCTNS)	National crime database, interoperability

Source: Compilation of various AI / Digital Policing Initiatives in India

In Himachal Pradesh, the use of tools such as helmet-detection cameras, ANPR cameras, smart CCTV networks, and cyber-intelligence platforms has improved operational efficiency. However, these developments have not been accompanied by a dedicated state-level AI governance policy or a statutory privacy framework. Significant gaps remain in publicly available records concerning algorithmic accuracy, data storage practices, access control policies, consent procedures, and grievance redress mechanisms (Himachal Pradesh Police, 2024). These concerns underscore the need to examine how Himachal Pradesh can balance AI-driven policing with constitutional safeguards, protect civil liberties, and maintain operational effectiveness.

This paper therefore examines the theme of *AI and Privacy on the Slopes: Governing Algorithmic Policing in Himachal Pradesh* from a techno-legal and policy perspective, situating developments in Himachal Pradesh within wider national and international debates. It explores the current adoption of AI tools in the state, the interaction between these deployments and privacy protections under *K.S. Puttaswamy v. Union of India* (2017) and the Information Technology Act, 2000, the present state of governance, and the structural reforms required to ensure that AI-enabled policing is ethical, accountable, and constitutionally sound.

LITERATURE REVIEW

Artificial intelligence (AI) has gained global traction in law enforcement, particularly through technologies such as predictive policing, facial recognition, and real-time surveillance (Fitzgerald, 2024; Hahn, 2025). These technologies offer potential benefits in crime prevention, information analysis, and resource allocation. However, they also raise significant ethical, privacy, and constitutional concerns, especially in democratic contexts where the protection of fundamental rights is paramount (Rani, 2025). In India, the adoption of AI in policing must be considered alongside the constitutional guarantee of privacy and the evolving legal framework for data protection and digital governance, particularly following *K.S. Puttaswamy v. Union of India* (2017). This literature review summarises contemporary scholarship on AI-driven policing, with particular emphasis on sources relevant to the Indian and regional context.

AI in Policing: Tools and Applications

Recent research highlights the growing use of AI in predictive crime analysis, automated surveillance, and legal support functions. Hahn (2025) presents a cross-national comparison of AI-driven predictive policing models and argues that algorithmic crime prediction can improve the allocation of law enforcement resources, although weak regulation may reinforce existing biases. Similarly, Fitzgerald (2024) focuses on the operational challenges associated with AI in law enforcement, particularly issues relating to accuracy, data quality, and model transparency, and argues that algorithmic interventions should be subject to continuous verification in order to prevent systematic errors. Kavidharani (2025) examines predictive policing technologies in the Indian context and contends that, without robust oversight mechanisms, AI-based systems may disproportionately affect disadvantaged groups and deepen social inequalities. Collectively, these studies emphasise that technological efficiency must be accompanied by ethical safeguards.

Ethical and Privacy Concerns

The integration of AI into law enforcement raises major ethical and privacy concerns. Singh (2025) examines the tension between security and privacy in India, arguing that unregulated AI-driven surveillance may violate constitutional rights. Kumar (2025) further notes that AI policing may have downstream effects on criminal justice processes, particularly where decisions are based too heavily on algorithmic outputs, thereby increasing the risk of unjust outcomes. Rani (2025) discusses the constitutional limits of AI-enabled policing and stresses the importance of proportionality, necessity, and judicial review in preventing privacy infringements in AI-assisted law enforcement. Together, these studies demonstrate that although AI may enhance policing capabilities, significant ethical risks remain, including unfair decision-making, lack of consent, and unauthorised use of data.

AI Governance and Oversight

Robust governance structures are essential for the responsible deployment of AI. Batool et al. (2023) examine global models of responsible AI governance and emphasise the importance of transparency, accountability, and auditing standards. Mirishli (2025) advocates privacy-preserving methods of data collection, including data minimisation, anonymisation, and controlled access. Singh and Mohapatra (2025) propose policy strategies for embedding ethical safeguards within the use of AI in the public sector. Taken together, these studies suggest that AI policing can be aligned with democratic values only through institutional oversight, external auditing, and clearly defined operational guidelines.

Legal and Constitutional Dimensions

India's constitutional framework, particularly the right to privacy under Article 21, sets a high threshold for government surveillance and algorithmic intervention. Drawing on the principles established in *K.S. Puttaswamy v. Union of India* (2017), Rani (2025) and Kavidharani (2025) argue that AI applications in policing must be governed by the principles of legality, necessity, proportionality, and transparency. They also stress that data interception and AI-enhanced surveillance should remain subject to judicial oversight so that technological efficiency does not come at the expense of civil liberties. Hahn (2025) reinforces this argument through comparative analysis, showing that strong legal regulation reduces the risk of misuse of AI in policing across jurisdictions.

Regional and Indian Context

The introduction of artificial intelligence into Indian state police forces, including pilot initiatives in Himachal Pradesh, illustrates the dual nature of technological adoption. On the one hand, it offers significant opportunities to improve operational effectiveness; on the other, it introduces complex legal, ethical, and governance challenges. Empirical studies (Kumar, 2025; Singh, 2025) indicate that law enforcement agencies in India are beginning to use predictive analytics and automated surveillance for functions such as traffic management, cybercrime detection, and intelligence gathering. However, deficiencies in policy transparency, judicial oversight, and technical safeguards remain evident, highlighting the need for a more systematic governance framework. Rani (2025) and Kavidharani (2025) therefore argue for the urgent establishment of effective AI governance mechanisms, independent ethics committees, and stronger public reporting practices to ensure that AI deployments serve the public good without undermining constitutional protections.

RESEARCH GAPS

Despite the growing body of literature, several important gaps remain. First, few empirical studies have examined state-level AI policing projects in India, particularly in smaller states such as Himachal Pradesh. Second, there is limited assessment of algorithmic bias and accuracy within Indian settings, where demographic and infrastructural conditions may differ significantly from those in other jurisdictions. Third, there is an absence of formal oversight mechanisms relating to judicial review, public accountability, and remedies in the context of AI-based policing. Addressing these gaps is necessary in order to develop policies that support the responsible and sustainable use of AI in policing while protecting fundamental rights.

RESEARCH OBJECTIVES

The objectives of this study are as follows:

1. To assess the use of AI-based policing technologies in Himachal Pradesh.
2. To examine the privacy and legal implications of AI-enabled policing in the state.
3. To evaluate existing governance mechanisms and propose measures for accountable and ethical AI deployment.

RESEARCH METHODOLOGY

Research Design

This study adopts an exploratory and descriptive research design to analyse the application of artificial intelligence in policing and the associated privacy concerns in Himachal Pradesh. The methodology is based exclusively on secondary data sources in order to ensure accuracy, reliability, and legal relevance.

Data Sources

Data were collected from verified secondary sources, including the following:

- Government reports, including those produced by the Ministry of Home Affairs, Himachal Pradesh Police, and NCRP/I4C
- Judicial documents, including Supreme Court judgments and a UK Court of Appeal case
- Publications from reputable policy think tanks, including the Vidhi Centre for Legal Policy, the Internet Freedom Foundation, and the Centre for Internet and Society
- International regulatory documents, including the European Union AI Act
- Academic literature from recognised journals addressing AI ethics, surveillance, and policing

DISCUSSION

Legal and Constitutional Framework

The implementation of AI-based policing by the Himachal Pradesh Police (HPP) must align with India's constitutional privacy protections and broader legal constraints. Under Section 69 of the Information Technology Act, 2000, the state has the power to intercept, monitor, or decrypt information. However, following the Supreme Court's decision in *K.S. Puttaswamy v. Union of India* (2017), any infringement of privacy must satisfy the requirements of legality, necessity, and proportionality under Article 21 of the Constitution.

Within this constitutional framework, the burden of justification is particularly high. Surveillance must be narrowly tailored, time-bound, and minimally intrusive, and it should be accompanied by procedural safeguards and, ideally, judicial oversight.

However, AI applications such as facial recognition technology, predictive analytics, and automated CCTV systems raise more complex concerns. These technologies can facilitate large-scale and persistent tracking, indefinite data retention, and algorithmic inference that extends beyond the original purpose of collection. Their internal logic, including training data, calibration processes, and confidence thresholds, is often opaque, thereby increasing the risks of error propagation, misidentification, and discriminatory effects. When combined with the absence of binding statutory protections or standardised audit regimes in India, this lack of transparency poses a serious threat to privacy and procedural fairness.

Accordingly, although digital surveillance may have a formal legal basis under Section 69 and related provisions, the use of AI without clear governance and accountability mechanisms significantly heightens the risk of constitutional overreach.

CASE STUDY: HIMACHAL PRADESH'S AI POLICING ECOSYSTEM

a) Strategic Coordination and Intelligence Sharing

Recent institutional developments indicate growing investment in AI-assisted policing in Himachal Pradesh. In late 2024, the Northern Region Police Coordination Committee convened a meeting in Shimla to discuss counter-terrorism, drug trafficking, cyber fraud, and misinformation, including the potential role of AI systems in cross-jurisdictional policing. This reflects a broader shift towards multisectoral interoperability and data-driven criminal intelligence exchange. Although such coordination may improve responsiveness to cross-border threats, it also expands the scope of surveillance and increases the number of data streams involved, thereby intensifying privacy and governance risks.

b) Academia-Police Institutional Collaboration

The Memorandum of Understanding (MoU) between HPP and IIT Mandi (2020–2025) formalises a strategic partnership in AI-driven criminogenic analysis, cybercrime detection, traffic management, and threat monitoring, thereby strengthening the technical infrastructure of policing. Although collaboration between academic institutions and law enforcement can provide significant benefits in terms of capacity building and innovation, it also raises important questions about algorithm design, data management, and accountability. These issues are especially important where there is limited public transparency regarding system specifications or auditing procedures.

c) AI Governance and Capacity Building

Himachal Pradesh has also demonstrated investment in AI-related capacity building. The *AI for Good Governance* workshop held in May 2025 trained more than 100 officials in areas such as transparency, risk mitigation, and digital governance planning, while the iCAST-25 Cybersecurity Workshop in April 2025 strengthened police capacity in digital forensics, cyber hygiene, and incident response. These initiatives suggest that the institution recognises the risks associated with AI and is taking a proactive approach to governance preparedness. However, episodic training alone is insufficient. Long-term oversight must be institutionalised through regular audits, standard operating procedures (SOPs), and citizen-facing redress and transparency mechanisms.

d) Technological Deployments

Smart traffic cameras with AI-based helmet-detection and number-plate recognition capabilities were introduced in Himachal Pradesh in 2021, primarily to strengthen traffic enforcement and road safety monitoring. Although these systems offer clear enforcement benefits, their integration with wider intelligence databases may transform them into broader surveillance tools. Given the documented risks of bias and misidentification in AI-based vision systems, particularly under adverse conditions such as low light and changing landscapes, these applications require rigorous validation. Research on facial recognition systems internationally has identified discriminatory accuracy errors, especially among underrepresented population groups.

In addition, coordination meetings have included discussions about expanding CCTV networks through AI modules capable of behaviour detection, cross-border movement tracking, and live surveillance. Unless properly regulated, such systems may effectively turn public spaces into extensive zones of data collection.

e) Digital Case Management and e-Courts Integration

At the national level, the e-Courts Phase III programme introduces AI into judicial processes through natural language processing (NLP), optical character recognition (OCR), and predictive scheduling. Although these systems may modernise case management and improve efficiency, the extent to which law enforcement agencies may access or rely upon related metadata or system outputs remains legally unclear.

In the absence of clear legal limits and controls, there is a risk of data leakage or misuse, which may undermine both privacy and procedural fairness.

PRIVACY, OVERSIGHT, AND ACCOUNTABILITY

a) Judicial Supervision and Public Transparency

Given the privacy implications of AI-assisted policing, both judicial oversight and public transparency are essential. The *Puttaswamy* judgment makes clear that any surveillance activity must be authorised by law, pursue a legitimate aim, and remain proportionate to that aim.

However, in Himachal Pradesh, there is no publicly available policy document clarifying how surveillance orders are authorised, who approves them, how data are managed, or what retention periods apply, particularly where AI tools such as CCTV analytics or automatic number-plate recognition (ANPR) are used. In the absence of clear procedures, the legitimacy of AI policing remains uncertain.

b) Technical Accuracy and Bias Mitigation

Both comparative international research and local empirical studies indicate substantial limitations in AI-based facial recognition and optical surveillance technologies. A recent audit of facial processing systems using an Indian demographic sample reported higher error rates across gender and age categories, with significantly poorer performance among women and certain other demographic groups. Such findings raise serious concerns regarding the accuracy, fairness, and reliability of these systems in operational policing contexts.

AI policing applications are also often trained on historical crime data in order to generate forecasts and surveillance alerts. However, researchers have noted that such historical data may already reflect patterns of selective enforcement or broader socio-economic bias. Algorithms trained on these data may therefore reproduce, or even amplify, such biases in subsequent policing decisions (Barocas & Selbst, 2016; Ferguson, 2017). In practice, this may lead to disproportionate surveillance of particular localities or social groups, thereby reinforcing structural inequalities in law enforcement. For this reason, AI-assisted policing should incorporate regular algorithmic audits, bias testing, and transparent reporting processes to ensure that technological tools do not inadvertently reproduce discriminatory outcomes.

Accordingly, before implementation, the Himachal Pradesh Police should require all AI-enabled devices, including helmet-detection cameras, number-plate recognition units, and integrated CCTV-AI systems, to undergo independent auditing, peer review, and validation under the state's distinctive environmental conditions, including mountainous terrain, variable lighting, and adverse weather. Agencies should establish and publicly report confidence thresholds, minimum error-rate expectations, and performance ceilings. In addition, low-confidence matches should be excluded from operational decision-making in order to reduce the risk of false identification and discriminatory outcomes.

c) Consent, Data Minimisation, and Purpose Limitation

AI surveillance practices should be governed by clear principles of data minimisation and purpose limitation. For example, cameras deployed for traffic monitoring or helmet detection should not automatically be repurposed for crowd monitoring or behavioural analysis without proper legal authorisation. Data retention policies should specify how long footage or biometric metadata may be retained, access controls should clearly define who may access such data and under what conditions, and appropriate safeguards should include role-based access, anonymisation, and encryption. Without such protections, the routine use of AI tools may contribute to the emergence of a broad and potentially unconstitutional surveillance infrastructure.

A related concern arises from the wider expansion of AI-enabled surveillance systems. Although technologies such as automatic number-plate recognition, facial recognition networks, and smart CCTV systems may improve operational efficiency, they may also contribute to the gradual normalisation of surveillance in public spaces. Scholars of surveillance governance warn that the large-scale collection of behavioural and biometric data can shift the balance of power between the state and individuals in ways that may undermine democratic accountability unless robust protections are in place (Brayne, 2020). Thus, without strict regulation, transparency, and oversight, the use of AI in policing may gradually develop into a permanent surveillance infrastructure. Regulatory frameworks must therefore ensure that technological development does not erode constitutional rights to privacy and civil liberty.

COMPARATIVE ETHICAL AI GOVERNANCE FRAMEWORKS

The use of artificial intelligence in policing has prompted governments across the world to establish regulatory frameworks intended to ensure the responsible and ethical deployment of algorithmic systems. One notable example is Canada's *Directive on Automated Decision-Making*, introduced by the Treasury Board of Canada Secretariat in 2019. Under this policy, federal institutions are required to conduct an Algorithmic Impact Assessment (AIA) before deploying automated decision systems in public administration. This assessment evaluates risks relating to transparency, bias, privacy, and accountability, and it supports the protection of these values through human oversight, public disclosure, and regular system audits.

Similarly, the European Union has adopted the Artificial Intelligence Act, under which certain AI applications, including biometric identification and predictive policing, are treated as high-risk systems. These systems must comply with strict regulatory requirements concerning data governance, transparency, risk assessment, and independent oversight (European Commission, 2021).

These international frameworks demonstrate that the integration of AI into public-sector decision-making must be supported by institutional oversight, transparency, and accountability. For Indian states such as Himachal Pradesh, these models offer useful benchmarks for the development of governance structures that balance technological innovation with constitutional protection and democratic responsibility.

REDRESS AND REMEDY

Citizens must have access to effective redress mechanisms in order to preserve constitutional fairness. Individuals subject to AI-enhanced surveillance should have the right to access and review their data, challenge its accuracy, request correction or erasure, and receive meaningful explanations where algorithmic outputs inform enforcement decisions. AI-generated evidence alone, including a facial recognition match, should not be treated as sufficient in the absence of corroboration from a non-AI source. In addition, an independent oversight body, such as a parliamentary watchdog, ombudsman institution, or state privacy commission, should be established to monitor compliance, adjudicate complaints, and promote transparency.

CONCLUSION

The introduction of artificial intelligence into the policing structure of Himachal Pradesh represents a significant shift from traditional enforcement practices towards data-driven governance. However, as this study has shown, the deployment of AI systems, including smart highway cameras, predictive analytics, and the possible future use of facial recognition, occurs within a complex legal, constitutional, and ethical environment. Indian constitutional jurisprudence, particularly the landmark Supreme Court ruling in *K.S. Puttaswamy v. Union of India* (2017), clearly recognises privacy as a fundamental right and restricts state surveillance through the requirements of legality, necessity, and proportionality. These principles apply directly to AI-driven policing technologies, which, by their nature, enable routine data extraction, automated profiling, and expanded surveillance capabilities.

The Himachal Pradesh Police has demonstrated proactive engagement with AI through strategic partnerships, such as its collaboration with IIT Mandi, and governance-related training initiatives, including *AI for Good Governance* (2025) and the iCAST-25 Cybersecurity Workshop (2025). Although such initiatives contribute to institutional readiness, they cannot substitute for legislative protections or transparent systems of oversight and accountability. Scholarship on artificial intelligence consistently shows that AI-based surveillance tools may suffer from accuracy limitations, demographic bias, and error propagation. These concerns are supported by empirical studies of facial recognition systems in India, which have reported significant performance disparities and limited operational precision (Coe & Atay, 2021). In the absence of independent audits and externally validated performance standards, the expansion of AI systems in Himachal Pradesh risks reproducing these documented shortcomings.

These governance concerns are further intensified by the absence of a comprehensive and enforceable data protection framework. Although Section 69 of the Information Technology Act, 2000 provides a legal basis for certain forms of AI-related surveillance, it does not by itself resolve the broader governance challenges raised by algorithmic policing. International scholarship repeatedly warns that algorithmic policing without clear legal safeguards may lead to reduced transparency, excessive discretion, and erosion of public trust (Brayne, 2020; Ferguson, 2017). This challenge is particularly acute in Indian states, where surveillance systems are often expanding more rapidly than the regulatory frameworks designed to govern them. Himachal Pradesh reflects this wider pattern: despite the adoption of increasingly sophisticated technologies, there are currently no publicly available policy documents outlining data retention periods, algorithmic accountability mechanisms, or citizen complaint procedures.

These findings support the argument that algorithmic policing is not merely a technological upgrade; rather, it represents a shift in the balance of power between the state and its citizens. As Barocas and Selbst (2016) argue, algorithmic systems may unintentionally encode and reproduce social biases, and when used in law enforcement, such biases may generate outcomes that conflict with the principles of equality and due process. In a socially and culturally diverse country such as India, the risk of disproportionate effects is even greater.

This study therefore concludes that AI-based policing in Himachal Pradesh has significant potential to improve crime detection, interstate intelligence coordination, and public safety, but only if it is supported by strong legal safeguards, regular auditing, and effective systems of oversight and accountability. Intrusive surveillance should be subject to judicial authorisation, standard operating procedures should be transparent, access controls should be role-based, public reporting mechanisms should be established, and independent review boards should be created to ensure alignment with constitutional requirements. The state must also ensure that AI deployments remain grounded in the principles of purpose limitation, minimal intrusion, and meaningful human oversight.

Ultimately, the sustainability of AI policing in Himachal Pradesh depends not on the sophistication of the technology alone, but on the adequacy of its regulation. Himachal Pradesh could become a model for ethical and constitutionally compliant AI governance in Indian policing if it institutionalises core protections relating to privacy, accountability, and democratic oversight. At the same time, the issues identified in this case study reflect a broader global challenge: many policing institutions are adopting artificial intelligence technologies more quickly than the legal and ethical safeguards required to govern them effectively.

FUTURE PERSPECTIVES AND POLICY RECOMMENDATIONS

Strengthening governance systems has become increasingly important in a period of rapid administrative transformation in India. Emerging pressures, including technological disruption and more complex socio-economic conditions, require proactive policies and adaptable regulatory frameworks. In this context, it is essential to identify future directions that can improve administrative effectiveness while also strengthening public trust. The following section outlines key future perspectives and policy recommendations that may guide the next phase of administrative reform in India.

Establishing a State-Level AI Governance Framework

The development of a dedicated and comprehensive AI governance policy for policing should be a central priority for Himachal Pradesh. This framework should clearly define the objectives, scope, and operational boundaries of AI systems while ensuring consistency with constitutional principles. It should include explicit provisions governing data collection, storage, deletion, and access control. A statutory policy framework would provide predictability, transparency, and consistency in the use of AI tools across the state.

Such a framework could draw on international governance models, including Canada's *Directive on Automated Decision-Making* and the European Union's Artificial Intelligence Act, both of which prioritise algorithmic transparency, risk assessment, and institutional oversight.

Implementing Independent Algorithmic Audits

The expansion of artificial intelligence in surveillance, traffic policing, and predictive policing creates a clear need for continuous scrutiny of accuracy, fairness, and safety. Independent external audits are more likely to ensure objectivity than internal departmental review alone. These audits should assess algorithmic bias, error rates, compliance with operational standards, and the effectiveness of risk-mitigation measures. Publicly available audit reports would enhance transparency and strengthen public confidence in AI-driven policing.

Strengthening Human Oversight and Police Capacity

Within law enforcement, AI should function as a decision-support tool rather than an autonomous decision-maker. Future policy must therefore invest in capacity building so that officers develop digital literacy, algorithmic reasoning skills, cyber-investigation capabilities, and ethical decision-making competence. Continuous professional development, including systematic training, advanced qualifications, and simulation-based learning, should be embedded within police institutions to improve understanding of AI limitations and reduce the risks of misuse and overreliance.

Ensuring Community-Centred AI Governance

Community engagement is essential to maintaining democratic legitimacy and participatory governance. Mechanisms such as public consultations, citizen advisory boards, annual transparency disclosures, and grievance redress platforms could be implemented in Himachal Pradesh. Incorporating public feedback would help ensure that AI systems remain responsive to local realities, cultural contexts, and community expectations, thereby reducing technocratic detachment.

Preparing for Technological Convergence

The coming decade is likely to bring deeper integration between AI, Internet of Things (IoT) devices, mobile governance infrastructure, geospatial analytics, and broader digital government systems. Himachal Pradesh should anticipate these developments by establishing interoperability standards, limiting functional creep, and regulating the role of private technology vendors in policing. Strategic foresight in this area would help ensure that implementation remains scalable without compromising privacy protections or democratic accountability.

Positioning Himachal Pradesh as a National Model

Himachal Pradesh has the potential to emerge as a national leader in ethical AI policing, given its relatively small population, active governance institutions, and established partnerships with academic organisations. By embedding fairness, transparency, and accountability into its regulatory framework, the state could demonstrate that technological advancement need not come at the expense of civil rights. A rights-respecting model of AI policing in Himachal Pradesh could therefore serve as a prototype for other Indian states.

REFERENCES

Barocas, S., & Selbst, A. D. (2016). Big data's disparate impact. *California Law Review, 104*(3), 671–732.

Batool, A., Kalhoro, H. B., & Bano, M. (2023). Responsible AI governance: A systematic literature review. *arXiv*. https://arxiv.org/abs/2401.10896

Brayne, S. (2020). *Predict and surveil: Data, discretion, and the future of policing*. Oxford University Press. DOI: 10.1093/oso/9780190684099.001.0001

Coe, J., & Atay, M. (2021). Evaluating impact of race in facial recognition across machine learning and deep learning algorithms. *Computers, 10*(9), 113. DOI: 10.3390/computers10090113

European Commission. (2021). *Proposal for a regulation laying down harmonised rules on artificial intelligence (Artificial Intelligence Act).* https://eur-lex.europa.eu

Ferguson, A. G. (2017). *The rise of big data policing: Surveillance, race, and the future of law enforcement.* New York University Press. DOI: 10.18574/nyu/9781479854608.001.0001

Fitzgerald, E. (2024). AI in predictive policing and its ethical challenges. *International Journal of Artificial Intelligence and Machine Learning*. https://itaimle.com/index.php/ijaiml/article/view/245

Government of India. (2000). *The Information Technology Act, 2000.* Ministry of Law and Justice. https://www.indiacode.nic.in

Hahn, J. (2025). Predictive policing and the implications of AI across global frameworks. *Cornell International Law Journal, 57*(3). https://publications.lawschool.cornell.edu/cilj/2025/08/28/predictive-policing-and-the-implications-of-ai-across-global-frameworks

Himachal Pradesh Police. (2024). *Annual report and digital modernization overview.* Government of Himachal Pradesh. https://hppolice.gov.in

Ministry of Electronics and Information Technology (MeitY). (2025). *iCAST-25 cyber security workshop proceedings.*

Internet Freedom Foundation. (2021). *Panoptic surveillance in India: A study of facial recognition deployments.* https://internetfreedom.in

Kavidharani, R. (2025). Predictive policing and constitutional morality: An evaluation of AI-based crime forecasting technologies in India. *LIJDLR, 3*(2), 903–913. https://lijdlr.com/2025/07/31/predictive-policing-and-constitutional-morality-an-evaluation-of-ai-based-crime-forecasting-technologies-in-india

Kumar, N. (2025). From surveillance to sentencing: Evaluating AI's role in Indian criminal justice. *Science Bulletin, 30*(1), 68–78. https://sciendo.com/article/10.2478/bsaft-2025-0008

Mirishli, S. (2025). Ethical implications of AI in data collection: Balancing innovation with privacy. *arXiv*. https://arxiv.org/abs/2503.14539

National e-Governance Division. (2025, April 8). *Cyber Security Workshop iCAST-25.*

National e-Governance Division. (2025, May 20). *AI for Good Governance: Driving transparency, efficiency, and impact (Press Release).*

Press Trust of India. (2024). *HP: Ways to integrate AI in policing deliberated upon at northern regional police meeting*. The Print.

Rani, S. (2025). Digital surveillance and predictive justice: Constitutional boundaries in AI-enabled law enforcement. *Civil Law Journal, 5*(2), 166. https://www.civillawjournal.com/archives/2025.v5.i2.C.166

Singh, P. (2025). Mass surveillance in the age of AI: The Indian dilemma of security versus privacy. *International Journal of Civil Law and Legal Research, 5*(2), 74–78. https://www.civillawjournal.com/archives/2025.v5.i2.A.146. DOI: 10.22271/civillaw.2025.v5.i2a.146

Singh, S., & Mohapatra, H. (2025). AI ethics, governance and privacy in a rapidly advancing digital world. *Systemic Analytics, 3*(2), 135–151. https://www.sa-journal.org/index.php/systemic/article/view/49

Supreme Court of India. (2017). *K.S. Puttaswamy (Retd.) v. Union of India,* (2017) 10 SCC 1, AIR 2017 SC 4161.

Treasury Board of Canada Secretariat. (2019). *Directive on automated decision-making*. Government of Canada.

UK Court of Appeal. (2020). *R (Bridges) v. Chief Constable of South Wales Police & Others,* EWCA Civ 1058.

Chapter 3
The Strategic Integration of Artificial Intelligence in Police Investigations:
Frameworks, Use Cases, and Governance Challenges

Muhammad Usman Tariq
http://orcid.org/0000-0002-7605-3040
Abu Dhabi University, UAE & University College Cork, Ireland

ABSTRACT

Artificial Intelligence (AI) is gradually shaping the future of modern investigative policing with enhanced operational effectiveness, predictive capability, and evidence analysis. This chapter examines the strategic application of AI in law enforcement, focusing on its applications, benefits, limitations, and guidelines for ethical and responsible implementation. While AI offers powerful technologies for crime prediction, digital forensic analysis, and monitoring, it also poses phenomenal risks with regard to privacy, bias, and transparency. Effective deployment depends on a multi-stakeholder strategy that incorporates technical readiness, cultural sensitivity, legal safeguards, and co-design through user participation. Drawing on examinations of world models of governance, sectoral cases, and evolving AI threats such as deepfakes and self-operating machines, this book stresses the importance of proactive governance and continuous monitoring.

DOI: 10.4018/979-8-3373-5228-2.ch003

INTRODUCTION

Artificial intelligence (AI) is gradually revolutionizing the nature of policing, and thus, it is becoming a critical part of modern law enforcement. In the last decade, new data-driven technologies such as machine learning, natural language processing, facial recognition, predictive analytics, and other AI-powered tools have empowered the police to rethink how they police. These technologies have become the need of the day in dealing with the challenges of contemporary policing today, such as greater sophistication in crimes, cyber-attacks, limited budgets, and fairness and transparency in policing (Tsabedze et al., 2025). With the world becoming more digital by the day, AI is not just a helpful technology but a necessity for law enforcement units worldwide to deal with challenges responsibly and efficiently (Tsabedze et al., 2025). One of the biggest ways in which AI is transforming policing is by processing and analysing vast quantities of data. For example, machine learning can use crime reports, camera footage, license plate data, and social media posts to target suspects or make educated guesses about perpetrators. AI helps detectives make more informed decisions by providing data-driven analysis, but it does not replace their jobs.

AI is also used in predictive policing, which is a controversial topic. This method uses historical crime data to make informed estimates of where crime will occur, so that police can deploy their resources better. If done fairly and openly, it can be an effective tool for lowering crime and making police work more efficient. However, if the underlying data contain antiquated prejudices, it poses tremendous questions of privacy, surveillance, and justice. Despite these shortcomings, the ability to forecast criminal behaviour is a giant step towards making police work proactive rather than reactive to crime. AI works best when dealing with intricate crimes on the Internet, including cybercrime, fraud, and online exploitation. AI can further scan dark web activity to detect illegal transactions involving firearms, drugs, or stolen data. These functions are essential because an increasing number of crimes are conducted online. AI also supports the daily work of police (McDaniel & Malik, 2023). Facial recognition can quickly match people of interest in any surveillance network and is faster and more accurate than traditional methods. AI-driven voice technologies can recognize urgency, fraud, or stress in emergency calls and help the police respond more quickly. AI-powered drones can perform aerial surveillance, patrol crowds at venues, and reach isolated areas during searches. These technologies not only make the police's work more efficient, but they also make officers safer by exposing them to fewer dangerous situations.

Knowing the many types of AI being applied to policing helps with understanding how they are utilized differently. Data analytics, computer vision, natural language processing, machine learning, and robotics are all types of AI used for policing

(Dahal et al., 2023). Data analytics software brings together and analyses a great deal of data from many sources into patterns of crime, network maps, and trends for forecasting. Computer vision features facial and object recognition to assist with real-time surveillance, suspect detection, and evidence collection. Natural language processing is all about the processing and making use of human language by computers. It is used to identify threats, perform emotion analysis, and filter information. The police might apply it to monitor threats to safety on social media or filter case files.

Although AI holds considerable promise in policing, it raises significant ethical questions. One of the main issues is algorithmic bias, where AI learns and reproduces past biases from training data. If historical data are racially or economically biased, the resulting AI can produce discriminatory conclusions, undermining police credibility and further polarizing community relations. It is important that AI technologies applied in policing are tightly controlled, made transparent, and have mechanisms to hold someone accountable. There must also be regulations on the use of evidence created through AI in investigations or court proceedings to avoid abuse and abuse of power (Aljanaahi et al., 2025).

Another significant challenge is human-AI collaboration. AI technology is only as good as the humans who create, train, and implement it. Police officers must be educated to understand what AI can and cannot do, for example, the accuracy of its predictions and the dangers of over-reliance on it. AI can be helpful, but never in place of human judgment, especially when it comes to issues of freedom and justice. Training programs must teach officers to question AI results and not simply accept them at face value. There is also the issue of making different systems work together. Most police forces have separate and unconnected technological systems (He et al., 2021). For AI to work effectively, it must be in an integrated digital system with secure data sharing, up-to-date information, and partnerships. This requires investment not only in technology but also in people understanding technology, dealing with change, and working together across agencies.

Despite these hurdles, the use of AI in police work has significant potential. It can support faster and more accurate decision-making, potentially save lives and improving public safety outcomes. AI can also perform some of the tedious work so that officers have more time to serve the public. It can also make investigations more precise, which might lead to more crimes being solved. It can help police maximize the use of their resources, particularly when budgets are constrained and public expectations are increasing. The future of AI in policing will be grounded in effective management, open practices, and commitment to democratic values. As AI becomes increasingly sophisticated and utilized in policing, it is important that it is created with technical expertise, as well as legal, ethical, and societal considerations (Kim et al., 2025). All parties involved, such as technical experts, police administrators, legislators, civic groups, and the communities being served, must work together to create AI technologies that are fair, accurate, and promote justice and security. Thus, AI can help police perform their work more fairly without violating people's right.

This chapter therefore examines how artificial intelligence can be integrated into police investigations in a way that is operationally effective, legally defensible, and ethically accountable. It explores the principal investigative applications of AI, including predictive analysis, facial recognition, risk assessment, and digital forensics, while also considering the organisational, legal, cultural, and technical barriers that often hinder adoption. The chapter argues that successful implementation depends not only on technological capability, but also on strategic leadership, workforce readiness, transparent governance, human oversight, and public trust. In doing so, it positions AI not as a replacement for professional judgement, but as a tool whose value in investigative policing depends on careful design, responsible use, and alignment with democratic principles.

LAW ENFORCEMENT APPLICATIONS IN INVESTIGATIVE CONTEXTS

Artificial intelligence is becoming increasingly common in law enforcement to enhance investigations, particularly as crimes grow more complex often involving digital networks, cross-border activity, and large volumes of data which are more difficult to detect and analyses using traditional investigative methods. AI helps predict where crimes might occur, find areas with high crime rates, and analyse a large amount of digital information. These tools are used in everyday police work and major investigations. While they bring new efficiencies, they also raise important questions regarding ethics, accuracy, and the rights of individuals. As police use more technology, it is important to carefully consider how these tools are implemented (He et al., 2021). One major use of AI in policing is in predictive policing. This method uses data and machine learning to identify places or people who might be involved in future crimes based on past data. It looks at previous crime reports, time patterns, where crimes happened, and social factors to predict where crimes might happen or who might commit them again. This can help the police use their resources better and stop crimes before they occur. However, predictive policing has faced criticism for its issues and ethical problems. A major concern is the quality and bias of the data used to train these models. For example, if the data is based upon older, biased policing practices such as disproportionately targeting certain areas or groups, the AI may replicate those biases. This may lead to over-policing in communities that are already disadvantaged, increasing the likelihood of unfair suspicion or arrests, and potentially contributing to miscarriages of justice. In addition, predictive models often do not explain how their decisions are made, making it difficult to question or challenge their outcomes. Although data-driven policing has its benefits, it requires safeguards to prevent unfair treatment and ensure accountability (Tariq, 2025).

Another area where AI is making an impact is facial recognition technology, which is used in both real-time surveillance and after an event for forensic investigation. In cities with many CCTV cameras, AI-enhanced facial recognition systems can scan live video feeds for known suspects or people of interest. This facilitates the police searching and trace individuals instantly, which may deter crime or catch persons in real time (Schiff et al., 2025). During criminal incidents, facial recognition can help identify suspects by comparing photographs from security cameras with existing databases, such as mugshots or official identification documents. This has been found to be helpful in the case of coverage spanning wide mass events, such as demonstrations, sports competitions, or public transport hubs, where people cannot be identified manually. The use of facial recognition systems is important but poses serious privacy and technical issues. False positives are a source of concern, especially where technology is used in multicultural populations. Studies show that facial identification technology works less well on minorities, women, and those who are extremely young or old, making false identification and discriminatory arrest a possibility (Boehme et al., 2024). In addition to these technical limitations, there are more general concerns about bulk surveillance and anonymity erasure in public life. The feeling of being constantly watched can hinder civil liberties, and calls will be made for regulation, transparency, and strict guidelines on the use of the technology.

Although this technology is powerful, it must be carefully controlled to prevent abuse. Artificial intelligence risk assessment models are also novel tools used in investigations to help identify and evaluate threats and manage incidents. These systems consider various variables, such as the type of incident, the criminal history of victims and suspects, crime patterns in the area, and other factors, to make judgments about whether a case is likely to be serious or timely. For example, in busy dispatch centres with many calls, risk models can help prioritize the situations that are most likely to turn violent or the offenders who pose the greatest threat to public safety (Das et al., 2025). This allows the police to make better use of their resources and respond more rapidly to emergency situations. Similarly, risk assessments in advance of trials are used to decide if a defendant is likely to offend again or fail to appear, and this decides whether he/she should be released or held. Although this data-based system can assist in making decisions more efficiently and fairly, it raises questions about fairness, due process, and transparency. Critics argue that such models can be discriminatory against certain groups, provided that the data hold prevailing prejudices. Additionally, the fact remains that most of these models are "black boxes," and it is difficult for defendants, counsel, or even judges to understand why they yield specific results or replicate outcomes. When such models are applied in investigations, they must be tested meticulously, and the police must ensure that they are used to augment, not replace, human judgment. The potential of future AI to prevent loss of life and cause prevention is assuring, but there needs to be clearly defined regulations in place to create public confidence and to protect human rights (Broeders et al., 2023).

Digital forensics is also a significant area where AI is making significant inroads, especially in the investigation of cybercrime, financial fraud, and child exploitation on the Internet. In today's world, digital evidence is often the key to establishing a case. They comprise emails, social media messages, browser history, digital images, text messages, and digital file metadata. Examples include emails, social media messages, browser history, digital images, text messages, and digital file metadata. Traditional forensic methods require a considerable amount of time and effort to process large amounts of data. AI tools are now helping to automate much of this process. They can quickly find relevant files, spot unusual activity, organize content, and even point out possible illegal material. For example, image recognition tools can scan thousands of photos to find signs of child exploitation, whereas text analysis tools can detect suspicious language or communications in large datasets. These tools are not only faster but also more consistent than the traditional manual methods. They can help identify connections or clues that might otherwise be missed, especially in complex cases with many digital interactions. However, the use of AI in digital investigations presents new challenges. One major issue is the reliability of the findings from AI. While these tools can identify suspicious content, they cannot always understand the full context, which is important in legal cases (Schiff et al., 2025). A message or file that appears to be suspicious might be harmless, and relying too much on AI might lead to misunderstandings or escalate the situation. Moreover, it is unclear whether evidence found using AI can be used in court. Lawyers on the other side for the defence might question how the evidence was handled, whether the algorithms were fair, or whether digital records were kept properly. These problems show that AI tools used in forensics must be open, checkable, and meet legal standards. Investigators not only need to learn how to use these tools but also understand their limitations and the need to confirm AI results using traditional methods (Tariq, 2025).

The use of AI in digital forensics raises privacy concerns (Das et al., 2025). When collecting and reviewing personal data from devices, whether it is a suspect's phone or a cloud account, it can uncover private and personal information. There is a thin line between what is needed for an investigation and what is too much, especially when the data includes information from people who are not part of the case. There must be clear rules to ensure that only the correct data are accessed, investigations are kept focused, and privacy rights are respected. responsibilities. These tools can accelerate investigations, identify evidence more quickly, and help focus on the most serious threats, which is crucial in an increasingly digital world. It is not enough to ask what AI can do for policing; we also need to ask how it can be used in a way that is responsible, fair, and in line with democratic values. Only by finding this balance can AI help make justice happen in both ways.

BARRIERS TO AI ADOPTION IN INVESTIGATIVE POLICING

There is great potential for artificial intelligence to assist police investigations. It can make work more effective, improve decision-making, and arm law enforcers with better tools to tackle more sophisticated crimes. However, making AI a common solution is challenging (Cui et al., 2025). There are various challenges, including cultural, ethical, legal, and technical, that would hamper its implementation. These challenges are more than just operational problems; they resonate with how police operate, engage with people, and promote justice in society. It is necessary to address these issues to apply both AI intelligently and justly in police investigations in the future.

One major obstacle is that the police force tends to resist change. Policing has been a formalized line of work with its own way of doing things, strict hierarchies, and established routines (He et al., 2021). AI represents a major shift in the manner of investigation. This requires new skills, new ways of working, and a different attitude toward technology (Cui et al., 2025). Some officers will be resistant to AI and think that it will take away their judgment or make them less important. Others might not even realize how it relates to their day-to-day work or might believe that the technology is too complex to use. Such resistance can lead to officers not using AI tools appropriately or refusing to use them altogether. To change this perception, merely introducing additional software is insufficient. Departments must attempt to change their culture by training officers, involving them in the process, and showing them how AI helps in actual cases. Leadership is everything; when senior officers are convinced about AI, others will be too (Kotter, 1995).

This raises significant ethical concerns. There are concerns that AI will lead to additional spying, discrimination, and unfair outcomes because of biased algorithms. AI-powered tools such as facial recognition, predictive policing, and social media monitoring can constantly watch people, analyse them, and make decisions without clear explanations. In investigations, these tools can help find suspects or assess risks, but if they are not fair or transparent, they can target people unfairly. Biases in the data used to train these systems can also pose a problem. If the data show that specific groups were targeted in the past, then AI will be able to learn to presume that those specific groups are more likely to commit crimes, even when they are not (Schiff et al., 2025). This can lead to a system where specific neighbourhoods or groups are targeted more, and therefore unjust treatment increases, while public trust in the police erodes. Achieving this ethically means developing good rules, being engaged with society, and holding algorithmic biases accountable. This also means broaching a larger debate about what policing should do in a democracy and the extent to which the government should have power in the virtual world.

Legal and data management issues are also major challenges (Hall et al., 2022). Policing is extremely regulated, and new technology must be integrated with privacy regulations, accountability regulations, and evidentiary rules pertaining to courts. AI will draw on a large amount of personal data from phones, social media, and surveillance cameras. This raises issues about who is in control of the data, where it is stored, who sees it, and why it is collected. Regimes such as the GDPR in the EU provide stringent rules over the use of individuals' data, with the requirement of transparency and equity (Schiff et al., 2025). Even in the absence of such regimes, people are more concerned about their rights and do not wish to be shrivelled by the government. Apart from privacy, when AI makes a mistake, the question of who is responsible is also an issue. If an AI tool misidentifies a person or yields an erroneous risk score, who is to blame? Responsibility may lie with the individual who designed the tool, the police force, or the officer using it—or, in some cases, no single individual. It may also extend to those responsible for inputting inaccurate or biased data into the system. These matters are not yet sorted out, and without clear guidelines, police may be hesitant to use AI tools because they would be legally liable (Tariq, 2025).

In addition, it is not always clear whether evidence generated by AI can be used in court. Standard evidence rules are intended for human testimony and tangible evidence, not for computer output. A prosecutor who wants to use something such as an AI risk assessment score or facial match as evidence would need to prove how it works, its reliability, and how it was used in a case. Most AI programs are black boxes in nature, and it is not clear always how they operate, even for the people who develop them. This is a major problem in legal affairs, where a fair trial means being able to object to evidence. Judges, lawyers, and jurors may be unaware of how to properly assess AI evidence, and without standards, it could harm legal processes instead of helping them to be more efficient. Courts and lawyers must develop new standards for AI evidence to ensure that it offers the same level of reliability, relevance, and fairness as traditional evidence (Allertseder et al., 2022). They do not have the right hardware, such as servers and safe storage, or the right software that is compatible with current systems. One major issue is that the police use a mix of old, non-networked systems. If an AI product works wonderfully in a vacuum, it will not be of much use if it cannot share or obtain data from other tools used by investigators. To solve this, it is necessary to standardize data formats, make data easier to secure and share, and build central sites for data processing. However, all of this takes time, money, and coordination across agencies.

Another significant challenge is that police officers are not trained in technology. AI tools are sophisticated and require specialized skills to use, repair, and understand (Schiff et al., 2025). Therefore, agencies must also invest in human expertise to support AI implementation, including hiring technical specialists, collaborating with colleges and universities, and engaging external partners for training and knowledge development. It is important to have a workforce that can handle technology and understand the real world of policing so that AI is used effectively and appropriately. As criminals become more adept at exploiting technology, such as encrypted messaging and advanced methods of hiding their tracks, the equipment police employ must keep pace. This makes AI deployment a target that is always moving, with conditions continually changing, and agencies need to be ready to pivot and develop new ideas more frequently.

In short, even though AI may have a tremendous effect on the way police operate, it is difficult to implement. There is resistance in police forces, anxiety about bias and disproportionate monitoring of individuals too much, issues regarding the legality of privacy and evidence, and technical constraints. These cannot be addressed by a single, quick fix. Instead, they require numerous inputs from the police community, lawmakers, technical people, lawyers, and communities (He et al., 2021). Only by combining their strengths through talk, conventions, training, and smart spending can AI be put to work so that it truly serves justice, public security, and the law. The dividends are substantial, but so are the hurdles. With sagacious vision and an eye for democratic ideals, AI can become an asset that makes policing fairer and more efficient.

STRATEGIC IMPLEMENTATION FRAMEWORKS

To effectively integrate artificial intelligence into investigative policing requires more than procuring cutting-edge gadgetry. It requires a carefully conceived and thought-out plan that synchronizes novel technology with the organizational culture, legislation, everyday operations, and moral precepts. The change AI brings is not just about hardware; it has a significant effect on how people work, decisions are made, citizens' trust, and the way the workforce speaks. The application of change management models that help structure change is one of the first key actions in any AI adoption. Kotter's 8-Step Change Model is particularly useful. This calls for generating a sense of urgency, coalition building to implement change, and vision making (Scher & Vera, 2025; Schein, 2010). Within policing, this might mean showing how cybercrime or online scams are growing and how current tools are inadequate. Assembling a team of technology-savvy officers, leaders, and external experts can help define the vision with operations as well as technical know-how. Once a plan has been implemented, open communication, instant successes such as successful pilot projects, and continued reinforcement are needed to engrain AI in the company culture. The ADKAR model, which considers Awareness, Desire, Knowledge, Ability, and Reinforcement, is also adaptable to policing (Shaw et al., 2024). Staff and officers need to know why AI is important (awareness), want to participate (desire), be skilled at new technology (knowledge), be capable of using them (ability), and receive positive reinforcement and support (reinforcement). ADKAR is effective at the individual level, ensuring that all police force members are walked through the change. There are severe limitations in transparency, documentation, human oversight, and fairness for high-risk systems, such as law enforcement. The UK's National Police Chiefs' Council (NPCC) also developed its own model the Covenant for Using Artificial Intelligence in Policing which sets out ethical principles for the use of data and technology in policing (National Police Chiefs' Council, 2023). For any police force rolling out AI, combining operational capabilities such as those outlined by Europol (2022) with legal protections from the EU or UK frameworks can provide a strong foundation for the responsible use of AI.

To illustrate how this works in practice, consider a real but anonymized mid-sized UK police force serving approximately 800,000 citizens. The force recently implemented a staged approach to using AI in investigative policing. The first step was to assess their readiness, technology check, data quality, legal readiness, and disposition towards workers interacting with AI. Surveys showed mixed responses; frontline officers were concerned about losing practical skills and professional autonomy in decision-making, while senior officers viewed AI as a means of reducing case backlogs and improving investigative accuracy. Based on these findings, the force launched a six-month pilot using AI technology to scour digital devices for illegal material related to online child exploitation. This technology speeded up the process compared to manual checking. Human investigators made the final judgment calls, which helped build trust. Simultaneously, a legal advisory board was established, involving legal experts, ethicists, and community representatives, to oversee the pilot and ensure transparency. When the pilot was successful, defined by a faster case review and more guilty pleas, the force extended the application of AI technology for case file scrutiny and risk assessment in domestic abuse cases. Each successive stage involved staff training, the establishment of new data policies, and open communication with the public. The deployment also benefited from the technical advice of a nearby university to analyse how well the algorithms functioned and remained neutral. This example shows how incremental, strategic planning and collaborative governance can take high-level intentions and turn them into concrete results that fit the local policing environment opportunity to link to the one of the change models. Intersector lessons offer further suggestions that can be applied to make the use of AI in policing more effective. Such intersector lessons highlight how cross-industry practices can inform more responsible, efficient, and ethically grounded implementation of AI in law enforcement. The focus on obtaining informed consent and the possibility of being able to check the decisions of AI has led to systems that are practical and dependable. The same requirements can be mandated for law enforcement to ensure that investigators are aware of how AI solutions work and that their outputs can always be checked. Furthermore, medicine utilizes teams of experts to examine new technology, a paradigm that the police can use to balance AI implementation with people's rights (Das et al., 2025). For example, in the defence sector, training and simulation based on real-world scenarios are used to enable personnel to practise AI-supported decision-making in controlled environments; similar approaches could be applied in policing to allow officers to test investigative tools safely before deploying them in live cases.

Another aspect that healthcare and defence have shown us is how critical testing and feedback are. Neither sector assumes that new technology is perfect when it is first introduced (Shaw et al., 2024). Instead, technologies are introduced in incremental steps, pilot-tested, and refined depending on what happens in the field. In policing, this might involve starting with a low-barrier-to-entry example, such as analysing electronic evidence in fraud cases, and then developing up to more complex applications, such as behaviour analysis or forecasting. In receipt of feedback from officers, analysts, lawyers, and members of the public, will help to make such systems effective and aligned with what the police need and society's expectations. Both sectors also prioritize the use of systems that are easy to upgrade and integrate into current platforms. Policing often end up with tools that are hard to adapt to or integrate with other systems. Learning from where flexibility is also important can help avoid such problems (Tariq, 2025).

The successful implementation of AI in police work depends on strategy, good leadership, and a desire to learn from other industries. It is not just learning a tool, but how work is done, how people are trained, and how ethical controls are built into the daily processes. Models such as Kotter's and ADKAR help to manage that change from within (Kotter, 1995). Standards from institutions such as Interpol, the EU, and local bodies such as the NPCC offer external measures of responsibility and best practices (Ba et al., 2025). Real-world examples from policing in the UK demonstrates how these ideas are applied in practice, especially when introducing changes in stages, designing with feedback from multiple stakeholders and engaging the public. Lessons from the defence and healthcare sectors suggest that AI can be used cautiously and effectively if it is introduced cautiously, extensively tested, and accompanied by human judgment (Tariq, 2025). If police view AI integration as an ongoing process rather than a one-time investment, they can not only benefit from technological advancements but also lead in its safe, ethical, and thoughtful application in the pursuit of justice.

GOVERNANCE, TRANSPARENCY, AND PUBLIC TRUST

With the greater application of AI in police work, the demand for transparency and trust from the public, in addition to clear rules, has increased. AI has the potential to assist police work in becoming more accurate, faster, and fair (Das et al., 2025). However, the use of AI can only be depended upon if it is felt that the AI will be utilized fairly and non-discriminatory. Police rely on the cooperation of the communities they serve, and that cooperation only exists perceived that it will be with trust that the police are honest and fair. If AI is introduced without guidelines and transparency, it could destroy this trust. To employ AI in a legal and fair manner, it is essential to develop systems that will explain decisions, including checks and balances, and engage public groups and independent experts from the outset. One major issue in controlling AI in policing is that many systems are difficult to understand. Machine-learning algorithms, especially deep-learning ones, are called "black boxes" because even their creators do not fully understand how they arrive at their conclusions. This kind of inscrutability is a grave issue in policing because incorrect conclusions have the potential to impact on people's liberty, reputation, or lives.

Considering how these challenges can be addressed, particularly in relation to transparency and accountability, is important. For more complex AI models, techniques such as feature attribution can be used to identify which variables most influence a decision. In addition, tools such as Local Interpretable Model-Agnostic Explanations (LIME) and Shapley Additive Explanations (SHAP) are commonly employed to provide interpretable insights into how models generate their outputs. Developers are also required to design user interfaces that transparently show the reasoning behind AI decisions. If an investigator uses an AI system to rank suspects that is, to prioritise or order individuals based on their assessed likelihood of involvement in a crime the system should clearly indicate which criteria contributed to each assessment, such as past offences, geographic proximity, or online activity. Warning labels about the potential for mistakes and limitations of the system need to be displayed so that users know that it is a supporting tool rather than an absolute one that the outcome is based upon an AI tool and is not an absolute. These safeguards must be made available for internal checks, judicial reviews, and unbiased audits. Auditability helps identify errors, such as wrongful arrests or racial bias in the use of technology, and to understand how the system works (Tariq, 2025). Without audit trails, it becomes impossible to demonstrate integrity and accountability, and trust in both the police and the technology is undermined. Transparency from the public is also necessary. Most people care about AI in policing not so much for what the technology does, but because sometimes things happen out of sight or without adequate explanation (Aljanaahi et al., 2025). People want to understand how AI devices work, whether they deal with individuals fairly, and what safety measures are being implemented. Transparency does not equate to the disclosure of every technical subtlety, which would be insecure or excessive, but rather towards uncomplicated and understandable explanations of what tools are used, why and how they are deployed, and who is tasked with handling them. On the other hand, openly reporting the boundaries of the system, the legal basis for it, and the safeguards in place can help make the public aware and accept its deployment. Openness is not an extra step; it is part of building trust in the age of cyberspace.

Consultation with these communities from the beginning resolves problems before they occur. Civil rights, racial justice, and criminal justice reform groups can also offer useful information about how AI can affect different communities, especially those systematically targeted by law enforcement. Ethics committees, including lawyers, technologists, sociologists, and human rights experts, can act as a check on the use of AI in law enforcement. These communities must have the power to be critical about new on new AI tools before they are implemented, ensure that they comply with ethical standards and the law, and suggest changes or veto tools that have high risks (Adams et al., 2025). Records should be published to ensure that everything being done is transparent. Oversight groups, whether current watchdogs, proposed regulators, or legislative committees, should also be able to monitor AI systems, conduct investigations of complaints, and ensure that investigators are not misusing them. It is very important that such groups are independent and have adequate resources to perform their role without being hindered by the people or groups they are regulating.

The benefits of engaging with these communities does not stop at reducing risks; they also make AI policing products more accepted and trusted (Das et al., 2025). If the public can identify that organizations such as civil society, ethicists, and independent regulators have played a genuine role in the deployment of AI, they will be more likely to believe that the systems are being used equitably and with sensitivity. This further increases the support for technological development in law enforcement. Public trust does not remain constant; it is built through regular discussions, openness, and wanting to be held accountable. The second vital area for building trust is ensuring that people's privacy rights and data are safeguarded. They demonstrate respect for people's freedom and dignity.

Public consultation is not necessarily a one-way process. Trust is built by listening to what people have to say and responding to them (Prakash et al., 2023). Police forces should create mechanisms for regular dialogue with communities, such as town forums, citizen advisory boards, online surveys, or partnerships with community organizations. These communities must be represented by a diverse spectrum of voices, especially those targeted or routinely silenced by the police. Direct communication with the most affected communities can help identify issues and make the design and application of AI technologies more effective. Additionally, involving the public in the development of governance frameworks offers some assurance that these systems reflect societal expectations, rather than solely the priorities of those in positions of authority.

Finally, applying AI to investigative policing is less a question of technology and more akin to a social deal. It works on trust, fairness, and good governance, as well as accuracy or effectiveness (Devlin, 2023). By being explainable and auditable, AI systems enable the police to ensure that their decisions are transparent and responsible. Being transparent and honest enables them to gain the confidence of the public and demonstrate that they are using technology appropriately. Involving civil society, review bodies, and ethics committees at the beginning incorporate democratic values into the design of the AI system.

FUTURE DIRECTIONS: BUILDING ADAPTIVE AI STRATEGY FOR LAW ENFORCEMENT

As policing shifts, it becomes evident that reliance on only the tools that are presently available in AI will not suffice. The rate at which technology is changing and the way criminals are working, are such that agencies need methods that can adapt, stay ahead, and respond quickly to new threats that continuously evolving. The newest threats include, deepfakes, autonomous systems, and using AI to spread disinformation. In addition, AI systems that learn and adapt to changing trends in crime must be developed, as well as governance that is future-proof and can predict and prepare for future risks (Das et al., 2025). One of the emerging challenges faced by the police is deepfakes, which are false videos, audio, or images created using AI that are very realistic. These deepfakes can be used to fabricate false evidence, produce false alibis, impersonate authentic individuals such as police or officials, or pass on false information that makes it difficult to investigate. Criminals can use deepfakes to make evidence seem questionable, mislead investigators, or lead the public to distrust investigators. Studies confirm that the justice system is at risk as deepfakes become increasingly simple to create, and the techniques to identify them are not keeping pace with the tools used to create them.

Another danger is the use of autonomous systems, such as drones, bots, or autonomous AI, operating without human oversight. Such systems can be used to commit crimes including intercepting communications, smuggling, cyberattacks, and the spread of disinformation. The more prevalent AI is in crime, the more decentralized it becomes and harder to trace it becomes. Police must prepare for scenarios in which offenders use AI systems to commit crimes remotely or indirectly, without direct physical involvement. For example, Europol has warned that organized crime groups already use AI to automate communication, impersonation, and spread false information in various languages. Crime groups are using AI to grow and render their activities more flexible (Bowen & Pashentsev, 2025). Misinformation, especially generated by AI, is a major issue. Disinformation, disinformation media, deepfakes, and AI-generated news can damage public trust, change the way citizens think, and interfere with police work and court trials. AI technologies can spread false information rapidly and widely across the globe before the truth is established, leading to confusion, creating mistrust in evidence gathering, and hindering investigations. Police must be able to prepare to track, authenticate media, and act quickly to counteract false information.

It is crucial to have systems in place that learn and adapt when new information is obtained (Bowers & Johnson, 2024). Dynamic AI systems are not permanent; they should learn from new information, evolve with changing crime, and update as trends change. For example, predictive systems that are not updated with new crime methods become outdated or even inaccurate. These systems may have mechanisms to take advantage of feedback from past questions to retrain models or recognize new patterns that lie beyond past information. These AI systems need to be adaptive, as they need to process new information, adjust threat models, and function even when some inputs are in doubt. However, adaptive AI has its drawbacks. Systems can start to work less effectively if the environment around them changes (also known as model drift), they can learn in damaging forms (e.g., bias), and they need to be tested to ensure that they are still equitable, legal, and accountable. They must be continuously monitored, audited, and overseen by humans. Fraud detection software, for example, needs to identify new fraud methods without triggering false positives for regular behaviour. To achieve this, law enforcement requires effective data governance, solid technology, and personnel who understand both policing and machine learning (Tariq, 2025).

To counteract these new risks and the demands of adaptive AI, law enforcement must employ anticipatory governance and scenario planning (Tsabedze et al., 2025). Instead of waiting for problems to arise, agencies must design structures that enable them to anticipate potential future scenarios, test policies and systems in advance, and consider ethical, legal, and societal implications. They should assist in challenging existing legislation, investigations, and raising public awareness (Broeders et al., 2023). By addressing these scenarios, agencies can identify gaps in their legal, technical, ethical, or operational configurations and prepare for them in advance. This may include revising laws, increasing forensic capacity, or developing public communication contingency plans. Anticipatory governance also includes implementing policies and regulations that may evolve with technology. This may include setting standards for digital evidence authentication, transparency regulations on AI, or setting ethics boards that can reallocate priorities as new technologies emerge. Another aspect of meeting the future is working collaboratively across borders, with businesses, universities, and the public. Many of these issues are global deepfakes spread internationally, AI-driven disinformation disregards borders, and criminals can develop tools in one location and exploit them elsewhere so police must cooperate transnationally and share information. Shared standards and regulatory processes can support this effort, including common approaches to identifying synthetic media and shared databases containing unique markers of artificially generated content.

Throughout this process, police must build resilience and establish contingency measures. Plans should include provisions for managing errors, ensuring human oversight, enabling external review, and maintaining clear procedures for when AI systems fail. Public trust depends on how such failures are addressed, being open, fixing, and revealing the issues. Flexible plans need to incorporate not only robust technology but also effective error handling, feedback mechanisms, transparency, and accountability. Therefore, capacity development and training are critical. Police officers, forensic specialists, legal practitioners, and leaders must remain educated on the newest AI threats, detection methods, and limitations. Some AI threats are adversarial in nature; for example, deep-fake manufacturers can evade detection. Having awareness of how detection works, especially where it fails, enables the prediction of what adversaries will do. It is equally important to ensure that forensic equipment is updated. This requires ongoing investments in research, equipment production, and facilities. Policymakers must participate in future-scanning and shaping governance that can respond to issues that have yet to arise. Public openness is also important. Trust can be easily lost if the public perceives that law enforcement is misusing AI or if sensationalized media bypass rectifications rapidly (Das et al., 2025). Transparency about the AI technologies used, how evidence is verified, and what safeguards are in place to stop deepfakes and misinformation is important. The benefits and limitations of AI must be understood. Collaborating with the media, civil society, and community groups makes these strategies more accessible and credible, confirming the legitimacy and effectiveness of law enforcement. In general, building an adaptive AI strategy for law enforcement involves more than just facing today's threats. It entails foreseeing future challenges, building systems capable of evolving and adapting as crime evolves, creating governance that is flexible and accountable, and including a diverse range of stakeholders.

RECOMMENDATIONS FOR POLICYMAKERS AND POLICE LEADERSHIP

Regarding the implementation of AI in law enforcement, it is reasonable to have a strategy that covers a multitude of aspects. At the technological level, police agencies must begin by examining how well they can manage AI. This entails agencies examining the data they possess, the quality of the data, the capacity of their computer systems to store and protect the data, and the potential for integrating their current technology with new AI technology. They will also need to establish guidelines for data gathering and processing. For instance, the need to ensure the use of data that is fair and pre-tested against bias, so that AI make unbiased decisions (He et al., 2021). They must ensure that any AI systems they procure include features such as explainability (the ability to provide clear reasons for decisions), robust error-checking mechanisms, and long-term maintainability. AI systems must be frequently audited for fairness, accuracy, dependability and security. Agencies must also project plan for updates and changes in the future.

The right culture within police departments is also vital. Leaders must promote AI positively and not merely consider it as another tool. Leaders must ensure that everyone in the department is aware of the benefits and drawbacks of AI. Training must encourage officers to critically evaluate AI outputs and their alignment with desired outcomes. Everyone, from grassroots practitioners to executives, must be engaged in deciding how AI is used. It is necessary to address fears of job loss, reduced autonomy, and ethical concerns. Being transparent and truthful about decision-making and AI deployment reduces potential resistance. Working with change management models, for example, small pilots to provide evidence of benefits, user feedback, and early celebration of success, can help make AI a normal part of day-to-day work (Das et al., 2025). Law and ethical readiness must be accompanied by technical and cultural readiness. Policymakers need to legislate to capture topics such as privacy, surveillance, bias in AI, and how evidence assembled using AI may be presented in court. Regulations should also state who is accountable if something goes wrong, such as misidentifications or misinformation. Human rights, equity, and openness must be upheld by ethical guidelines. These must be incorporated into the processes of acquiring, deploying, and auditing AI systems and related processes. Independent scrutiny must take place, as well as parties participating in key decisions and the collection of minimum data with full consent (Tariq, 2025).

Police leaders and policymakers must collaborate with a wider range of international stakeholders, including law enforcement agencies, regulatory bodies, technology developers, and academic institutions, to address the cross-border nature of AI-enabled crime. Crime is often committed in other nations, such as cybercrime or Internet fraud, and AI threats are global. No single law enforcement entity can deal with these issues individually (Teece, 2022). Sharing information, data, and best-practice agreements between nations is essential. Organizations such as INTERPOL, the OECD, and national and regional organizations can help create standards and tools for enhanced cooperation. Common platforms from which to draw on each other's experiences can speed up the adoption of AI use. Common laws for data protection and cross-border legal cooperation among nations are also crucial.

A further critical component of collaboration is joining universities, technology companies, and local organizations. Such communities are known to develop new AI technologies, and therefore, police can benefit from partnerships with them. Research, applications, and techniques can be communicated to ease the police's use of better instruments (Cosenz & Noto,2016). Activist networks and community members can propose different solutions to address equity and cultural differences, making AI systems more ethical and widely accepted.

Investment in education and building capabilities is another essential area of focus. Police services require people who are knowledgeable in data science, machine learning, cybersecurity, and ethics. This would involve hiring new personnel, reskilling the current workforce, or establishing specialist teams for AI. Training is not merely a matter of learning how to use AI tools, but also of critically evaluating their outputs, understanding their limitations, maintaining human oversight, and monitoring their performance. Leaders must also be trained in the broader implications of AI development and implementation, ensuring informed and responsible decision-making.

Cooperation with users or user-influenced AI tools is also essential. Involving officers, investigators, and others will make AI systems usable, integrate them into day-to-day practices, and ensure compliance with ethical standards (Das et al., 2025). This keeps the people operating the tools, believing and cooperating with them. Having the public help formulate strategies, ethical guidelines, or bodies of regulation makes the system fairer and more trustworthy. In brief, good AI policies require attention at many different levels. This includes having resilient technology, changing the way organisation's function, setting ethics and legislation, working with other countries and sectors, investing in humans and co-designing, and providing transparency and accountability. When all of these elements are managed well, AI can help law enforcement become more efficient, fair, and trustworthy.

CONCLUSION

The radical changes in policing with the advent of artificial intelligence (AI) demonstrate its strategic value. It is not just a minor improvement but something that can fundamentally change the way the police work. Today, policing is faced with issues that would have been unthinkable only a couple of decades ago: internet-based crimes that know no borders, editable digital evidence, the public's concerns for mass surveillance, internet radicalization, disinformation, and computers that can nearly think like humans. AI does not help a little, it can completely transform the way investigations are conducted. They can sense, predict, analyse, and respond to threats in ways that were previously impossible (He et al., 2021). Devices that can process and interpret vast quantities of information, interlink data across multiple sources, and identify hidden patterns in social networks, financial transactions, or online activity are not simply additional features; they are essential for modern policing. To fulfil its role in protecting the public, advancing justice, and preventing crime, the use of AI in policing must become a core element of future strategic planning. It can speed up investigations, make the use of limited resources more effective, improve knowledge of what is happening in real time, and in some cases, restore public confidence by making things fairer, more transparent, and accountable. Moreover, AI has the potential to transform policing from a passive response to crime to proactive prevention of harm, ahead of time.

However, in such potential lies great danger. Although the benefits are compelling, they are by no means assured. Just because technology is advanced does not necessarily mean it will work well or be employed wisely. In the absence of adequate oversight, AI tools can be used for illness, induce bias, undermine civil rights, or harm already vulnerable communities Therefore, police leaders, policymakers, technical experts, and the public must approach AI with both hope and caution (Boehme & Mourtgos, 2024). Ethics cannot be an afterthought in the application of AI in policing; it must be integral. Ethical mistakes can lead to wrongful arrests, discriminatory suspicion, lost trust that makes communities unwilling to work with police, and legal repercussions that waste time, reputation, and resources. However, if principles such as fairness, necessity, proportionality, transparency, and accountability are driving change and application, AI can enhance the legitimacy of policing. This is more than just penning down rules; it entails putting ethics into the that manner AI is acquired, created, supervised, trained, and regulated. This entails having the courage to say "no" if certain uses of AI are too risky or unjustified. This also implies a willingness to continue monitoring and adjusting as technology evolves.

Engaging communities in the utilization of AI naturally follows from a robust ethical foundation. Policing is, by definition, embedded in its communities, and its legitimacy rests on how the community sees it, gives permission for it to act, and works with it. If AI is deployed without listening to the voices of these communities, especially those who were wrongly targeted in the past, there is a high risk that it will reinforce existing injustices rather than correcting them (He et al., 2021). Co-designing AI tools with police officers, civil society, ethicists, lawyers, and community members ensures that the tools are practical, relevant, accepted, and ready to use. Inclusive implementation further entails an understanding of who is likely to be affected, how, and creating channels for them to provide feedback, voice concerns, and monitor the process. Being open and honest with the public about what tools are being used, why they are being used, their limitations, and how they are being protected can mitigate fear, uncertainty, and suspicion. This trust is at the heart of effective policing because communities that feel respected, heard, and protected are more likely to offer information, cooperate with the police, and help prevent violent actors from exploiting distrust.

Policing leaders must build into their plans not only the ability to use technology, but also the ability to manage it effectively within their organizations (He et al., 2021). This includes the right technical infrastructure, good quality data, ability to interoperate across systems, trained staff, legal and governance arrangements, and regulation. AI deployment must be realized as an incremental, extended process: pilot in small steps, evaluation, feedback, improvement, and growth only when the benefits become clear and the risks are comprehended and managed. They need to ensure that the systems are resilient to errors, changes in threats, and malefactors. Systems must be designed to manage and respond to errors effectively, with clear mechanisms for human intervention and well-defined procedures for addressing failures. Policies should ensure that errors are acknowledged, corrected, and systematically reviewed to inform continuous learning and improvement.

Policymakers have a specific role to play in creating legislation and regulations that enable innovation to happen, but also hold individuals to account, safeguard rights, clarify who is responsible, establish standards for what can be used as evidence in court, and check. Ambiguous or outdated legislation can lead to abuse, legal entanglements, and rights violations (Mourtgos et al., 2022). Ethical standards are important but are not sufficient without actual enforcement, oversight, and the ability to correct mistakes. Expenditures on independent auditing, transparency to the public, data privacy, and building capacity for individuals and institutions are all necessary. One of the most valuable lessons learned is that AI can improve policing but will never replace human judgment, experience, and accountability. No algorithm can be implemented without questioning. Critical judgments should not be left to something we do not understand. Human judges, courts, officials, and review panels must have control, make the final call, and review and correct mistakes. This system, in which people are woven in, step by step, does not stall progress; rather, it keeps power under control and guarantees justice and fairness even as technology becomes more advanced.

As crime becomes increasingly technology-driven, evidence more digital, and public expectations grow not only for effective outcomes but also for fairness and accountability, policing must adapt. AI offers powerful assets such as pace, scale, perception, and foresight. However, these assets must be used thoughtfully, with consideration and cooperation. Society ought to be hopeful but guided by our moral and ethical choices. Inclusion must guide how AI is developed and structured in an equitable and transparent manner with clear rules (Raffaelli et al., 2025).

REFERENCES

Adams, I. T., McCrain, J. M., Schiff, D. S., Schiff, K. J., & Mourtgos, S. M. (2025). Police reform from the top down: Experimental evidence on police executive support for civilian oversight. *Journal of Policy Analysis and Management*, *44*(2), 403–427. DOI: 10.1002/pam.22620

Aljanaahi, A., Hakeem, M. K., Aljanaahi, A., & Shah, I. (2025). A review of analytical and chemometric strategies for forensic classification of homemade explosives. *Analytical Science Advances*, *6*(1), e70010. DOI: 10.1002/ansa.70010 PMID: 40242023

Allertseder, S., Okon, G., & Schweer, T. (2022). Chances and challenges of predictive policing for law enforcement agencies. In Markarian, G., Karlović, R., Nitsch, H., & Chandramouli, K. (Eds.), *Security technologies and social implications*. DOI: 10.1002/9781119834175.ch12

Ba, B., Ge, H., Kaplan, J., Knox, D., Komisarchik, M., Lanzalotto, G., Mariman, R., Mummolo, J., Rivera, R., & Torres, M. (2025). Political diversity in U.S. police agencies. *American Journal of Political Science*, *69*(4), 1–19. DOI: 10.1111/ajps.12945 PMID: 40881318

Boehme, H. M., & Mourtgos, S. M. (2024). The effect of formal de-policing on police traffic stop behavior and crime: Early evidence from the LAPD's policy to restrict discretionary traffic stops. *Criminology & Public Policy*, *23*(3), 517–542. DOI: 10.1111/1745-9133.12673

Bowen, S. A., & Pashentsev, E. N. (2025). AI, biases and cultures. In Cheng, Y., & Verčič, D. (Eds.), *AI and strategic communication*. DOI: 10.1002/9781394275434.ch12

Bowers, K., & Johnson, S. (2024). Facing the future of crime: A framework for police use of technology. *The Political Quarterly*, *95*(3), 480–488. DOI: 10.1111/1467-923X.13426

Broeders, D., Cristiano, F., & Kaminska, M. (2023). In search of digital sovereignty and strategic autonomy: Normative power Europe to the test of its geopolitical ambitions. *Journal of Common Market Studies*, *61*(5), 1261–1280. DOI: 10.1111/jcms.13462

Cosenz, F., & Noto, G. (2016). Applying system dynamics modelling to strategic management: A literature review. *Systems Research and Behavioral Science*, *33*(6), 703–741. DOI: 10.1002/sres.2386

Cui, M., Li, W., & Kamoche, K. (2025). Building trust in decision-support artificial intelligence: A boundary spanning perspective. *Information Systems Journal*, •••, 1–22. DOI: 10.1111/isj.70015

Dahal, A., McNevin, D., Chikhani, M., & Ward, J. (2023). An interdisciplinary forensic approach for human remains identification and missing persons investigations. *WIREs Forensic Science*, *5*(4), e1484. DOI: 10.1002/wfs2.1484

Das, S., Malik, P. K., & Pandey, A. (2025). Challenges and advances in underwater sonar systems and AI-driven signal processing for modern naval operations: A systematic review. *Journal of Field Robotics*, •••, 1–33. DOI: 10.1002/rob.70077

Devlin, K. (2023). Power in AI. In Gallagher, M., & Montiel, A. V. (Eds.), *The handbook of gender, communication, and women's human rights*. DOI: 10.1002/9781119800729.ch8

Europol. (2022). *Artificial intelligence and policing*. Publications Office of the European Union.

Hall, S. W., Sakzad, A., & Choo, K.-K. R. (2022). Explainable artificial intelligence for digital forensics. *WIREs Forensic Science*, *4*(2), e1434. DOI: 10.1002/wfs2.1434

He, Q.-C., Nie, T., Yang, Y., & Shen, Z.-J. (2021). Beyond repositioning: Crowdsourcing and geo-fencing for shared-mobility systems. *Production and Operations Management*, *30*(10), 3448–3466. DOI: 10.1111/poms.13442

Kim, S., Khoreva, V., & Vaiman, V. (2025). Strategic human resource management in the era of algorithmic technologies: Key insights and future research agenda. *Human Resource Management*, *64*(2), 447–464. DOI: 10.1002/hrm.22268

Kotter, J. P. (1995). Leading change: Why transformational efforts fail. *Harvard Business Review*, *73*(2), 59–67.

McDaniel, J. L. M., & Malik, N. (2023). Managing allegations concerning Black and Asian police officers, cultural competence and reflective practice under the Police (Conduct) Regulations 2020. *The Modern Law Review*, *86*(2), 498–517. DOI: 10.1111/1468-2230.12785

Mourtgos, S. M., Adams, I. T., & Nix, J. (2022). Elevated police turnover following the summer of George Floyd protests: A synthetic control study. *Criminology & Public Policy*, *21*(1), 9–33. DOI: 10.1111/1745-9133.12556

National Police Chiefs' Council. (2023). *Covenant for using artificial intelligence (AI) in policing*. https://science.police.uk/delivery/resources/covenant-for-using-artificial-intelligence-ai-in-policing/

Prakash, L. N. C. K., Ravva, S. K., Rathnamma, M. V., & Suryanarayana, G. (2023). AI applications of drones. In S. N. Mohanty, J. V. R. Ravindra, G. Surya Narayana, C. R. Pattnaik, & Y. Mohamed Sirajudeen (Eds.), *Drone technology*. DOI: 10.1002/9781394168002.ch7

Raffaelli, R., Zuzul, T., Gulati, R., & Rivkin, J. (2025). Outcome and process frames: Strategic renewal and capability reprioritisation at the Federal Bureau of Investigation. *Strategic Management Journal*, *46*(6), 1325–1362. DOI: 10.1002/smj.3697

Schein, E. H. (2010). *Organizational culture and leadership* (4th ed.). Jossey-Bass.

Schiff, K. J., Schiff, D. S., Adams, I. T., McCrain, J., & Mourtgos, S. M. (2025). Institutional factors driving citizen perceptions of AI in government: Evidence from a survey experiment on policing. *Public Administration Review*, *85*(2), 451–467. DOI: 10.1111/puar.13754

Shaw, M. S., Toliver, S. R., & Tanksley, T. (2024). The internet does not exist in the sky: Literacy, AI, and the digital middle passage. *Reading Research Quarterly*, *59*(4), 690–705. DOI: 10.1002/rrq.537

Tariq, M. U. (2025). The role of AI-powered learning analytics in enhancing student engagement and performance. In J. Moore, S. Gupta, M. Sharma, A. Garg, & H. Josephine V. L. (Eds.), *Transforming education with data science in the AI era* (pp. 123–148). IGI Global Scientific Publishing. DOI: 10.4018/979-8-3373-2185-1.ch005

Tariq, M. U. (2025). Integration of artificial intelligence and machine learning in business intelligence: Enhancing decision making and operational efficiency. In Ishtaiwi, A., Al-Qerem, A., Al Khaldy, M., & Alauthman, M. (Eds.), *Driving modern business intelligence architecture for operational efficiency* (pp. 279–306). IGI Global Scientific Publishing. DOI: 10.4018/979-8-3373-2125-7.ch009

Tariq, M. U. (2025). Innovation and agility: Adapting business strategies for sustainable growth in dynamic markets. In Ananthan, S., Kohli, A., Manickam, T., & Dhanabalan, T. (Eds.), *New business development strategies for achieving sustainable growth* (pp. 113–140). IGI Global Scientific Publishing. DOI: 10.4018/979-8-3373-2048-9.ch005

Teece, D. J. (2022). A wider-aperture lens for global strategic management: The multinational enterprise in a bifurcated global economy. *Global Strategy Journal*, *12*(3), 488–519. DOI: 10.1002/gsj.1462

Tsabedze, L. T., Akinnuwesi, B. A., Dlamini, B., Mbunge, E., Fashoto, S. G., Olabanjo, O., Mashwama, P., Metfula, A. S., Nxumalo, M., Badeji-Ajisafe, B., & Egenti, G. (2025). Enhancing public safety in Eswatini: A machine learning–driven predictive policing model. *Human Behavior and Emerging Technologies, 9939274*(1), 9939274. Advance online publication. DOI: 10.1155/hbe2/9939274

Chapter 4
Strategic Architectures for AI-Integrated Reconstitution of Police Education:
A Multilevel Governance Framework

Ashraf Alam
http://orcid.org/0000-0001-6178-1187
Alliance University, Bengaluru, India

ABSTRACT

This chapter presents a governance sensitive architecture for AI integrated police education that treats officer formation as ontological reconstitution rather than technical retrofit. It integrates andragogy, experiential and situated cognition, diffusion and sociotechnical adoption theory, and competency-based engineering to build simulation intensive, adaptive, analytically instrumented curricula. The chapter details cyber-physical simulation, algorithmic personalization, multimodal assessment, and stackable micro credentials across the career arc, and specifies an operating model that synchronizes curriculum, incentives, oversight, and financing with mitigations for culture, infrastructure, privacy, and budgets. Polycentric governance, fairness by design, and public dashboards convert learning into civic legitimacy, while trajectories in augmented and mixed reality, quantum scaled scenarios, and federated metaverse hubs remain constrained by legal, ethical, and participatory safeguards that anchor innovation within democratic accountability.

DOI: 10.4018/979-8-3373-5228-2.ch004

INTRODUCTION

Epistemological Reframing of Police Pedagogy within AI Governance Regimes

The accelerating digitization of law enforcement has displaced apprenticeship-only training with a datafied decisional ecology in which predictive analytics, automated sensing, natural language processing, and high dimensional forensic inference recalibrate evidentiary generation, risk estimation, and operational coordination (Steventon, 2025; Mansoor, 2026; Ahmed et al., 2025). These systems function as socio-technical institutions that configure human attention, standardize procedural pathways, and delimit lawful discretion, therefore the central curricular problem is not technological supplementation but ontological reconstitution of what counts as police knowledge, prudential judgment, and professional identity (Alda, 2025; Afzal & Panagiotopoulos, 2025). Classical drill, static scenario rehearsal, and tacit mentorship, once adequate for local and visible crime, now underperform in environments saturated with probabilistic signals, adversarial manipulation, and latency-sensitive coordination. Instructional design must therefore migrate from content transmission to competence orchestration, that interleaves algorithmic reasoning, uncertainty quantification, causal interpretation, and constitutional constraint with affective regulation and intercultural communication (Schiff et al., 2025; Chowdhury, 2023; Alam, 2023a). In this reframing, education is tasked with producing agents who can interrogate model provenance, audit data lineage, read calibration plots, and translate AI outputs into defensible action while remaining accountable to community expectations and judicial scrutiny (Ganguli, 2025; Ersöz et al., 2025). The resulting pedagogical telos is a synthesis of computational literacy, ethical discernment, and procedural mastery that renders officers credible interpreters of AI mediated reality rather than passive consumers of technological prescription.

Ontic Reconfiguration of Officer Agency, Hermeneutics, and Praxis

The contemporary officer operates as an interpreter of noisy signals, an ethical adjudicator of AI recommendations, and a mediator across human communities, statutory regimes, and automated infrastructures, which requires cognitively elastic repertoires that blend evidentiary hermeneutics with computational pragmatics (Johnson et al., 2022; Maathuis, 2024). Predictive mapping supplies spatial hypotheses conditioned by historically contingent data that may embed measurement bias, hence officers must perform counterfactual reasoning, sensitivity analysis, and proportionality review before resource deployment (Chen & Meng, 2024; William et al.,

2023). Digital forensics pipelines surface latent structures in unstructured corpora, yet admissibility and chain-of-custody integrity remain human responsibilities that depend on transparent documentation and reproducible analytical steps. Cybercrime investigations demand fluency in adversarial tactics, protocol forensics, and anomaly detection, integrated with privacy safeguards and transnational cooperation norms (Fan et al., 2024; Alikhademi et al., 2022). Pedagogy consequently centers epistemic humility regarding model fallibility, interpretive justice that resists the reification of biased priors, and digital reflexivity that continuously recalibrates human judgment within AI-assisted feedback loops. Competence must be assessed not only through outcome accuracy but also through process metrics such as decision latency under cognitive load, adherence to legal sequence constraints, linguistic neutrality during interviews, and contamination avoidance during evidence handling. When curricula institutionalize these metrics, officers acquire metacognitive control over when to defer to automation, when to contest it, and how to articulate reasons that satisfy supervisory audit as well as public reason.

Programmatic Architecture for Multilevel Stewardship and Legitimation

The research–practice interface remains underdeveloped in police education, since scholarship has privileged operational deployments of analytics while neglecting the didactic architectures that sustain trustworthy adoption, which leaves institutions vulnerable to fragmented pilots, tool fetishism, and legitimacy erosion. A corrective requires a multilevel governance schema that links micro-level learner analytics, meso-level academy routines, and macro-level regulatory guardrails into a single evidentiary pipeline (Buades-Rotger et al., 2025; Partridge & Zaghloul, 2025; Darehbidi, 2025). At the micro level, adaptive platforms must generate interpretable learning traces that support formative feedback and defensible credentialing. At the meso level, academies must codify procurement transparency, scenario diversity audits, data retention limits, and independent moderation of assessment models. At the macro level, statutory alignment, standardized documentation, external review cadences, and public dashboards convert internal improvement into civic accountability (Harris & Burke, 2021; Springs, 2024; Adams, 2025). This chapter advances this program by synthesizing andragogical theory, experiential and situated cognition, diffusion and sociotechnical adoption models, and competency-based assessment into a coherent design grammar for AI literacies in policing. The intended endpoint is an institutional ecology where AI systems are domesticated by law and ethics, where officers achieve calibrated autonomy within AI partnerships, and where communities perceive measurable reductions in procedural error and disproportionate harm that validate the profession's democratic warrant.

THEORETICAL AND CONCEPTUAL FOUNDATIONS FOR AI INTEGRATED POLICE EDUCATION

Artificial intelligence reconfigures police pedagogy by replacing episodic knowledge transfer with an ecology of continuous inference, where probabilistic modeling, multimodal sensing, and human machine teaming coalesce into a new epistemic infrastructure for decision making. A defensible foundation therefore fuses adult learning science with organizational change scholarship and competency engineering so that curricular forms mirror the cognitive and institutional realities of AI practice (Mugari & Obioha, 2021; Bowers & Johnson, 2024). Andragogical principles prioritize self-direction and problem orientation while cognitive load theory calibrates sequencing, spacing, and interleaving to prevent extraneous burden as learners confront uncertainty quantification, causal attribution, and adversarial robustness. Sociocultural learning frames expertise as participation in communities of practice, which aligns with simulation rich environments that stage authentic constraints such as data scarcity, legal proportionality, and public scrutiny. Organizationally, diffusion theory, institutional isomorphism, and sociotechnical systems analysis clarify why tools thrive only when routines, incentives, and governance artifacts coevolve. Competency based design then anchors outcomes through observable behaviors, decision latencies, calibration awareness, and documentation fidelity so assessment attests to lawful process as well as tactical effect. Absent this scaffolding, AI appears as a miscellany of software demonstrations that neither alter tacit schemas nor survive rotation, audit, or litigation, whereas a theory informed architecture yields durable literacies that social actors can explain, contest, and legitimate across academy, courtroom, and community (Kanwel et al., 2023; Gültekin-Várkonyi, 2022).

Integrated Learning and Adoption Theories for AI Literacy

A rigorous synthesis of learning theories and adoption models situates AI literacy within measurable cycles of experience, reflection, and institutional uptake. Andragogy specifies autonomy and immediate applicability, which adaptive platforms operationalize through self-paced pathways aligned with caseload archetypes such as AI risk interpretation, intrusion triage, and multilingual engagement mediated by translation systems. Experiential learning transforms high fidelity simulation into knowledge by coupling branching contingencies with structured after-action review, so concrete episodes feed abstract schemata that generalize under pressure. Vygotskian constructivism and dialogic pedagogy position AI as an intelligent mediator that curates evidence, surfaces contradictions, and scaffolds cross rank deliberation in tasks like cross border trafficking investigations where legal norms collide. Situated learning advances novices from peripheral observation to central participation through rehearsals that embed legal sequence constraints, evidentiary hygiene, and community interaction within dynamic uncertainty. Transformative learning targets identity level reframing through perspective taking modules, that cultivate epistemic humility and interpretive justice when historical data encode bias. Adoption durability follows Technology Acceptance and Unified Theory logics, in which perceived usefulness and effort expectancy rise when analytics shorten documentation, fortify interview quality, and standardize chain of custody. Diffusion dynamics locate early adopters in cyber and data units whose visible wins enroll the early majority, while sociotechnical alignment prevents assessment telemetry from being nullified by legacy promotion practices, thereby converting tool novelty into institutional normativity.

Competency Based Architecture for AI Ready Policing

Competency based education operationalizes the promise of AI by specifying granular capabilities, instrumenting performance, and credentialing mastery through reproducible evidence rather than attendance signals. Digital literacy expands from generic computing to AI reasoning, feature sensitivity, prompt engineering for investigative retrieval, and cyber hygiene under adversarial conditions (Saini & Kaur, 2023; Kumar et al., 2024). Ethical cognition is exercised through case reconstructions that require legality checks, proportionality tests, and articulation of reasons that withstand supervisory and judicial review while analytics probe for confirmation bias and disparate impact. Cultural competence matures through language mediation, dialect exposure, and community authored vignettes that force reconciliation of procedural rigor with contextual dignity (Edco et al., 2025; Khan & Ullah, 2024; Kumar et al., 2025). Resilience becomes measurable when biofeedback captures heart rate variability, gaze stability, and micro motor control so coaching can down regulate arousal without degrading situational awareness and after-action visualization links physiology to decision quality. Assessment synthesizes multimodal traces into interpretable narratives that explain what changed, why it matters for safety and rights, and how to consolidate gains (Cucoreanu, 2024; Kayalvili et al., 2023; Shapiro, 2023). Micro credentials then certify discrete capacities such as interview neutrality, contamination avoidance, digital triage, and cross-cultural negotiation, which stack into transparent career lattices that align specialization with operational demand. Workforce planners use aggregated telemetry to forecast readiness, identify systemic bottlenecks, and target mentoring resources, thereby transforming AI from a collection of tools into a disciplined system that produces officers who are data literate, ethically grounded, culturally adept, and procedurally reliable.

GLOBAL LANDSCAPE AND CROSS-SECTOR ANALOGUES

Adoption Trajectories and Regional Anchors in AI Mediated Police Pedagogy

Across jurisdictions the incorporation of artificial intelligence into police education has proceeded through path dependent assemblages of infrastructure, regulation, and organizational habitus that yield distinct pedagogical ecologies (Yen & Hung, 2021; Riley & Dixon, 2024). Canadian programs have operationalized immersive simulation for judgmental use of force and crisis negotiation with conversational agents that branch in response to prosody, latency, and semantic framing, thereby coupling experiential learning with measurable after-action analytics (Alakayleh, 2025; He & Wang, 2025; Archbold, 2025; Alam, 2023b). Australian academies have scaled decision trees for hostage dialogue and critical incident management that capture thousands of trainee choices and feed curriculum refinement through error taxonomies. Dutch crowd management instruction integrates agent-based models of pedestrian flow and sentiment dynamics so proportionality planning can be rehearsed before mass gatherings, while German financial crime curricula simulate sanctions evasion and shell networks using graph analytics to cultivate forensic reasoning over transactional complexity. British interviewing schools employ natural language processing to flag coercive prompts and rights defects at transcript level, which stabilizes procedural justice as a teachable skill. United States laboratories train digital evidence triage with pipelines that accelerate lawful extraction and documentation while preserving chain integrity. Singapore's Home Team Academy and South Korean cyber units rehearse intrusion response with synthetic corpora that scale to multi-terabyte images and ransomware propagation, aligning technical remediation with evidentiary admissibility. High capability systems therefore display a stitched architecture in which simulation, adaptivity, and credentialing are interlocked rather than bolted onto legacy lecture formats.

Heterogeneous Capacities, Constraint Regimes, and Normative Harmonization in Transnational Training

Middle income jurisdictions have pursued hybridization that tethers classroom instruction to mobile microlearning and lightweight simulation so that AI concepts diffuse without prohibitive capital expenditure. Brazilian state schools deliver adaptive modules on crowd communication, local legal parameters, and de-escalation, capturing performance traces that route individualized practice even when facilities lack high fidelity suites. Indian and Kenyan services leverage translation systems for multilingual community engagement that double as training artifacts by expanding dialect sensitivity and pragmatic competence while producing analytics for targeted vocabulary reinforcement. These trajectories seldom replicate the full stack of wealthy settings yet they cultivate foundational literacies and legitimacy dividends during incremental infrastructure growth. International bodies have converged on scaffolds for lawful and ethical adoption. UN drug control specialists have urged capacity building that couples digital transformation with AI literacy and rights aware pedagogy. The INTERPOL Innovation Centre convenes shared modules in predictive analytics, digital forensics, and governance that standardize vocabulary and minimal competence across dozens of services. The Council of Europe has recommended safeguards against discrimination, opacity, and unbounded surveillance for law enforcement uses of AI, and several academies now embed such principles into scenario authoring and assessment governance. These frameworks do not mandate tool uniformity. They instead instantiate portable requirements for transparency, documentation, human supervision, redress, and interoperability that reduce coordination frictions in cross border operations and anchor public accountability.

Cross Sectoral Heuristics Transferable to Police Andragogy under Algorithmic Conditions

Domains with entrenched safety cultures and simulation traditions offer importable design grammars for police education under AI. Healthcare demonstrates how instrumented practice reduces iatrogenic error through objective structured assessments, motion trajectory analytics, and stress regulation feedback, that together render procedural accuracy teachable at scale. The policing analogue involves contamination avoidance during evidence handling, interview neutrality under cognitive load, and de-escalation choices that preserve dignity and safety while remaining auditable. Aviation supplies a template for dynamic simulation and harmonized standards where scenario engines adapt to operator choices, inject cascading failures, and enforce checklists under acute time pressure, which maps onto crowd control, pursuit, and incident command, while highlighting the value of international protocols that allow skills to travel. Contemporary military schooling advances adversary modeling through AI agents, that learn from trainee moves, forcing red teaming and collateral risk quantification while embedding humanitarian restraint within tactical excellence, a coupling that policing can emulate to prevent capability from outrunning legality. Corporate governance adds analytics for leadership development, bias detection, and impact dashboards that translate internal telemetry into external trust through lucid public reporting. Together these analogues indicate that successful AI enriched police pedagogy requires rigorous instrumentation, scenario diversity, fairness auditing, and transparent credentialing so that technical mastery, ethical cognition, and intercultural fluency cohere into interoperable professionalism rather than isolated vendor demonstrations.

AI-ENABLED METHODS - SIMULATION, ADAPTIVITY, ASSESSMENT, AND CPD

Cyber-Physical Simulacra for High-Risk Competency Formation

Artificial intelligence has transfigured police simulation into a cyberphysical simulacrum, that fuses conversational agents, agent-based crowd models, and sandboxed network emulations to generate contingencies that unfold in response to prosody, kinesics, and evidentiary choices (Torsu, 2024; Aguilar-Ortiz et al., 2025). The pedagogical utility derives from fidelity that is functional rather than merely photoreal, where lawful sequencing, chain of custody integrity, and proportionality auditing are encoded as constraints that modulate scenario branching. Trainees rehearse crisis negotiation while sentiment analyzers track accommodation, dominance, and rapport repair, then experience crowd dynamics emergent from heterogeneous agents whose goals and thresholds shift with weather, topology, and messaging (Syed & Albalawi, 2024; Umanah et al., 2024; Adams, 2024; Alam, 2023c). Cybercrime laboratories synthesise malware propagation and credential theft within isolated architectures so that containment, logging, and forensic imaging can be practiced without operational risk (Mangkhalasiri & Poothakool, 2025). Cognitive load is regulated through graduated complexity, worked example fade outs, and retrieval practice that reintroduces earlier skills under interference. Presence and immersion are evaluated alongside procedural accuracy to ensure affective arousal does not degrade legality or safety. Linguistic and cultural mediation is embedded through perspective taking vignettes authored by community partners, that require respectful address, accommodation of disability, and multilingual turn taking. The result is an epistemic environment where signal detection, uncertainty quantification, and ethical deliberation are learned as coupled habits, and where after-action analytics transform tacit experience into explicit schemata that can be audited, iterated, and transferred across units and jurisdictions.

Algorithmically Orchestrated Personalization for Mastery Learning

Personalization governed by machine intelligence converts exposure into mastery by aligning practice with an officer's latent knowledge state inferred from performance traces. Bayesian knowledge tracing, item response theory, and contextual bandit algorithms estimate difficulty and select the next task that maximizes expected learning while constraining cognitive load. A trainee who misorders evidence sealing steps receives a micro scenario with additional distractors and time pressure until sequencing and labeling stabilize under stress. Natural language models compare interview excerpts to exemplar corpora and recommend drills that strengthen open prompts, neutrality markers, and rights advisories. Spaced repetition algorithms schedule interleaved refreshers so skills that decay are resurfaced before failure returns, while elaborative interrogation and self-explanation prompts promote durable transfer to novel contexts. The platform surfaces interpretable features such as hesitation points, error classes, and decision latency distributions so instructors act as diagnosticians who design targeted coaching and capstones rather than delivering uniform lectures. Cohort analytics reveal curricular blind spots when mastery plateaus cluster around specific subskills or scenario archetypes, which triggers content diversification rather than superficial difficulty inflation (Albrecht & Den Heyer, 2025; Gupta et al., 2025; Basharat et al., 2025). Privacy preserving aggregation protects individuals while still enabling institutional improvement. The net effect is a mastery pipeline that respects adult autonomy, accelerates competency acquisition, and produces reproducible gains in lawful precision, communicative clarity, and situational calm across varied operational ecologies.

Multimodal Analytics for Valid and Reliable Formative Evaluation

Assessment has migrated from episodic testing to continuous multimodal inference that integrates language, motion, attention, and physiology to produce high resolution feedback with documented validity. Natural language processing detects coercive phrasing, compound questioning, and missed rights advisories in interview transcripts, while computer vision models quantify stance stability, muzzle discipline, and team spacing with interpretable overlays that enable targeted remediation (Tabi et al., 2023; Alam & Mohanty, 2023a). Eye tracking and heart rate variability supply indices of cognitive load and vigilance that are linked to decision quality without pathologizing normal arousal (Eke, 2025; Tang, 2024; Zuwanda et al., 2024). Measurement theory underwrites fairness and reliability through construct validity studies, generalizability analyses, and tests for differential item functioning to ensure scores are invariant across dialects, genders, and body types. Predictive models estimate readiness for specialized roles by relating micro behaviors and latency profiles to later performance in complex scenarios, yet human adjudication remains decisive through structured rubrics that consider legality, proportionality, and narrative justification (Qiu, 2025; Sarzaeim et al., 2023). Calibration curves, discrimination statistics, and Brier score audits verify that risk estimations and readiness scores align with observed outcomes rather than spurious correlates (Roksandić et al., 2022; Adams et al., 2024). Transparent data lineage, retention limits, and role-based access controls sustain trust by separating developmental analytics from disciplinary use, and audit logs permit independent review of model versions and parameter changes (Bag et al., 2024). In this ecology, assessment becomes an instructional instrument that shapes learning trajectories while satisfying evidentiary expectations of courts, oversight bodies, and communities.

Credential Ecologies and Mentorship Informatics for Continuous Development

Continuous professional development (CPD) operates as an ecosystem where micro credentials, skills ontologies, and mentorship analytics align individual aspiration with organizational demand. Competency frameworks decomposed into observable behaviors support digital badges in interview neutrality, contamination avoidance, digital triage, drone operations, and cross-cultural negotiation, each earned through performance in instrumented scenarios rather than attendance alone (Davies & Krame, 2023; Bacalu, 2021; Sager et al., 2025; Alam & Mohanty, 2023b). Badges stack into transparent pathways that open rotations, specialist selection, and promotion while recognition of prior learning prevents redundancy for experienced officers. Recommender systems trained on skills graphs, assignment histories, and reflective journals curate concise modules that fit operational tempo and resurface when telemetry signals drift, thereby replacing annual refresher rituals with timely micro interventions (Awoyemi et al., 2025; Harris, 2022). Graph embeddings and constrained matching link recruits to mentors whose complementary strengths and availability promise maximal learning gain, while human oversight safeguards fit quality and psychological safety (Bag et al., 2024; Egbert & Esposito, 2024; Yu & Carroll, 2022). Communities of practice are sustained through moderated debriefs where anonymized analytics seed discussion and ethical reflection. Portfolios aggregate artifacts, feedback narratives, and credential histories that travel with the officer across units and jurisdictions, enabling portability without sacrificing local specificity (Dempsey et al., 2023). Governance policies secure privacy through consent, minimization, and deletion windows, and firewall developmental data from punitive use. This ecology turns CPD into a living system that couples merit, equity, and operational readiness with an auditable trail of learning evidence.

Lifecycle Coupling of Learning, Performance, and Workforce Planning

The most consequential innovation is the coupling of simulation, personalization, assessment, and credentialing into a single lifecycle that spans recruit induction to mid-career specialization and supervisory stewardship. A recruit begins with a domestic conflict scenario that probes interview clarity and evidence hygiene, receives adaptive drills that remediate compound questioning and labeling errors, and earns micro credentials that unlock community assignments where those skills are consequential. Mentorship signals prompt co practice with exemplars of calm scene control, while biofeedback modules teach breath pacing and gaze anchoring that stabilize performance under crowd noise and time pressure (Riccio et al., 2024; Rani, 2024). The same telemetry later informs readiness decisions for negotiation teams or cyber forensics units without reliance on opaque exams detached from practice. At the institutional tier, aggregated and privacy protected data reveal systemic bottlenecks such as contamination spikes when more than three actors are present, which triggers scenario redesign, briefing updates, and equipment tweaks (Davies & Krame, 2023; Al-Shamsi & Ahmad, 2024). Workforce planners use competency heat maps to forecast coverage, prioritize hiring, and target upskilling grants where mission risk is highest (Tulinov et al., 2022; Alam & Mohanty, 2023c). Oversight boards review fairness dashboards that display scoring parity, badge attainment, and outcome gains with plain language caveats about causality and cohort size. In this integrative architecture, AI functions as connective tissue that links learning and labor, strengthens legitimacy through measurement and transparency, and enables a defensible claim that training reduces the errors that communities most want to see diminished.

IMPLEMENTATION AND BARRIERS

The integration of artificial intelligence into police education succeeds only when pedagogy, institutional routines, and governance are redesigned as a single system. Pilots that sit outside core curriculum rarely persist beyond a single budget cycle because instructors revert to legacy drills, procurement fragments, and evaluation focuses on novelty rather than outcomes. Durable implementation follows a coherent pathway that begins with disciplined curriculum integration, proceeds through a streamlined change sequence with aligned incentives, embeds multistakeholder oversight, and anticipates barriers with targeted mitigations and financing. The result is an operating model in which simulations, adaptive practice, and multimodal assessment are not stand-alone tools, but connected capabilities that raise competence, compress error rates, and strengthen community legitimacy.

Curricular Systems Engineering for AI Literacy and Operant Model Design

Implementation begins with a forensic needs analysis that links recurrent operational harms to explicit competencies and measurable learning data. Academies inventory contamination events, interview defects, miscalibrated force in volatile scenes, and latency in digital triage, then translate each failure mode into instrumented scenarios with observable behaviors, tolerance bands, and timing thresholds. Competency maps thread AI reasoning, data hygiene, legality sequencing, and equity heuristics through doctrinal law, tactics, wellness, and community interaction, so that AI literacy appears in context rather than as elective novelty (Gkougkoudis et al., 2022). Timetables reserve protected blocks for simulation, coaching, and reflective synthesis, while learning platforms ingest telemetry from conversation, kinematics, gaze, and stress indices to generate interpretable feedback. Capstones combine technical execution with narrative justification and proportionality review, and pass gates require both correct outcomes and lawful process. Micro-credentials align with local risk profiles so that urban services weight interview integrity, chain of custody discipline, and crowd proportionality, whereas rural services emphasize solo decision making, radio pragmatics, and interagency coordination during disaster operations. The operating model specifies analytic review cadences, remediation triage, and conversion of verified mastery into badges that count for selection and promotion. By treating curriculum, analytics, and credentialing as a single cybernetic loop, institutions replace performative pilots with a disciplined architecture that increases competence, compresses error variance, and demonstrably improves legitimacy (Khoei & Singh, 2024). Such integration stabilizes instructor practice, clarifies accountability pathways, and accelerates iterative evidence-based refinement over time.

Sequential Change Mechanics and Incentive Alignment for Institutional Uptake

Successful adoption follows a concise sequence that synthesizes classical change literatures into a pragmatic choreography of urgency, coalitioning, routinization, and incentive redesign (Yavorsky & Mikheeva, 2022; Dubravova et al., 2024). Urgency is grounded in local evidence such as suppressed cases attributed to digital mishandling, complaint spikes after communication failures, and near misses during crowd operations, which reframes AI pedagogy as risk mitigation rather than gadgetry. A cross-rank coalition that includes instructors, supervisors, labor representatives, civil society partners, and technical staff codesigns scenarios, metrics, and governance artifacts so legitimacy is distributed rather than administrative (Pei, 2025; Apostolakis et al., 2022). Early wins are engineered by replacing low yield lectures with measured simulations that halve a recurrent error class within one cohort and survive staff rotation. Standard operating procedures fix roles, cadences, documentation, and review meetings, thereby translating novelty into habit. Incentives then anchor the shift through promotion points for verified micro-credentials, recognition for data informed coaching, procurement preferences for interoperable tools with auditability, and time allowances for reflective debriefs (Dworzecki & Nowicka, 2021; Mandavilli, 2025; Haley & Burrell, 2025). Communication remains continuous and intelligible, detailing what tools record, how records are secured, how long data persists, and how competence is recognized, while public demonstrations and plain language dashboards connect training outputs to reductions in procedural errors and use of force. Uncertainty is handled in the open through published minutes and remedial actions so rumor does not fill vacuums. This parsimonious sequence prevents backsliding, lowers cynicism, and aligns motivation with professional identity across organizational strata.

Polycentric Governance, Assurance Oversight, and Prudent Procurement

Legitimacy emerges from polycentric governance that embeds legal compliance, ethical constraint, and technical assurance within curriculum decisions and procurement pipelines. A steering committee comprising jurists, ethicists, technologists, commanders, and community delegates reviews scenario families, dataset provenance, documentation sufficiency, and fairness test batteries before deployment, thereby converting abstract principles into operational guardrails (Blount, 2024; McDaniel & Pease, 2021; Alam & Mohanty, 2023d). Independent outcome boards evaluate whether AI enhanced education reduces specified error classes, shortens case cycle times, and improves community satisfaction, then publish accessible reports that disclose methods, limitations, and remedial plans. Procurement discipline prevents vendor lock in and quality drift through mandatory disclosures of model purpose, data lineage, subgroup evaluation, update cadences, cybersecurity posture, and service continuity guarantees (Apene et al., 2024; Al Shamsi & Safei, 2023; Kaufmann, 2024). Contracts incorporate audit rights, bias testing tooling, price stabilization, and exit clauses that secure data portability and functional replacement without interruption. Interoperability standards cover identity, rostering, outcome schemas, scenario descriptors, and telemetry so modules from different suppliers can coexist and be upgraded without retraining instructors or losing historical traces. Data governance policies specify role-based access, encryption at rest and in transit, retention schedules, consent management, and redress processes that separate developmental analytics from disciplinary systems (Chukaieva & Matulienė, 2023; Berk, 2021). Together these mechanisms institutionalize accountability, deter opacity, and encourage iterative improvement. When governance artifacts are public and comprehensible, communities perceive AI enabled education as professionalization aligned with rights rather than as inscrutable instrumentation of control. Such transparency stabilizes trust, disciplines vendors, and strengthens jurisdictional cooperation.

Barrier Taxonomy with Contextualized Mitigation and Risk Containment

Adoption barriers cluster across culture, infrastructure, privacy, and finance, and each requires context specific mitigation, that treats officers and communities as stakeholders rather than obstacles. Cultural resistance often derives from fears of deskilling, loss of autonomy, and punitive surveillance, which is countered by publishing precinct level evidence of error reduction and time savings, erecting developmental firewalls that prohibit training analytics in misconduct proceedings, and granting officers rights to inspect, correct, and contest records (Ishchenko et al., 2024; Lin, 2025; Haley & Burrell, 2025). Technical fragility appears as bandwidth bottlenecks, aging endpoints, and brittle integrations, addressed through staged architectures that cache locally while rendering and analytics occur in the cloud, open standards that enable gradual replacement, and mobile first micro simulations that capture event logs even under weak connectivity. Privacy risk emerges when realistic datasets include sensitive particulars or when biometrics are captured without meaningful consent, mitigated through synthetic or differentially private corpora, rigorous de identification, explicit opt ins, and fairness testing across dialects, genders, and experience levels (Mugari & Obioha, 2021; Bowers & Johnson, 2024). Budget scarcity threatens continuity, so multiyear business cases quantify avoided harms, shared services pool costs across regions, and agreements mandate knowledge transfer to reduce vendor dependence. By treating mitigation as a design discipline rather than a rhetorical appendix, institutions convert skepticism into participation and transform fragile pilots into resilient programs with measurable dividends in safety, efficiency, and legitimacy (Kanwel et al., 2023; Gültekin-Várkonyi, 2022). Iterative retrospectives document lessons learned and recalibrate controls as operational ecologies evolve over successive cycles.

Multilevel Coupling and Sustainability through Adaptive Governance

Coherence across micro, meso, and macro strata determines longevity, therefore implementation must synchronize learner pathways, academy routines, and national oversight into a mutually reinforcing system. At the micro tier officers receive adaptive plans tied to caseload archetypes, mentors are matched through analytics for complementary strengths, and protected time is reserved for simulation, coaching, and reflective synthesis so learning does not compete with shift demands (Saini & Kaur, 2023; Kumar et al., 2024). At the meso tier academies redesign schedules, workload formulas, and instructor recognition so preparation for instrumented teaching and after-action review is valued labor rather than invisible commitment, while data pipelines flow into curriculum councils that update scenarios when aggregated telemetry reveals bottlenecks. At the macro tier ministries promulgate AI literacy standards aligned with rights, mandate interoperable data formats, and create funding formulas that reward measured improvement rather than raw adoption counts, while external audits report fairness, effectiveness, and remedial actions in accessible language (Edco et al., 2025; Khan & Ullah, 2024; Kumar et al., 2025). Sustainability follows continual improvement cycles that retire stale content, add incidents drawn from recent cases, recalibrate scoring thresholds as competence rises, and test for stereotype drift or unintended incentives. Vendor ecosystems are diversified to avoid single points of failure, second source arrangements are secured for critical components, and internal authoring capacity is cultivated so expertise remains public (Cucoreanu, 2024; Kayalvili et al., 2023; Shapiro, 2023). Through such coupling, AI education becomes a durable public infrastructure that strengthens professionalism and social license while enabling transparent governance across federated training consortia worldwide.

GOVERNANCE, ETHICS, AND MEASUREMENT

The viability of AI in police education rests on governance architectures that make legality, fairness, and accountability operational rather than aspirational. Training is a public good funded by taxpayers, therefore the systems that create data about recruits and serving officers must be transparent, reviewable, and proportionate (Alakayleh, 2025; He & Wang, 2025; Archbold, 2025; Yen & Hung, 2021; Riley & Dixon, 2024). Governance anchors the why and how of AI use; ethics specifies the limits and protections; measurement connects internal learning gains to external legitimacy. When these strands are braided together into audits, fairness testing, and public reporting, institutions can modernize pedagogy without eroding trust.

Juridical Consonance and Institutional Accountability Infrastructures

Legal alignment functions as the basal lamina upon which every pedagogical and computational layer must be seated, therefore governance design specifies traceability, contestability, and proportionality as operative constraints rather than aspirational slogans. Training systems that simulate law enforcement decision making require documented model provenance, data lineage maps, and human oversight at points of consequential allocation so that decisional authority remains reviewable under administrative and judicial standards (Torsu, 2024; Aguilar-Ortiz et al., 2025; Alam & Mohanty, 2024). Curriculum councils institute privacy by design through minimization, purpose limitation, and role-based access, while procurement templates mandate AI transparency statements, security attestations, and portability guarantees that preclude vendor lock in. Scenario repositories undergo equality screening to prevent protected attributes or their proxies from silently steering outcomes, and impact assessments record foreseeable risks, mitigation controls, and residual uncertainties before deployment (Syed & Albalawi, 2024; Umanah et al., 2024; Adams, 2024). Developmental analytics are sequestered from personnel processes through firewalled databases, explicit retention schedules, and redress channels that allow officers to inspect, correct, or expunge inaccurate traces within lawful windows. Federated academies harmonize schemas and redress procedures so protections travel with learners across jurisdictions, and oversight boards composed of jurists, ethicists, technologists, and community delegates ratify releases, pause updates, and commission remedial action when noncompliance is detected (Mangkhalasiri & Poothakool, 2025). Accountability thus becomes continuous practice rather than episodic performance, since documentation, audit logs, and version registers render institutional memory machine readable and civically legible, enabling external review to validate that training gains do not come at the expense of legality, equity, or due process.

Ethical Guardrails and Fairness by Design Paradigms

Ethical adequacy begins with epistemic hygiene in the data pipeline and extends through interface affordances to consequence governance, therefore fairness is architected ex ante rather than appended ex post. Scenario content privileges synthetic or rigorously de-identified corpora and community authored vignettes over raw operational files, with consent workflows, masking routines, and time bounded retention to curtail unregulated reuse (Albrecht & Den Heyer, 2025; Gupta et al., 2025; Basharat et al., 2025). Generative pipelines are instrumented for stereotype leakage detection so that visual tropes, linguistic cues, or narrative arcs do not couple protected identity with criminal propensity, and library composition is balanced across gender, age, ethnicity, disability, and urban rural topologies to blunt overfitting. Fairness operates at three strata that interlock. Scenario fairness assures exposure to multiple lawful resolution pathways, so learners are not rewarded for a single coercive style (Tabi et al., 2023). Model fairness interrogates natural language and vision components for differential error across dialects, accents, skin tones, mobility profiles, and experience tiers using calibration curves, sensitivity parity, and error symmetry. Outcome fairness monitors score distributions, badge attainment, and progression rates after controlling for preparation and access to mentoring, with root cause analysis distinguishing content bias, tool bias, and structural inequities, then documenting dated remediations. Transparency norms require intelligible notices that specify what is collected, why, for how long, and how to contest inaccuracies, while opt in is the default for physiological telemetry and eye tracking with viable non-invasive alternatives to avoid coercion (Eke, 2025; Tang, 2024; Zuwanda et al., 2024). Ethical governance therefore cultivates trust by converting dignity, equity, and autonomy into testable and enforceable design properties.

Auditability Regimes and Civic Dashboarding for Epistemic Transparency

Oversight achieves credibility when verification is methodological, recurrent, and intelligible to lay publics and expert audiences, hence audit regimes triangulate technical, scenario, and pedagogical evidence streams. Internal conformance reviews confirm that procurement clauses, documentation standards, access controls, and retention schedules match promulgated policy, while independent technical audits replicate performance on holdout corpora, retest subgroup parity, and verify calibration and discrimination metrics against declared baselines (Qiu, 2025; Sarzaeim et al., 2023). Scenario audits interrogate scripts, visuals, and branching graphs for stereotype drift, legality lapses, and perverse incentives, and require corrective commits that are recorded in version control with action owners and dates. Pedagogical audits compare pre and post adoption cohorts on contamination errors, missed rights advisories, decision latency under stress, and interview neutrality scores using matched samples and sensitivity checks for confounders. Where thresholds are breached, rollback procedures disable automated scoring while qualitative feedback continues, and remediation timelines are published (Roksandić et al., 2022; Adams et al., 2024). Public dashboards close the loop by presenting a compact canon of outcome indicators that communities value, including reductions in specified procedural error classes, time to lawful digital evidence processing, cultural competence badge completion, and trend lines in complaints for units whose officers completed defined modules, with uncertainty bands and narrative caveats about attribution. Accessibility features and multilingual interfaces broaden reach, and open data extracts potentially allow researchers and journalists to interrogate series independently, thereby converting internal improvement into externally verifiable legitimacy.

Measurement Integration within Reflexive Governance Cycles

Measurement becomes the vertebral column of governance when every module ships with an articulated theory of change that links inputs to proximal learning markers and distal operational outcomes, and when findings recursively reconfigure content, policy, and resourcing (Bag et al., 2024). Proximal markers include accuracy under time budgets, adherence to legally sequenced procedures, linguistic neutrality indices in interviews, contamination avoidance rates, and stress regulation indicators derived from heart rate variability and gaze stability, each validated for reliability and invariance across demographic groups. Distal outcomes include charge sustainability, suppression motion losses avoided, cycle times for digital evidence, sentinel event reduction, community satisfaction after contacts, and supervisor assessments anchored in structured rubrics (Davies & Krame, 2023; Bacalu, 2021; Sager et al., 2025). Mixed methods designs integrate quantitative series with ethnographic debriefs that explain why a metric moved or stalled, and longitudinal cohorts support durability inferences while monitoring unintended effects such as speed gains that erode thoroughness or confidence gains that inflate risk appetite. Causal identification leverages difference in differences, synthetic controls, or interrupted time series with robustness checks for policy shocks and cohort composition (Awoyemi et al., 2025; Harris, 2022). Findings drive curriculum refactoring, tool configuration, mentoring allocation, and procurement renewal, and also inform funding so budgets follow demonstrated impact rather than novelty. When measurement is braided with legal alignment, ethical guardrails, and public dashboarding in a fixed cadence, AI enabled pedagogy becomes simultaneously more effective and more legitimate, since the very instruments that personalize learning also generate the evidentiary record required to prove fairness, efficacy, and societal value.

CONCLUSION AND WAY FORWARD

The coming decade will conjoin augmented and mixed reality, quantum enhanced computation, and federated simulation ecologies to reshape police pedagogy into a coherent socio technical system. These capacities will not appear as curiosities but as instruments domesticated by policy, curriculum, and civic accountability, so machine intelligence augments prudent judgment rather than displacing it. Heads up displays with context aware overlays can bridge rehearsal and field practice by cueing lawful sequence, contamination avoidance, and calm language while instructors reconstruct attention paths and decision points from privacy safeguarded telemetry. Quantum inspired scenario engines will expand state spaces for contingency planning, permitting city scale exercises that couple infrastructure failure, information cascades, and adversarial adaptation while preserving auditable guardrails for legality and proportionality. Persistent shared worlds will permit transnational cohorts to practice interoperability with AI agents filling non-critical roles to maintain tempo without erasing human oversight. Governance must specify scope, retention, opt in consent, and redress so that training traces do not drift into mass collection or punitive surveillance. Fairness by design must test rendering, voice synthesis, attention cueing, and scoring for differential effects across dialects, skin tones, mobility profiles, and experience tiers. Measurement must track reductions in procedural error classes, improvements in interview neutrality, and cycle time for evidence processing with uncertainty explained to the public. Only when capability, constraint, and transparency remain braided can these futures elevate competence while strengthening legitimacy.

Legitimacy will be determined by the granularity of guardrails and the equity of access strategies rather than by spectacle or novelty. Developmental firewalls must keep training analytics separate from misconduct adjudication, while consent workflows for physiological telemetry, gaze traces, and AR vision feeds provide alternatives and revocation rights. Procurement governance should enforce interoperability, data portability, second sourcing, and vendor disclosure of model objectives, data lineage, subgroup performance, and updates so pedagogy is not captured by proprietary ecosystems. Financing should pool capital through shared hubs, while mobile first variants deliver compressed assets to low bandwidth jurisdictions, so micro credentials can be earned despite infrastructure gaps. Mentorship informatics should match recruits with exemplars using skills graphs, and leadership analytics can identify supervisors who model fair discipline and inclusive teams for scaling through promotion criteria. Community co-design should become routine in scenario authoring so advocates, disability groups, youth councils, and minority associations shape narratives and harm maps that improve fidelity and reduce stereotype drift. Public dashboards should report fewer contamination events, fewer missed rights advisories, and faster decisions under stress, while fairness indicators display score parity and progression rates across protected classes. By aligning financing, governance, mentorship, and participation, institutions can avert stratification where elite academies monopolize fidelity suites while others stagnate. The aim is a federated learning commons where capability accrues to officers and communities and where trust grows with gains.

The strategic lesson of this chapter is pragmatic synthesis rather than technological celebration, since credible reform couples capability with constraint and converts internal learning into value. AI integrated education reconceives professional identity by binding computational literacy, ethical discernment, intercultural fluency, and lawful procedure into one repertoire that withstands legal scrutiny and evaluation. Institutions align micro level practice, meso level routines, and macro level standards so literacy, interoperability, and audit cadence travel with officers across roles and regions. Cross sector importation from healthcare, aviation, and the military shows that simulation and checklist discipline raise accuracy, shorten decisions, and temper risk when governance is explicit. Forward motion requires policy commitments to open standards, data portability, second sources, and transparent dashboarding, along with workforce investments that cultivate internal authoring and fairness testing capacity. Community co-design must remain central, so narratives and harm mapping reflect lived realities, while oversight bodies retain authority to pause modules that normalize bias or yield no measured improvement. When measurement, ethics, and law operate in a fixed cadence, augmented reality stabilizes procedural memory under stress, quantum inspired scenarios surface blind spots in complex cascades, and federated worlds normalize cross border collaboration without surrendering accountability. If police education treats artificial intelligence as connective tissue and embeds democratic guardrails at every layer, services will graduate officers who are data literate, grounded, culturally competent, and accountable, thereby strengthening safety and trust.

REFERENCES

Adams, I. T. (2024). Large language models and artificial intelligence for police report writing. *CrimRxiv*. DOI: 10.21428/cb6ab371.779603ee

Adams, I. T. (2025). Automation and artificial intelligence in police body-worn cameras: Experimental evidence of impact on perceptions of fairness among officers. *Journal of Criminal Justice*, *97*, 102373. DOI: 10.1016/j.jcrimjus.2025.102373

Adams, I. T., Barter, M., McLean, K., Boehme, H. M., & Geary, I. A.Jr. (2024). No man's hand: Artificial intelligence does not improve police report writing speed. *Journal of Experimental Criminology*, •••, 1–18. DOI: 10.21428/cb6ab371.4a6d42e9

Afzal, M., & Panagiotopoulos, P. (2025). Data in policing: An integrative review. *International Journal of Public Administration*, *48*(7), 411–430. DOI: 10.1080/01900692.2024.2360586

Aguilar-Ortiz, J., Zamudio-García, V. M., & Simancas-Acevedo, E. (2025). Sustainable Development Goal 16 Peace and Justice Criminal Justice and Artificial Intelligence Applications for a More Efficient and Fair System. In *Machine and Deep Learning Solutions for Achieving the Sustainable Development Goals* (pp. 435-460). IGI Global Scientific Publishing. DOI: 10.4018/979-8-3693-8161-8.ch022

Ahmed, S., Khan, M. F., Singh, B., Singh, N., & Sharma, B. (2025). Enhancing Crime Scene Analysis: The Impact of AI Technologies on Evidence Processing. In *Forensic Intelligence and Deep Learning Solutions in Crime Investigation* (pp. 63-84). IGI Global Scientific Publishing. DOI: 10.4018/979-8-3693-9405-2.ch004

Al-Shamsi, A., & Ahmad, N. B. (2024). Opportunities and Challenges of AI Adoption by the Abu Dhabi Police: A Review Study. *International Journal of Academic Reserach in Economics and Management Sciences*, *13*(3). Advance online publication. DOI: 10.6007/IJAREMS/v13-i3/22719

Al Shamsi, H. R. S., & Safei, S. A. (2023). Artificial intelligence adoption in predictive policing to predict crime mitigation performance. *International Journal of Sustainable Construction Engineering and Technology*, *14*(3), 289–298. DOI: 10.30880/ijscet.2023.14.03.025

Alakayleh, O. (2025). The Use of Artificial Intelligence Systems in Crime Detection and Prevention: Applications and Challenges. Available at *SSRN* 5132225. DOI: 10.2139/ssrn.5132225

Alam, A. (2023a). Media multitasking with M-learning technology in real-time classroom learning: Analysing the dynamics in formal educational settings for the future of E-learning in India. In *2023 2nd International Conference on Smart Technologies and Systems for Next Generation Computing (ICSTSN)* (pp. 1-6). IEEE. DOI: 10.1109/ICSTSN57873.2023.10151509

Alam, A. (2023b). The secret sauce of student success: Cracking the code by navigating the path to personalized learning with educational data mining. In *2023 2nd International Conference on Smart Technologies and Systems for Next Generation Computing (ICSTSN)* (pp. 1-8). IEEE. DOI: 10.1109/ICSTSN57873.2023.10151558

Alam, A. (2023c). Leveraging the power of 'modeling and computer simulation' for education: An exploration of its potential for improved learning outcomes and enhanced student engagement. In *2023 International Conference on Device Intelligence, Computing and Communication Technologies, (DICCT)* (pp. 445-450). IEEE. DOI: 10.1109/DICCT56244.2023.10110159

Alam, A., & Mohanty, A. (2023a). Implications of virtual reality (VR) for school teachers and instructional designers: An empirical investigation. *Cogent Education, 10*(2), 2260676. DOI: 10.1080/2331186X.2023.2260676

Alam, A., & Mohanty, A. (2023b). Design, development, and implementation of software engineering virtual laboratory: A boon to computer science and engineering (CSE) education during Covid-19 pandemic. In *Proceedings of third international conference on sustainable expert systems: ICSES 2022* (pp. 1-20). Singapore: Springer Nature Singapore. DOI: 10.1007/978-981-19-7874-6_1

Alam, A., & Mohanty, A. (2023c). From bricks to clicks: The potential of big data analytics for revolutionizing the information landscape in higher education sector. In *International Conference on Data Management, Analytics & Innovation* (pp. 721-732). Singapore: Springer Nature Singapore. DOI: 10.1007/978-981-99-1414-2_51

Alam, A., & Mohanty, A. (2023d). Learning on the move: a pedagogical framework for state-of-the-art mobile learning. In *International Conference on Data Management, Analytics & Innovation* (pp. 735-748). Singapore: Springer Nature Singapore. DOI: 10.1007/978-981-99-1414-2_52

Alam, A., & Mohanty, A. (2024). Framework of Self-Regulated cognitive engagement (FSRCE) for sustainable pedagogy: A model that integrates SRL and cognitive engagement for holistic development of students. *Cogent Education, 11*(1), 2363157. DOI: 10.1080/2331186X.2024.2363157

Albrecht, J. F., & Den Heyer, G. (Eds.). (2025). *Special Topics in Policing: Critical Issues and Global Perspectives* (Vol. 3). Springer Nature., DOI: 10.1007/978-3-032-06680-0

Alda, E. (2025). Productivity on patrol: Measuring efficiency gains from AI-assisted police reports with a global malmquist index. *CrimRxiv*. DOI: 10.21428/cb6ab371.d923f490

Alikhademi, K., Drobina, E., Prioleau, D., Richardson, B., Purves, D., & Gilbert, J. E. (2022). A review of predictive policing from the perspective of fairness. *Artificial Intelligence and Law*, *30*(1), 1–17. DOI: 10.1007/s10506-021-09286-4

Apene, O. Z., Blamah, N. V., & Aimufua, G. I. O. (2024). Advancements in crime prevention and detection: From traditional approaches to artificial intelligence solutions. *European Journal of Applied Science. Engineering and Technology*, *2*(2), 285–297. DOI: 10.59324/ejaset.2024.2(2).20

Apostolakis, K. C., Dimitriou, N., Margetis, G., Ntoa, S., Tzovaras, D., & Stephanidis, C. (2022). DARLENE–Improving situational awareness of European law enforcement agents through a combination of augmented reality and artificial intelligence solutions. *Open Research Europe*, *1*, 87. DOI: 10.12688/openreseurope.13715.2 PMID: 37645167

Archbold, C. A. (2025). Special issue on police reform. Policing. *Policing (Oxford, England)*, *19*, paaf013. Advance online publication. DOI: 10.1093/police/paaf013

Awoyemi, O., Attah, R. U., Basiru, J. O., & Leghemo, I. M. (2025). A community-policing innovation model to build sustainable trust and effectively reduce crime in urban areas. DOI: 10.54660/.IJMRGE.2025.6.1.848-853

Bacalu, F. (2021). Digital policing tools as social control technologies: Data-driven predictive algorithms, automated facial recognition surveillance, and law enforcement biometrics. *Analysis and Metaphysics*, *20*(0), 74–88. DOI: 10.22381/AM2020215

Bag, A., Roy, S., & Pandey, A. (2024). Harnessing the Power of Artificial Intelligence in Law Enforcement: A Comprehensive Review of Opportunities and Ethical Challenges. *Exploring the Ethical Implications of Generative AI*, 121-145. DOI: 10.4018/979-8-3693-1565-1.ch008

Bag, A., Shashikant, S., Mishra, P., & Pradhan, A. (2024, March). Using artificial intelligence in US law enforcement-a review. In. AIP Conference Proceedings: Vol. 2816. *No. 1* (p. 050002). AIP Publishing LLC., DOI: 10.1063/5.0179536

Basharat, M. F., Sajid, N., Fattah Shah, S. A., & Kazmi, S. G. A. (2025). National Policy and Legislative Framework for AI Governance in Law Enforcement Agencies and Criminal Justice System of Pakistan. *Available at SSRN* 5248649. DOI: 10.2139/ssrn.5248649

Berk, R. A. (2021). Artificial intelligence, predictive policing, and risk assessment for law enforcement. *Annual Review of Criminology*, *4*(1), 209–237. DOI: 10.1146/annurev-criminol-051520-012342

Blount, K. (2024). Using artificial intelligence to prevent crime: Implications for due process and criminal justice. *AI & Society*, *39*(1), 359–368. DOI: 10.1007/s00146-022-01513-z

Bowers, K., & Johnson, S. (2024). Facing the Future of Crime: A Framework for Police Use of Technology. *The Political Quarterly*, *95*(3), 480–488. DOI: 10.1111/1467-923X.13426

Buades-Rotger, M., Martínez Catena, A., Recio, G., Cano Gallent, M., Niñerola i Maymí, J., Figueras Masip, A., & Gallardo-Pujol, D. (2025). Personality predicts internalizing symptoms and quality of life in police cadets: A comparison of artificial intelligence and parametric approaches. *Health & Justice*, *13*(1), 43. DOI: 10.1186/s40352-025-00351-7 PMID: 40613989

Chen, Y., & Meng, J. (2024, November). Agility and Resilience: The Governance of Ethical Alienation in Police Artificial Intelligence. In 2024 8th Asian Conference on Artificial Intelligence Technology (ACAIT) (pp. 274-276). IEEE. DOI: 10.1109/ACAIT63902.2024.11021763

Chowdhury, M. (2023). Going cyberpunk: Conceptualizing the smart (er) artificially intelligent firearm for policing's Utopian future. *International Journal of Police Science & Management*, *25*(3), 324–337. DOI: 10.1177/14613557231184689

Chukaieva, A., & Matulienė, S. (2023). Possibilities of applying artificial intelligence in the work of law enforcement agencies. *Scientific Journal of the National Academy of Internal Affairs*, *3*(28), 28–37. DOI: 10.56215/naia-herald/3.2023.28

Cucoreanu, C. (2024). Public Order and the Technological Revolution: Implications for Police and Citizen Safety. *European Journal of Law and Public Administration*, *11*(1), 39–52. DOI: 10.18662/eljpa/11.1/219

Darehbidi, Z. N. (2025). The Use of Artificial Intelligence Technology in Preventing Female Delinquency: A Novel Approach to Situational Crime Prevention. *Legal Studies in Digital Age*, *4*(1), 1–10. DOI: 10.61838/kman.lsda.131

Davies, A., & Krame, G. (2023). AI-Driven Innovation in Law Enforcement: The Synergistic Potential of Police Body Cameras and Drones as a Complementary Policing Tool for Tactical and Operational Enhancement. *Policing (Oxford, England), 17*(1), 1–13. DOI: 10.1093/police/paad083

Davies, A., & Krame, G. (2023). Integrating body-worn cameras, drones, and AI: A framework for enhancing police readiness and response. *Policing. Policing (Oxford, England), 17*, paad083. Advance online publication. DOI: 10.1093/police/paad083

Dempsey, R. P., Brunet, J. R., & Dubljević, V. (2023). Exploring and understanding law enforcement's relationship with technology: A qualitative interview study of police officers in North Carolina. *Applied Sciences (Basel, Switzerland), 13*(6), 3887. DOI: 10.3390/app13063887

Dubravova, H., Cap, J., Holubova, K., & Hribnak, L. (2024). Artificial intelligence as an innovative element of support in policing. *Procedia Computer Science, 237*, 237–244. DOI: 10.1016/j.procs.2024.05.101

Dworzecki, J., & Nowicka, I. (2021). Artificial intelligence (AI) and ICT-enhanced solutions in the activities of police formations in Poland. In *Artificial Intelligence and Its Contexts: Security, Business and Governance* (pp. 161–181). Springer International Publishing., DOI: 10.1007/978-3-030-88972-2_11

Edco, H., Simbolon, W., Nita, S., & Koto, Z. (2025). Optimization of Predictive Policing Technology for Prevention of Brawling Crimes at Bekasi City Metro Police Station. *Journal of Law. Politic and Humanities, 5*(3), 1447–1457. DOI: 10.38035/jlph.v5i3.1313

Egbert, S., & Esposito, E. (2024). Algorithmic crime prevention. From abstract police to precision policing. *Policing and Society, 34*(6), 521–534. DOI: 10.1080/10439463.2024.2326516 PMID: 38974932

Eke, R. N. (2025). Adopting Artificial Intelligence-Based Predictive Policing in Nigeria: Prospects and Difficulties. *African Journal of Advances in Science and Technology Research, 18*(1), 142–164. DOI: 10.62154/ajastr.2025.018.010680

Ersöz, F., Ersöz, T., Marcelloni, F., & Ruffini, F. (2025). *Artificial Intelligence in Crime Prediction: A Survey With a Focus on Explainability*. IEEE., DOI: 10.1109/ACCESS.2025.3553934

Fan, X., Salehzadeh, R., Korivand, S., Bordbar, F., Cousin, C., Griffin, D. J., & Jalili, N. (2024). Exploring law enforcement officers' expectations and attitudes about communication robots in police work. *Human Technology, 20*(1), 25–44. DOI: 10.14254/1795-6889.2024.20-1.2

Ganguli, P. (2025). Digital policing: Using social media surveillance to tackle cybercrime. *Available at SSRN* 5124657. DOI: 10.2139/ssrn.5124657

Gkougkoudis, G., Pissanidis, D., & Demertzis, K. (2022). Intelligence-led policing and the new technologies adopted by the Hellenic Police. *Digital*, *2*(2), 143–163. DOI: 10.3390/digital2020009

Gültekin-Várkonyi, D. G. (2022). Predictive Policing and Bias in a Nutshell: Technical and Practical Aspects of Personal Data Processing for Law Enforcement Purposes. *Digital Criminal Justice: A Studybook Selected Topics for Learners and Researchers. Krisztina Karsai, Adem Sözüer, Liane Wörner (eds.). Istanbul.* DOI: 10.2139/ssrn.4238774

Gupta, M., Sood, R. P., & Singh, R. (2025). Artificial Intelligence in Criminal Investigation: Transforming Law Enforcement and Forensic Analysis. In *Rethinking the Police for a Better Future: Navigating Policing Challenges with Accountability and Trust* (pp. 311-323). Cham: Springer Nature Switzerland. DOI: 10.1007/978-3-031-83173-7_21

Haley, P., & Burrell, D. N. (2025). Integrating Artificial Intelligence into Law Enforcement: Socioeconomic and Ethical Challenges. [SEC]. *SocioEconomic Challenges*, *9*(2), 60–77. Advance online publication. DOI: 10.61093/sec.9(2).60-77.2025

Haley, P., & Burrell, D. N. (2025). Using Artificial Intelligence in Law Enforcement and Policing to Improve Public Health and Safety. *Law. Economics and Society*, *1*(1), 46–p46. DOI: 10.30560/les.v1n1p46

Harris, H. (2022). Artificial intelligence and policing of financial crime: a legal analysis of the state of the field. *Financial technology and the law: Combating financial crime*, 281-299. DOI: 10.1007/978-3-030-88036-1_12

Harris, H., & Burke, A. (2021, October). Artificial Intelligence, Policing and Ethics–a best practice model for AI enabled policing in Australia. In *2021 IEEE 25th International Enterprise Distributed Object Computing Workshop (EDOCW)* (pp. 53-58). IEEE. DOI: 10.1109/EDOCW52865.2021.00032

He, D. S., & Wang, T. S. (2025). An exploration of the service and crime prevention performance of the municipal police departments of Taiwan's counties: The perspective of broken windows theory. *Policing*, *48*(1), 136–156. DOI: 10.1108/PIJPSM-05-2024-0088

Ishchenko, T., Nikitina, I., & Das, B. (2024). Innovations in Law Enforcement Education: the Impact of Artificial Intelligence Tools. DOI: 10.32782/2078-3566-2024-4-27

Johnson, T. L., Johnson, N. N., McCurdy, D., & Olajide, M. S. (2022). Facial recognition systems in policing and racial disparities in arrests. *Government Information Quarterly*, *39*(4), 101753. DOI: 10.1016/j.giq.2022.101753

Kanwel, S., Khan, M. I., & Usman, M. (2023). From bytes to bars: The transformative influence of artificial intelligence on criminal justice. *Qlantic Journal of Social Sciences*, *4*(4), 84–89. DOI: 10.55737/qjss.059046443

Kaufmann, M. (2024). AI in policing and law enforcement. In *Handbook on Public Policy and Artificial Intelligence* (pp. 295–306). Edward Elgar Publishing., DOI: 10.4337/9781803922171.00031

Kayalvili, S., Rajulu, G. G., Changala, R., & Kumbhkar, M. (2023, October). Integration of Machine Learning and Computer Vision to Detect and Prevent the Crime. In *2023 International Conference on New Frontiers in Communication, Automation, Management and Security (ICCAMS)* (Vol. 1, pp. 1-5). IEEE. DOI: 10.1109/ICCAMS60113.2023.10526105

Khan, I. A., & Ullah, A. (2024). The Role of Artificial Intelligence in Enhancing Social Governance: A Framework for Ethical Implementation and Policy Development in Pakistan. *Journal of Management & Social Science*, *1*(4), 274–289. DOI: 10.63075/9fzpbn74

Khoei, T. T., & Singh, A. (2024). A survey of Emotional Artificial Intelligence and crimes: Detection, prediction, challenges and future direction. *Journal of Computational Social Science*, *7*(3), 2359–2402. DOI: 10.1007/s42001-024-00313-3

Kumar, J. S., Amiruzzaman, M., Bhuiyan, A. A., & Bhati, D. (2024). Predictive Analytics in Law Enforcement: Unveiling Patterns in NYPD Crime through Machine Learning and Data Mining. *Research Briefs on Information and Communication Technology Evolution*, *10*, 36–59. DOI: 10.64799/rebicte.v10.3

Kumar, M., Kumar, M., Dabur, S., Yadav, R., Kumar, K., & Tyagi, M. (2025, April). Exploring the Implementation of Artificial Intelligence in the Indian Legal System. In *2025 3rd International Conference on Communication, Security, and Artificial Intelligence (ICCSAI)* (Vol. 3, pp. 1545-1551). IEEE. DOI: 10.1109/ICCSAI64074.2025.11064188

Lin, L. S. (2025). Integrating Artificial Intelligence in Police Education: An Analysis of the Top-Down Approach at Taiwan's Central Police University. In *Transforming Vocational Education and Training Using AI* (pp. 131-164). IGI Global Scientific Publishing. DOI: 10.4018/979-8-3693-8252-3.ch006

Maathuis, C. (2024, November). Insights into Building VR Solutions in the Police Domain. In *Proceedings of the International Conference on Education Research.* Academic Conferences and publishing limited. DOI: 10.34190/icer.1.1.2800

Mandavilli, V. K. C.VENKATA KALYAN CHAKRAVARTHY MANDAVILLI. (2025). SAP AI Applications Across Diverse Sectors: Education, Law Enforcement, and Art. *World Journal of Advanced Research and Reviews*, *26*(2), 2012–2019. DOI: 10.30574/wjarr.2025.26.2.1887

Mangkhalasiri, P., & Poothakool, K. (2025). Data Science in Policing in Thailand: Challenges and Future Directions–A Review From International Perspectives. *Journal of Contemporary Social Sciences and Humanities*, *12*(2), 18–34. DOI: 10.59796/jcsh.v12i2.18-34

Mansoor, S. I. U. (2026). AI and the Rule of Law in Urban Security: Upholding Police Accountability in Smart Cities. In AI-Driven Policing and Urban Security in Smart Cities (pp. 55-80). IGI Global Scientific Publishing. DOI: 10.4018/979-8-3373-0245-4.ch003

McDaniel, J. L., & Pease, K. (Eds.). (2021). *Predictive policing and artificial intelligence*. Routledge, Taylor & Francis Group. DOI: 10.4324/9780429265365

Mugari, I., & Obioha, E. E. (2021). Predictive policing and crime control in the United States of America and Europe: Trends in a decade of research and the future of predictive policing. *Social Sciences (Basel, Switzerland)*, *10*(6), 234. DOI: 10.3390/socsci10060234

Partridge, J., & Zaghloul, F. (2025). Policing the data: Can data analytics help law enforcement? *Journal of Information Technology Teaching Cases*, *15*(1), 90–94. DOI: 10.1177/20438869231212214

Pei, Y. (2025). The Integration of Artificial Intelligence into Smart Policing Systems: Applications and Risk Governance. *Advances in Management and Intelligent Technologies*, *1*(4). Advance online publication. DOI: 10.62177/amit.v1i4.486

Qiu, Y. (2025). Policing AI-generated crimes: An ethnographic study on anti-cybercrime police in China. *Security Journal*, *38*(1), 34. DOI: 10.1057/s41284-025-00491-3

Rani, M. (2024). Impacts and ethics of using Artificial Intelligence (AI) by the Indian Police. *Public Administration and Policy*, *27*(2), 182–192. DOI: 10.1108/PAP-06-2023-0081

Riccio, V., Jia, D., & Das, D. K. (Eds.). (2024). *Challenges of Contemporary Policing: Higher Education, Technology, and Officers' Well-Being*. Taylor & Francis., DOI: 10.4324/9781003452379

Riley, B. K., & Dixon, A. (2024). Emotional and cognitive trust in artificial intelligence: A framework for identifying research opportunities. *Current Opinion in Psychology*, *58*, 101833. DOI: 10.1016/j.copsyc.2024.101833 PMID: 38991423

Roksandić, S., Protrka, N., & Engelhart, M. (2022, May). Trustworthy Artificial Intelligence and its use by Law Enforcement Authorities: where do we stand? In *2022 45th jubilee international convention on information, communication and electronic technology (MIPRO)* (pp. 1225-1232). IEEE. DOI: 10.23919/MIPRO55190.2022.9803606

Sager, M. A., Arshad, M., Ahmed, T., Abbas, S. S., & Khan, M. S. (2025). Enhancing Police Effectiveness in Punjab: Integrating Training and Capacity Building Initiatives for Sustainable Impact. *Journal of Social Sciences Review*, *5*(1), 526–537. DOI: 10.62843/jssr.v5i1.517

Saini, I. S., & Kaur, N. (2023, July). The power of predictive analytics: forecasting crime trends in high-risk areas for crime prevention using machine learning. In *2023 14th International Conference on Computing Communication and Networking Technologies (ICCCNT)* (pp. 1-10). IEEE. DOI: 10.1109/ICCCNT56998.2023.10306731

Sarzaeim, P., Mahmoud, Q. H., Azim, A., Bauer, G., & Bowles, I. (2023). A systematic review of using machine learning and natural language processing in smart policing. *Computers*, *12*(12), 255. DOI: 10.3390/computers12120255

Schiff, K. J., Schiff, D. S., Adams, I. T., McCrain, J., & Mourtgos, S. M. (2025). Institutional factors driving citizen perceptions of AI in government: Evidence from a survey experiment on policing. *Public Administration Review*, *85*(2), 451–467. DOI: 10.1111/puar.13754

Shapiro, A. (2023). Optimizing the immeasurable: On the techno-ethical limits of predictive policing. In *Artificial intelligence and the city* (pp. 240–257). Routledge., DOI: 10.4324/9781003365877-18

Springs, D. (2024). Smart city planning focused on the US cities in need of policing innovations and public health safety technologies and strategies. *Health Economics and Management Review*, *5*(1), 117–128. DOI: 10.61093/hem.2024.1-09

Steventon, M. (2025). Policing in Practice. In *Understanding Policing and Professional Practice* (pp. 123–140). Routledge., DOI: 10.4324/9781041057758-10

Syed, S., & Albalawi, E. M. (2024). Transforming Law Enforcement: Exploiting Big Data Science and Data Analytics for Precision Decision-Making and Crime Pattern Anticipation in Police Operations. DOI: 10.21203/rs.3.rs-4677394/v1

Tabi, C., Hewage, C., Bakhsh, S. T., & Ukwandu, E. (2023). Contemporary issues in child protection: police use of artificial intelligence for online child protection in the UK. In *Digital Transformation in Policing: The Promise, Perils and Solutions* (pp. 85–107). Springer International Publishing., DOI: 10.1007/978-3-031-09691-4_5

Tang, X. (2024). Innovative Paradigms in Policing: A Quantitative Study of Technology, Training, and Community Engagement in China. *European Journal on Criminal Policy and Research*, •••, 1–29. DOI: 10.1007/s10610-024-09608-7

Torsu, L. A. (2024). Crime prevention in the digital age: Challenges and technologies for policing in Aflao border township in Ghana. *The Police Journal*, 0032258X241309190. DOI: 10.1177/0032258X241309190

Tulinov, V. S., Bilykh, I. V., Merdova, O. M., Volobuieva, O. O., & Veselov, M. Y. (2022). Activities of Law Enforcement Agencies in the Context of the Introduction of Innovative Technologies (Comparative Legal Aspect). *Cuestiones Políticas*, *40*(72), 145–163. Advance online publication. DOI: 10.46398/cuestpol.4072.08

Umanah, E. A., Willie, C. E., & Daniel, U. S. (2024). Implications of Emerging Technologies on Social Behaviour and Crime Control in the 21st Century. *Journal of Advanced Research and Multidisciplinary Studies*, *4*(3), 152–162. DOI: 10.52589/JARMS-JL2NFQ57

William, P., Shrivastava, A., Shunmuga Karpagam, N., Mohanaprakash, T. A., Tongkachok, K., & Kumar, K. (2023). Crime analysis using computer vision approach with machine learning. In *Mobile Radio Communications and 5G Networks: Proceedings of Third MRCN 2022* (pp. 297-315). Singapore: Springer Nature Singapore. DOI: 10.1007/978-981-19-7982-8_25

Yavorsky, M. A., & Mikheeva, S. V. (2022, April). The Use of Artificial Intelligence Technologies and Big Data in Law Enforcement. In *Proceedings of the International Conference Engineering Innovations and Sustainable Development* (pp. 669-675). Cham: Springer International Publishing. DOI: 10.1007/978-3-030-90843-0_76

Yen, C. P., & Hung, T. W. (2021). Achieving equity with predictive policing algorithms: A social safety net perspective. *Science and Engineering Ethics*, *27*(3), 36. DOI: 10.1007/s11948-021-00312-x PMID: 34075448

Yu, S., & Carroll, F. (2022). Insights into the next generation of policing: understanding the impact of technology on the police force in the digital age. In *Artificial Intelligence and National Security* (pp. 169–191). Springer International Publishing., DOI: 10.1007/978-3-031-06709-9_9

Zuwanda, Z. S., Lubis, A. F., Solapari, N., Sakmaf, M. S., & Triyantoro, A. (2024). Ethical and Legal Analysis of Artificial Intelligence Systems in Law Enforcement with a Study of Potential Human Rights Violations in Indonesia. *The Easta Journal Law and Human Rights*, *2*(03), 176–185. DOI: 10.58812/eslhr.v2i03.283

Section 2
Criminal Application and Policing and Law Enforcement Use Cases of Artificial Intelligence

Chapter 5
The Criminal Application of Artificial Intelligence:
How Offenders Are Exploiting AI to Facilitate, Enhance, or Conceal Crime

Petros Violakis
http://orcid.org/0000-0002-6789-0592
Rabdan Academy, UAE

ABSTRACT

The rapid evolution of Artificial Intelligence (AI) has not only transformed industries and governance but has also introduced novel methods for criminal exploitation. This chapter investigates how offenders leverage AI technologies to facilitate, enhance, and conceal criminal activity. Grounded in criminological and socio-technical theories—including Routine Activity Theory and Cyber Routine Activity Theory, Rational Choice Theory, Script Theory, and Dual-Use Technology Theory—the study develops a comprehensive offender classification framework based on motivation, technical skill, role, and access model. Through a 15-question empirical questionnaire distributed among professionals in law enforcement, cybersecurity, and academia, the research examines offender profiles, AI misuse patterns, and systemic gaps in detection and policy. The chapter concludes with policy recommendations that emphasize AI-specific detection tools, regulation of generative models, and offender-targeted intervention strategies.

DOI: 10.4018/979-8-3373-5228-2.ch005

INTRODUCTION

The speed and spread of Artificial Intelligence (AI) has changed modern societies dramatically in every area including governance, commerce, communication, education and security. AI systems are now being used to assist a myriad of useful applications ranging from data analysis to automation to predictive decision-making and generative content production. Yet the same technologies that improve productivity, innovation and public service delivery are creating new potential for criminal exploitation. As access to AI tools becomes more widespread, scalable, and embedded in the daily digital space, offenders become more capable of using them to support, enrich and mask criminal efforts. This constitutes an emerging challenge for criminology, cybersecurity, and public policy, with fundamental conceptions of offending being challenged by technologies that automatically obscure deception, increase reach, and minimize operational effort and make them more difficult to detect.

The criminal exploitation of AI must be viewed in the context of an extended historical development of digitally enabled offending. Earlier phases of cyber-enabled crime were already influenced by the use of automation, scripting, phishing kits, botnets, malware reuse and cybercrime-as-a-service server infrastructures, all of which have facilitated the process of offenders industrialising new forms of deception, expanding the ways in which targets are selected, and lowering the demand for advanced bespoke expertise. What is different in the current phase of AI is not that earlier models of cybercrime have been fully replaced, but that an increasing number of systems able to produce persuasive text, realistic synthetic media, adaptive and automated decision support, are available at low cost and with only minimum technological know-how requirements. In this sense, AI is continuing a broader trend where digital tools have made it easier to identify targets, act as means of imitation of trusted communication and also serve as a means of organising criminal activity (Yamin, Ullah, Ullah, & Katt, 2021; Kaur, Gabrijelčič, & Klobučar, 2023; Choi, Dearden, & Parti, 2024; Treleaven, et al., 2023; NCSC, 2024).

Recent scholarship suggests that the technology of generative, as well as machine-learning systems, has been aiding this transition by making sophisticated forms of deception and targeting accessible to a far more extensive pool of users. Schmitt and Flechais highlight how generative AI is enhancing social engineering through its capacity for realistic content creation, sophisticated targeting and personalisation, and automatic attack infrastructures (Schmitt & Flechais, 2024), whereas Parti, Dearden and Choi (2023) highlight the fact that AI can increase criminal activity during the stages of reconnaissance, targeting, execution, and concealment (Choi, Dearden, & Parti, 2024). Broader cybersecurity scholarship has also argued that AI is a dual-use capability, which can enhance defensive detection, but also increases adversarial possibilities, particularly in relation to phishing attacks, malware support and synthetic content abuse (Bécue, Praça, & Gama, 2021; Gupta, Akiri, Aryal, Parker, & Praharaj, 2023; Taddeo, McCutcheon, & Floridi, 2021). These academic findings are backed by official assessments, for example, the UK National Cyber Security Center (NCSC) who warn that the cyber threat is already changing as a consequence of AI (NCSC, 2024), and is lowering barriers to entry; or the Federal Bureau of Investigation (FBI IC3, 2024) who state that criminals are using generative AI to make fraud and social engineering attacks more convincing and easier to carry out.

The criminal use of AI is not exclusive to very skilled cyber actors or adversaries with state related connections. Rather than that, AI is bringing down barriers to entry over a wide range of offending through access to high-level capabilities via commercial platforms, open-source tools, and easy-to-use generative systems. Tasks that once required specialist expertise, took much time, or required coordinated effort can now be assisted or accelerated by AI-enabled systems. Some of these are phishing, impersonation, disinformation, fraud, surveillance, identity manipulation, social engineering, reconnaissance and concealment. In this sense, AI does not just create a new tool in the offenders arsenal, it changes the circumstances under which crime can be planned, executed, enacted on a massive scale and concealed. It also is changing the profile of potential offenders, by widen access to capabilities which were previously limited to more technically-skilled or better resourced actors.

AI-enabled crime differs from previous forms of cybercrime less in the creation of entirely new types of offence than in the enhancement of existing criminal methods. The most important shift is functional: AI has the ability to make familiar forms of offending faster, cheaper, more scalable, more persuasive and more adaptive. Academic research is starting to emphasize that generative AI is a key factor in social engineering as it provides a higher level of linguistic quality, contextual plausibility, precision targeting and automation capabilities in an effort to enable offenders to generate convincing content for phishing, impersonation and fraud at scale (Schmitt & Flechais, 2024; Choi, Dearden, & Parti, 2024; Ferrag, et al., 2024). Related work also points towards LLMs and adjacent AI systems now being materially relevant to phishing work flows, cyber threat intelligence, malware assistance and other phases of cyber operations activity, even if their impact to date may largely be on enhancing existing tactics rather than replacing them wholesale (Jaffal, Alkhanafseh, & Mohaisen, 2025; Kasri, et al., 2025; NCSC, 2025).

A further distinction, however, has to do with realism and the cognitive effect. Earlier cybercrime had relied on detectable linguistic mistakes, low-grade impersonation or substantially static templates. By contrast, the modern AI-enabled offending is able to use synthetic text, cloned voices, manipulated images and deepfake video to try and exploit trust with a greater sense of authenticity. Research on deepfakes and synthetic media shows that these innovations complicate verification operations, heighten privacy and reputational threats (such as the verification process of media content and the implication for privacy, etc.), as well as contribute to a rising detection arms race (Hynek, Gavurová, & Kubák, 2025; Gambín, Yazidi, Vasilakos, Haugerud, & Djenouri, 2024; Kaur, Hoshyar, Saikrishna, Firmin, & Xia, 2024). Europol and INTERPOL have both given similar warnings about deepfakes, fake identities and AI facilitated deception while the FBI has explicitly pointed out the role generative AI plays in enhancing the plausibility of fraud as well as multilingual targeting (FBI IC3, 2024; Europol, 2025; INTERPOL, 2024). The distinguishing feature, therefore, is not just digital offending, it is digitally enabled offending function augmented with adaptive, realistic, and widely accessible AI capability.

This study explores offender exploitation and use of AI in relation to support, improvement of criminal conduct and concealment activity while paying attention to offender characteristics, the patterns of AI misuse and broader governance and structural implications of AI enabled crime. It fills an important gap in current scholarship. Although there is a growing concern about the misuse of AI, much of the existing discussion revolves around the technology itself, its risks, or its regulatory implications, rather than the offender as an individual decision-maker in changing opportunity structures. There is still a need for a more offender centred structured understanding of who is exploiting AI and how and why they are interested in the use of these tools and which stages of the criminal process AI is most useful. This chapter therefore places the offender at the centre of analysis, and aims to link technological change and criminological explanation. In so doing, it goes beyond descriptive accounts of AI risk and offers an analytical model that connects motivation, capability, crime stage and dual use dynamics into the study of AI-enabled offending. This is consistent with recent scholarship calling for greater offender focused and ecosystem based analysis of how AI is misused, versus just 'technical' or 'tool centred' types of accounts (Choi, Dearden, & Parti, 2024; Treleaven, et al., 2023; Schmitt & Flechais, 2024).

To this end, the study is based on relevant criminological and socio-technical perspectives, such as Routine Activity Theory, Script Theory, and Dual-Use Technology Theory. Together, these perspectives are useful for understanding how AI changes opportunities for crimes, becomes integrated into various stages in the offending process, and why technologies developed for legitimate civilian purposes may be used for harmful or illegal purposes. Building on these foundations, the study introduces an extensive offender classification framework using motivational, technical skill, operational role and access models. The aim is not only to describe AI misuse, but also to improve the understanding of the variety of different actors involved, from the opportunist's low-skill activities using commercially available tools to the more technically competent perpetrators that are capable of adapting AI systems for complex forms of crime.

The research is focused by the more general proposition that AI is transforming both the means and the logic of offending. First, AI-enabled tools may reduce the technical and operational barriers that previously restricted involvement in sophisticated forms of crime, in doing so opening it to people with little expertise to undertake activities requiring advanced knowledge. Second, AI may enable an increase in the speed, frequency, and scalability of criminal behaviour by automating the process of phishing, targetting, surveillance, and manipulating identity. Third, AI may reinforce the concealment process by allowing offenders to cover intent, create false content, evade attribution, and minimize visibility of harmful behaviour, using tools such as deepfakes or anonymization platforms, adversarial manipulation, etc. Fourth, the offenders exploiting AI are unlikely to constitute a uniform category of criminals; on the contrary, they are expected to differ significantly in their motivation to offend, their skill level, their role, and their access to technological resources for offense. These differences are important analytically, as they determine the ways in which offending behavior is conducted with AI tools by offenders and how preventive, detection, and policy responses can be shaped.

In light of these concerns, the study is organized around various fundamental research questions. It raises the question of which phase of the criminal lifecycle AI is being most commonly applied in, whether it be planning, execution, or concealment. It examines knowledge about how professionals view the probable characteristics of offenders targeting AI-such as age, educational background and skills profile. It examines the techniques that are most common or emerging due to AI enabled by AI technologies in criminal settings and how these technologies impact the ability of experts to detect, prevent, and respond to them in the current environment. It also asks for professional input on the best ways to reduce the misuse of AI, and asks whether it is possible to systematically classify offenders based on motivation, technical skill, operational role and access to AI tools. These questions are designed to encourage the discussion to go beyond the concern about AI-enabled offending, toward a more structured understanding of AI-enabled offending.

Empirically, the research is based on a set of 15 questions sent to people working within law enforcement, cybersecurity and academia. This approach, based on expert opinions, aims to capture the knowledgeable perceptions of profiles of offenders, emerging uses-misuse patterns, and the system weaknesses of current responses. Preliminary findings suggest that AI is perceived as being particularly valuable in the execution and concealment phase of the crime, and the misuse of AI is often linked to technically competent, adaptive and profit-driven actors. At the same time, the findings highlight relevant detection and governance gaps, which suggest the need for better tailoring of existing responses to the unique dynamics of AI enabled offending.

Open-source and official reporting points to the fact that AI-enabled offending is emerging in an already vast cyber-fraud environment. In 2024, the Internet Crime Complaint Center of the Federal Bureau of Investigation had a total of 859,532 complaints with USD 16.6 billion in reported losses, with the highest number of complaints (193,407) being for phishing and spoofing (FBI IC3, 2024). The same report documented especially severe financial damage among elderly victims, with the group that is 60 and older reporting losses of around USD 4.8 billion (FBI IC3, 2024). These figures do not identify AI as a separate reporting category, but show the scale of the fraud environment that AI is now being used in. That interpretation is consistent with the interpretation from academic work that argues that AI should not be treated as a new type of crime, but as a multiplier of capabilities, which adds to a new level of efficiency, adaptability, and reach of current criminal ecosystems (Choi, Dearden, & Parti, 2024; Treleaven, et al., 2023; Ferrag, et al., 2024).

At the same time, both official and academic sources are increasingly identifying generative AI as a multiplier of fraud and deception. The FBI has said that criminals are using generative AI to make social engineering, spear phishing, romance fraud, investment fraud, and other confidence schemes just that much easier and realistic (FBI IC3, 2024). The NCSC has likewise determined that AI is leading to a rise in the number and scale of cyber attacks and a reduction in the entry barriers (NCSC, 2025; NCSC, 2024). Academic literature generally shares this view. Schmitt and Flechais suggest that generative AI enhances social engineering capabilities by adding realism, targeting and automation and Jaffal et al. and Kasri et al. demonstrate that several LLMs act within a larger cybersecurity context of both useful applications and exploitable weaknesses (Schmitt & Flechais, 2024; Kasri, et al., 2025; Jaffal, Alkhanafseh, & Mohaisen, 2025). Broader reviews of the role of AI in cybersecurity have also emphasized that technologies for detection and defence could be repurposed in an offensive way, confirming the twin use dilemma at the heart of crime enabled by artificial intelligence (Salem, Azzam, Emam, & Abohany, 2024; Kaur, Gabrijelčič, & Klobučar, 2023; Taddeo, McCutcheon, & Floridi, 2021).

However, the availability of systematic offender-level statistics is still very limited. This point seems especially important when responding to calls for clearer offender profiling. However, the availability of systematic offender-level statistics is still very limited. This point seems especially important when responding to calls for clearer offender profiling. INTERPOL have explicitly stated that there is a lot more information or knowledge about fraud methods and modi operandi than offender profile and about the organisational structures behind them (INTERPOL, 2024). Academic research comes to a similar conclusion: there is more rich literature on attack methods, the dynamics of social engineering, deepfakes, AIs aiding cyber operations than on verified offender demographics or stable typologies based on large-scale empirical data (Choi, Dearden, & Parti, 2024; Schmitt & Flechais, 2024;

Hynek, Gavurová, & Kubák, 2025). This evidentiary gap strengthens the value of offender-centred analytical frameworks and expert-perception studies such as the present one which attempt to classify emerging patterns in the absence of completeness of data from the offender side.

By combining theoretical insight and empirical observation, this study adds to the new discourse on intelligent threat actors and the misuse of AI in criminal activities. Its broader purpose is both analytical and practical: analytically, in seeking to understand more clearly the manner in which AI is changing criminal opportunity, the nature of offender behaviour and concealment strategies; and practically, in addressing more targeted responses to prevention, detection and regulation in this area. In doing so, it suggests that the key to understanding the exploitation of AI is not just looking at what AI system capability can do, but also looking more deeply at offender motivations, the patterns of offender adaptation and the 'dual use' nature of modern AI systems. As AI continues to spread to the commercial and social environments, the importance of adaptive governance and offender-centric measures to combat it becomes increasingly critical.

THEORETICAL FRAMEWORK

Typologies and Classification of Criminal Application of Artificial Intelligence

The current research is based on four interrelated theoretical perspectives that are used to understand the use of Artificial Intelligence (AI) by offenders to support, facilitate, or obscure criminality: Routine Activity Theory (RAT), Cyber Routine Activity Theory (CRAT) (RAT and CRAT are combined), Script Theory, Rational Choice Theory and Dual-Use Technology Theory. Together, these frameworks support the conceptual development of the AI-Enabled Crime Dynamics Framework (ACDF) which attempts to examine how AI-enabled crime can be understood as the result of interaction between structural vulnerabilities, offender decision-making, crime sequencing and the affordances of dual-use technologies.

Routine Activity Theory (RAT) & Cyber Routine Activity Theory (CRAT)

Routine Activity Theory (RAT), which was first established to explain variations in crime through changes in routine activities of everyday life, has become one of the most commonly used frameworks to study cyber-enabled harm (Cohen & Felson, 1979). Its central proposition is that crime is the convergence of a motivated offender, a suitable target, and a lack of able guardianship, in terms of time and space. This logic has been thoroughly tested, modified, and transferred to digital realms (Yar, 2005; Holt & Bossler, 2009; Leukfeldt & Yar, 2016). Over time, this resulted in the development of Cyber Routine Activity Theory (CRAT), which reformulates opportunity based explanations for cyberspace. A systematic study of this literature also show the lasting analytical relevance of RAT/CRAT in the context of cybercrime, while also discloses the increasing limitations when these theories are applied to AI-enabled forms of criminality (Ahmad & Thurasamy, 2022).

According to RAT, crime is more likely to occur when three conditions all coincide: a motivated offender, a suitable target, and lack of sufficient guardianship (Cohen & Felson, 1979). In the context of AI-enabled crime, AI empowers offender ability through automation of reconnaissance activities, identification of weakly protected assets and support of deceptive communications on a large scale, lowering the threshold for committing crime (Dzuba, 2025; Grinbaum & Adomaitis, 2024; UNICRI & UNCCT, 2021).AI can thus help to minimize the practical limitations that historically have reinforced the function of guardianship (e.g. the cost of surveillance, difficulties in tailored targeting and the detectability of malicious communications), and maximize the suitability of targets (Dzuba, 2025; Grinbaum & Adomaitis, 2024; UNICRI & UNCCT, 2021).

Early theoretical work was questioned about the meaningfulness of RAT - which was built on concepts of physical co-presence and of spatial convergence to explain cybercrime and online harms. Yar argued that although there is no physical proximity in cyberspace, this still creates patterned opportunities for victimisation with information becoming the central "target" as opposed to physical property (Yar, 2005; Wall, 2007). This conceptual shift was critical in the development of CRAT in which visibility, accessibility and guardianship were redefined as digital rather than purely spatial phenomena (Yar, 2005; Vakhitova, 2025).

Cyber Routine Activity Theory takes this reasoning further to the digital context where online routines, platform architecture and transnationally networked processes influencing exposure to danger are examined (Yar, 2005; Leukfeldt & Yar, 2016; Holt & Bossler, 2009; Ahmad & Thurasamy, 2022). AI intensifies these processes through supporting the cross-platform data mining, profiling of behaviour and targeted influence campaigns which widen the reach of offenders beyond the usual geographical constraints (Ganaie, 2026; UNICRI & UNCCT, 2021; Liang, 2023).

Subsequent empirical studies focused on the explanatory value of RAT variables in cyber settings. In research conducted by Leukfeldt and Yar based on survey evidence on a large sample of RAT victims, the authors reported that certain RAT variables, especially visibility and accessibility, maintained statistical significance in cyber victimisation whereas others, such as target value and technical guardianship, had diminishing or conflicting effects (Leukfeldt & Yar, 2016; Holt & Bossler, 2009;

Pratt, Holtfreter, & Reisig, 2010).These findings are important as they suggest that RAT explains where and under what circumstances cyber harm occurs, but is less successful in explaining why certain actors engage in such conduct. This is a limitation suggesting integration with Rational Choice Theory and associated motivational approaches (Williams, 2016).

Field work extensions have also shown that cybercrime clusters in specific environments as a result of the interaction of routine activities and broader structural conditions which shape target availability and offender opportunity (Kigerl, 2011; Bossler & Holt, 2010; Pyrooz, Decker, & Moule, 2013). Related work in the fields of community and place-based criminology once again emphasised the significance of micro-contexts, situational dynamics and institutional responses, indicating that opportunity structures are not static but are created by arrangements in organisational, technological and governance dimensions (Taylor, 2015; Clarke & Eck, 2005; Weisburd, Groff, & Yang, 2013). These insights have a great deal of relevance to platform-mediated and algorithmically-structured digital environments.

By the early 2010s, a growing number of scholars questioned the way that the elements of RAT were treated as binary conditions. Drawve, Thomas, and Walker associated RAT with post-event outcomes such as arrest and demonstrated that offender motivation, awareness of the situation, and misreadings of guardianship influence not only the occurrence of crime, but also enforcement outcomes (Drawve, Thomas, & Walker, 2014). This expanded the scope of RAT from causal antecedents to system responses. A more important step forward, however, was provided by Schaefer and Mazerolle who suggested a processual interpretation of RAT. Rather than conceiving guardianship as existing or not, they approached the concept of crime control as differing by the concept of relationality, relativity, and responsibility (Schaefer & Mazerolle, 2017). This reframing reintroduced social process and structural context into RAT because it became evident that opportunity control is something that develops, as opposed to something that occurs instantaneously.

Recent empirical work reinforces this complexity. Huber et al., show that in some cases, having more powerful forms of physical or personal guardianship does not necessarily enhance cybercrime victmatisation and their results imply that some protective measures may have a false sense of security as they motivate riskier behaviour online and thus increase exposure to cyber threats (Huber, Pospisil, Sauter, & Treytl, 2025). Such findings suggest that in digitally saturated environments forms of guardianship could produce new exposures through feedback loops, offender adaptation and variation in crime types.

Across the RAT/CRAT literature, there is wide agreement on a number of issues. First, patterned online exposure is primary in understanding digital victimisation and targeting. Second, RAT/CRAT are particularly useful in terms of explaining opportunity structures and target choice. Third, is that guardianship is the most volatile and contested element of the framework. This limitation is more evident within adjacent studies of online harm. Hawdon et al., for example, show that opportunity-based explanations are insufficient for explaining participation in online hate attacks; particularly where engagement is all about identity, narratives, and social meaning (Hawdon, Costello, Barrett-Fox, & Bernatzky, 2019). supports the view that RAT/CRAT shed their light on the exposure and opportunity, but under-explain mobilisation and behavioural escalation.

There has also been more divergence in the literature. Some scholars still accept RAT as a flexible schema that is adaptable to cybercrime and even AI mediated offending, but others note the strain that automation, platformisation and algorithmic mediation place on the theory. There remains controversy regarding the extent to which models of cybercrime can explain criminal harms involving symbolic manipulation, social engineering, reputational harm or concerted deception in which strategic communication plays a central explanatory role. Even so empirically, the routine activity logic still is relevant to ideologically tinged or politically charged cyber harms, particularly in providing the opportunity structures and the suitability of the target (Holt, Turner, Freilich, & Chermak, 2021).

However, when applied to AI-enabled crime, a number of limitations are visible. Both RAT and CRAT are essentially human-centred models that assume that offenders, targets, and guardians are all discrete agents who make conscious and situation-specific decisions. This assumption is no longer as credible in digital spaces, where exposure, targeting and communication have become greatly influenced by recommender systems, generative AI and AI-driven content creation. RAT also does not provide a fully developed account of algorithmic guardianship. Although recent scholarship is aware of technical and institutional guardians of information, it still struggles to articulate how AI systems monitor, prioritises, amplifies or suppresses content and activity such that it actively restructures opportunity. Finally, RAT/CRAT struggle to account for scale and pace, introduced by the availability of AI tools, which help to compress time and minimize the skills and allow mass targeting in ways that defy the assumptions of routine activity as being a 'gradual patterned process'.

Taken together, the development of RAT and CRAT indicate that these theories remain highly useful to explaining how criminal opportunities are developed online, exposure to risk is created, and how appropriate targets are identified by offenders in digital environments. Yet they are only a partial basis for analysing AI-enabled crime. In order to understand how offending appears as a structured series of acts, and not as a situational coincidence, analysis must focus less on the converging of opportunities and more on theories that explicitly model action sequences and operational progression and, most notably, Script Theory.

Script Theory and Sequencing Criminal Activity in the AI Era

While Routine Activity-based approaches do help to explain the development of criminal opportunities, they can not provide much insight into the development of criminal activity as a process. Script Theory overcomes this limitation, conceptualising crime as not a single, discrete event, but a series of actions, which occur in sequence and over time. Originating in the work of Cornish, Script Theory offers an analytical framework for decomposing complex criminal behaviour into preparatory, execution and post-event stages; each made up of smaller decision-dependent steps (Cornish, 1994). This view has been particularly influential in studies of crime prevention and security, in which interventions are modeled on attempts to interfere with certain steps in harmful activity, rather than on focus on motivation alone.

Script Theory views criminal behaviour as a script which unfolds from preparation, to execution and aftermath (Cornish, 1994). In regards to AI-enabled crime this enables researchers to trace back how the AI tools are used at various points: selecting targets, finding victims, crafting customized messages, automating malicious communications, carrying out fraud or intrusion and concealing traces after the fact. Generative AI for example can be used to write phishing emails, create synthetic audio or video to impersonate, write convincing documentation or automate narratives of post incident deception and denial (Weimann, Winter, Köhler, & Brzuszkiewicz, 2024; Lakomy, 2023; Nelu, 2024).

This logic was previously anticipated indirectly. According to Pech and Slade, the media exposure and symbolic narratives can spread “aggressive scripts” which will be played out by later actors (Pech & Slade, 2005). Although not presented explicitly in terms of crime scripting their work recognised that harmful activity often follows repeatable templates that can be copied, modified and re-enacted. This insight is very relevant in the case of AI-enabled offending in which template-based fraud, automated persuasion and repetition-based campaigns of deception can be created and scaled rapidly.

Parallel work in social psychology led to the development of the theory of script at an affect and motivational level. Drawing on affect theory, Greco and Stenner conceptualised scripts as behaviours that are enduring structures of narrative that bind emotions, identities and expectations into patterned behaviour (Greco & Stenner, 2008). Under this view, scripts are not only behavioural guides, but also frameworks which help maintain the meanings, expectations and identities that are shared across time. This is a useful perspective in understanding AI-enabled offending, where grievances, opportunism and claims to identity can be organised into a coherent narratives which come before or justify criminal conduct.

The most systematic operationalisation of Script Theory, however, has been developed from the crime scripting literature. Dehghanniri and Borrion's review has shown the importance of allowing crime scripts to be utilised to model offences on a step-by-step basis, identify the points of intervention, and aid the implementation of situational prevention strategies within organised crime, cybercrime and similar areas of crime. They also reveal major limitations such as inconsistent definitions of scripts; weak empirical validation; and the lack of evaluation of the effectiveness of script-based interventions to actually reduce harm. Importantly, they clearly discuss the relevance of cyber systems, digital traces and data-driven environments for future script construction (Dehghanniri & Borrion, 2019). This observation is especially salient in the AI context, where we have automated tools able to construct, optimise and adapt crime scripts much faster and on a much greater scale than processes involving humans alone.

Across the Script Theory literature there is a huge degree of convergence around the idea that harmful activity is processual and decomposable. Whether analyzed in the context of the affective narratives (Greco & Stenner, 2008),patterns of imitation (Pech & Slade, 2005) or the process of offender sequencing (Dehghanniri & Borrion, 2019), scripts always appear to be understood as structured pathways through time. This makes Script Theory very well suited to the study of AI enabled crime where offences will rarely take place without some preparation, execution routine, and some form of post-event concealment or monetisation.

Divergence remains, however, both in level of analysis and in methodology maturity. Motivational script approaches discuss the formation and sustainability of narratives and identities while the crime scripting approach examines how motivations encode into concrete actions spanning a series of situational stages. Few studies do successfully integrate these levels to tell us how motivations are translated into operational criminal behaviour. As Das notes, research on this topic is still fragmented across different fields of academia, which is problematic at a time when there is a more urgent need for integrated analytical models (Das, 2022).

Several gaps emerge when Script Theory is applied to the fields of crime, which is enabled by AI. First, the active role of AI as a script generator has not been fully theorised in the literature. Scripts have typically been viewed as learned, copied or designed by humans, while generative AI is now capable of creating fraudulent narratives, operational content, synthetic identities, phishing scripts and post-event deception, multiply criminal scripts and accelerate criminal narratives, scripts. Second, existing work often isolates particular stages of activity rather than modelling an end-to-end of a criminal pipeline. Script Theory provides conceptual tools to link target selection, preparation, the execution, the concealment and the aftermath in a chain, but this potential has not yet been well developed in the context of AI. Third, prevention-oriented scripting has yet to fully consider disruption, in a way that AI is adapting scripts dynamically, across the platforms and jurisdictions.

Overall, Script Theory goes beyond opportunity because it demonstrates how AI-enabled crime operates as a sequenced and staged process (as opposed to a situational coincidence). It assists in determining where AI tools are used in the lifecycle of offences, how they change the decision points and where interventions may be more effective. Nevertheless, existing scholarship on the subject has not yet extended the theory of Script Theory adequately to account for environments that would increasingly be characterized by automation, generative content and cross-platform connectivity. Addressing such gaps is crucial for understanding the nature of contemporary AI enabled offending as well as emphasizing the importance of the Rational Choice Theory, which describes how offenders make strategic decisions by weighing costs, benefits and risks within the changing technological condition.

Rational Choice Theory and Criminal Decision Making for Offenders in the Age of Artificial Intelligence

Rational Choice Theory (RCT) conceptualises crime as the outcome of purposeful decision-making in which actors weigh up perceived costs, benefits and risks when deciding on tactics, targets and methods. Early economic and criminological approaches to offending tended to assume that it is a rational choice, based on an understanding of the constraints and opportunities, and that illicit behaviour is chosen because it is perceived to have higher utility than its legal alternatives (Das, 2022; Crenshaw, 1981; Becker, 1968; Sandler & Enders, 2004). Within this tradition, offenders are therefore not irrational actors, but are strategic actors reacting to incentives, constraints and information environments (Kydd & Walter, 2006; Enders & Sandler, 2012).

RCT considers that offenders weigh up costs, rewards and risks of detection prior to deciding to offend (Becker, 1968; Clarke & Cornish, 1985). In the AI context the attractiveness of AI is the promise of higher impact with lower perceived effort, lower exposure and higher scalability. AI chatbots can be used to automate customised interactions on a larger scale, deepfake and voice-cloning applications may be reused for low cost, and automated translation can help cross borders and increase audience penetration (Lakomy, 2023; Makuch, 2025).In the criminal world such capabilities are useful not only for direct fraud and cyber intrusion, but also for deception, impersonation, market manipulation and digital concealment.

Foundational work in RCT has always emphasised cost benefit calculation, on both organisational and individual levels. Offenders change behaviour in relation to levels of enforcement, perceived sanctions and returns (Crenshaw, 1981; Sandler & Enders, 2004; Clarke & Cornish, 1985). Later work indicated that offenders do not always act with perfect rationality and that they may be motivated by some factors such as identity, recognition, grievance, and symbolic gain (Das, 2022; Victoroff

& Kruglanski, 2009; Adams, 2021). This has particular relevance when it comes to AI-enabled crime, where the motives could be profit, influence, prestige, revenge, or experimentation, rather than financially motivated.

Recent scholarship has further challenged narrow materialist seemingly simple interpretations of rationality in an effort to show that actors are often interested in functioning to transform broader social and informational structures in ways that go beyond simply maximizing immediate material gain. Boyle makes a distinction between possession goals and milieu goals, and it demonstrates that many malicious campaigns will not simply aim for material results, but also control the social, informational and psychological mix in which they are operating (Boyle, 2023). This is directly relevant to that of AI enabled crime, where visibility, narrative domination, reputational damage and disruption may be as valuable as direct theft (Toros & Gunning, 2009).

Empirical studies provide support for the relevance of RCT by demonstrating that ideologically or strategically motivated actors are sensitive to situational risk, chances of detection as well as intensity of enforcement. Barnum and Logan, for example, uncover that ideologically motivated offenders strategically control the risk and tailor their tactics to mitigate the chances of apprehension, indicating that the two sets of considerations, ideology and strategic reasoning, often overlap (Barnum & Logan, 2023; Horgan, 2005; Gill & Deckert, 2014). Similar logic applies to AI-enabled offending, where the incentives coupled to low risks in the physical domain, remote execution, high automation and anonymity make technologically mediated crime more attractive.

In digital contexts, RCT has been used, to an increasing extent, to explain movement into cyber-enabled offending and harms. Research indicates that actors are attracted to cyber environments due to anonymity, low operational costs, low physical exposure and global-reach (Hoffman & Schweitzer, 2015; Golose, 2022). This is consistent with the broader findings that cyberspace lowers operational barriers to support a variety of harmful functions with relatively lower exposure and cost (Liaropoulos, 2014; Kapsokoli, 2023; Conway, 2017). Cybersecurity research also demonstrates that the offender effort and the defender cost can often be highly asymmetric, and also that AI further emphasizes this asymmetry by automating labour and compressing time (Hojda, Mieila, Mieila, & Dafina, 2024; Anderson, 2006).

Artificial Intelligence fundamentally alters the cost benefit calculations that drive rational offending behaviour. Through automation of the reconnaissance process, optimisation of target selection, refinement of communicative persuasion, and reduction of the technical specific skills, AI compresses the duration of decision rationalisation and changes the way the offender assesses the operational risk. It enhances the expected utility by reducing operational costs and the range of potential impact, hence, AI-mediated tactics become appealing even for actors who have scarce resources and/or expertise (Golose, 2022; Boyle, 2023; UNICRI & UNCCT, 2021).

At the same time, the literature is divided regarding the limits of rationality in harmful behaviour. Some scholars focus on strategy and adaptability when it comes to explaining rational action (Kydd & Walter, 2006; Boyle, 2023; Barnum & Logan, 2023) whereas others maintain that feelings, moral beliefs, and a belief in injustice also contribute to the perception of what is rational by offenders (Adams, 2021; McCauley & Moskalenko, 2008). These perspectives do not oppose RCT, but indicate that rational decisions are affected by social conditions, mental processes, and the expanding role of information systems powered (electronically) by artificial intelligence.

There are important gaps when it comes to using RCT in the context of AI-enabled crime. First, much of the literature treats AI as a neutral tool and does not consider adequately the way by which algorithmic optimisation and machine assisted decision making may alter human cost-benefit assessments. Second, a collective and distributed rationality is underdeveloped in the literature concerning networked environments in which decisions are fragmented across human-machine assemblages. Third, while RCT contributes to explaining why offenders choose to adopt AI, it is far less useful at explaining how AI alters the sequencing and execution of operations, which is more directly explained by Script Theory.

Thus, although RCT is indispensable to analyse criminal AI exploitation, it is merely insufficient as a stand alone explanatory framework. It provides a strong framework to understanding why offenders turn to AI, how tactics are replaced, and how strategic adaptation takes place but would need to be combined with CRAT and Script Theory to explain digital exposure, the sequencing of criminal activity, and machine assisted decision making. AI does not remove rationality in offending but instead transforms it by bringing down barriers to taking certain actions, opening up perceived opportunties, and altering the way offenders perceive risk.

Dual-Use Technology Theory and AI facilitated Crime

Dual-Use Technology Theory is about technologies having legitimate civilian purposes, but can be used for military, harmful, or malicious purposes. The intellectual roots of dual-use technology are to be found in Cold War discussions of nuclear, chemical and biological weapon development where advances in science and computing generate ongoing dilemmas between innovation, diffusion and security (National Research Council, 2004; Miller & Selgelid, 2007). Over time, this framework has gone beyond just the physical weapons systems, to include software, cyber capabilities, and AI systems (Herr & Rosenzweig, 2014; Lupovici, 2021).

Dual-use governance scholarship also points to large differences in regulatory approaches across policy areas, particularly to concerns about verification, attribution and enforcement. Such challenges can best be observed in the field of information technology because of the longstanding governance gaps, alongside the emergent migrations of dual-use risks into AI ecosystems (Herr & Rosenzweig, 2014; Wenger & Cavelty, 2022; Bois & Reyes, 2023).

In the case of AI, Dual-Use Technology Theory brings to the forefront ethical and governance dilemmas posed by systems with a dual-purpose of aiming to benefit as much as harm. Recent scholarship on AI as a dual-purpose capacity in both the cyber and physical environment suggests the regulatory challenge presented by powerful general purpose models capable of supporting health, education, productivity while also being repurposed for disinformation, cyberattacks, fraud, impersonation, and any other criminal activity (Wasil, Grinbaum, & Adomaitis, 2024; DCAF, 2025). In the area of crime, this view emphasizes the challenge of conventional lines between licit and illicit use with various generative AI, LLMs and autonomous (or semi-autonomous) systems.

These concerns are being greatly amplified by the general purpose nature of today's AI. Large language models, generative media, and autonomous decision support systems are not created with a single function, but with the flexibility to be adapted by the various sectors, users, and threats. Policy-oriented assessments take a similar unvarnished perspective of AI as an expanding dual-use enabler in harmful activity particularly in the form of generative media, automated persuasion and semi-autonomous systems that are embedded in commercial ecosystems (Rawat & Kaushal, 2026). Unlike traditional weapons, these systems are to a great extent software-based, reproducible and developed at extremely low marginal cost, making attribution, export control and enforcement much harder (UNICRI & UNCCT, 2021; Herr & Rosenzweig, 2014).

Under the dual use paradigm, the AI is best approached not only as a tool, but as a capability multiplier, even more so, a capability multiplier which is difficult to contain as a result of its software-centric design, low barriers to entries and reliance by capabilities on global distributed infrastructures. Generative AI systems can be trained, fine-tuned, and redeployed without any physical transfer, which means that the traditional regimes of control only work to some extent (National Research Council, 2004; Herr & Rosenzweig, 2014).

One of the most important contributions of the dual use literature is that it has shown how technologies can have significant impact on the threat landscape without necessarily their deliberate weaponisation, as security threats often arise through diffusion, adaptation and repurposing, rather than their original design intent. Herr and Rosenzweig's PrEP model (Propagation-Exploit-Payload) illustrates this tactic of malicious systems often arising from technologies which are inherently dual-use (Herr & Rosenzweig, 2014). Applied to AI-enabled crime this means that data-scraping technologies, generative models, recommender systems and automated translation technologies, all widely used for legitimate ends, can be used by offenders, without any traditional regulatory triggers kicking in.

There is also recent scholarship placing AI into a wider dual-use security dilemma in which ambiguities in intent, capability and use create spirals of insecurity (Lupovici, 2021). In criminal situations, A.I.-enabled surveillance, content moderators and predictive analytics can make security better, although they can also give rise to flexible counter-measures, with offenders experimenting with deception, evasion and automation. Defensive innovation and offensive adaptation therefore have reciprocal interaction which undermines rather than produces stability.

The literature shows that there is considerable convergence on one point: harmful actors very often don't need to develop frontier AI systems independently. Instead, they increasingly resort to commercial tools, open-source models, and systems that are not adequately secured to be efficiently used for propaganda, recruitment, reconnaissance, cyber actions, fraud, impersonation, psychological operations, and other harmful goals (UNICRI & UNCCT, 2021). Practitioner informed literature also highlights the concept of re-useability of commercially available AI tools for operational support and psychological effect rather than the development of completely new systems (Aslam, 2025).

Divergence in literature is most evident on governance feasibility. Some scholars promote adaptive forms of regulation based on Dual-Use Research of Concern (DURC) such as risk tiering, disclosure control and institutional oversight (Wasil, Grinbaum, & Adomaitis, 2024; DCAF, 2025). Others remain sceptical arguing that commercial incentives, norms of openness and geopolitical competition place significant constraints on the effectiveness of upstream regulation (Herr & Rosenzweig, 2014; Lupovici, 2021).

A major gap in the literature exists in terms of the limited level to which Dual-Use Technology Theory is integrated with models of the crime process. While numerous research studies report potential misuse scenarios, fewer are more systematic about how dual use AI is altering the entire criminal lifecycle, including discovering, preparing, executing, concealing, and then amplifying the effect later. Limited attention has also been paid to the interaction of dual-use dynamics with decentralised, low capability or loosely networked forms of offending where AI might be substituting for organisational hierarchy, specialised expertise, or infrastructure.

Dual-Use Technology Theory therefore offers an important macro-structural perspective. It describes the reasons AI can lead to long-lasting security risk even in the absence of bad intent, and the limited response to governance. Yet the theory does not explain why the certain offenders choose to incorporate AI or how they value its operational utility. Those questions call for an engagement with **Rational Choice Theory** that deals with the perceptions of costs, risks, benefits that are re-calibrated under conditions of AI enabled capabilities expansion (Yar, 2005; Cohen & Felson, 1979).

Understanding Artificial Intelligence Enabled Crime through an Integrated Framework

Taken together, these four strands of theory offer a very good but incomplete explanation of criminal AI exploitation if left in isolation. To promote the synthesis, this chapter adopts the AI-Enabled Crime Dynamics Framework (ACDF). The ACDF conceptualises AI-enabled crime as the outcome of interacting processes of vulnerability by structural factors, offender decision-making, staging logic of criminal action and affordance of dual use technologies. It draws on the perspectives of RAT and CRAT to understand the power of AI to restructure opportunities and degrade guardianship, the perspective of Script Theory to understand the reality of AI in terms of planning, execution, and concealment stages, and the classical perspective of Rational Choice Theory to understand why criminal offenders perceive AI as a low risk and high reward enabler, as well as the Dual-Use Technology Theory to capture ethical ambiguity and regulatory complexity of AI systems. In this way, the ACDF can provide a holistic view of how AI is being used to facilitate, augment and conceal crime, and also help to inform more specific policy responses with regard to prevention, detection and school responses.

Thus, for the study of criminal use of AI, Rational Choice Theory is indispensable but incomplete. It provides an appropriate framework for understanding offender incentives, tactical substitution and strategic adaptation under circumstances of technological change. It helps to explain the attractiveness of AI to offenders: combination of reducing operational effort, uniqueness of exposure and increasing speed and scale; as well as often improving the perceived return from any illicit activity. In this sense, AI doesn't eliminate rationality in offending and instead it just changes its configuration through shifting the perceived balance of cost, risk, and reward. At the same time, Rational Choice Theory, by itself, cannot adequately explain how AI-enabled crime unfolds as it moves from stage to stage, how opportunity structures are re-shaped as a result of digital environments, or how general-purpose AI tools cross the boundaries into assembling a criminal enabler due to dual-use dynamics. For that reason, it has to be combined with Script Theory, CRAT, dual use technology theory to encompass the complete logic of AI enabled offending.

METHODOLOGY

This research uses a descriptive-exploratory, mixed-methods approach in order to explore the use of artificial intelligence (AI) by offenders in attempting to facilitate, enhance, or conceal criminal activity. A descriptive-exploratory approach is suitable because the criminal use of AI is an emerging and not yet sufficiently mapped field that needs both structured measurement and interpretive insight. The mixed-methods research design enables the study to engage the combination of quantitative pattern together with qualitative depth to support a wider picture of offender behaviour, as well as AI misuse practices, and the wider implications in governance and security of AI-enabled crime.

The main research tool used is a 15-item question survey with closed-ended and open-ended questions. The closed-ended questions aimed at capturing patterned responses on issues relating to familiarity with AI-enabled crime, offender characteristics, stages of the crime, AI-enabled methods of the crime, perceived reduction of effort and risk of detection and the effectiveness of existing detection or policy responses. The open-ended questions were added to give the respondents an opportunity to elaborate more on offender motivation, emerging trends of misuse, shortcomings in policy, and real-life examples. This combination of item-types serves to strengthen the study by allowing rich professional judgement that cannot be measured entirely by fixed-response categories to be collected along with the perceptions that can be measured.

The survey instrument was created using a theory-informed approach, which was aligned with the AI-Enabled Crime Dynamics Framework (ACDF). The ACDF combines four theoretical perspectives, namely Cyber-Routine Activity Theory (CRAT), Script Theory, Rational Choice Theory (RCT), and Dual-Use Theory. This theoretical alignment was meant to ensure that the instrument did not just collect empirical data, but that it also contributed to the analysis of the framework per se.

More specifically, Cyber-Routine Activity Theory provided information for questions relating to exposure to digital vulnerability, weaknesses in guardianship, and limits to detection and response. Script Theory influenced on items exploring where AI is used in criminals process, but particularly the phases of planning, execution and concealing. Rationale choice theory had been used to guide questions regarding offender incentives, perceptions of reduced effort, risk minimisation and the appeal of AI as a low-cost, high-reward enabler. Dual-Use Theory was used as the basis for items relating to the abuse of AI systems that were designed for legitimate civilian, commercial or productive purposes. In this way the structure that the questionnaire took was that of an empirically informed instrument linked to wider theoretical explanation, as opposed to one functioning purely descriptively.

A purposive strategy was used in order to reach out to participants who had relevant expertise and professional experience. The focus population was people working in either law enforcement, cybersecurity, academic or policy related sectors as these are in particularly good positions to understand current and new forms of AI misuse. This non-probability sampling approach has been chosen because the study is not aiming to obtain general public opinion, but rather informed opinions from the respondents directly involved in crime prevention, cyber threats analysis, AI governance or operational for related fields of research related to AI. The value of this approach is the depth and relevance of the expert insight and not statistical representativeness.

Data collection was made using a digital survey format, which permitted accessibility to many and efficient involvement regardless of the location. The survey was disseminated in the form of an electronic version, which allows respondents to complete the survey remotely and at their convenience. Participation was completely voluntary and anonymous, which was designed to encourage open and honest answers and decrease possible hesitation or social desirability bias. Digital delivery was also used to support practical advantages, which included ease of dissemination, response management and safe storage of data.

The methodological decision to use both closed and open-ended questions are particularly relevant when it comes to AI enabled crime. On the one hand, closed items give the basis for identifying recurring perceptions and dominant patterns with regard to offender profiles, methods and institutional gaps. On the other hand, open-ended answers allow the participants to think about the more complex issues, such as why the offenders are attracted to the use of AI tools, how criminal practices are changing, and what are the forms of policy or operational response that are most urgently needed. This increases the descriptive value of the study without losing the exploratory nature of the study.

Ethical considerations were viewed as a fundamental part of the research design. The study was conducted in accordance with standard academic ethics procedures and principles of informed consent, anonymity, and confidentiality. All participants were fully informed of the purpose of the study, the voluntary nature of participation and the right to withdraw from the study at any stage prior to submission. No personally identifying information was collected and all the responses were anonymised before analysis. Data were stored in secure digital environments that were restricted access and used only for academic research purposes. The study was carried out following relevant institutional ethical requirements and principles of good practice of data protection in general, and good practice relating to GDPR (where applicable).

The survey also shows clear internal consistency with the ACDF with its distribution of questions into the four theoretical strands. Questions relating to offender age, education, perceived reduction in effort, and risk reduction have linkages that mostly fall under Rational Choice Theory as these questions assist in understanding offender decision-making under the conditions of changing technology. Questions concentrating on crime stages and real cases reflect Script Theory, because they inform us about how AI gets embedded in sequential stages of criminal action. Items based on the detection gaps, weakness in guardianships, policy shortcomings reflect RAT/CRAT and how digital environments are changing opportunities and weakening the traditional forms of protection. Finally, questions about the familiarity with misuse of AI, regulation, the emerging methods, and legitimate tools being repurposed for crime, reflect the Dual-Use Theory, emphasising the ethical ambiguity and regulatory issues for general-purpose AI systems.

Taken together, this methodological design helps to support the study's larger purpose, developing a grounded understanding of criminal AI exploitation. The descriptive-exploratory mixed methods approach seems well suited to a rapidly changing field where empirical evidence is still limited, offender practices are diverse and government responses are uneven. A survey that employed a combination of theory-informed survey design, expert sampling, digital anonymous data collection and robust ethical protections allows the present study to provide a structured underpinning for the analysis of the ways in which AI is being used to facilitate, enhance or implement concealment of criminal activity.

This methodological design also should be interpreted in the context of current data limitations. Open-source and law enforcement reporting on AI-enabled crime is growing, however, there is still a lack of robust offender-level data sets while official knowledge is still stronger on offence methods, than verified offender profiles or organisational structure (INTERPOL, 2024). Academic research is also still more advanced in relation to phishing, social engineering, deepfakes, LLM abuse, adversarial AI, than it is in relation to stable empirical offender typologies (Choi, Dearden, & Parti, 2024; Schmitt & Flechais, 2024; Jaffal, Alkhanafseh, & Mohaisen, 2025). Accordingly, the current study does not purport to measure offender behaviour directly; it records the perceptions of experts regarding emerging patterns, emerging risks and classifications in an area where offender-side evidence is still incomplete.

Theoretical Mapping of Questionnaire

Table 1. Mapping questions to theories

Questions	Question Topic	Linked Theory	Justification
Q2	Familiarity with AI in crime	Dual-Use Theory	Familiarity levels to determine awareness of ethical ambiguity and dual functionality on AI tools.
Q3	Offender age group	Rational Choice Theory	Helps in inferring decision making trends among age cohorts; younger users may possibly see lower risk because of being digitally fluent.
Q4	Offender education level	Rational Choice Theory, Dual-Use Theory	Suggests offender capacity to exploit complex AI tools, supports decision making and dual use misuse potential.
Q5	Open-ended: who exploits AI and why	Rational Choice Theory, Script Theory, Dual-Use Theory	Gives subjective insight of motivations, modus operandi, and access to technology.
Q6	Stages of crime where AI is used	Script Theory	Directly linked to the sequencing of crime - the planning of the crime, execution, concealment - essential to script theory and ACDF lifecycle integration.
Q7	AI-enabled methods encountered	Dual-Use Theory, Script Theory, CRAT	A reflection of adaptation of dual use tool into criminal scripts and erosion of traditional guardianship.
Q8	Emerging trends in AI misuse	Dual-Use Theory, Script Theory, CRAT	Underscores the creativity of offenders, shows gaps in the existing security and regulation.
Q9	AI reduces effort	Rational Choice Theory	Touches on offender cost benefit calculus and crime facilitation.
Q10	AI reduces risk of detection	Rational Choice Theory, CRAT	Reinforcement of perception of AI as a low-risk, high-rewards tool and implication of weakening of guardianship/detection mechanisms.
Q11	Effectiveness of detection tools	CRAT	Focused on guardianship - major in Routine Activity frameworks Cyber-RAT
Q12	Gaps in policing/policy/legal framework	CRAT, Dual-Use Theory	Discusses weaknesses in structures and regulations.
Q13	Opinion on AI regulation	Dual-Use Theory	Directly probes attitude towards managing ethical ambiguity and restrict dual use AI access.
Q14	Open-ended policy recommendations	CRAT, Dual-Use Theory, Script Theory	Supports all of the 3: Policy gaps (CRAT), Dual-Use Control (Dual-Use), and Criminal script disruption.
Q15	Open-ended real-world cases	Script Theory, Rational Choice Theory, Dual-Use Theory	Allows full demonstration theory into action - sequencing (Script), motivation (RCT), Tool nature (Dual-Use).

FINDINGS STRUCTURE

This chapter presents the results of the study through the structure of the instrument with 15 questions. The objective is to consider how an artificial intelligence (AI) is perceived by professionals in its criminal use, in particular in connection with the profiles of offenders, the patterns of misuse, the motives, the difficulty of detection and the reactions from regulating bodies. This is especially important given that not only official but also academic evaluations highlight the growing disparity between the known scope of cyber-enabled fraud and the comparatively small state of knowledge about offender profile, in which expert-informed classification schemes are highly valuable at this point of AI-enabled crimes research (FBI IC3, 2024; FBI IC3, 2024; INTERPOL, 2024; Choi, Dearden, & Parti, 2024).

The chapter is divided into thematic sections, and displays the items from the survey in line with each section.

Section A: Participant Background

A very clear majority of respondents had directly been exposed to AI-enabled criminality in professional or research activities. This finding suggests that crime facilitated by AI has reached the operational and investigative environments rather than being a theoretical or speculative issue. The presence of respondents with direct experiences enhances a reliability of a data-set since their responses are likely to be informed by actual observation or professional involvement with emerging digital threats.

Respondents that indicated exposure most often made references to incidents involving "deepfakes", "AI-generated phishing", "voice cloning" and "synthetic identity fraud". These references pointed to the fact that practitioners already see AI-based techniques in fraud investigations, cybersecurity monitoring and digital forensics. The responses therefore support the wider observation that the misuse of AI is becoming increasingly visible across a variety of areas including financial crime, cyber intrusion and online manipulation.

Q1. What is your professional background?

Figure 1.

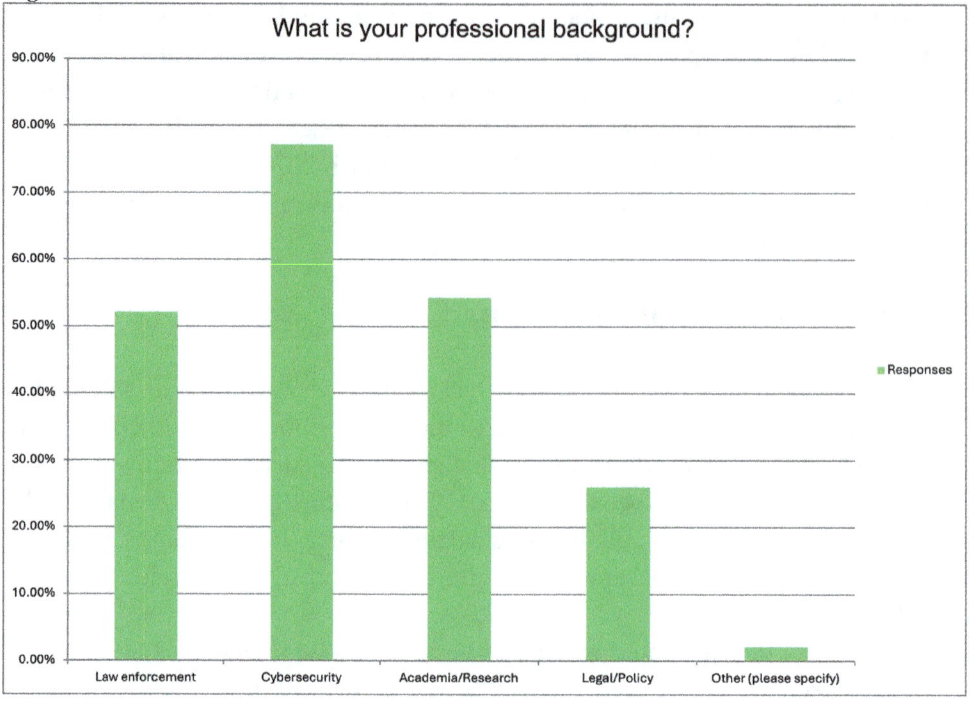

The multidisciplinary nature of the respondent pool is important as AI-enabled crime is at the intersection of technology, security, governance and law. Respondents from "law enforcement" provide insights into investigation and detection issues. Participants from "cybersecurity" bring technical viewpoints of vulnerabilities and new methods of attack. Meanwhile, analytical interpretations and governance views are provided by those respondents coming from "academia" and "policy" fields. This diversity enhances the quality of the interpretive process in the survey because AI misuse cannot be understood through a single disciplinary lens. Instead, the phenomenon calls for perspectives that lead to a combination of operational knowledge, technical understanding, and regulatory analysis.

Q2. How much do you know about criminal application of Artificial Intelligence (AI)?

Figure 2.

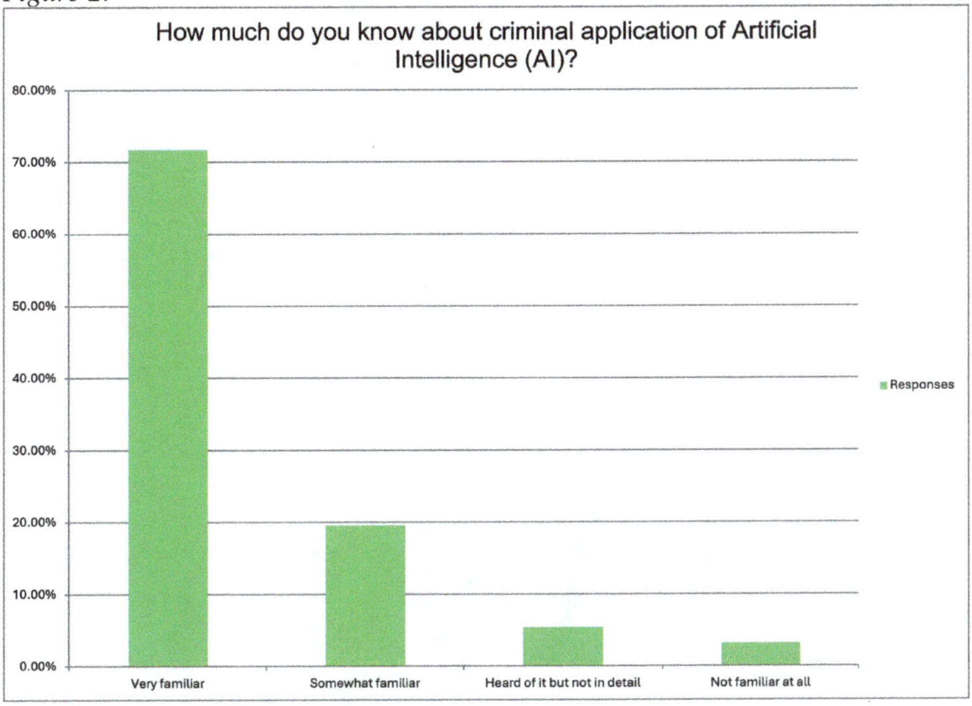

The high level of respondents indicating "very familiar" state indicates that crimes done using AI body are widely known among professionals working in the field of security and digital technologies. The respondents identified that they have heard of several AI abuses including "deepfake impersonation", "AI-generated phishing emails", "voice cloning fraud", and "automated cyberattacks".

This level of familiarity means that abuse of AI is not seen as a technological threat in the future but a challenge in work today. Many professionals seem to already confront or learn about AI-driven criminal techniques in their work environments. The findings therefore strengthen the relevance of the research topic, and confirm the fact that the questionnaire catches some of the insights from people who are active and aware of what is happening with crime through AI.

Section B: Offender Profile (Perceived)

Q3. What is the most common age group of offenders who use AI?

Figure 3.

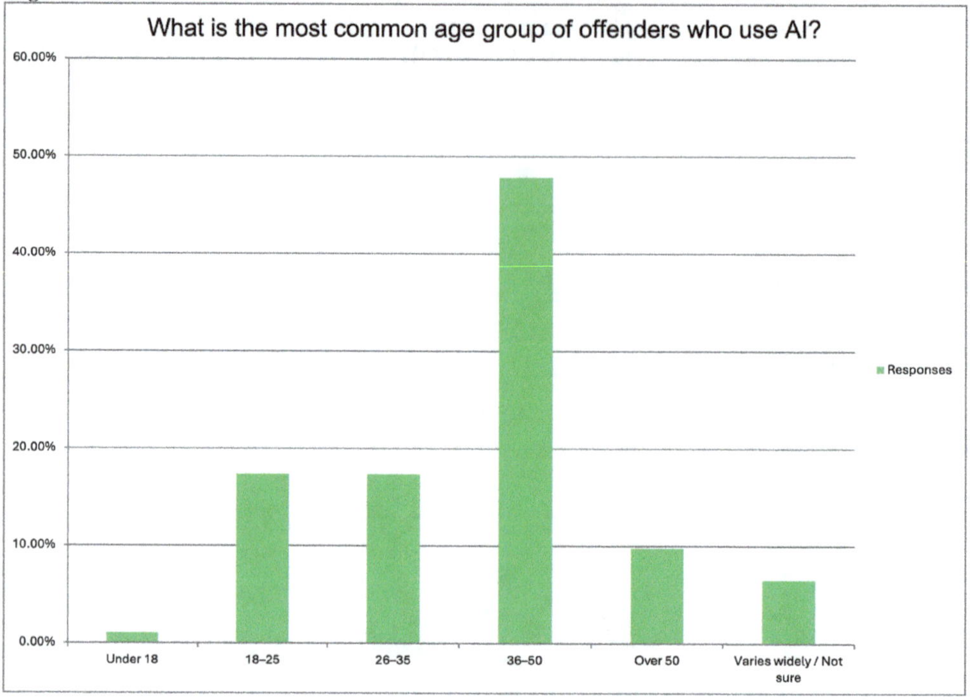

The 36-50 age range was most commonly reported as being linked with offending by AI technology. This finding is notable because it challenges the popular assumption that technology driven crime is dominated by very young offenders.

Instead, respondents seem to associate misuse of AI with those who are likely to have professional experience, technical competence or organisational ties. The perception that offenders may be mid-career individuals implies the need for a combination of technical literacy, professional access and strategic awareness through AI-enabled crime. The relatively low number of responses identifying offenders under 18 suggests respondents do not consider AI misuse as the result of inexperienced youth experimentation. Rather, the offender profile that emerges from the survey seems to involve actors who may have greater expertise and capability.

Q4. What is the education level of offenders using AI tools, generally?

Figure 4.

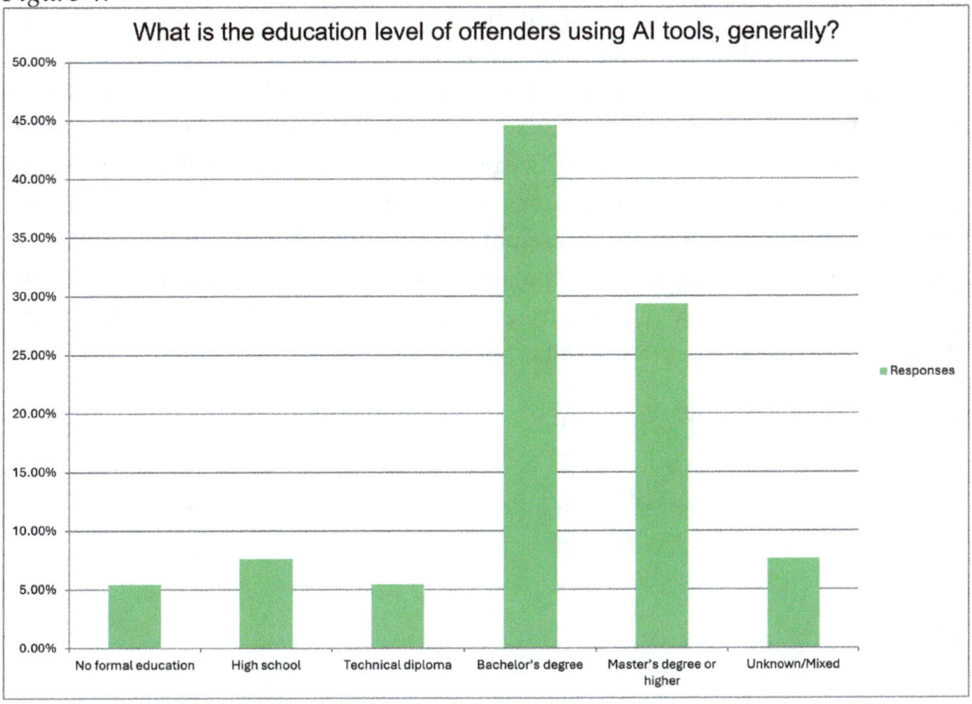

Respondents strongly link AI-enabled offending to relatively high educational attainment. Many respondents view offenders as at least having undergraduate education and a good proportion identified the education level of postgraduate education as typical.

This perception could be due to the technological nature of many AI tools and some of the skills needed to effectively manipulate or adapt them. Activities such as producing "deepfake media", creating "synthetic identities" or taking advantage of "adversarial machine learning techniques" can be considered as demanding technical competence. However, it is also important to consider that generative AI systems are becoming more user-friendly. This means that while some types of misuse of AI may require specific types of knowledge, others may be available to those who lack advanced technical experience.

> **Q5.** In your opinion, who or what groups are most likely to abuse AI for criminal means, and why?

The qualitative responses indicate that the misuse of AI is not limited to a certain type of offender. Instead, respondents define a varied ecosystem of actors.

Many of the responses highlight the activity of "organized crime networks" and "fraud syndicates". This means that they have become more embedded in organized crime operations rather than merely being utilized by isolated individuals. Several respondents mentioned "technically skilled individuals" and "insiders" too, which seems to suggest that access to technical knowledge or institutional resources could be playing an important role in facilitating AI misuse. Additionally, some of the respondents pointed out to "state-sponsored actors" and "disinformation actors", underscoring the fact that AI tools are potentially applicable not only for financial crime, but also for information manipulation and strategic influence as well. These responses show AI misuse may occur across different motivations including profit, influence, espionage and ideological aims.

Section C: Typology of Use

Q6. In which stage(s) of criminal activity is AI most often used?

Figure 5.

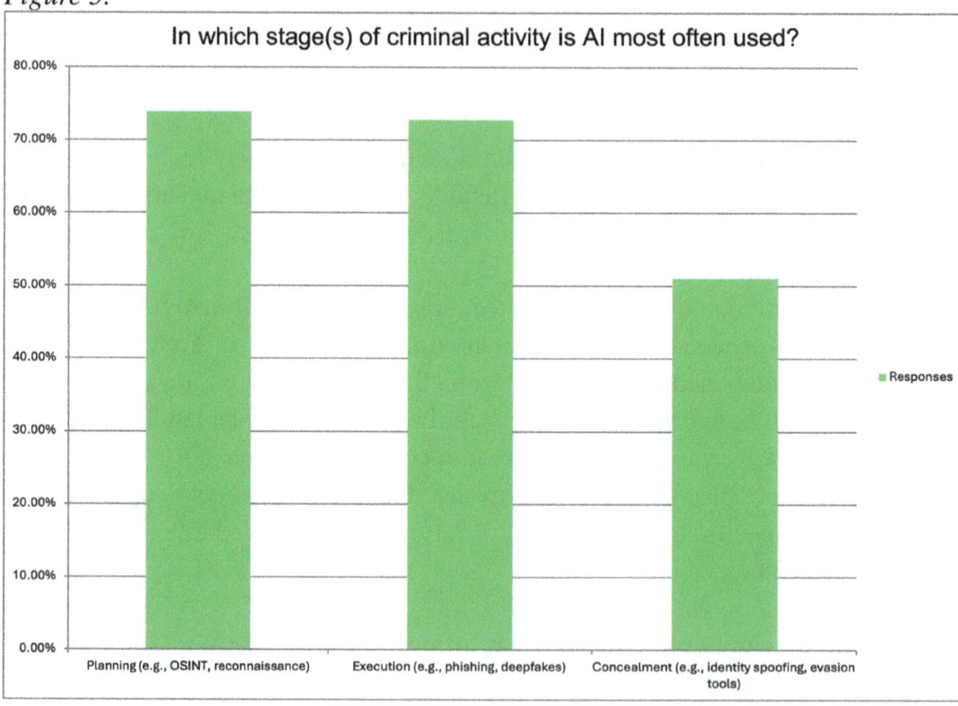

The distribution of responses shows that AI tools are applied at multiple points in criminal activity. Respondents were often linking AI to stages of the planning and execution process suggesting AI is useful to offenders during both preparation stages and operational implementation.

Examples that use planning stage include "OSINT automation", "data scraping" and "target identification". Execution-stage applications are, "deepfake impersonation", "AI-generated phishing messages", and "automated cyberattacks". The following concealment stage uses: "synthetic identities", "identity spoofing", "evasion tools". This distribution makes it easy to see how AI abuse is process-oriented. Rather than working as a single tool that is used at a single moment in time, AI seems to work as an enabling technology which is capable of influencing various stages of criminal behavior.

Q7. Which AI-enabled criminal methods are you aware of or have come across?

Figure 6.

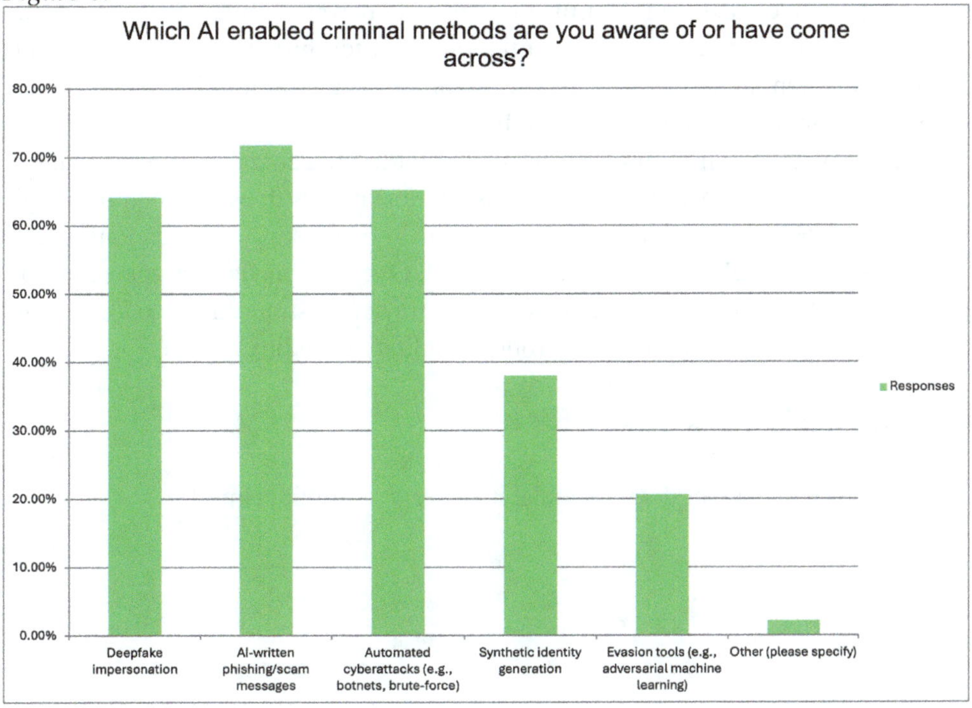

The responses indicate that AI is primarily being used to enhance traditional forms of digital crime. For example, "phishing campaigns" is not something new, but AI can compose a convincing message at scale and at specific targets. Similarly "impersonation scams" have been in existence for decades, but "deepfake video" and "voice cloning" technologies certainly make them much more credible.

The results therefore suggest that AI does not necessarily create completely new categories of crimes. Instead, it is acting as a capability multiplier that enhances the efficiency, scale and persuasiveness of existing criminal tactics.

Q8. From your experience, are there new or emerging ways in which offenders are using AI that are unknown or not widely known?

This dataset is considerably less valuable for analysis because most answers to this question are extremely short (or non-substantive answers). The main pattern that comes out of this isn't so much the variety of ways people were familiar with misuse of AI, but rather the absence of detailed articulation from people. The percentage of minimal responses implies that they may be aware of the emerging criminal uses of AI, but that they did not expand on or provide examples of specific forms and mechanisms of use. This could mean one of three things: (i) limited respondent time/engagement, confusion regarding newer criminal applications, or (ii) that some respondents have taken the question too broadly and answered the question in a non-analytical way, or (iii) inability or non familiarity to significant cases, which in turn creates a vulnerability.

Even so, what few meaningful things all point to the general awareness that the misuse of AI is growing, although the dataset unfortunately does not go into enough detail to pick out strong recurring themes such as "deepfakes", "voice cloning", or "automated phishing" as previous datasets did. Overall, this dataset appears to be supportive but weak evidence and is most useful to demonstrate an acknowledgment of the issue and not for drawing any robust qualitative findings.

Section D: Motivation and Risk

Q9. To what extent does AI make it easier to commit crimes?

Figure 7.

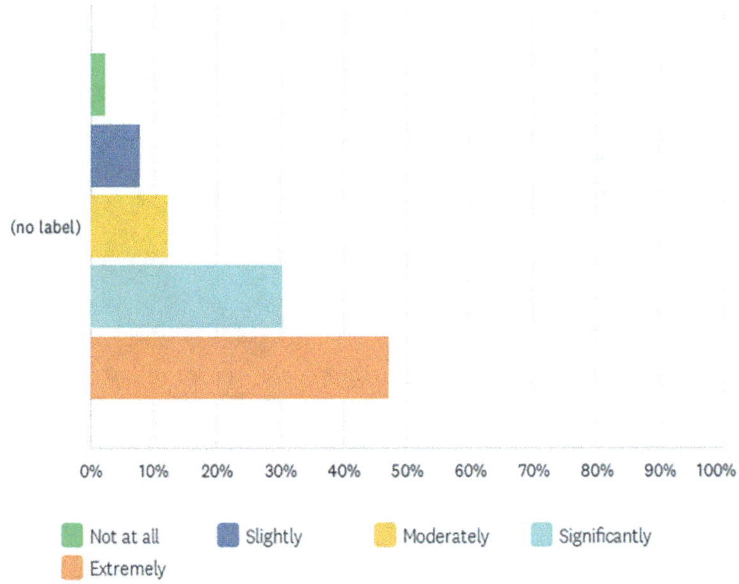

Respondents agree very strongly with the statement that the use of AI makes it easier to commit crime. This is presumably due to the automation capabilities of AI tools, which can create text, images, or audio immediately. Activities that would have previously required a great deal of preparation can now be done in a fast-paced manner with generative AI systems.

Q10. To what extent does AI decrease the risk of detection?

Figure 8.

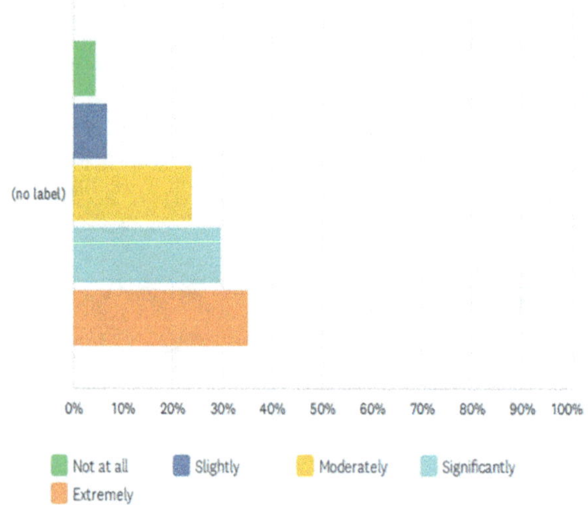

Respondents generally agree that the risk of detection is reduced through the use of AI. This may be related to the ability of AI systems to generate realistic synthetic content or automate attacks in ways that would make it difficult to attribute them.

Section E: Detection, Policy and Response

Q11. How effective are existing technological solutions (e.g. antivirus, cyber forensics) for the detection of AI-enabled crimes?

Figure 9.

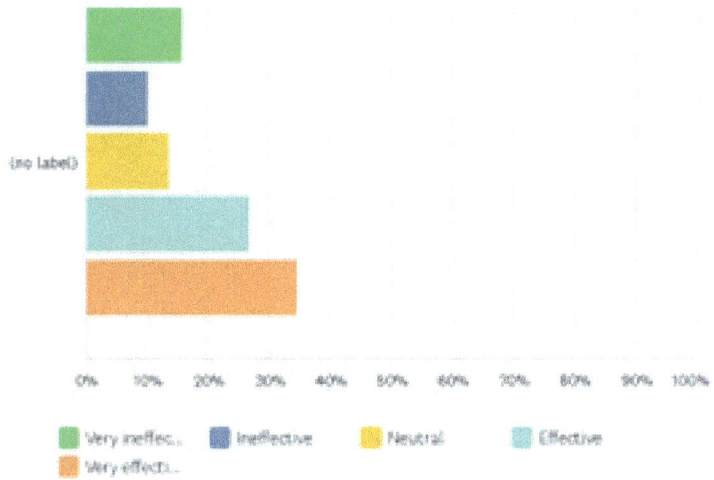

The moderate rating indicates the view that respondents don't think current detection technologies show sufficient capability to assertively tackle the evolving challenges supported by AI enabled crime.

Q12. What are the gaps in the existing policing, cybersecurity, or legal frameworks which prevent response to AI-enabled criminal activity?

Respondents clearly emphasised that there was some disconnect between technological development and institutional preparedness. In particular, the need for the legal frameworks to adapt to crimes involving "generative AI", "synthetic media" or "automated deception" was underlined by many participants. Training and capability gaps were also mentioned quite often. Law enforcement agencies might not have any specialized knowledge on certain areas, such as "AI forensics" or "deepfake detection". Additionally, the transnational nature of many AI-enabled crimes causes problems of jurisdiction that create complicated investigation and prosecution.

Q13. Should access to powerful open-source or generative AI tools be restricted/regulated to avoid misuse?

Figure 10.

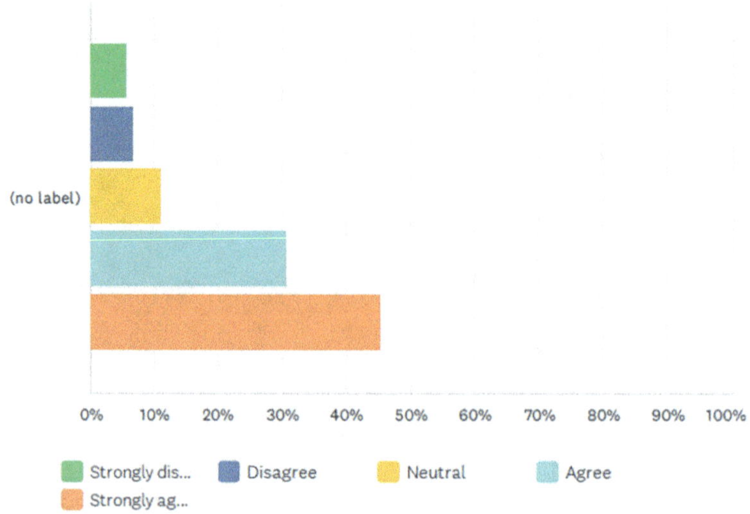

Most respondents said that they support some level of regulation/oversight of powerful AI tools. This is because of concerns about the dual-use potential of AI technologies, which can be used for both beneficial and harmful purposes. Respondents seem to realize that AI innovation should not have to be restricted at all. However, many believe that some type of safeguards or governance mechanisms may be required to avoid misuse, especially when dealing with "synthetic media" or "automated deception" and/or "large scale content generation".

> **Q14.** What specific solutions, policies, regulations, or innovations do you recommend to prevent and respond to AI-driven crime better?

The recommendations provided by the respondents highlight the importance of multi-layered solutions. Technical responds such as "deepfake detection systems", need to be combined with institutional reforms such as better training of investigators and stronger regulatory frameworks. Many of the respondents highlighted the importance of "international cooperation" also, in line with the transnational nature of digital crime. Additionally, there were several responses on the need for "public digital literacy" to enable individuals to recognize deception and manipulation.

> **Q15.** Please share any real-world example, case study, or personal observation regarding the use of AI in criminal acts (e.g. fraud, impersonation, deception, cyberattack).

This is a more restricted but useful data set on perceived AI-enabled crime. Many responses are short or non-substantive, which do not allow for much qualitative analysis. However, the stronger responses still have clear thematic consistency. The predominant scheme is "impersonation" particularly "deepfake impersonations", "impersonating someone's voice" and executive style fraud such as "it's me, the ceo, i need you to send me money". These responses indicate that respondents mainly link AI misuse with deception, simulation of identity, and comma exploiting trust. A second major theme is financially motivated fraud, which is reflected in keywords such as "fraud", "wire fraud" and "asking for money". This means that AI is perceived as a tool to boost the credibility and success of scam attempts.

Communication based attacks are also prominent such as "phishing attacks", "suspicious messages" and "scam link". In addition, there are some response containing mentions of "address books hacked", "personnel information leaked" and manipulated visuals such as "formation of images" and "photoshop" showing concern of data exploitation and synthetic media.

POLICY RECOMMENDATIONS

This research recommends the set of targeted and layered interventions to deal with the growing threat of crime, enabled by AI. First, it is necessary to create AI-specific detection and forensic tools that can be able to identify "deepfakes", "voice cloning", "AI-generated phishing", "synthetic identities" and other deceptive or manipulated content. Given that respondents repeatedly identified the central risks of impersonation, fraud and deception through communication forms it requires defensive tools to be designed not only for technical detection, but also for more practical use as part of the investigation effort.

Second, policymakers should introduce basic safeguards for open-source and dual-use systems of artificial intelligence systems so that powerful generative models are used responsibly and with the appropriate oversight. These can be embedded (e.g. scanners cannot scan and print paper currency due to software lock). The results strongly indicate a need for regulation, particularly where AI tools can be applied to "fraud", "wire fraud", "phishing attacks", and "deepfake impersonations".

Third, it is necessary to revise (and keep revising regularly) current law enforcement, and investigative training programs to involve AI profiling, trace of digital evidence, synthetic media, and scenario-based learning about the misuse of investigation using AI. Respondents repeatedly identified areas of capability deficiencies in policing and cybersecurity which raises the policy implication that the institutional adaptation is lagging behind offender innovation.

Fourth, governments, industry and civil society should foster public digital literacy (including education system) to make individuals and organizations better able to spot "suspicious messages", manipulated media, attempts at impersonation and other AI-assigned fraud techniques. Since many of the most frequently cited threats require interaction with human trust, public and organizational level resilience is essential.

Fifth, better cross sector and international cooperation is needed. Respondents repeatedly mentioned legal fragmentation, attribution problems and cross border enforcement problems. Effective prevention and response will therefore require a level of coordination between law enforcement, cybersecurity actors, financial institutions and regulators, and technology companies.

Finally, intervention strategies need to be refined with respect to offender classification models that match the preventative and investigative response to offender motivations, technical capability and access patterns. Because respondents identified a wide range of likely offenders, including "cybercriminal groups", "organized crime networks", "technically skilled individuals", "insiders" and in some cases "state-sponsored actors", a one-size-fits-all response is unlikely to be effective. Tailored interventions will enhance policy and operational responses which will be more precise and of greater value.

CONCLUSION

Criminal exploitation of AI is complicated, adaptive and on the rise. The results of this chapter indicate that respondents most strongly associate misuse of AI with "deepfakes", "voice cloning", "AI-generated phishing", "synthetic identities" and related synthetic identity and impersonation fraud and scams. AI is not viewed as the creation of a new type of crime, but rather a tool that makes crime faster, more realistic, larger in scope and easier to hide.

The survey also suggests that AI-enabled crime is linked to a wide network of offenders that include technically competent individuals, organized criminal actors and other networked groups that are able to use dual-use technologies for malicious purposes. At the same time, respondents repeatedly refer to important weaknesses in current legal, regulatory, technical and institutional responses. Existing governance and detection systems are considered to be only partially useful to keep up with the speed and sophistication of modern misuse by AI.

This study has therefore established both a conceptual and also empirical basis for understanding how offenders exploits AI to facilitate, enhance or conceal crime. By bringing together theory, survey evidence and insights from qualitative analysis methods it provides a practical basis for a more robust policy, more adaptive law enforcement design, more effective regulatory design and future research in AI enabled criminal behaviour.

REFERENCES

Adams, P. A. (2021). Terrorism as the quest for justice in contemporary Nigeria. *UJAH: Unizik Journal of Arts and Humanities*, *22*(2), 85–102.

Ahmad, R., & Thurasamy, R. (2022, July 17). Routine activity theory and cyber-crime: A systematic literature review. *Journal of Cyber Security and Mobility*, *11*(1).

Anderson, R. (2006). The economics of information security', 314(5799), pp. 610–613. *Science*, *314*(5799), 610–613. DOI: 10.1126/science.1130992 PMID: 17068253

Aslam, M. M. (2025, July 6). High-tech terrorism: The use of AI in terrorism industry. Retrieved from Islamic Military Counter Terrorism Coalition (IMCTC) eLibrary.: https://www.imctc.org/en/eLibrary/Articles/Pages/article1762025.aspx

Barnum, T. C., & Logan, M. K. (2023). Radicalized environmental extremism and situational decision-making. *Journal of Research in Crime and Delinquency*, *61*(3), 406–444. DOI: 10.1177/00224278231152439

Becker, G. S. (1968, March-April). Crime and Punishment: An Economic Approach. *Journal of Political Economy*, *76*(2), 169–217. DOI: 10.1086/259394

Bécue, A., Praça, I., & Gama, J. (2021, June). Artificial intelligence, cyber-threats and Industry 4.0: Challenges and opportunities. *Artificial Intelligence*, *54*(5), 3849–3886.

Bois, R. D., & Reyes, A. T. (2023). *Dual-use and cyber-surveillance: EU policies and current practices. European Parliament Briefing No. 754439*. European Parliament.

Bossler, A. M., & Holt, T. J. (2010). Bossler, A.M. and Holt, T.J. (2010) 'The effect of self-control on victimization in the cyberworld', Crime & Delinquency, 56(4), pp. 539–568. *Crime and Delinquency*, *56*(4), 539–568.

Boyle, M. J. (2023). The choice for terrorism: Possession and milieu goals among terrorist groups. *Perspectives on Terrorism*, *17*(3), 1–22.

Choi, S., Dearden, T., & Parti, K. (2024). Understanding the Use of Artificial Intelligence in Cybercrime. *International Journal of Cybersecurity Intelligence and Cybercrime*, *7*(2), 1–3. DOI: 10.52306/2578-3289.1185

Clarke, R., & Cornish, D. (1985). Modeling offenders' decisions: A framework for research and policy. In Andresen, M. A., Brantingham, P. J., & Kinney, J. B. (Eds.), *Crime Opportunity Theories: Routine Activity, Rational Choice and their Variants* (pp. 157–195). Taylor and Francis.

Clarke, R. V., & Eck, J. E. (2005). *Crime Analysis for Problem-Solvers in 60 Small Steps*. U.S. Department of Justice, Office of Community Oriented Policing Services.

Cohen, L., & Felson, M. (1979). Social change and crime rate trends: A routine activity approach. *American Sociological Review, 44*(4), 588–608. DOI: 10.2307/2094589

Conway, M. (2017). Determining the Role of the Internet in Violent Extremism and Terrorism: Six Suggestions for Progressing Research. *Studies in Conflict and Terrorism, 40*(1), 77–98. DOI: 10.1080/1057610X.2016.1157408

Cornish, D. (1994). The procedural analysis of offending and its relevance for situational prevention. In R. V. Clarke (Ed.), Crime prevention studies (Vol. 3, pp. 151–196). Criminal Justice Press. Crime prevention studies, 3, 151-196.

Crenshaw, M. (1981). The causes of terrorism. *Comparative Politics, 13*(4), 379–399. DOI: 10.2307/421717

DCAF. (2025, February 17). The double-edged sword of artificial intelligence in security sector governance. Geneva Centre for Security Sector Governance. Retrieved from DCAF: https://www.dcaf.ch/double-edged-sword-artificial-intelligence-security-sector-governance#

Dehghanniri, H., & Borrion, H. (2019). Crime scripting: A systematic review. *European Journal of Criminology, 18*(4).

Drawve, G., Thomas, S. A., & Walker, J. T. (2014). The Likelihood of Arrest: A Routine Activity Theory Approach. *American Journal of Criminal Justice, 39*(3), 450–470. DOI: 10.1007/s12103-013-9226-2

Dzuba, C. (2025). Artificial intelligence in social engineering: A literature review through the lens of routine activity theory. *Issues in Information Systems, 26*(2), 452–465.

Enders, W., & Sandler, T. (2012). Enders, W. and Sandler, T. (2012) The Political Economy of Terrorism. 2nd edn. Cambridge: Cambridge University Press. Cambridge: Cambridge University Press.

Europol. (2025). Steal, Deal and Repeat. The Hague: Europol. Retrieved from Internet Organised Crime Threat Assessment (IOCTA: https://www.europol.europa.eu/publication-events/main-reports/steal-deal-and-repeat-how-cybercriminals-trade-and-exploit-your-data

FBI IC3. (2024). Federal Bureau of Investigation - Internet Crime Report 2024. Washington, DC: Internet Crime Complaint Center. Retrieved from https://www.google.com/search?q=FBI+IC3+(2024b)+2024+IC3+Annual+Report.+Washington%2C+DC%3A+Internet+Crime+Complaint+Center%2C+Federal+Bureau+of+Investigation.&rlz=1C5CHFA_enAE1042AE1042&oq=FBI+IC3+(2024b)+2024+IC3+Annual+Report.+Washington%2C+DC%3A+Inter

FBI IC3. (2024, December 3). Criminals Use Generative Artificial Intelligence to Facilitate Financial Fraud. Retrieved from FBI Public Service Announcement: https://www.ic3.gov/PSA/2024/PSA241203

Ferrag, M. A., Alwahedi, F., Battah, A. A., Cherif, B., Mechri, A., Tihanyi, N., . . . Debbah, M. (2024). Generative AI in Cybersecurity: A Comprehensive Review of LLM Applications and Vulnerabilities. arXiv:2405.12750, 1-52.

Gambín, Á. F., Yazidi, A., Vasilakos, A., Haugerud, H., & Djenouri, Y. (2024). Gambín, Á.F., del Ser, J., Etxaniz, J. and Muguerza, J. (2024) 'Deepfakes: Current and future trends', Artificial Intelligence Review, 57, article 64. *Artificial Intelligence Review*, *57*(64), 1–32.

Ganaie, N. A. (2026, January 6). The role of artificial intelligence in radicalisation, recruitment and terrorist propaganda: Deconstructing violent extremism and reimagining counterterrorism in contemporary digital ecosystems. *Frontiers in Political Science*, *7*, 7. DOI: 10.3389/fpos.2025.1718396

Gill, P. H., & Deckert, P. (2014). Bombing alone: Tracing the motivations and antecedent behaviors of lone-actor terrorists. *Journal of Forensic Sciences*, *59*(2), 425–435. DOI: 10.1111/1556-4029.12312 PMID: 24313297

Golose, P. R. (2022). Cyber Terrorism- A Perspective of Policy Analysis. *International Journal of Cyber Criminology*, *16*(2), 149–161.

Greco, M., & Stenner, P. (Eds.). (2008). *Emotions: A social science reader*. Routledge.

Grinbaum, A., & Adomaitis, L. (2024). Dual use concerns of generative AI and large language models. *Journal of Responsible Innovation*, *11*(1), 2304381. DOI: 10.1080/23299460.2024.2304381

Gupta, M., Akiri, C., Aryal, K., Parker, E., & Praharaj, L. (2023). From ChatGPT to ThreatGPT: Impact of Generative AI in Cybersecurity and Privacy. *IEEE Access : Practical Innovations, Open Solutions*, *11*, 80218–80245. DOI: 10.1109/ACCESS.2023.3300381

Hawdon, J., Costello, M., Barrett-Fox, R., & Bernatzky, C. (2019). Hawdon, J., Costello, M., Barrett-Fox, R., & Bernatzky, C. (2018). The perpetuation of online hate: A criminological analysis of factors associated with participating in an online attack., 15(1), 157–181. *Journal of Hate Studies*, *15*(1). Advance online publication. DOI: 10.33972/jhs.166

Hoffman, A., & Schweitzer, Y. (2015). Cyber Jihad in the Service of the Islamic State (ISIS). Strategic Assessment, 18(2).

Hojda, M. H., Mieila, M., Mieila, C., & Dafina, L. C. (2024). Rational Choice And Cybersecurity. [Constantin Brancoveanu University]. *Contemporary Economy Journal*, *9*(4), 60–67.

Holt, T., & Bossler, A. (2009). Examining the applicability of lifestyle-routine activities theory for cybercrime victimization. *Deviant Behavior*, *30*(1), 1–25. DOI: 10.1080/01639620701876577

Holt, T. J., Turner, N. D., Freilich, J. D., & Chermak, S. M. (2021). Examining the Characteristics That Differentiate Jihadi-Associated Cyberattacks Using Routine Activities Theory. *Social Science Computer Review*, *40*(6), 1614–1630. DOI: 10.1177/08944393211023324

Horgan, J. (2005). *The Psychology of Terrorism*. Routledge.

Huber, E., Pospisil, B., Sauter, T., & Treytl, A. (2025). Cybercrime Victimisation and Categorization – A View from the Perspective of Routine-Activity-Theory (RAT). Kriminologie - Das Online-Journal | Criminology - The Online Journal, 7, 100-123.

Hynek, N., Gavurová, B., & Kubák, M. (2025). Risks and benefits of artificial intelligence deepfakes: Systematic review and comparison of public attitudes in seven European Countries. *Journal of Innovation & Knowledge*, *10*(100782), 1–19. DOI: 10.1016/j.jik.2025.100782

INTERPOL. (2024). *Beyond Illusions: Unmasking the Threat of Synthetic Media for Law Enforcement*. INTERPOL.

INTERPOL. (2024). *Global Financial Fraud Assessment*. INTERPOL.

Jaffal, N. O., Alkhanafseh, M., & Mohaisen, D. (2025). Large Language Models in Cybersecurity: Applications, Vulnerabilities, and Defense Techniques. arXiv:2507.13629, 1-21.

Kapsokoli, E. (2023). Cyberterrorism A New Wave of Terrorism or Not? In Ferrag, M. A., Kantzavelou, I., Maglaras, L., & Janicke, H. (Eds.), *Hybrid Threats, Cyberterrorism and Cyberwarfare*. Routledge.

Kasri, W., Himeur, Y., Alkhazaleh, H. A., Tarapiah, S., Atalla, S., Mansoor, W., & Al-Ahmad, H. (2025). From Vulnerability to Defense: The Role of Large Language Models in Enhancing Cybersecurity. *Computation (Basel, Switzerland)*, *13*(30), 1–59. DOI: 10.3390/computation13020030

Kaur, A., Hoshyar, A. N., Saikrishna, V., Firmin, S., & Xia, F. (2024, May 29). Deepfake video detection: Challenges and opportunities. *Artificial Intelligence Review*, *57*(159), 1–47.

Kaur, R., Gabrijelčič, D., & Klobučar, T. (2023). Artificial intelligence for cybersecurity: Literature review and future research directions. Information Fusion, 97(article 101804), 1-29.

Kigerl, A. (2011). Kigerl, A. (2012) 'Routine activity theory and the determinants of high cybercrime countries', 30(4), pp. 470–486. *Social Science Computer Review*, *30*(4), 470–486. DOI: 10.1177/0894439311422689

Kydd, A., & Walter, B. (2006). The strategies of terrorism'. *International Security*, *31*(1), 49–80. DOI: 10.1162/isec.2006.31.1.49

Lakomy, M. (2023, December 15). Artificial intelligence as a terrorism enabler? Understanding the potential impact of chatbots and image generators on online terrorist activities. Retrieved from Global Network on Extremism & Technology: https://gnet-research.org/2023/12/15/artificial-intelligence-as-a-terrorism-enabler-understanding-the-potential-impact-of-chatbots-and-image-generators-on-online-terrorist-activities/

Leukfeldt, E., & Yar, M. (2016). Applying routine activity theory to cybercrime: A theoretical and empirical analysis'. *Deviant Behavior*, *37*(3), 263–280. DOI: 10.1080/01639625.2015.1012409

Liang, C. S. (2023). Terrorist digitalis: Preventing terrorists from using emerging technologies. In Institute for Economics and Peace (Ed.), Global Terrorism Index 2023 (pp. 72-74).

Liaropoulos, A. (2014). On cyber-terrorism: Redefining terror in cyberspace. Politika, Annual Journal, 41-88.

Lupovici, A. (2021). Lupovici, A. (2021). The dual-use security dilemma and the social construction of insecurity. Contemporary Security Policy, 42(3), 257–285. *Contemporary Security Policy*, *42*(3), 257–285. DOI: 10.1080/13523260.2020.1866845

Makuch, B. (2025, December 21). Extremists are using AI voice cloning to supercharge propaganda. Experts say it's helping them grow. Retrieved from The Guardian: https://www.theguardian.com/technology/2025/dec/21/ai-voice-cloning-nazis-islamic-state-extremism

McCauley, C., & Moskalenko, S. (2008). Mechanisms of political radicalization: Pathways toward terrorism'. *Terrorism and Political Violence*, *20*(3), 415–433. DOI: 10.1080/09546550802073367

Miller, S., & Selgelid, M. J. (2007). Ethical and philosophical consideration of the dual-use dilemma in the biological sciences. *Science and Engineering Ethics*, *13*(4), 523–580. DOI: 10.1007/s11948-007-9043-4 PMID: 18060518

National Research Council. (2004). *Biotechnology Research in an Age of Terrorism. Washington (DC)*. National Academies Press.

NCSC. (2024). *NCSC Annual Review 2024*. National Cyber Security Centre.

NCSC. (2025). Impact of AI on Cyber Threat from Now to 2027. Retrieved from National Cyber Security Centre.: https://www.ncsc.gov.uk/report/impact-ai-cyber-threat-now-2027

Nelu, C. (2024, June 10). International Centre for Counter-Terrorism. Retrieved from Exploitation of generative AI by terrorist groups.: https://icct.nl/publication/exploitation-generative-ai-terrorist-groups

Pech, R. J., & Slade, B. W. (2005). Imitative terrorism: A diagnostic framework for identifying catalysts and designing interventions. *Foresight*, *7*(1), 47–60. DOI: 10.1108/14636680510581312

Pratt, T., Holtfreter, K., & Reisig, M. (2010). Routine online activity and Internet fraud targeting: Extending the generality of routine activity theory. *Journal of Research in Crime and Delinquency*, *47*(3), 267–296. DOI: 10.1177/0022427810365903

Pyrooz, D. C., Decker, S., & Moule, R. K. (2013). Criminal and routine activities in online settings: Gangs, offenders, and the Internet. *Justice Quarterly*, *30*(4), 1–30.

Rawat, R., & Kaushal, N. (2026, January 6). AI in terrorism: Emerging threats for state security. Retrieved from Observer Research Foundation (ORF): https://www.orfonline.org/expert-speak/ai-in-terrorism-emerging-threats-for-state-security

Salem, A. H., Azzam, S. M., Emam, O. E., & Abohany, A. A. (2024). Advancing cybersecurity: A comprehensive review of AI-driven detection techniques. *Journal of Big Data*, *11*(105), 1–38. DOI: 10.1186/s40537-024-00957-y

Sandler, T., & Enders, W. (2004, June). An economic perspective on transnational terrorism. *European Journal of Political Economy*, *20*(2), 301–316. DOI: 10.1016/j.ejpoleco.2003.12.007

Schaefer, L., & Mazerolle, L. (2017). Putting process into routine activity theory. *Security Journal*, *30*(1), 266–289. DOI: 10.1057/sj.2015.39

Schmitt, M., & Flechais, I. (2024). Digital deception: Generative artificial intelligence in social engineering and phishing. *Artificial Intelligence Review*, *57*(12), 1–18. DOI: 10.1007/s10462-024-10973-2

Taddeo, M., McCutcheon, T., & Floridi, L. (2021, April 30). Trusting Artificial Intelligence in Cybersecurity, a Double-Edged Sword. *SSRN*, 1-12. DOI: 10.1007/978-3-030-81907-1_15

Taylor, R. B. (2015). *Community criminology: Fundamentals of spatial and temporal scaling, ecological indicators, and selectivity bias*. NYU Press. DOI: 10.18574/nyu/9780814724187.001.0001

Toros, H., & Gunning, J. (2009). Exploring a critical theory approach to terrorism studies. In Jackson, R., Smyth, M. B., & Gunning, J. (Eds.), *Critical Terrorism Studies: A New Research Agenda* (pp. 87–108). Routledge.

Treleaven, P., Barnett, J., Brown, D., Bud, A., Fenoglio, E., Kerrigan, C., & Schoernig, M. (2023). The future of Cybercrime AI and Emerging Technologies are creating a Cybercrime tsunami. *SSRN*, 1-34. DOI: 10.2139/ssrn.4507244

UNICRI, & UNCCT. (2021). UNICRI, & UNCCT. (2021). Algorithms and terrorism: The malicious use of artificial intelligence for terrorist purposes. United Nations Interregional Crime and Justice Research Institute & United Nations Office of Counter-Terrorism. Retrieved from UNICRI: https://unicri.org/News/Algorithms-Terrorism-UNICRI-UNOCCT

Vakhitova, Z. I. (2025, January 22). Cyber-Routine Activity Theory. Oxford Research Encyclopedia of Criminology.

Victoroff, J., & Kruglanski, A. (Eds.). (2009). *Psychology of Terrorism: Classic and Contemporary Insights*. Psychology Press.

Wall, D. (2007). *Cybercrime: The Transformation of Crime in the Information Age*. Polity Press.

Wasil, A. R., Grinbaum, A., & Adomaitis, L. (2024, October 7). Governing dual-use technologies: Case studies of international security agreements and lessons for AI governance (SSRN Working Paper). Retrieved from SSRN: https://papers.ssrn.com/sol3/papers.cfm?abstract_id=4946527&mirid=1 DOI: 10.2139/ssrn.4946527

Weimann, G., Winter, C., Köhler, D., & Brzuszkiewicz, S. (2024). Generating terror: The risks of generative AI exploitation. *CTC Sentinel*, *17*(1), 17–24.

Weisburd, D. L., Groff, E. R., & Yang, S.-M. (2013). *The Criminology of Place: Street Segments and Our Understanding of the Crime Problem*. Oxford University Press.

Wenger, A., & Cavelty, M. D. (2022). The ambiguity of cyber security politics in the context of multidimensional uncertainty. In Wenger, A., & Cavelty, M. D. (Eds.), *Cyber Security Politics*. Routledge.

Williams, M. L. (2016). Guardians Upon High: An Application of Routine Activities Theory to Online Identity Theft in Europe at the Country and Individual Level. *British Journal of Criminology*, *56*(1), 21–48. DOI: 10.1093/bjc/azv011

Yamin, M. M., Ullah, M., Ullah, H., & Katt, B. (2021). Weaponized AI for cyber attacks. *Journal of Information Security and Applications*, *57*, 1–35. DOI: 10.1016/j.jisa.2020.102722

Yar, M. (2005). The novelty of "cybercrime": An assessment in light of routine activity theory. *European Journal of Criminology*, *2*(4), 407–427. DOI: 10.1177/147737080556056

APPENDIX

Full Questionnaire

Criminal Application of AI – How Offenders are Exploiting AI to Facilitate, Enhance, or Conceal Crime

Section A: Participant Background

Q1. What is your professional background? *(Cloze)*
Law enforcement Cybersecurity Academia/Research Legal/Policy
Other (please specify): _______

Q2. How much do you know about criminal application of Artificial Intelligence (AI)? *(Cloze)*
Very familiar Somewhat familiar Heard of it but not in detail Not familiar at all

Section B: Offender Profile (Perceived)

Q3. What is the most common age group of offenders who use AI? *(Cloze)*
Under 18 18–25 26–35 36–50 Over 50 Varies widely / Not sure

Q4. What is the education level of offenders using AI tools, generally? *(Cloze)*
No formal education High school Technical diploma Bachelor's degree
Master's degree or higher Unknown/Mixed

Q5. In your opinion, who or what groups are most likely to abuse AI for criminal means, and why? *(Open-ended)*

Section C: Typology of Use

Q6. In which stage(s) of criminal activity is AI most often used? *(Cloze – multi-select)*
Planning (e.g., OSINT, reconnaissance)
Execution (e.g., phishing, deepfakes)
Concealment (e.g., identity spoofing, evasion tools)

Q7. Which AI enabled criminal methods are you aware of or have come across? *(Cloze – multi-select)*
Deepfake impersonation
AI-written phishing/scam messages
Automated cyberattacks (e.g., botnets, brute-force)

Synthetic identity generation
Evasion tools (e.g., adversarial machine learning)
Other (please specify): _______

Q8. From your experience, are there new or emerging ways in which offenders are using AI that are unknown or not widely known? *(Open-ended)*

Section D: Motivation and Risk

Q9. To what extent does AI make it easier to commit crimes? *(Cloze – Likert scale)*

Not at all　Slightly　Moderately　Significantly　Extremely

Q10. To what extent does AI decrease the risk of detection? *(Cloze – Likert scale)*

Not at all　Slightly　Moderately　Significantly　Extremely

Section E: Detection, Policy & Response

Q11. How effective are existing technological solutions (e.g. antivirus, cyber forensics) for the detection of AI-enabled crimes? *(Cloze – Likert scale)*

Very ineffective　Ineffective　Neutral　Effective　Very effective

Q12. What are the gaps in the existing policing, cybersecurity or legal frameworks which prevent response to AI-enabled criminal activity? *(Open-ended)*

Q13. Should the access to powerful open source or generative AI tools be restricted/regulated to avoid misuse? *(Cloze)*

Strongly disagree　Disagree　Neutral　Agree　Strongly agree

Q14. What specific solutions, policies, regulations/innovations do you recommend to prevent and respond to AI driven crime better? *(Open-ended)*

Q15. Please share any real world example(s), case study or personal observation regarding the use of AI in criminal acts (e.g. fraud, impersonation, deception, cyberattack). *(Open-ended)*

Chapter 6
The Promise and Issues of Artificial Intelligence and Predictive Policing: A Case Study of the United States

Angelo Kevin Brown
http://orcid.org/0000-0001-8167-5090
Arkansas State University, USA

ABSTRACT

The chapter examines the use of Artificial Intelligence (AI) in modern law enforcement in the United States of America. This includes the technological foundations, performance, legal, and social issues of AI policing tactics, including predictive policing, facial recognition technology (FRT), and other automated systems. As a result of academic literature, government reports, and more, the potential gains of AI in policing, such as efficiency, are contrasted with its risks. The use of case studies in cities such as Los Angeles, Chicago, and New Orleans shows that there were many failures in oversight, transparency, and efficiency. A comparison of EU regulation with the fractured American model highlights the pros and cons of distinct governance styles. The chapter ends with policy recommendations for responsible use of AI in policing so that justice, accountability, and support of the public is not lost with the continued integration of AI.

INTRODUCTION

The use of artificial intelligence (AI) in policing is being adopted by many law enforcement agencies and is affecting American police in various ways that may

DOI: 10.4018/979-8-3373-5228-2.ch006

raise concerns about citizens' rights. While many AI-based technologies support administrative tasks such as report writing, this chapter will primarily focus on how AI aids patrol operations through predictive policing, investigative tactics, and related technologies in the United States of America (USA). Traditionally, policing has often been reactive, responding to crimes after they occur. With AI integration, the hope is that police can become more proactive. AI tools, with their powerful computing capabilities and vast amounts of data, can enhance proactive, information-driven policing (Joh, 2017). Police agencies must keep pace with evolving data-driven technologies and increasingly complicated criminal threats, such as organized transnational crime and cybercrimes, while staying within budget. They are turning to AI as a powerful assistant to help meet these challenges (Chukaieva & Matulienė, 2023). The goal of using AI is to achieve new levels of effectiveness and efficiency in policing.

This technological hope is being called into question as empirical evidence shows a gap between AI's promises and its reality in the United States (US). What was promoted about AI in policing was its potential to transform the field, but this was often done without acknowledging the known risks (Lum & Isaac, 2016). AI supporters argue that AI is an efficient and accurate system capable of reducing crime and eliminating human bias, but the literature reveals inaccuracies and overlooked errors (Isaac, 2017).

The algorithms used in many of these systems have compounded systemic racism by being trained on past discriminatory data, which often reproduces over-policing in communities (Berk, 2021). The widespread adoption of AI-driven surveillance technologies raises additional concerns for civil rights (Haley & Burrell, 2025). Despite these issues, AI may offer great opportunities for policing when used carefully.

The history of AI as a tool for increasing efficiency has transformed the relationship between the state and citizens. A responsible approach to the use of AI in police work must be carefully monitored in a democratic nation that emphasizes a human rights-based approach to governance. This chapter will explore the effectiveness, bias, and issues with AI governance, arguing that such a model in the USA should be grounded in empirical evidence, accompanied by ethical guidelines and legal accountability to protect values of justice, fairness, and human rights.

AI IN US POLICING: SCOPE AND OPERATIONAL APPEAL

To understand the implications of artificial intelligence in policing, it is important to define the key terminology and concepts of what artificial intelligence entails. AI is a broad set of technologies transforming police work in many significant ways. AI is generally a computer-based program that is usually based on Machine Learning ML and Large Language Models (LLMs), which are advanced models that are argued to be able to learn and make decision-making procedures (Mundlamuri et al., 2025). With law enforcement, AI is not yet about sentient robots; it is currently about creating predictive models to help predict crime, profile criminals, gather intelligence, and analyze evidence such as DNA, voice, or video.

ML is behind most law enforcement-related AI applications. ML is a common type of AI in which systems are trained on large datasets to identify patterns and improve predictive accuracy over time, rather than having rules explicitly coded into them. Policing is an information-intensive setting, with law-enforcement agencies having access to vast amounts of historical information on arrests and crime locations, as well as a variety of public and private information on people and locations. ML algorithms use historical data to perform tasks such as predicting future criminal activity locations, identifying people likely to commit a crime, or identifying public safety issues.

Another application of machine learning is computer vision (CV), which trains computers to recognize and interpret data from images and videos (Shah et al., 2021). This can facilitate the use of standard AI tools in policing and has been adopted by agencies in the US to free up resources, increase surveillance, and attempt to reduce crime while increasing public safety. One of the most well-known applications is facial recognition technology (FRT), which also includes DNA systems, automated license plate readers, and the ability to automatically analyze surveillance videos to identify a specific object, such as a weapon or potential criminal activity that would not be generally observed as efficiently by just a human (Rani, 2024).

A subcategory of ML is Natural Language Processing (NLP), which enables machines to interpret human language. NLP has found its use in policing in the US by automating administrative tasks, such as police report writing (Rani, 2024). Audio captured by an officer's body-worn camera can now be transcribed with a live narration to create an initial draft of a police report, and the officer should revise and verify it before submission. NLP is also used to analyze camera footage to record interactions that will be reviewed by supervisors, including actions that may be used in performance evaluations and could lead to promotion, intervention, or even potential legal consequences.

AI APPLICATIONS IN US POLICING

The applications of AI technology in law enforcement operate within a functional framework alongside human officers and by taking over mundane information-based tasks, helping relieve officers and administrators so they can focus more on other duties, including computer-aided dispatch systems that help prioritize calls for response (Greene & Patterson, 2018). AI can also increase human capabilities by augmenting them, including machine learning that processes large crime datasets or vision processing that analyzes thousands of hours of video to find the suspect's face in a crowd. AI can, in some areas, replace humans with fully automated processes. These AIs that operate without human control, such as self-directed cameras that regulate traffic. Improved infrastructure is critical to implementing these operations because of the risk of making errors, while a system to help with paperwork has different insecurities than a system that autonomously determines a law enforcement decision.

The description of AI as an assistant is a framing created by AI companies and adopted by agencies that have implemented it. This definition of AI technology and its capabilities can help alleviate our concerns about technology. A focus has been on efficiency improvements rather than a more serious argument about whether mass surveillance or risk-scoring people based on predictive models is an ability that should be used at all. The effect is that the policy environment is created to ask how to employ technology ethically, rather than whether to employ it. The way these tools are defined can affect how they are accepted and used and may distract people from their influence on society.

Predictive Policing

The term predictive policing refers to the use of analytical skills and quantitative techniques to identify areas likely to be targets of police intervention and to prevent or solve crimes through statistical projection. It uses place-based models that identify geographic locations with high risk and person-based models that assign individuals risk scores to inform resource allocation and action before risks occur. Predictive policing has been around long before AI; in some capacity, it dates back to the early 19th century in France, with the use of crime mapping by researchers and statisticians André-Michel Guerry and Adriano Balbi (Andresen & Hodgkinson, 2025).

The RAND Corporation identified four categories of prediction on which such systems base their decisions (Perry et al., 2013). First are crime prediction methods. These are the most widespread, and they are also known as place-based or hotspot policing. They use past statistics to predict the likelihood of crime in specific spaces and times, indicating a higher risk of property crimes, such as burglary or auto theft. Next are procedures for predicting offenders. These person-based systems attempt to identify those at the greatest risk of future criminal involvement, usually by computing a risk score based on variables such as criminal history, age, and known associates. Third is the perpetrators' prediction methods. Crime scene data collected in the past is used in these methods to generate profiles that may then help predict perpetrators' identities in unsolved cases. The last aspect is ways to predict who will become crime victims. These are like offender predictions in that they identify who or what is likely to become a victim of crime, thereby enabling preventive outreach.

These models, especially place-based systems, have a theoretical foundation in criminological research, including recurring patterns and contagion effects (Hernandez, 2013). This theory suggests that crimes occur spatially and temporally and that a new crime is a substantial predictor of another crime of the same nature in the nearby area in the immediate future. By routinely entering crime data, typically including the type, time, and location of an incident, into algorithms, the systems can produce predictions on a regular basis. The promise from AI supporters is a positive shift in policing toward a proactive, rather than a reactive, style. The technology is said to support crime prevention in a highly efficient manner, increasing community safety and deterring victimization by allocating limited police resources where they can have the greatest impact.

Facial Recognition, Biometrics, and Mass Surveillance

Forensic and investigative analysis is also being used, with AI facilitating the analysis of physical and digital evidence. These tactics include interpreting crime-scene DNA evidence, analyzing digital evidence on a computer, and ballistic analysis (Faqir, 2023). Biometric identification and surveillance are methods of tracking individuals based on distinctive physiological or behavioral characteristics (Haley, 2025). This often involves facial recognition technology, but it also uses fingerprints, DNA, and even gait analysis, all of which are faster and more scalable through AI and can be applied to drones and other robots.

Concerns about a reduction in personal privacy and civil freedom surround facial recognition technology (FRT) and biometric surveillance in general. When presented as an effective instrument for detecting criminals and locating missing people, FRT's use by law enforcement has arguably been tainted by various instances of technical prejudice, raising civil rights concerns (Ruhrmann, 2019). The technical standards for the technologically driven competition to enhance the technology's accuracy have placed themselves far ahead of the legal and ethical codes that regulate its application.

The National Institute of Standards and Technology (NIST)-led Face Recognition Vendor Test (FRVT) is a technical assessment of FRT (Grother, 2022). The community has frequently treated the FRVT as the international standard for assessing the performance of computer facial recognition algorithms, developed by commercial and academic developers worldwide. The program consists of furnishing objective, independent data to aid governmental agencies and other parties in making well-informed choices. The FRVT conducts tests of algorithms like black boxes (developers pack up their code and send it to NIST, which runs it on large, segregated government datasets of photographs). The datasets are visa photos, police mugshots, and border-crossing photos, to test under a variety of conditions. The evaluations take two basic scenarios into account. This is used to evaluate how an algorithm determines whether an identity claim is valid by comparing two images (a person's face and their passport photo). The False Match Rate (FMR) and False Non-Match Rate (FNMR) are frequently used as performance indicators (Schuckers, 2010). With improvements in recent years, there have been reports of an overall increase in algorithmic accuracy (El Fadel, 2025).

Investigative and Generative AI in Reporting and Administrative Practice

AI is quickly becoming part of everyday policing, such as filling out reports, processing forensic evidence, and gathering intelligence. These applications are usually seen as a positive efficiency mechanism for addressing police burnout and improving the efficiency of the investigative process, but they also pose a different, more complicated risk to evidentiary integrity and legal responsibility, and they may undermine human judgment in the criminal justice system.

Paperwork is one of the most significant administrative tasks in contemporary policing. Research indicates that police officers may be required to devote around 40 percent of their work to report writing, which pulls them off the street and contributes to officer burnout and attrition, especially in understaffed agencies. Technology companies have been relying on AI that would help write reports. The well-known version is by Axon, a generative AI program named 'Draft One' (Brems, 2025). The system takes as input the audio recorded by an officer on a body-worn camera during an event. The officer is prompted to describe what is happening as it occurs, and the AI uses the audio to create a first draft of the narrative section of a police report. The officer should then revise, correct, and add more information to the draft before submitting.

Several of the police departments have adopted it early. The police departments have stated that the tool significantly saved officers time spent creating reports, made them better and easier to read through verbatim quotations, and made them more accountable because the video can confirm the narrative. Axon states that the tool can reduce time spent on reports by up to 82 percent, freeing officers to focus more on proactive policing (Adams et al., 2024). The narrative here faces significant resistance from critics, including those in police departments, and real-world testing showed no significant time savings (Adams et al., 2024).

A key factor in administrative AI systems such as Draft One is a narrative strongly centered on addressing officer wellness and staffing issues. With this in mind, it is easy to see that technology is quite appealing to police management, but the risk to evidence integrity should be prioritized. A vulnerability is introduced by the application of generative AI throughout the legal procedure. A police report is an administrative and a governing document that can be used to determine a person's freedom. The new point of failure in court and in the law is created because of the system's issues. This is likely to cause many pre-trial issues regarding the trustworthiness of technology, making prosecutors hesitant to risk dismissal, as AI-aided reports, created to speed up the justice process, may not turn out as advertised.

AI IN FORENSIC AND INVESTIGATIVE ANALYSIS

In forensic labs, people are being supported by AI as analysts struggle to handle an increasing volume of digital and biological evidence (Herke, 2026). AI, with its ability to analyze large datasets faster than a human, is a current response to this problem. The amount of data from a single investigation can be up to terabytes across dozens of device types, making manual review of this information take months. AI-enabled systems developed by companies such as Cellebrite and Magnet Forensics can process such data much quicker, potentially flagging significant evidence such as images containing child sexual abuse material, suspicious financial activity, or communication indicating a criminal network, among many others (Jarrett & Choo, 2021; Ramesh Babu et al., 2024). This not only speeds up the process but also reduces investigators' exposure to the material's traumatic nature.

The National Institute of Justice (NIJ) has supported research on AI applications, including in the interpretation of DNA mixtures, such as when DNA from more than one person is in the same sample (Rigano, 2019). AI can pick up patterns and isolate individual profiles, which may be too complex for humans to analyze. AI can also be used in gunshot detection, where audio files are analyzed to determine the number and type of firearms involved. AI can also be used to improve and analyze poor-quality images and videos, identifying license plates or suspects that would not have otherwise been recognizable (Memon et al., 2026).

It is important to consider the errors that can arise in forensic AI applications. The performance of these systems depends on training on high-quality data, which can be costly to obtain. The legal questions associated with the increasing complexity of these models have not yet been fully resolved. AI systems that are not able to be explained by the users on how they make their decisions, referred to as black boxes, could be challenged in court because even an AI expert might not be able to articulate how the AI made its decision (Alimardani & Istiqomah, 2025).

Robotics, Drones, and Emerging Autonomous Policing Tools

AI is transforming the physical aspect of policing through autonomous robotics. Policing currently uses robotics, especially Unmanned Aerial Vehicles (UAV's) as a primary auxiliary instrument in targeted investigations. They are used to generate 3D reconstructions of traffic accidents and crime scenes, to help with investigations, and to provide situational awareness in high-risk incidents such as the rescue of a hostage, the engagement of an active shooter, or the pursuit of an armed suspect on the run. Agencies are also starting to use robotics to respond to incidents, assessing the situation before officers even arrive, which enhances the safety of field officers but can also raise privacy concerns because they can enhance officers' vision and collect information (Joh, 2022). These activities can be improved using unmanned drones with autonomous capabilities, but there is an important ethical concern about the use of force by non-human robots (Joh, 2016).

The future of robotic policing will lead to less human involvement. The possibilities of autonomous robotic patrols, robot-assisted crowd control, and arming human officers with augmented reality (AR) smart glasses that display real-time data overlays, facial recognition, and database access are currently being considered. The outcomes of such applications raise significant legal concerns, particularly regarding the use of force by autonomous systems and privacy issues arising from their surveillance capabilities, as they can view areas that the human eye would not be able to because of the different type of senses and waves they can detect and the ability to fly and get a point of site that would not be possible for a person (Gavrilovic, 2016).

Autonomous use of robots increases surveillance significantly, and this is the Pandora's box that remains unopened regarding applying automated force on civilians. The current stage of the trade-off involves the tension between automating these challenging tasks and the possibility of new systems that are difficult to spot systematic errors, the de-skilling of police officers, officers' loss of a sense of ownership, and the loss of the critical human context and understanding of empathy in policing.

CROSS-CUTTING PROBLEMS IDENTIFIED ACROSS U.S. APPLICATIONS

Predictive policing is among the most controversial police tactics in the country. Used as a proactive crime prevention device, it has experienced widespread failures to deliver on its potential. An analysis of predictive policing shows that the application of the technology often operates in a biased fashion, using past crime data to produce a system that can magnify injustice in the name of scientific precision (Berk, 2021).

The empirical basis for the effectiveness of predictive policing is filled with inconsistencies. AI companies have reported success, but recent reviews of the academic and independent communities have found little substantial evidence of the technology's promised crime-reduction effects, for example, a 2015 study of the Los Angeles Police Department (LAPD) program found that patrols driven by predictions from the epidemic-type aftershock sequence (ETAS) model resulted in a statistically significant decrease in targeted crimes compared with a control group (Mohler et al., 2015). Various cities have implemented a predictive crime system like PredPol, and patrols have recorded a significant drop in burglaries (Gerstner, 2018).

A literature review by Meijer and Wessels (2019) revealed a contrast between the research's interest in the possible benefits and drawbacks of predictive policing and the availability of empirical evidence. Their study demonstrates there is evidence of crime reduction, but overall, there is a lack of evidence of predictive policing efficacy. US Senators have demanded that the Department of Justice stop funding predictive policing programs due to their inaccuracy and discrimination (Sankin, 2024).

Some of the issues are related to considerable methodological difficulties. It is very difficult to set up proper control groups or to isolate the effects of predictive policing outcomes from confounding factors, such as other changes occurring simultaneously in policing and the community. The net effect is that of a technology that has been rapidly adopted on the promise that it is hard to quantify through research.

Historical Data, Bias, and the Predictive Policing Feedback Loop

The fundamental criticism of predictive policing is not in its unproven usefulness, but rather in its very basis, which is the data on which it relies (Hobart, 2025). The systems are models of historical police records, including the data about reported crimes and arrests. The fatal assumption in this model is that this information constitutes an objective account of crime, but in reality, it does not, especially when it relies on official data.

Because the history of exposure to police data is filled with well-documented examples of discriminatory policing practices, which are in themselves biased toward Black and Brown communities in countless databases, the data does not properly correct the bias; instead, it learns, internalizes, and reinforces it. This creates a self-reinforcing cycle in which the point of algorithmic unfairness in policing is the biased input (Ugwudike, 2023). Algorithms developed with training data representing past data that account for more stops of minorities, since they have been over-policed in the past, not due to higher crime prevalence behind the trends.

According to biased prediction, the algorithm memorizes this trend and concludes that these neighborhoods will be hotspots of future crime again. Disproportionate deployment is another issue; the police have historically concentrated their resources unevenly in these areas (Wheeler, 2020).

The larger the police presence, the more low-level crimes they will observe and the more stops and arrests that will occur in the areas (Bennett Moses & Chan, 2018). The new arrest records then serve as input into the system, providing evidence that the initial estimate was correct, and even more statistical relationships between the neighborhood and crime are found.

The feedback loop transforms predictive policing into the process of legitimizing historical bias. It implements past human choices and turns them into the apparently objective, data-driven requirements of the future. The outcome is that the cycle of over-policing damages the community's trust and exacerbates existing social inequalities. Instead of a neutral device, technology becomes a tool that augments the very biases it was intended to eliminate.

CASE STUDIES

As theoretically analyzed, predictive policing has played out in the real world, but with many more challenges than the proponents predicted. Cities across the US that were held out as the wave of the future of policing have gone quiet and have either been decommissioned or sharply reduced after audits, internal and external, found them to be ineffective, discriminatory, or both. These case studies raise the accusation that technology is being used without sufficient oversight of its contents.

Los Angeles

Since the Los Angeles Police Department (LAPD) was an early and eager adopter, another case study in the predictive policing lifecycle is its experience. The department adopted two major initiatives: Place-based prediction of property crime, which was intended to focus on predicting hotspots of crime (PredPol) and program; and person-based program named Operation LASER (Los Angeles Strategic Extraction and Restoration), which was developed with military contractor, Palantir, and assigned individuals a score based on their tendencies to commit crimes (González, 2024). An internal audit by the Inspector General of the LAPD in 2019 delivered a devastating review of its algorithmic systems (Ferguson, 2021). The audit found that the programs were the victim of a lack of centralized control and informal training, resulting in uneven and problematic implementation across the city. The audit allayed fears of civil rights advocates and found that out of the people in the LASER chronic offender list, nearly 80 percent were either Black or Latino men (Apolinar, 2023). The system's efficacy was similarly considered problematic.

Chicago

One of the most notable examples of person-based predictive policing experiments in the US was the Strategic Subject List (SSL), commonly referred to as the Heat List, developed and implemented by the Chicago Police Department (CPD), together with the researchers of the Illinois Institute of Technology (Cheng, 2025). Although it has been argued that the program's objectivity, the program itself was discriminatory, and no evidence of its influence was shown. The results showed that the SSL was disproportionately labeling young Black men with the designation of being a high risk. An official evaluation of the program by the RAND Corporation found that, whatever the status of an individual on the list, there was no significant statistical difference in the probability of an individual becoming a victim of a homicide or a shooting, and the program was not a successful tool in reducing gun violence (Saunders et al., 2016). In late 2019, it closed the program.

New Orleans

This incident in New Orleans illustrates that predictive policing is exceptionally problematic when used in a culture of secrecy and based on biased data (Winston, 2018). The New Orleans Police Department (NOPD) has been in a secretive collaboration with Palantir Technologies since 2012 to run a predictive policing initiative. The agreement was reported to be a type of in-kind donation to circumvent formal procurement procedures and operate without the city council's or residents' awareness or consent. A troubling aspect of such secrecy was the NOPD's record. Another investigation by the Department of Justice (DOJ) had revealed that NOPD was involved in a pattern of unconstitutional behavior with racially biased stops and arrests and a systematic record of biased data (Richardson, et al., 2019). The Palantir system was established directly over this data, where inputs such as field interview cards were known to reflect discriminatory tendencies. It perpetuated these tendencies, creating target lists of people who were predominantly young, Black males. After journalists exposed the program in 2018, the backlash led to its termination. In 2020, the New Orleans City Council enacted a broad ordinance severely limiting the use of predictive policing and other surveillance technologies, though some of the limits were reversed when the city experienced a rise in violent crime.

The results of all these high-profile failures represent an important lesson about predictive policing. The very mechanism of technology doing what it does best, which is to see patterns within the information, is the worst aspect when the information itself is a document of systematic injustice (Van Brakel, 2025). The better the algorithm understands historical bias, the more effectively it can express injustice in the future, thereby continuing to jeopardize public safety and trust.

FACIAL RECOGNITION AS AN INVESTIGATIVE LEAD: PROMISE AND MISIDENTIFICATION RISK

Despite these significant improvements in the overall performance of AI systems in general and FRT systems, there remains a systematic difference in error rates across demographic groups. This has been reported repeatedly by both NIST and other examiners. A 2019 NIST report (NISTIR 8280), which used 189 algorithms submitted by 99 developers, reported that, across a majority of systems tested, the pattern of demographic differentials was present. In the one-to-many match case, the report found that algorithms used returned false positives 100 times more often on East Asian and African American faces than on Caucasian faces (Patrick et al., 2019). The report also found higher rates of erroneous returns among women and the elderly than among men (Benedict, 2022).

Studies have shown that commercial gender classification systems have gender biases. Their experiments yielded an error rate of up to 34.7 percent in identifying the gender of darker-skinned females, and 0.8 percent as the highest error rate in identifying the gender of lighter-skinned males (Buolamwini & Gebru, 2018). These differences can be attributed to two basic causes. First, these algorithms were trained on extensive, unrepresentative datasets that mainly include white, male faces. In a situation when a system is not already trained on a diverse set of faces, it is less capable of recognizing people who belong to underrepresented groups. Second, there are technical reasons that could result in low-quality images that the algorithm cannot analyze. These factors include default camera settings that are not well optimized to capture the specifics of darker skin tones.

The real-world implications of AI in law enforcement have now been reported, with instances of wrongful arrests resulting from FRT mismatches. Six of them were Black, including Robert Williams, Nijeer Parks, Randal Reid, and Porcha Woodruff, individuals who were arrested or jailed because of a mistake made by a computer (Fraerman, 2024). These cases show the mistake that has been made when biased technology is deployed into a system in which racial differences have always existed.

Law enforcement agencies should not use FRT alone to make an arrest based solely on a match (Jones, 2020). Many policy documents state that any action based on FRT should be overridden by independent evidence found by officers. The number of wrongful arrests indicates a gap between policy and practice. These cases show that automation bias is affecting police, creating overconfidence in the output of an automated system that treats FRT results as objective facts. The problem is revealed by the fact that, in numerous cases, police officers routinely fail to follow proper protocol and instead immediately arrest the most likely match, as shown by the computer, without conducting an independent investigation.

As AI has a perception of scientific certainty, it can override human choice and due process. They do not just give back one match; they often provide the digital lineup of possible candidates. Even in the case when the right person is among them, there is no surety about the fact that it will be chosen by a human reviewer whose personal cognitive shortcomings may prejudice. Such an issue can make this laboratory-tested precision rating misleading when applied to the reliability of investigations.

CONSTITUTIONAL AND CIVIL LIBERTIES IMPLICATIONS OF BIOMETRIC SURVEILLANCE

The use of FRT, especially real-time mass surveillance, conflicts with constitutional values and the safeguard of a reasonable expectation of privacy guaranteed by the Fourth Amendment to the US Constitution, which protects citizens against unreasonable searches and seizures of their persons, property, and private data. In the US, police generally need to have a warrant to search and seize property within a private location, unless they have exceptions to this, such as consent from the owner, during an emergency where there is an imminent threat to life, they have plain view of a crime in progress, or during a hot pursuit.

The use of the third-party doctrine, which establishes a presumption in the courts, is that individuals cannot treat as private and confidential information that they share with other parties. AI is creating more opportunities for this type of information to be shared (Nicolella, 2023). Carpenter v. United States led to a change in the US, holding that a warrant was required to obtain long-term cell-site location data (Nicolella, 2023). Although the Court did not break much new ground on privacy rights, it acknowledged that new technologies that enable the easy, comprehensive collection of revealing personal information warrant heightened Fourth Amendment protections, even when a third party, such as a private corporation, retains the information.

AI surveillance is often viewed as a form of third-party search. The capacity to scan the streets of a city in real time and measure people's movements, along with the ability to create an account of associations and activities, significantly improved the surveillance state's capabilities. Such capabilities can have a serious effect on their First Amendment rights of freedom of speech, assembly, and expression, discouraging individuals from participating in protests, religious services, and political organizing, and raising concerns that they would be identified and that a profile of their ties and activities would be created. While people in public do not have the same legal right to privacy as they do in private spaces, this has led to the argument that such powerful technology still reduces civil liberties (Allen & Muhawe, 2025).

A report on facial recognition concluded that, with few exceptions, the US lacks appropriate regulations and laws to address issues related to FRT (National Academies of Sciences, Engineering, and Medicine, 2024). This is the government's inability to keep up with technology, perhaps the gravest risk of all. With such a degree of interest in advancing the technical accuracy of FRT, influenced by events such as NIST's FRVT, the need to focus on governance and rights (Swaminathan & Danks, 2024) has been shown. The civil liberties community also has concerns that an accurate FRT would still be too powerful a device to entrust to the state, as the AI-driven surveillance network creates a massive power imbalance between citizens and the state. This shows a systematic mismatch that can arise from the increased use of FRT technology and the governing of its legal regulation.

Market pressures and government contracts encourage technology companies to optimize a few performance metrics (Friedman et al., 2022). AI developers and officials need to be able to solve the downstream societal problems that security systems generate, for there to be hope of mitigating these issues. This can create a gap in which the technology's ability to cause harm at scale exponentially increases, while the legal and ethical systems necessary to regulate that power fall far behind, posing a serious threat. This innovation, intended to improve technology, is separated from the process needed to control it, thus creating a gap between competence and responsibility.

A serious issue with these systems is the plausible deniability and accountability that AI-generated reports and evidence can provide officers in cases where a mistake appears in them (Ferguson, 2025). Law enforcement could now find themselves in a situation where a report contains incorrect information, but it could also be argued in court that the AI wrote it and experienced an AI-hallucination, raising issues of evidence reliability. Critics are concerned that a language model cannot easily transcribe the intricate details of a police officer encounter, such as sarcasm, local accents, street lingo, non-English terms, and other aspects of confrontation. The AI has been shown to be inaccurate in its portrayal of important, subjective words, even when the official video recording contradicts that description.

Doubtful benefits of great time savings are also being uncovered through evaluations of AI systems. Anchorage Police Department reported that after completing a three-month trial of Draft One, they found that the technology did not save time and did not retain it (Guariglia, 2025).

The possibility of a non-human author in a chain of evidence has created problems for prosecutors. In Seattle, Washington state, prosecutors have advised police not to rely on AI to file reports in severe cases, citing concerns that inaccuracies may threaten the entire trial (Ferguson, 2025). District attorneys have been wary of evaluating how defense attorneys will question the admissibility and reliability of such AI-produced reports in court.

GOVERNANCE, REGULATION, AND THE ACCOUNTABILITY DEFICIT

The blending of artificial intelligence into law enforcement has been a test fraught with errors, underscoring the necessity of governance. The technological capabilities of AI have advanced so quickly that control has lagged, leaving legal, ethical, and policy guidelines required to properly contain it and reduce harm. With every reported failure and the erosion of public trust, people are starting to understand that the right direction for responsible AI in policing is not to enhance algorithms, but to prioritize strong governance systems that prioritize accountability.

The European Union AI Act

The European Union (EU) has arguably been a step ahead of the US in AI regulation by taking a comprehensive, proactive, and rights-based approach through its AI Act. The Act restricts AI systems with unacceptable risks to fundamental rights (Davtyan, 2025). After FRT in the United Kingdom (UK) faced serious public scrutiny and legal challenges, they began revising their policies to limit AI use in policing (Gentile, 2024). The Covenant for Using Artificial Intelligence, endorsed by police throughout the UK, establishes principles for the ethical use of AI, such as transparency, accountability, and fairness, with a focus on unbiased outcomes, human-in-the-loop protocols in which humans make the final decisions, and legal and proportionality principles. The International Criminal Police Organization (INTERPOL) and the United Nations Interregional Crime and Justice Research Institute (UNICRI) have created a toolkit to advise on the responsible use of AI, ensuring it is lawful, ethical, and trustworthy (Zagaynov, 2025). The Toolkit for Responsible AI Innovation in Law Enforcement, published in June 2023, is intended to minimize harm while assisting police efficiently.

The Fragmented United States

The US lacks a general federal regulatory framework for AI use compared to the EU (Davtyan, 2025). The Police in the US are generally controlled by the states under the Tenth Amendment to the Constitution, which allows the federal government to influence state policy and practice through funding. US regulations combine state and local laws, voluntary federal recommendations, and non-binding federal guidance. Its status has been that of permissionless innovation, and it uses the post hoc process of litigation to address wrongs that occur. At the federal level, the activity has been guided by aspirational guidelines, such as the non-binding White House Plan known as the Blueprint for an AI Bill of Rights, and agency policy statements (Schildkraut et al., 2023).

Most states have proposed AI-related bills, but the strategy has been piecemeal. It is common to find them focused on specific technologies, such as facial recognition systems. Some states, such as Washington in 2020 (Senate Bill 6280) and Colorado's in 2022 (Senate Bill 113), have already enacted laws requiring accountability reports and warrants to use FRT, whereas California, by Assembly Bill (AB) 1215 in 2019, has suspended its use in body cameras, and other jurisdictions have prohibited its use in certain situations (Tracol, 2025), but there is a lack of comprehensive laws in the US regulating all AI-related policing practices at the state or federal levels (Davtyan, 2025).

More cities are enacting Community Control Over Police Surveillance (CCOPS) ordinances to update policies governing police surveillance (Southerland, 2023). New surveillance systems cannot be purchased unless they are approved and publicly discussed in city council meetings. Some cities, such as San Francisco and Boston, and states like Maine have greatly restricted government facial recognition (Lee & Chin, 2022).

The result of this divergence in regulation has led to a global geopolitical AI divide. The EU's strict system may take longer to implement, but it is likely to lead to a market with more trustworthy, standardized, and legally secure technologies. The US laissez-faire model allows innovation to occur more rapidly but at the cost of greater harm (Davtyan, 2025). Such a situation allows the use of possibly unsafe tools, making independent law enforcement agencies unwilling beta testers. It can result in even greater high-profile failures and false arrests, and cause a reactive, disorderly chain reaction of backlashes, lawsuits, and disjointed laws, which is relatively ineffective compared to having a proactive, principled framework in place in the first place.

PRINCIPLES FOR RESPONSIBLE AI USE IN US POLICING

The regulation of AI in policing needs to continue, and a need for agreements on developing fundamental principles of an ethical framework of AI in policing, with coordination from organizations like the African Union, Europol, Interpol, the UN, and others, which some have already helped contribute to creating a blueprint for governance of AI, like UNICRI's AI toolkit. An ethical framework must include a requirement for transparency; law enforcement agencies, when they utilize AI systems, must publicly disclose the type of system they are using, its purpose, and provide an understandable evaluation of the system's role in the process.

AI systems need to enhance, not substitute for, human judgment; officers need to be trained to use these systems responsibly and not rely on or trust AI as the primary decision-maker, which could deprive a person of their rights and freedoms. They need to understand that human decision-making can be undermined by automation bias; human ethical thinking should not be lost in policing.

COMMUNITY ENGAGEMENT

The legitimacy of AI in policing needs the trust of the communities in which it is used. The use of surveillance and predictive tools without considering their biases can erode the relationship between law enforcement and communities. People have expressed serious doubts about AI, especially among groups exposed to more discrimination, who show lower levels of trust (Sagana et al., 2025). Legitimacy relies on procedural justice when citizens believe the government behaves fairly and respectfully.

Community participation supports good governance. Community members need to be consulted in the decision-making process before implementing AI technologies. The CCOPS ordinances, which give the public the right to know how they are policed, make this right enforceable. The trust of the people is a major part of legitimate democratic policing.

POLICY IMPLICATIONS FOR RESPONSIBLE AI USE IN US POLICING

Artificial intelligence offers innovative possibilities in law enforcement, but the current course of governance and technological solutionism is at risk of eroding civil liberties. Proper regulation will enable responsible innovation and the implementation of AI in policing, with specific, evidence-based recommendations for law enforcement agencies and policymakers.

Police departments and AI developers share responsibility for the legal and ethical application of AI. Police need to implement strict procurement processes for AI to ensure the technology they use is legal and ethical. They should not accept the marketing claims of AI systems, but they must have tested evaluations before acquiring

AI systems. An effective governance structure should consider those affected by these systems and ensure that victims have a practical way to dispute wrongdoing.

Transparency, Disclosure, and Community Participation

Policies need to specify what the tool may or may not be used for to limit mission creep. It should describe which data the system uses, how it is stored and secured, and include requirements for human oversight. The policy should use systems outputs as recommendations only and have independent verification when an officer acts on a lead provided by AI. Transparency guidelines should consider the availability of information about the algorithm's design. Black-box systems, in which functionality is hidden, should be avoided. Independent, third-party verification of a tool's accuracy and fairness should be part of the testing.

Explainability is an important part of transparency for law enforcement agencies that use AI. The system should be explainable so that the output it produces can be explained to the officers who use it (Zocholl et al., 2025). Agencies that generate risk scores or other AI-based recommendations need an auditable record. They should also have readable use policies. AI tools should be implemented with a transparent policy on their use, taking into account community and legal participation.

Human Oversight and Limits on Automation

Error protocols can be important in circumstances where a human's judgment does not align with the AI's recommendation. It is important to develop a method of recording and auditing such disagreements. There is a need for continuous training of those working with the technology, as it will be less effective if used by unskilled personnel. Officers need to understand the AI's limitations, errors, and biases. Training should include how AI can reinforce prejudice and the constitutional standards that AI can interview. Agencies can develop a culture in which officers feel empowered by a challenge, examine, and overrule AI suggestions.

Implementing common data entry standards can maintain consistency within the organization and enhance collaboration with other agencies. Data auditing and cleaning processes should be performed to detect and eliminate errors and inconsistencies, which can help with the problem of data creating biased outputs. Federal, state, and local policymakers all need to understand the issues related to AI frameworks and establish expert oversight agencies for AI systems and non-adversarial expert bodies, such as a national police technology ethics commission and state-level counterparts, composed of a group of multidisciplinary experts, including those in technology, law, and ethics, and representatives of the communities they serve. These agencies would examine and certify AI tools, create binding norms, and examine complaints.

Along with policies to promote compliance with proper local ordinances, so that individuals, following democratic principles, make a clear decision about surveillance technology purchases after considering input from citizens of the jurisdiction that will be affected. Auditing and publishing disparities is important, as it can identify performance gaps and be done openly.

Governance Standards for High-Risk Police AI

Congress and legislators should not just regulate specific technologies one at a time, but also create broad policies governing the use of all "high-risk" AI systems in policing by applying essential foundations similar to those in the EU AI Act. This kind of legislation should have mandatory transparency measures. Make law enforcement agencies publicly disclose what AI and technologies they use. Policy should also require all high-risk AI systems to be regularly and independently audited to determine their accuracy, effectiveness, and non-discrimination. Improve the issues of historical crime and other forms of publicly available data, which are known to be racially and systematically biased in training predictive policing algorithms.

Governments give substantial funding to local law enforcement. This money should be utilized to encourage the use of responsible AI. Policies can tie federal and state grant money to the condition that the grant recipient agency adheres to a proper code of ethics, transparency provisions, and independent decision-making standards. All funding for predictive policing systems and other AI systems that are ineffective or have a discriminatory effect on individuals must be stopped to support due process protections. Companies that develop and sell AI systems to law enforcement should be required to meet ethical and social responsibility in making their systems fair and accountable. This goes back to the development of diverse and representative datasets, which produce less homogeneous training datasets, leading to bias.

Reducing the issues of Black Box Model of AI systems can be done by placing greater emphasis on the development of explainable AI (XAI). The systems sold to law enforcement agencies should also ensure that their decisions can be mapped or tracked and that their working processes can be explained to users or oversight bodies. High-risk systems should not be covered under "trade secret" claims to avoid the scrutiny they require.

CONCLUSION

AI use within US policing, explored in this chapter, is at risk of perpetuating a history of algorithmic prejudice that creates serious threats to civil liberties. The responsible and fair implementation of AI in law enforcement should be supported by improved code and proper policy. The illusion of technological solutionism has been displayed by scholars and critics. The presumption that an advanced algorithm will provide a solution to our crime issues has so far proven significantly misleading. The future of policing and criminal justice will likely have an increase and advancement of AI technologies. Effectiveness and predictive abilities will likely also improve significantly in the coming years, but the promise of a safe AI surveillance society, and the result of authoritarian control, is a potential future we should attempt to avoid by protecting civil rights. The future is possible, where AI serves as a valuable tool that enhances people's safety without undermining their trust or the civil rights of our society.

REFERENCES

Adams, I. T., Barter, M., McLean, K., Boehme, H. M., & Geary, I. A.Jr. (2024). No man's hand: Artificial intelligence does not improve police report writing speed. *Journal of Experimental Criminology*, 1–18.

Allen, A. L., & Muhawe, C. (2025). Is Privacy Really a Civil Right? *Berkeley Technology Law Journal*, *40*, 1.

Alimardani, A., & Istiqomah, M. (2025). Beyond black boxes and biases: Advancing artificial intelligence in sentencing. *Current Issues in Criminal Justice*, 1–21. DOI: 10.1080/10345329.2025.2527994

Apolinar, C. (2023). *Examining the Secondary Effects of the Los Angeles Police Department's Operation LASER on Los Angeles Neighborhoods* (Master's thesis, University of California, Irvine).

Andresen, M. A., & Hodgkinson, T. (2025). Il Y a Quelque Chose sur la Carte: A Modern Spatial Analysis of Crime in Early 19th Century France. *American Journal of Criminal Justice*, *50*(4), 565–584. DOI: 10.1007/s12103-025-09798-8

Benedict, T. J. (2022). The computer got it wrong: Facial recognition technology and establishing probable cause to arrest. *Washington and Lee Law Review*, *79*, 849.

Bennett Moses, L., & Chan, J. (2018). Algorithmic prediction in policing: Assumptions, evaluation, and accountability. *Policing and Society*, *28*(7), 806–822. DOI: 10.1080/10439463.2016.1253695

Berk, R. A. (2021). Artificial intelligence, predictive policing, and risk assessment for law enforcement. *Annual Review of Criminology*, *4*(1), 209–237. DOI: 10.1146/annurev-criminol-051520-012342

Buolamwini, J., & Gebru, T. (2018, January). Gender shades: Intersectional accuracy disparities in commercial gender classification. In *Conference on fairness, accountability and transparency* (pp. 77-91). PMLR.

Brems, R. (2025). Transforming police reporting with generative AI: Insights from the Oklahoma City Police Department. *The Police Journal*, 0032258X251346365.

Cheng, S. (2025). Predictive Policing in Practice: A Case Study of Chicago's Strategic Subject List.

Chukaieva, A., & Matulienė, S. (2023). Possibilities of applying artificial intelligence in the work of law enforcement agencies. *Scientific Journal of the National Academy of Internal Affairs*, *3*(28), 28–37. DOI: 10.56215/naia-herald/3.2023.28

Davtyan, T. (2025). The us approach to ai regulation: federal laws, policies, and strategies explained. *Journal of Law, Technology, & the Internet, 16*(2), 223.

El Fadel, N. (2025). Facial Recognition Algorithms: A Systematic Literature Review. *Journal of Imaging, 11*(2), 58. DOI: 10.3390/jimaging11020058 PMID: 39997560

Faqir, R. S. (2023). Digital criminal investigations in the era of artificial intelligence: A comprehensive overview. *International Journal of Cyber Criminology, 17*(2), 77–94.

Ferguson, A. G. (2021). Surveillance and the tyrant test. *Geological Journal, 110*, 205.

Ferguson, A. G. (2025). Generative Suspicion and the Risks of AI-Assisted Police Reports. *Nw. UL Rev., 120*, 299.

Fraerman, A. (2024). Relying on Unreliable Tech: Unchecked Police Use of Algorithmic Technologies. *Santa Clara High-Technology Law Journal, 40*, 115.

Friedman, B., Heydari, F., Isaacs, M., & Kinsey, K. (2022). Policing police tech: A soft law solution. *Berkeley Technology Law Journal, 37*, 701.

Gavrilovic, N. (2016). The All-Seeing Eye in the Sky: Drone Surveillance and the Fourth Amendment. *U. Det. Mercy L. Rev., 93*, 529.

Gentile, G. (2024). Does big brother exist?: facial recognition technology in the United Kingdom.

Gerstner, D. (2018). Predictive policing in the context of residential burglary: An empirical illustration on the basis of a pilot project in Baden-Württemberg, Germany. *European Journal for Security Research, 3*(2), 115–138. DOI: 10.1007/s41125-018-0033-0

Greene, D., & Patterson, G. (2018). Can we trust computer with body-cam vidio? Police departments are being led to believe AI will help, but they should be wary. *IEEE Spectrum, 55*(12), 36–48. DOI: 10.1109/MSPEC.2018.8544982

Grother, P. (2022). Face recognition vendor test (FRVT) part 8: Summarizing demographic differentials. [NIST]. *National Institute of Standards and Technology, 8429*, 8. DOI: 10.6028/NIST.IR.8429.ipd

González, R. J. (2024). Algorithmic policing: Part 1. Tech startups, venture capital and law enforcement in America. *Anthropology Today, 40*(5), 23–27. DOI: 10.1111/1467-8322.12916

Guariglia, M. (2025). *Anchorage police department: AI-generated police reports don't save time*. Electronic Frontier Foundation.

Haley, P., & Burrell, D. N. (2025). Integrating Artificial Intelligence into Law Enforcement: Socioeconomic and Ethical Challenges. *SocioEconomic Challenges (SEC), 9*(2).

Haley, P. (2025). The Impact of Biometric Surveillance on Reducing Violent Crime: Strategies for Apprehending Criminals While Protecting the Innocent. *Sensors (Basel), 25*(10), 3160. DOI: 10.3390/s25103160 PMID: 40431950

Herke, C. (2026). Automated Fingerprint Identification: The Role of Artificial Intelligence in Crime Scene Investigation. *Forensic Science, 6*(1), 6. DOI: 10.3390/forensicsci6010006

Hernandez, P. (2013). Is Crime Contagious? A Near-Repeat Pattern Analysis of Burglary Incidents in Winston-Salem, 2012. *Journal of Justice Studies, 3.*

Hobart, L. N. (2025). AI, Bias, and National Security Profiling. *Berkeley Technology Law Journal, 40*, 165.

Isaac, W. S. (2017). Hope, hype, and fear: The promise and potential pitfalls of artificial intelligence in criminal justice. *Ohio St. J. Crim. L., 15*, 543.

Jarrett, A., & Choo, K. K. R. (2021). The impact of automation and artificial intelligence on digital forensics. *WIREs Forensic Science, 3*(6), e1418. DOI: 10.1002/wfs2.1418

Joh, E. E. (2016). Policing police robots. *UCLA L. Rev. Discourse, 64*, 516.

Joh, E. E. (2017). The undue influence of surveillance technology companies in policing. *SSRN, 92*, 19. DOI: 10.2139/ssrn.2924620

Joh, E. E. (2022). Ethical AI in American Policing. *Notre Dame J. on Emerging Tech., 3*, 261.

Jones, C. (2020). Law enforcement use of facial recognition: Bias, disparate impacts on people of color, and the need for federal legislation. *NCJL & Tech., 22*, 777.

Lee, N. T., & Chin, C. (2022). Police surveillance and facial recognition: Why data privacy is imperative for communities of color. *The Brookings Institution. Erişim adresi:* https://www. brookings. edu/research/police-surveillance-and-facial-recognition-why-data-privacy-is-an-imperative-for-communities-of-color

Lum, K., & Isaac, W. (2016). To predict and serve? *Significance, 13*(5), 14–19. DOI: 10.1111/j.1740-9713.2016.00960.x

Meijer, A., & Wessels, M. (2019). Predictive policing: Review of benefits and drawbacks. *International Journal of Public Administration, 42*(12), 1031–1039. DOI: 10.1080/01900692.2019.1575664

Memon, M., Talpur, S., Narejo, S., Channa, A., & Pandey, J. K. (2026). Fundamentals of image processing for surveillance. In *Computational Intelligence in Surveillance Systems Using Image Processing* (pp. 13–24). Elsevier. DOI: 10.1016/B978-0-443-36408-2.00010-2

Mohler, G. O., Short, M. B., Malinowski, S., Johnson, M., Tita, G. E., Bertozzi, A. L., & Brantingham, P. J. (2015). Randomized controlled field trials of predictive policing. *Journal of the American Statistical Association, 110*(512), 1399–1411. DOI: 10.1080/01621459.2015.1077710

Mundlamuri, R., Gunnam, G. R., Mysari, N. K., & Pujuri, J. (2025). The Evolution of AI: From Classical Machine Learning to Modern Large Language Models. *IEEE Access : Practical Innovations, Open Solutions, 13*, 178302–178341. DOI: 10.1109/ACCESS.2025.3621344

National Academies of Sciences, Engineering, and Medicine. (2024). *Facial recognition technology: Current capabilities, future prospects, and governance.*

Nicolella, E. (2023). Evolving Privacy Protections for Emerging Machine Learning Data under Carpenter v. United States. *FIU L. Rev., 17*, 453.

Patrick, G., Mei, N., & Kayee, H. (2019). Face recognition vendor test (frvt) part 3: Demographic effects. *National Institute of Standards and Technology, Report NISTIR, 8280.*

Perry, W. L., McInnis, B., Price, C. C., Smith, S., & Hollywood, J. S. (2013). *Predictive policing: Forecasting crime for law enforcement.* RAND Corporation.

Ramesh Babu, B., Usha Rani, T., & Naga Kumari, Y. V. (2024). AI's Watchful Eye: Protecting Children from Sexual Abuse with Artificial Intelligence. In *Child Sexual Abuse: A Public Health Problem in India* (pp. 441–455). Springer Nature Singapore. DOI: 10.1007/978-981-99-8745-0_37

Rani, M. (2024). Impacts and ethics of using Artificial Intelligence (AI) by the Indian Police. *Public Administration and Policy, 27*(2), 182–192. DOI: 10.1108/PAP-06-2023-0081

Richardson, R., Schultz, J. M., & Crawford, K. (2019). Dirty data, bad predictions: How civil rights violations impact police data, predictive policing systems, and justice. *NYUL Rev. Online, 94*, 15.

Rigano, C. (2019). Using artificial intelligence to address criminal justice needs. *National Institute of Justice Journal, 280*(1-10), 17.

Ruhrmann, H. (2019). Facing the future: protecting human rights in policy strategies for facial recognition technology in law enforcement.

Sagana, A., Zhang, M., & Sauerland, M. (2025). Public attitudes towards police use of AI-driven face recognition technology. *Computers in Human Behavior*, 108821.

Sankin, A. (2024). *Senators Demand Justice Department Halt Funding to Predictive Policing Programs*. The Markup.

Saunders, J., Hunt, P., & Hollywood, J. S. (2016). Predictions put into practice: A quasi-experimental evaluation of Chicago's predictive policing pilot. *Journal of Experimental Criminology*, *12*(3), 347–371. DOI: 10.1007/s11292-016-9272-0

Schildkraut, P. J., Kim, J. W., Marotta, M., Courtney Jr, J. V., & Waters, P. J. (2023). The Blueprint for an" AI Bill of Rights". *The Journal of Robotics, Artificial Intelligence & Law, 6*.

Schuckers, M. E. (2010). False Non-Match Rate. In *Computational Methods in Biometric Authentication: Statistical Methods for Performance Evaluation* (pp. 47–96). Springer London. DOI: 10.1007/978-1-84996-202-5_3

Shah, N., Bhagat, N., & Shah, M. (2021). Crime forecasting: A machine learning and computer vision approach to crime prediction and prevention. *Visual Computing for Industry, Biomedicine, and Art*, *4*(1), 9. DOI: 10.1186/s42492-021-00075-z PMID: 33913057

Southerland, V. M. (2023). The Master's Tool and a Mission: Using Community Control and Oversight Laws to Resist and Abolish Police Surveillance Technologies. *UCLA Law Review. University of California, Los Angeles. School of Law*, *70*, 2.

Swaminathan, N., & Danks, D. (2024). Application of the NIST AI risk management framework to surveillance technology. *arXiv preprint arXiv:2403.15646.*

Ugwudike, P. (2023). Algorithms, policing, and race. *The Routledge International Handbook on Decolonizing Justice*, 146.

Wheeler, A. P. (2020). Allocating police resources while limiting racial inequality. *Justice Quarterly*, *37*(5), 842–868. DOI: 10.1080/07418825.2019.1630471

Winston, A. (2018). Palantir has secretly been using New Orleans to test its predictive policing technology. *The Verge, 27.*

Tracol, X. (2025). The Use of Facial Recognition Technologies by Law Enforcement Authorities in the US and the EU: Towards a Convergence on Regulation? *Technology and Regulation, 2025*, 289–315.

Van Brakel, R. (2025). Pre-emptive big data surveillance and its (dis) empowering consequences: The case of predictive policing. In *Exploring the boundaries of big data* (pp. 117–142). Routledge. DOI: 10.4324/9781003695202-7

Zagaynov, M. R. (2025). Interpol Activities and Artificial Intelligence Issues. *Sociopolitical Sciences, 15*(3), 93–99. DOI: 10.33693/2223-0092-2025-15-3-93-99

Zocholl, M., Stampouli, D., Wittfoth, M., & Mounier, G. (2025). Fundamental considerations for the use of explainable AI in law enforcement. *Frontiers in Political Science, 7*, 1605619. DOI: 10.3389/fpos.2025.1605619

Chapter 7

Facial Recognition in Policing: Human Rights, Bias, and Surveillance

Afshan Razzaq
http://orcid.org/0009-0008-8992-6593
University of Westminster, London, UK

ABSTRACT

In the absence of AI specific legislation in the UK, existing research has been clear in illustrating that Facial Recognition Technologies ('FRT') deliberately disregard fundamental human rights of individuals at the cost of catching and deterring criminals and increasing public safety. Therefore, this chapter argues from a proactive viewpoint and calls for new legal and regulatory frameworks to be passed that directly address the human right issues associated with FRT in policing before they arise. The aim of this chapter is to scope existing literature on FRT used in policing in the UK and its impact on fundamental human rights.

INTRODUCTION

Although first mentioned in the 20th century by Alan Turing, in his quest to discover whether computer machines could think like humans Artificial Intelligence ('AI') has, in the last decade, become a growing phenomenon in our everyday lives. From using a smart phone to auto-correct spelling mistakes, asking a Generative Pre-Trained Transformer such as ChatGPT ('GPT') for cake recipes and being medically diagnosed by a GPT to the use of autonomous weapons in wars and sophisticated self-driving cars, AI is rapidly changing landscapes in many industries

DOI: 10.4018/979-8-3373-5228-2.ch007

such as medicine, education, policing, engineering and law. AI is pioneering the way things are done by humans and paving the way forward for technology led cognitive intelligent systems to do tasks that would traditionally be done by human intellect. The growth of machine learning and technology has made industry led processes, procedures, data analysis and decision making more easier, more efficient and self-productive by automating the most repetitive and autonomous tasks, in some cases in a matter of seconds. This has led many to speculate how far artificial intelligence and technology could penetrate policing in the UK and how it will impact fundamental human rights, criminal justice and the rule of law.

In the absence of AI specific legislation in the UK, existing research has been clear in illustrating that Facial Recognition Technologies (FRT) disregards fundamental human rights of individuals at the cost of catching and deterring criminals and increasing public safety. Therefore, this chapter proactively calls for new legal and regulatory frameworks to be passed that directly address the current gaps in legislation and protect fundamental human rights. Nonetheless, the law authorises the police, being a public authority, to interfere with qualified rights subject to the interference being for a legitimate aim, necessary and proportionate in a democratic society. The aim of this chapter is to scope existing literature on FRT used in policing in the UK and its impact on fundamental human rights. The chapter will be set out in six subsections. The first details the case for the continued rollout of AI in policing. The second will investigate the case against law enforcements growing reliance on AI and FRT. The third will explore misidentification issues in FRT. The fourth will discuss issues that have arisen in the use of big data and watch lists by law enforcement agencies. The fifth subsection will focus on human rights considerations that arise from the deployment of AI surveillance in law enforcement contexts. The sixth will examine the emerging solutions and discuss whether these are sufficient in protecting the civil and political rights of individuals.

THE CASE FOR AI IN POLICING

According to IBM (2024) AI is 'technology that enables computers and machines to stimulate human learning, comprehension, problem solving, decision making, creativity and autonomy.' Amazon Web Services Inc. (2024) gives a more human centred definition by stating 'AI is technology with human-like problem solving capabilities.' However, both definitions fail to consider human emotions such as empathy and feelings that are relevant in the daily life of a police officer.

In my view, AI used in policing in England and Wales has, to some extent, exemplary benefits when it comes to detecting and deterring some street crime. I also recognise that the use of new technologies in policing such as FRT are here to stay and will become more advanced in the foreseeable future. The use of FRT is arguably valuable for police forces who want to swiftly identity and catch criminals and people of interest, potentially increasing police efficiency in times of scarcity of resources.

From a policing perspective, AI such as FRT is seen as an enhancement to help manage stretched resources. FRT can scan waves of faces in crowds in a matter of seconds to identify suspects, missing people and those wanted by the police - something a police officer on foot would not be able to do when patrolling large crowds, effectively saving officer time. The National Police Chiefs Council ('NPCC') lead for AI, Chief Constable Alex Murray (2024), perceives the use of AI in policing as having benefits of cost efficiency, greater productivity in fighting crime and providing swifter justice to individuals, families and wider communities. He states:

> *'Our remit is huge, from tackling online child abuse, organised crime through to preventing burglary and reassuring the public. In all these areas AI can make us more effective – it can be a tool for good. In addition, it can allow policing, which is ultimately paid for by the public, to be more efficient and productive (p. 1).*

However, this view glosses over the level of human engagement required in policing which includes clear communication, good listening, emotional intelligence, empathy and trust-building which are all reduced by reliance on AI.

Nevertheless, notable real-life examples have been provided by the Home Office in its fact sheet on the use of FRT, illustrating its effectiveness in fighting crime and bringing perpetrators to justice. In one notable incident, a sex offender was apprehended during the Kings Coronation thanks to a face match that flagged up from the use of a FRT camera. In another incident in Soho in 2023 the deployment of FRT on two Fridays led to 6 positive identifications and zero false identifications leading to 5 arrests of wanted individuals.

To support the inevitable rise of AI surveillance in policing some police forces in England and Wales have developed responsible use AI solutions which are aimed at responding to deficiencies relating to data bias and discrimination. The West Midlands Police ('WMP') have adopted an independent data ethics committee with the help of research conducted by Oswald et al (2024). The role of the Committee is to provide independent suggestions and advice to the West Midlands police Data Analytics Lab on any ethical risks posed by data intelligent programmes developed by the Lab. These programmes include, but are not limited to, identifying areas where crime is most likely to happen and individuals who are part of criminal networks. The WMP ethics committee consists of various stakeholders, including experts and the public. The research found advice from the committee has helped to promote the responsible use of AI and considered a wider range of human rights, ethical issues, scientific dilemmas and legal implications arising from the use and deployment of artificial intelligent systems than is apparent elsewhere. Given the notable problems with deploying AI in law enforcement environments, the adoption of a data ethics committee appears to be good practice for all UK police forces as it, potentially, helps to prevent human rights breaches from the design stage of AI technology.

From a public perspective, the positioning of AI in law enforcement has mixed views. A survey conducted jointly by The Alan Turing Institute and Ada Lovelace Institute on public perception on artificial intelligence in Britain found 70% of the 4000 adults surveyed thought the use of FRT at border control to increase the speed of processing people coming into the country was advantageous. This implies that public attitudes are favourable towards AI especially when the technology is used to reduce delays in law enforcement processing times. However, it is important to note that this public view only applies to FRT used at border control and thus somewhat supports the use of FRT in crime detection and prevention. For example, when a wanted criminal entering the country is flagged by FRT algorithms because they are placed on the border force watch list.

THE CASE AGAINST AI AND FRT

Discrimination and Bias

FRT is arguably a modern form of surveillance created by a dominant state which has the power to discipline and control ethnic minorities and marginalised groups in society through state institutions that are known to be racist. This includes the police who exercise authority using discriminatory practices and unconscious bias. These systematic failures are repeated when biased historical data is used to train FRT surveillance systems.

Public perceptions of efficiency in airport queues aside, several human right groups, academics and experts have criticised AI technological advancements in policing, highlighting the current bias and errors inherent in AI machine learning algorithms that can lead to ethnic/racial profiling, as well as a lack of accountability and transparency. This was illustrated at the Notting Hill Carnival where FRT technologies were placed to identify people on a Metropolitan Police watch list, discriminating against marginalised and ethnic minority groups in society. In 2022, The Gangs Violence Matrix ('GVM'), an artificial intelligence tool used by the Metropolitan Police to confirm the identify of violent gang members across London and risk assess gang violence to protect victims was found to be discriminatory. Eighty percent (80%) of the names on the matrix represented black people. Amnesty International (2022), another human rights organisation, initiated a 'ban the scan' campaign calling for a ban on FRT which supports racist policing. A more sensible approach might be to introduce new regulations and legislation that directly addresses racist policing in FRT.

The fact that 80% of the names on the GVM represented black people raises the important question of whether Metropolitan Police remain institutionally racist, this time through the disguise of innovative technology they cannot explain. The Macpherson Report (1999) written in light of the racially aggravated murder of an 18-year-old black male named Stephen Lawrence by a group of white males in 1993 defined institutional racism as:

'the collective failure of an organisation to provide an appropriate and professional service to people because of their colour, culture, or ethnic origin. It can be seen or detected in processes, attitudes and behaviour which amount to discrimination through unwitting prejudice, ignorance, thoughtlessness and racist stereotyping which disadvantage minority ethnic people' (p.49).

The Casey Report (2023) found:

'unfair outcomes in communities that result from under-protection, over-policing or from both and a culture of downplaying and denial of discrimination and repeated unwillingness to accept and deal with institutional failures that let down Londoners.' (p.330).

This draws a blatant likeness to AI in policing which appears to racially profile, over police and under protect certain groups in society. Therefore, it is arguable that AI surveillance is potentially the latest illustration of institutional racism in UK police forces because it is trained on existing processes, attitudes and behaviours in policing. This is problematic especially if police officers have been diagnosed as racist as this could, potentially, be reflected in AI algorithms and outcomes that have been trained using biased data and experience. This was highlighted in the Notting Hill Carnival where FRT focused on marginalised and ethnic minority groups and the GVM where 80% of names represented black people, demonstrating police bias and racism on both occasions. This again, calls for stricter regulatory frameworks that deals with racial discrimination in policing.

The above perception is supported by the work of Crenshaw (1991) whose theory of intersectionality has been an interesting perspective on the different strands of identity and how the domination of power works. Crenshaw (1991) explains the different strands of identity such as race, gender and class should not be looked at in isolation. Instead, she advocates for their combination to truly understand why certain members of society are marginalised by power structures that impact across multiple areas of disadvantage, illustrating how the rules of dominant powers work in practice. Crenshaw (1991) argues inequality is not the result of individual biases but of systematic failures by dominant societal institutions that allow racism and inequality to exist as they are presented as minority problems. In the context of FRT surveillance used in policing, the dominant power is the state that controls and disciplines marginalised members of society through the police who are themselves institutionally racist and allow inequality to exist. Criminal laws exist to favour the rich upper class and criminalise the poor.

Crenshaw's work is supported by examples to illustrate the theory. Historically, the concept of rape has been associated with the title 'a black convict and white victim' and the laws on rape and sexual violence have imposed strict discipline and control over black communities as a result. This illustrates how the social construction of crimes and dominant legal rules may function to promote inequality and biases.

Lamble and McElhome (2023) suggest racial inequality and discrimination are required in policing to maintain colonial capitalist structures first established in the 19th century. They advise the best way to deal with police racism is to curb police powers. In the context of FRT, one way to achieve this objective would be to have, legally enforceable, independent oversight on the decision to deploy FRT surveillance.

Police Suspicion and Discretion

It is an understatement to say that police suspicion and discretion naturally targets ethnic minorities and marginalised members of society. A wide level of discretion is given to police forces on who to add to the FRT surveillance watch list and where the FRT should be placed. It is arguable that FRT is consciously placed in geographical areas where there are higher numbers of ethnic minorities and marginalised individuals. While this may be rationalised as deployments to areas with high levels of street crime, it is equally arguable that FRT surveillance might be useful to discipline them to follow expected norms and values of society that are created by the rich and powerful.

Richardson, Schultz and Crawford (2019) have discovered that machine algorithms used by police departments to deter and detect crime can be racially biased towards certain ethnicities and marginalised members of the public. Their work analysed thirteen jurisdictions in the USA and found data used to train and build predictive systems used in policing is commonly distorted. It is based on police racial bias and, on occasions, obtained using improper, unethical conduct and police policies. This is referred to as dirty policing and leads to the existence of dirty data which consists of incorrect data based on the improper conduct and policies. The predictive systems then replicate this data to predict where crimes will take place and how to effectively deploy police resources. They provide an excellent example of how crime statistics in one jurisdiction, New York, were manipulated by senior officers to show lower crime rates and how officers convinced victims not to make complaints. Arrests and summon targets were met by corrupt police framing innocent people by placing illegal drugs on them or writing false reports. What is worrying is that there is little evidence to suggest that police forces using predictive policing systems and private technology companies providing the technology have addressed the dirty data issue – is the data included or excluded when building the systems? Therefore, it is questionable if the systems serve proper justice as they are reiterating police biases and improper practices to make predictions that are fundamentally flawed and unethical.

Wrongful Inferences

It is arguable that new legal and regulatory frameworks are required to prevent wrongful inferences being made by AI. If the inference can be explained it is easier to identify if it is reasonable and whether justice has been served equally.

Wachter and Mittelstadt (2018) recognise how dangerous wrongful inferences can be, especially when they are used to make life changing decisions about people. Therefore, they argue for a new right to be established in data protection law called *'the right to reasonable inferences'* (p. 2) which would expect the data controller to justify why the inference is reasonable in the circumstances. This will trigger open accountability and ensure data subjects have some control over how their personal data is used.

The 'Black Box' Issue

There appears to be a clear trade-off between promises of more efficient policing from AI deployment and being unable to explain how machine algorithms reach a decision; known as the black box AI issue. Bathaee (2018) defines the black box issue as *'an inability to fully understand an AI's decision-making process and the inability to predict the AI's decisions or outputs'* (p.905). This causes problems of a lack of transparency and accountability as police officers do not understand how AI has reached an outcome and are therefore unable to interpret the results to explain the reasoning of decisions to members of the public who are impacted by AI decisions. This may potentially result in criminal liability and incarceration of an entirely innocent person.

Brożek et al (2023) argue the how and why questions on outcomes from algorithmic processes are not answered due to the opaque nature of automated decision-making process. Consequently, this can lead to public trust and accountability issues if it remains not clear how a decision has been reached and who is responsible for making decisions – was it the machine algorithm or the police operator?

Wachter et al. (2017) rightly proposes that *'unconditional counterfactual explanations'* (p. 844) should be given to data subjects relating to automated decisions regardless of whether the effects of the decision are significant or legal in nature. Watcher (2017) rationalises counterfactual explanations by the following example:

'You were denied a loan because your income is £30,000. If your income had been £45,000 you would have been offered the loan' (p.844).

This shows the outcome decision but also explains how the desirable outcome could be achieved by the data subject through the counterfactual statement. In this example, through having an income of £45,000. This helps amend the algorithmic variables to produce the desired result but more importantly explains in easy-to-understand terms how the decision has been reached. Furthermore, counterfactuals help promote fairness by identifying variables that cause discrimination such as on the grounds of race, sex and gender, or indeed intersectional variations of these. However, Wachter et al. (2017) provides the counterfactual explanations in relation to GDPR which does not appear to offer a legal right to an explanation and does not apply to competent authorities such as the police to prevent, investigate, detect or prosecute individuals for crimes. For this reason, it is important for the UK government to improve its regulatory regime to cover the gaps in current legislation.

TECHNOLOGICAL ISSUES IN MISIDENTIFICATION

FRT surveillance has been highly scrutinised due to its ability to catch a sea of people, including those who are not on police watchlists, potentially invading our fundamental rights of privacy and peaceful assembly, using the justification of detecting and deterring crime. Arguably, FRT is an extension of Foucault's (1977) panopticon prison design theory, the difference is that instead of being observed by police guards behind a prison wall, everyone, whether criminal or not, freely going about their everyday business are now being monitored by the police, sometimes without their prior knowledge, I call this the 'open prison design'.

Although there is no universally accepted definition for FRT it can generally be agreed that these technologies use unique cameras designed to scan the facial features of individuals captured by the eye of the camera and form biometric maps of faces (also known as data sets). These maps are then fed through the special computer algorithm to see if there is a potential match against a bespoke 'watch list' that has been created by a police force. Watch lists are a back-end function that power AI front end applications. They consist of images extracted from the Police National Database ('PNC') and other intelligence sources. Front end technologies such as cameras, are then deployed widely in public places including peaceful protests, carnivals, sports events and more recently during the Coronation of King Charles III to scan as many people as possible that come within its vision.

Misidentification Issues

FRT has well documented problems principally concerning the misidentification of individuals. Problems include, using watch lists that are biased and police officers making decisions to stop individuals without matches being verified first. This was most recently highlighted in an incident in early 2024 where a black British man, Shaun Thompson, was stopped and questioned by police for 30 minutes following an incorrect match of his biometric facial data against a bespoke police watch list. Consequently, Shaun Thompson and Silki Carlo, the director of Big Brother Watch, a human rights campaign group, instructed barristers from Matrix Chambers on a judicial review of live FRT cameras deployed by Metropolitan Police in early 2024. This confirms Buolamwini and Gebru's (2018) findings that FRT skin classification algorithms perform less well when identifying darker males in comparison to lighter males. This creates a double jeopardy for black people who, at the back end of FRT, are subject to an institutionally racist police service and are more likely to be placed on police watchlists as indicated by GVM and the Casey Review. Alternatively, at front end of FRT black people are more prone to misidentification than white faces. Therefore, it is arguable that FRT magnifies the already existing problems with police racism. This may explain why technology superpowers such as Amazon, IBM and Microsoft have stopped selling FRT technologies to police forces.

On the contrary, the National Physical Laboratory conducted a study on behalf of Metropolitan Police on the accuracy of the FRT technology used by the force called NeoFace® Watch. It concluded that there had been a huge improvement in the accuracy of the FRT systems when deployed in different locations. This claim is supported by the private supplier of the technology, NEC Software Solutions UK (2024), which confidently states the system *'is designed to find a needle in a haystack'* (p.2). However, University of Essex researchers, Fussey and Murray (2019) state that only 8 matches were accurate out of the 42 matches flagged by the live FRT algorithms used by the Metropolitan Police in the 6 trials that ran from June 2018 to February 2019. The lack of consensus on the accuracy of the technology questions its reliability in detecting and deterring crime and suggests a sizeable amount of caution needs to be upheld before further rollout.

BIG DATA AND THE WATCHLIST

Big data generally refers to the gathering of large amounts of data from different sources. In the context of policing, this includes data obtained from crime reports, witness statements, victim statements, custody records, investigations, intelligence sources and online data relating to criminals, victims, witnesses and suspects. The data collected is used to train computer algorithms to form trends and patterns, predict and prevent future crimes, identify criminals and which locations crimes are likely to take place. Leslie et al. (2021) argue AI algorithms used in machine learning to predict patterns and trends are only as good as the information used to teach them. Therefore, if the information is already incorrect or contains biases then this may certainly lead to racial profiling, gender inequality and further discrimination against already marginalised populations. This view illustrates that racial profiling, and discrimination may already exist in the data used to train algorithms which can be seen as a by-product of police culture and attitudes at the time the data is collected. In the UK this is especially problematic given repeated findings of institutional racism, misogyny and harm caused to LGBTQ+ communities and citizens both within and from British policing.

In the context of FRT surveillance, police watch lists consist of images of individuals already held by the police from custody records and images provided by public bodies, private companies, individuals and other law enforcement agencies. According to the College of Policing (2022) guidance on watchlists, they should be compiled using intelligence authorised by an approving officer, related to a police objective and operation. Those that can be included on a watchlist are suspects of a criminal offence; or a person who is due to commit an offence; people on bail conditions; victims of crime; missing people; wanted people; or those that are at risk of harm. This illustrates the wide discretion provided to police officers about who to identify and watch, when to intervene and where to place the FRT surveillance systems on a larger scale. This wide discretion is arguably problematic given the reported research on bias and discrimination within policing. This more critical view of the discretion afforded to policing was supported by the Court of Appeal in R (on the application of Edward Bridges) v Chief Constable of South Wales [2020]. The Court stated the discretion given to individual police officers as regards to who to include on the watchlist and where to place FRT was too wide. The Surveillance Camera Code of Practice ('SCCP') and Standard Operating Procedure ('SOP') used by South Wales Police were found to be inadequate legal frameworks. Consequently, from a human rights lens, the interference with Bridges privacy right under Article 8(1) of the ECHR was not in accordance with the law as required by Article 8(2) of the ECHR. This appears to strengthen the argument that new legislation is required to curb wide police discretion used in FRT surveillance processes which do not hold the police accountable for discriminatory practices in interests of detecting and deterring crime.

The above findings all suggest the deployment of AI in law enforcement may not apply equally to everyone, meaning AI is potentially unfair, unethical, unlawful, biased and discriminatory in its application and so needs urgent recommendations to deal with its manifest problems. Workable solutions could include independent human oversight committees, human rights impact assessments, police training programmes on bias, bad data and how FRT algorithms work.

HUMAN RIGHTS CONSIDERATIONS

A human rights perspective is helpful to the analysis in this chapter because of the significant concerns FRT surveillance is raising in relation to fundamental human rights of citizens. Current debates on the topic highlight the highly invasive nature of FRT surveillance on every day private life as the technology captures the facial images of people in public places without their express consent. It also deters individuals from sharing their opinions and attending peaceful protests due to the fear of being criminalised and discriminates against marginalised and ethnic minority groups in society. Therefore, I call for legislation that is proactive rather than reactive towards human right breaches as this will help balance the scales of justice more fairly in support of human rights.

The Human Rights Act 1998 ('HRA') incorporates the rights and freedoms derived from the ECHR into domestic law in the UK. It is well established that surveillance conducted by the police through FRT engages important individual rights such as private life (Article 8(1) of the ECHR), freedom of expression (Article 10(1) of the ECHR), assembly and association (Article 11(1) of the ECHR) which are commonly referred to as qualified rights. This means the rights are not absolute and can be restricted by non-identical limitations set in the ECHR. The law authorises the police, being a public authority, to interfere with these rights subject to the interference being for a legitimate aim, necessary and proportionate in a democratic society. This is a balancing exercise that requires a thorough analysis of the doctrines of proportionality derived from law and the margin of appreciation advocated by the European Court of Human Rights ('ECtHR') based in Strasbourg. Section 6(1) of the HRA 1998 places an obligation on a public authority such as the police to not act in a way that is incompatible with the convention rights. A failure to act can also be seen as not adhering to convention rights unless domestic legislation states otherwise. As outlined earlier, the effects of police surveillance through FRT is that it is discriminatory when choosing who to put on the watch list and where to place FRT despite guidance in place which is legally unenforceable. FRT also causes a chilling effect deterring individuals from exercising their rights. There is strong evidence from academics, researchers and human rights organisations to suggest that fundamental human rights are being violated by using FRT surveillance in policing in England and Wales.

FRT surveillance is advantageous for private technology companies who develop FRT and sell these to public law enforcement agencies making a healthy profit in a low competition market. On the contrary, individuals want to protect their fundamental rights to private and family life under Article 8(1) of the ECHR, freedom of expression under Article 10(1) of the ECHR, freedom of assembly and freedom of association with others under Article 11(1) of the ECHR without being unlawfully discriminated against on grounds of sex, race and colour under Article 14 of the ECHR. However, FRT surveillance used by police forces is known to be highly invasive on every day private life as the technology captures the facial images of people in public places without their express consent. It deters individuals from expressing their opinions and attending peaceful protests due to the fear of being criminalised often referred to as the chilling effect and discriminates against marginalised and ethnic minority groups in society. To add to this controversy, no direct legislation applies to FRT surveillance undertaken by police forces in England and Wales that safeguards political and civil rights of individuals.

The following paragraphs focus on three fundamental human rights stated in the Convention; the right to respect for private and family life (Article 8(1) of the ECHR); freedom of expression (Article 10(1) of the ECHR) and freedom of assembly and association (Article 11(1) of the ECHR) which are all qualified rights protected by both the ECHR on an international level and the HRA at a domestic level. The parasitic right of prohibition of discrimination (Article 14 of the ECHR) which is dependent on the interference with one or more of the fundamental rights stated in the Convention will also be explored.

Article 8 of the ECHR

Article 8(1) of the ECHR states that 'everyone has the right to respect for his private and family life, his home and correspondence' (p.11). However, under Article 8(2) of the ECHR this is a qualified right which means public authorities can intervene with the right as long as it is:

'in accordance with the law and is necessary in a democratic society in the interests of national security, public safety or the economic well-being of the country and for the prevention of disorder or crime' (p.11).

This is a balancing exercise that requires the police to justify interference with the right to privacy by ensuring the deployment of FRT surveillance is in accordance with the law and is necessary in a democratic society in the interests of one or more of the provisions contained in Article 8(2) of the ECHR.

Expectations of private life differ between people, temporally and geographically, such that the definition of 'private life' has been open to contestation. Warren and Brandeis (1890) define privacy as 'the right to be let alone' (p.1).

In Von Hannover v Germany (2004), the Court stated:

'The guarantee afforded by Article 8 of the convention is primarily intended to ensure the development, without outside interference, of the personality of each individual in his relations with other human beings...there is therefore a zone of interaction of a person with others, even in a public context, which may fall within the scope of private life' (p.50).

On the other hand, in R (Razgar) v Secretary of State for the Home Department [2004], Lord Bingham of Cornwall said private life under Article 8 ECHR includes 'those features which are integral to a person's identity or ability to function socially as a person' (p. 9). In Pretty v United Kingdom [2002], the Court said, *'Article 8 also protects a right to personal development, and the right to establish and develop relationships with other human beings and the outside world'* (p. 61).

FRT surveillance has the potential to be highly intrusive on private life by scanning the facial features of crowds of people going about their usual everyday business in public places without their express or implied consent. The biometric facial data of every individual who is captured by the eye of the camera is irrelevant to the police, especially if the person is not a criminal and not on the bespoke police watchlist. However, this sensitive data is processed automatically by a machine that cannot be held accountable for its actions. Consequently, ethnic minorities and marginalised groups in society begin to self-govern their behaviour due to the threat of being silently watched by FRT. Human Rights campaign groups such as Liberty and Big Brother Watch have called for a complete ban on the use of the technology which is perceived to be highly intrusive and invasive on private life and is seen as a form of mass state surveillance. FRT surveillance is here to stay and is likely to become more advanced and sophisticated in the future, therefore a more robust approach would be to introduce new legislation for FRT that would protect human rights.

In the case of R (on the application of Bridges) v Chief Constable of South Wales Police & Ors [2020], the Court of Appeal ('CA') ruled that South Wales Police had breached the appellants right to respect for private and family life under Article 8(1) of the ECHR when they used an FRT camera in his hometown of Cardiff. The Court found that South Wales Police had a high level of discretionary power in deciding who would be included in the watchlist and where to deploy FRT when applying Article 8(2) of ECHR. The SCCP and SOP used by South Wales Police were found to be inadequate legal frameworks. This ruling illustrates there were insufficient legal rules and guidelines in place to monitor personal data processing and the use of FRT in policing. This case exemplifies the level of state power and control over innocent citizens by state institutions to detect and deter crime in marginalised societies. It further proves there are significant gaps in existing legal and regulatory frameworks which do not protect an individual's right to privacy. Therefore, to protect against potential human right breaches in the future much stronger legal and regulatory frameworks are necessary to deal with the problems inherent in FRT Surveillance by the police.

Yeung et al (2019) argue that an international human rights framework is the best standard that can be achieved for more ethical use of AI. Human rights should be considered at every stage of the design, development, testing, monitoring and deployment of AI technologies to deal with existing human rights concerns. This will allow for trial and error, and algorithmic decision-making systems can be adjusted to ensure human rights are adhered to. Additionally, robust legal rules should be implemented that enforce the framework alongside regulatory guidance and oversight.

Critically, current human rights frameworks have proven insufficient to deal with novel technologies such as FRT, whose deployment by UK law enforcement has repeatedly been found to breach several of these human rights.

Articles 10 and 11 of the ECHR

Article 10(1) of the ECHR states:

'Everyone has the right to freedom of expression. This right shall include freedom to hold opinions and to receive an impart information and ideas without interference by public authority and regardless of frontiers' (p.12).

This right is subject to restrictions in Article 10(2) of the ECHR *'as are prescribed by law and are necessary in a democratic society in the interests of national security...or the prevention of disorder or crime...'* (p.12).

Article 11(1) states *'everyone has the right to freedom of assembly and to freedom of association with others, including the right to form and to join trade unions for the protection of his interests'* (p.12). This right is subject to restrictions in Article 11(2):

'as are prescribed by law and are necessary in a democratic society in the interests of national security or public safety, for the prevention of disorder or crime...' (p.12).

Therefore, the law authorises the police, being a public authority, to interfere with these rights subject to the interference being for a legitimate aim, necessary and proportionate in a democratic society.

The Universal Declaration of Human Rights (1948) ('UDHR') states the freedom of expression includes 'the freedom to hold opinions and convey information and ideas through any medium irrespective of any borders' (art.19). Alternatively, Belyaeva et al (2010) define freedom of assembly as *'the international and temporary presence of a number of individuals in a public place for a common expressive purpose'* (p.15). On the other hand, Smith and Anker (2005) state freedom of association 'enables individuals to come together and collectively to express, promote, pursue and even defend common interests' (p.18).

FRT surveillance is being used extensively by the police at large public events from the Notting Hill carnival, Pro-Palestine protests, Formula 1 Grand Prix to football stadiums and shopping centres. The deployment of technology has been found to cause a chilling effect whereby individuals behave differently because they are conscious they are being watched by the police. They stop going to public places where FRT is being used due to the fear of being labelled a "criminal" as they can no longer remain anonymous.

Rautenberg and Murray (2024) argue that intimidating AI surveillance by the state forces change in the conduct of individuals because of the fear of being watched and the potential repercussions of behaving abnormally. This prevents individuals from developing their identity in creative ways and they simply continue complying with the status quo. This challenges the notion of a good life as individuals are unable to flourish through creativity, self -development and expression as there is no autonomy of the individual to determine how they flourish. They confidently state that human rights law is incapable of regulating intrusive AI surveillance by the state and protecting against the adverse impact of the chilling effect on democratic values such as peaceful assembly (Article 11 of the ECHR) and freedom of expression (Article 10 of the ECHR). They suggest the proposed solution to this problem is for human rights law to acknowledge a digital economy and to adapt accordingly by including potential harms to individuals to human rights compliance assessments.

Nussbaum (2011) articulates for a person to flourish in life and advance creative and intellectual capabilities they must have the autonomy to express their thoughts, opinions, beliefs and values freely. To live a good life a person should have the confidence to speak up individually or as part of a group in support of an idea or vision, without state interference. AI surveillance technologies should not intervene and harm these capabilities by triggering the chilling effect. This illustrates the devastating effects of AI surveillance technology on the freedom of expression and peaceful assembly as individuals are unable to be their true selves and develop their identities. Individuals appear to merge their appearance and behaviour with the expected norms of society at the cost of their freedom to think, speak and act freely.

Solove (2007) appears to contradict traditional views on the 'chilling effect' by arguing that it is difficult to know the extent of the chilling effect on actions and behaviours as there is little empirical evidence on how people behave and express themselves in the absence of state surveillance. Despite well documented concerns about the chilling effects of FRT surveillance in literature, Solove has a valid point.

Article 14 of the ECHR

Article 14 of the ECHR states the rights and freedoms in the Convention will apply without discrimination on grounds of *'sex, race, colour, language, religion, political or other opinion…'* (p.13). Therefore, this Article is not a standalone right and is designed to come into play when the enjoyment of a substantive right or freedom as stated in the Convention is interfered with, for example, by discriminatory rules, measures, policies and/or practices directed at a particular race or sex. This is highlighted in the following paragraphs in relation to the blatant biases and discriminatory data inherent in FRT.

Oswald and Paul (2024) refer to bias as unlawful discrimination on grounds of protected characteristics which include race, sex, gender, age and disability which arise more particularly in criminal justice cases. In R v Gough [1993] Lord Goff recognises unconscious bias in decisions; *'even-though a person may in good faith believe he is acting impartially; his mind may unconsciously be affected by bias'*(para.14). This reiterates the conundrum of subjective police bias in deciding who to watch, where and when to intervene once an outcome is made by FRT technologies.

Yeung (2018) argues that discrimination and bias can arise from the use of machine learning algorithms in a number of ways. Bias can arise from; developers who hold personal opinions when building the technology; the type of model used in creating the system; the data sets used to train machine algorithms and from the deployment of the technology. This was illustrated in the case of P E Manjang v Uber Eats UK Ltd and others [2022] which was funded by the Equality and Human Rights Commission. This case concerned automated FRT and detection technology used on an Uber Eats App to verify Manjang's identity as an Uber driver which was found to be biased and racially discriminatory by a UK Employment Tribunal. This case illustrates how the design, development and use of innovative technology is failing to consider and risk assess the impact on fundamental human rights despite clear guidance in Article 14 of the ECHR which prohibits discrimination on grounds of race, colour and other characteristics. This case signifies there is a need for a new AI specific legal and regulatory model framework that makes it compulsory for technology companies to consider, and risk assess the impact of FRT on human rights and how any potential risks can be mitigated.

EMERGING SOLUTIONS

This chapter advocates for a protective stance in favour of human rights and advocates for a more comprehensive legal and regulatory framework to be introduced that directly deals with FRT surveillance in policing and safeguards against, potential, human rights breaches. There appear to be greater benefits in legislation that is proactive rather than reactive towards human right breaches and caters for future technological advancements. This will help balance the scales of justice in support of human rights.

The European Union ('EU') has implemented the world's first legislation regulating artificial intelligence. The EU (AI) Act ('the Act') came into force on 1 August 2024 to deal with the potential dangers, risks and threats posed by the development and use of AI on EU citizens. The Act uses a risk-based approach to AI systems to promote its philosophy of trustworthy AI. There are four levels of risk in the use of AI under the Act: unacceptable risk; high risk, limited risk and minimal risk. Article 5 of the Act makes clear that unacceptable risks are totally prohibited such as social scoring; FRT databases; the categorisation of biometric data leading to an inference on sensitive data including race, political affiliation, trade union membership, religion, sex etc and real time biometric identification operated remotely unless an exception applies.

High-risk AI systems are heavily regulated by the Act, according to Article 6(2) these include but are not limited to biometric identification systems which are remotely operated and permitted under law; the categorisation of sensitive biometric data permitted under law; emotion recognition systems and AI systems used by or on behalf of law enforcement agencies for profiling purposes for the detection, investigation or prosecution of crime. Articles 8 to 17 impose additional obligations on the providers of high-risk AI systems such as having a risk management system; keeping records; governance of data; instructions for deployers on how to use the AI system; a requirement for human oversight and technical and quality management systems to ensure compliance. Therefore, the Act's effect on FRT is limited as it does not totally prohibit its use by law enforcement agencies despite its sensitive biometric nature. However, due to being a relatively new act there is no existing empirical evidence to illustrate that these assessments will prevent or stop human right breaches in the future from the use of FRT surveillance.

Gikay (2024) argues the Act is not useful as it aims to regulate AI systems across various sectors and categorises AI systems according to levels of risks without thinking about how AI technology will evolve, any false perceptions, how likely the risks are and political influence on the non-regulation of AI. The scope of the Act includes organisations that are not based in the EU but provide AI systems to the EU and where outcomes outside the EU are used in the EU, compliance can be expensive for organisations that provide/deploy AI systems outside the EU. Critics argue the increase in EU requirements could potentially stifle innovation. Furthermore, the Act does not capture AI systems that do not fall into one of the four categories even where serious risks are posed.

The UK government is taking a pro-innovative, global leadership approach to artificial intelligence and has not yet passed any regulatory legislation. Critically, it is arguable that the UK appears to be playing a game of 'catch me if you can' with

AI by reacting to fast paced technological developments rather than being proactive in preparing for future developments and uses of AI by developing a comprehensive legal and regulatory model framework. The Brussels effect whereby other countries begin to follow the leadership of the European Union in passing relevant legislation on artificial intelligence has not yet occurred in the sphere of AI regulation. This has led some human rights organisations to critically argue there is no lawful basis for using FRT which has discrimination built into algorithms. This is why AI specific legal and regulatory frameworks are encouraged to deal with the existing gaps in the law.

Despite the lack of AI-specific legislation there is a raft of primary legislation and statutory instruments that indirectly apply to the deployment and use of FRT technologies by UK Police forces. These include the common law and statutory duties of the police to detect and deter crime, the power to take, retain and disclose photographs under section 64A of the Police and Criminal Evidence Act 1984 (albeit there is no mention of photographs taken in public places) and the updated SCCP introduced under sections 29 to 31 of Protection of Freedoms Act 2012 ('PoFA 2012') relating to overt surveillance by public authorities. Additionally, there is regulatory guidance from the government's action plan; police practice guidelines such as the Model for Responsible Innovation and Authorised Professional Practice; SOP; local policy documents; a covenant for using AI in policing; codes of ethics; United Nations ('UN') model protocol and toolkit; privacy and data protection impact assessments and algorithm transparency recording standards ('ATRS') which directly apply to the use of FRT in policing. However, with the Labour government in power and the continued quest to make Great Britain an AI superpower there is a possibility of further soft regulations being introduced to deal with current gaps in legislation. Industry specific regulators such as the Information Commissioners Office ('ICO') and The Equality and Human Rights Commission ('EHRC'), respectively, provide guidance for complying with data protection and human rights legislation. Albeit there is little guidance on how public authorities using artificial intelligence can comply with the Equality Act 2010.

It is arguable that the above non-statutory initiatives are limited in effect as they are not legally binding and therefore not enforceable. However, on the other hand, the ICO 'which is the UK regulator for information rights has a stronger position. It has extensive power to issue fines for non-compliance with data protection principles which could potentially act as an effective deterrent for privacy violations if access to personal data is involved. However, these fines are likely to be issued after a data protection breach has already occurred. Therefore, this measure is reactive rather than proactive in preventing breaches. By this time the damage has already been done. Therefore, a new regulatory framework could better address problems associated with FRT technologies.

REFERENCES

Ada Lovelace Institute & The Alan Turing Institute. (2022). How do people feel about AI? A nationally representative survey of public attitudes to artificial intelligence in Britain. In Executive Summary. https://www.adalovelaceinstitute.org/wp-content/uploads/2023/06/Ada-Lovelace-Institute-The-Alan-Turing-Institute-How-do-people-feel-about-AI.pdf

Amazon Web Services Inc. (2024). What is Artificial Intelligence (AI)? https://aws.amazon.com/what-is/artificial-intelligence/#:~:text=Artificial%20intelligence%20(AI)%20is%20a,and%20make%20data%2Dbased%20predictions

Amnesty International. (2022). Ban the scan - Amnesty International. https://www.amnesty.org/en/petition/ban-the-scan-petition

Bathaee, Y. (2018). The artificial intelligence black box and the failure of intent and causation. *Harvard Journal of Law & Technology*, *31*(2), 905. https://www.questia.com/library/journal/1G1-547758123/the-artificial-intelligence-black-box-and-the-failure

Big Brother Watch. (n.d). Landmark legal challenges launched against facial recognition after police and retailer misidentifications. https://bigbrotherwatch.org.uk/press-releases/landmark-legal-challenges-launched-against-facial-recognition-after-police-and-retailer-misidentifications/

Big Brother Watch. (n.d). Stop Facial Recognition - Big Brother Watch. https://bigbrotherwatch.org.uk/campaigns/stop-facial-recognition

Brożek, B., Furman, M., Jakubiec, M., & Kucharzyk, B. (2023). The black box problem revisited. Real and imaginary challenges for automated legal decision making. *Artificial Intelligence and Law*, *32*(2), 427–440. DOI: 10.1007/s10506-023-09356-9

Buolamwini, J., & Gebru, T. (2018). Gender Shades: Intersectional accuracy Disparities in commercial gender classification. Proceedings of Machine Learning Research, 81, 1–15. https://proceedings.mlr.press/v81/buolamwini18a/buolamwini18a.pdf

College of Policing. (2022). Watchlist. https://www.college.police.uk/app/live-facial-recognition/watchlist

College of Policing. (n.d.). Code of Ethics. https://www.college.police.uk/ethics/code-of-ethics

Crenshaw, K. (1991). Mapping the Margins: Intersectionality, Identity Politics, and Violence against Women of Color. *Stanford Law Review*, *43*(6), 1241. DOI: 10.2307/1229039

EHRC. (2022). Artificial intelligence in public services. https://www.equalityhumanrights.com/guidance/artificial-intelligence-public-services?returnurl=https%3A%2F%2Fwww.equalityhumanrights.com%2Fsearch%3Fkeys%3DARTIFICIAL%2BINTELLIGENCE%2BIN%2BPUBLIC%2BPLACES

Foucault, M. (1977). *Discipline and punish: the birth of the prison*. Penguin Group.

Fussey, P., & Murray, D. (2019). Independent report on the London Metropolitan Police Service's trial of live facial recognition technology. In University of Essex Human Rights Centre. https://repository.essex.ac.uk/24946/1/London-Met-Police-Trial-of-Facial-Recognition-Tech-Report-2.pdf

Gikay, A. A. (2024). Risks, innovation, and adaptability in the UK's incrementalism versus the European Union's comprehensive artificial intelligence regulation. *International Journal of Law and Information Technology*, *32*, eaae013. Advance online publication. DOI: 10.1093/ijlit/eaae013

GOV.UK. (1984). Police and Criminal Evidence Act 1984, s. 64A https://www.legislation.gov.uk/ukpga/1984/60/section/64A

GOV.UK. (1998). Human Rights Act 1998, s. 6. Available at: Legislation.gov.uk. https://www.legislation.gov.uk/ukpga/1998/42/contents

GOV.UK. (2024). The model for responsible innovation. https://www.gov.uk/government/publications/the-model-for-responsible-innovation/the-model-for-responsible-innovation and Live facial recognition.

ICO. (2019). Information Commissioner's Opinion: The use of live facial recognition technology by law enforcement in public places. https://ico.org.uk/media/about-the-ico/documents/2616184/live-frt-law-enforcement-opinion-20191031.pdf

Leslie, D., Burr, C., Aitken, M., Cowls, J., Katell, M., & Briggs, M. (2021). Artificial intelligence, Human Rights, Democracy, and the Rule of Law: A primer. SSRN Electronic Journal. DOI: 10.2139/ssrn.3817999

National Police Chiefs' Council (NPCC). (2024). NPCC welcomes first ever lead for Artificial Intelligence (AI). https://news.npcc.police.uk/releases/npcc-welcomes-first-ever-lead-for-artificial-intelligence-ai

NEC Software Solutions. (2024). Facial Recognition Software. https://www.necsws.com/solutions/evidence-insights/facial-recognition-software/

Nussbaum, M. C. (2011). Creating capabilities: The human development approach. *Choice (Chicago, Ill.)*, *49*(02), 49–0784. DOI: 10.5860/CHOICE.49-0784

Oswald, M., Paterson-Young, C., McBride, P., Maher, M., Calder, M., Gill, G., Tiarks, E., & Noble, W. (2024). Ethical review to support Responsible Artificial Intelligence (AI) in policing: A preliminary study of West Midlands Police's specialist data ethics review committee. Northumbria University Research Portal. https://researchportal.northumbria.ac.uk/en/publications/ethical-review-to-support-responsible-artificial-intelligence-ai-

Oswald, M., & Paul, A. (2024). Bias. Handbook of Digital Criminology (De Gruyter, 2024, Forthcoming). https://papers.ssrn.com/sol3/papers.cfm?abstract_id=4738337

P E Manjang v Uber Eats UK Ltd and others (2022). Employment Tribunal, 3206212/2021. https://assets.publishing.service.gov.uk/media/62dab66b8fa8f5649dbef494/Mr_P_E_Manjang_-v-_Uber_Eats_UK_Ltd___Others_-_3206212_2021_-_Preliminary_Judgment.pdf

Parliament, U. K. (2021). Police Powers: An Introduction. House of Commons Library. https://commonslibrary.parliament.uk/research-briefings/cbp-8637/

Pretty v United Kingdom (2002) 35 EHRR 1, 61

R (on the application of Edward Bridges) v The Chief Constable of South Wales Police & Ors [2020] EWCA Civ 1058

R (Razgar) v Secretary of State for the Home Department [2004] 2 AC 368, 383, 9

Radiya-Dixit, E., & Neff, G. (2023). A sociotechnical audit: Assessing police use of facial recognition. *ACM Conference on Fairness, Accountability, and Transparency*, 1334–1346. https://doi.org/DOI: 10.1145/3593013.3594084

Rautenberg, N., & Murray, D. (2024). Making tangible the Long-Term harm linked to the chilling effects of AI-enabled surveillance: Can human flourishing inform human rights? *Human Rights Review (Piscataway, N.J.)*, *25*(3), 293–315. DOI: 10.1007/s12142-024-00727-6

Richardson, R., Schultz, J., & Crawford, K. (2019). Dirty data, Bad predictions: How civil rights violations impact police data, predictive policing systems, and justice. New York University Law Review Online, 192

Sir William Macpherson of Cluny. (1999). The Stephen Lawrence Inquiry Report of an Inquiry https://assets.publishing.service.gov.uk/media/5a7c2af540f0b645ba3c7202/4262.pdf

Solove, D. J. (2007). The First Amendment as criminal procedure. SSRN Electronic Journal. https://scholarship.law.gwu.edu/faculty_publications/946

The Office of the Police Chief Scientific Adviser (OPCSA). (n.d.). Science and Technology in Policing. Covenant for using Artificial intelligence (AI) in policing. https://science.police.uk/delivery/resources/covenant-for-using-artificial-intelligence-ai-in-policing/#:~:text=This%20Covenant%20outlines%20a%20set,Council%20on%2028%20September%202023

The white mask. (2024). The Guardian. https://www.theguardian.com/technology/audio/2024/mar/18/episode-5-the-white-mask

Turing, A. (2004). Computing Machinery and Intelligence (1950). In B. Jack Copeland (Ed.), The Essential Turing Seminal Writings in Computing, Logic, Philosophy, Artificial Intelligence United Nations. (2024). Practical toolkit for law enforcement officials to promote and protect human rights in the context of peaceful protests. https://www.ohchr.org/en/documents/tools-and-resources/practical-toolkit-law-enforcement-officials-promote-and-protect-human

United Nations General Assembly. (1948). Universal declaration of human rights, Article 19. (General Assembly Resolution 217A). https://www.un.org/en/about-us/universal-declaration-of-human-rights

R v Gough (1993). 2 WLR 883

Van Den Anker, R. K. S. C. (2005). The essentials of human rights. CiNii Books. https://ci.nii.ac.jp/ncid/BA75808387

Von Hannover v Germany (2004) 40 EHRR 23

Wachter, S., & Mittelstadt, B. (2018). A Right to Reasonable Inferences: Re-Thinking Data Protection Law in the Age of Big Data and AI. Columbia Business Law Review, 2019(2). https://papers.ssrn.com/sol3/papers.cfm?abstract_id=3248829

Wachter, S., Mittelstadt, S., & Russell, C. (2017). Counterfactual explanations without opening the black box: automated decisions and the GDPR. SSRN Electronic Journal, 844. https://doi.org/DOI: 10.2139/ssrn.3063289

Warren, S. D., & Brandeis, L. D. (1890). The right to privacy. *Harvard Law Review*, *4*(5), 193. DOI: 10.2307/1321160

Yeung, K. (2018). A study of the implications of advanced digital Technologies (Including AI Systems) for the concept of responsibility within a human rights framework. SSRN Electronic Journal. https://papers.ssrn.com/sol3/Delivery.cfm/SSRN_ID3286027_code830937.pdf?abstractid=3286027&mirid=1

Yeung, K., Howes, A., & Pogrebna, G. (2019). AI Governance by Human Rights-Centred Design, Deliberation and Oversight: An end to ethics washing. SSRN Electronic Journal. DOI: 10.2139/ssrn.3435011

Chapter 8
Crime Hotspot Detection in Streaming Data: A Multi-Factor Approach Using DenStream and CluStream

Apiwe Macingwane
http://orcid.org/0000-0002-7062-907X
University of the Western Cape, South Africa

Omowunmi E. Isafiade
http://orcid.org/0000-0002-3028-6180
University of the Western Cape, South Africa

ABSTRACT

Crime hotspot detection is crucial for identifying high-crime areas and guiding resource allocation. Within hotspots, crimes differ in severity and require weighted treatment. This chapter introduces a multi-factor crime type weight-based ranking mechanism for classifying crimes in streaming clustering models. Two algorithms are used: DenStream, applying exponential decay with potential and outlier micro-clusters, and CluStream, using an online–offline framework with pyramidal snapshots. Crime data from the Stats SA Western Cape dataset was streamed in 50-record batches. The core contribution is a three-factor weight Wi combining frequency, severity, and reporting consistency, ensuring hotspot ranking reflects crime volume, seriousness, and reliability. Models were evaluated using internal/external metrics, cluster count, time, and memory. Results show CluStream yields more compact and accurate clusters than DenStream, though slower, making it suitable for deployment. This method supports proactive resource allocation through efficient streaming clustering and weighted hotspot analysis.

DOI: 10.4018/979-8-3373-5228-2.ch008

INTRODUCTION

Crime hotspot detection is the process of identifying geographic areas experiencing high crime rates to assist with strategic resource deployment and law enforcement planning (Zhang et al., 2023). Hotspots can be identified through periodic batch clustering of historical data or real-time streaming of reported crime data, enabling law enforcement to address real-world problems (Zhang et al., 2023). The reported crimes are classified based on their severity and harm to victims (Baek et al., 2021; Curtis-Ham, 2022). Understanding the risk assessment within a hotspot enables faster and more informed responses to dangerous situations and more efficient resource allocation.

Clustering, an unsupervised machine learning (ML) technique, has emerged as a promising data-driven solution for hotspot analysis, grouping data into clusters based on intrinsic patterns and similarities without requiring pre-labelled data (Hosseinzadeh et al., 2022). Several clustering models have been widely applied in crime prevention, each with unique strengths (Sahu, 2022; Pramanik et al., 2023a; Kaza et al., 2005; Zubaroğlu & Atalay, 2021). However, static clustering methods such as Density-Based Spatial Clustering of Applications with Noise (DBSCAN) and Ordering Points To Identify the Clustering Structure (OPTICS) face significant limitations when applied to streaming data (Sahu, 2022). These methods suffer from reliance on manual parameter tuning, limited real-time implementation capabilities, fragmented evaluation metrics, insufficient integration of diverse data sources, and the absence of end-to-end proactive adaptive systems capable of effectively handling the dynamic nature of streaming crime data, where patterns evolve continuously and require immediate response (Ding et al., 2015; Ahmed et al., 2020; Zubaroğlu & Atalay, 2021; Sahu, 2022). Streaming clustering models present a promising technique for handling large datasets and real-world scenarios (Zubaroğlu & Atalay, 2021). However, most clustering models focus on forming clusters rather than adopting a prioritised clustering approach.

While existing work predominantly treats all crimes within a hotspot as equally significant or relies solely on incident frequency for prioritisation (Butt et al., 2021; Cesario et al., 2023; Sahu, 2022), this research aims to address a critical gap by integrating crime-type characteristics directly into the clustering evaluation framework (Sherman et al., 2016; Mohler et al., 2020; Wu & Meghanathan, 2023). Traditional hotspot detection methods identify where crimes concentrate, but few studies consider which types of crimes dominate each hotspot and how serious those crime compositions are.

Hence, this research introduces a three-factor weighting mechanism that combines frequency, severity, and reporting consistency to produce operationally meaningful, ranked hotspot clusters, enabling law enforcement to distinguish between hotspots requiring different intervention strategies. Furthermore, streaming clustering models (DenStream and CluStream) were employed to detect hotspots in incoming crime data, and a crime-type weight-based ranking mechanism was applied, integrating severity, frequency, and reporting consistency to generate weighted clusters for prioritisation. The dataset includes incident crime records derived from Stats SA crime data, along with police station coordinates (Heiduk, 2017). The models were evaluated using standard metrics such as Silhouette Score, Davies–Bouldin Index, Calinski–Harabasz Index, Adjusted Rand Index, Normalised Mutual Information, number of clusters, execution time, and memory usage, designed to assess both clustering quality and practical performance.

The experimental design is intended to deliver scalable, real-time performance on dynamic crime data streams while providing data-driven analytical accuracy for efficient, priority-based resource allocation (Cesario et al., 2023; Butt et al., 2021; Xie et al., 2022). By combining streaming clustering with multi-factor crime-type weighting, this work bridges the gap between spatial pattern detection and operational decision-making, offering a more actionable and context-aware approach to crime hotspot analysis. Importantly, the temporal analysis presented here is envisaged as a continuous analytical model that can inform spatial deployment decisions, thereby linking the efficiency of real-time temporal processing with the practical requirements of spatial resource allocation in policing environments.

RELATED WORK

Over the years, there have been significant improvements in the application of ML techniques to crime analysis (Isafiade & Bagula, 2017), with clustering models proposed as a promising method for hotspot detection (Dlamini, 2017; Sahu, 2022; Tulumello & Iapaolo, 2022; Pramanik et al., 2023b; Safat et al., 2021). Once hotspots are detected, the grouped data can be leveraged to enhance the decision-making capabilities of law enforcement agencies (Ezugwu et al., 2022; Ezugwu et al., 2021; Bhattacharjee & Mitra, 2021). Ranking these detected hotspots allows for more efficient resource allocation (Mohler et al., 2020). This section provides an overview of the literature and existing work that laid the groundwork for this research.

Hotspot Detection

Hotspot detection relies on various clustering algorithms, including partitional, density-based, model-based, grid-based, and streaming approaches (Oyewole & Thopil, 2023; Ezugwu et al., 2022; Zubaroğlu & Atalay, 2021). Appiah et al. (2022) applied a hybrid expectation–maximisation (E-M) and K-Means model to the violent crime dataset of West Midlands County (2017), using geodesic distance as the metric and evaluating performance with Bayesian Information Criterion (BIC), Sum of Squared Errors (SSE), and hotspot detection accuracy. Pramanik et al. (2023a) employed fuzzy clustering based on graph theory to detect overlapping clusters in crime reports; however, the models required sophisticated preprocessing and were parameter sensitive. Despite these limitations, the results displayed a high silhouette index and a low Davies–Bouldin Index (Pramanik et al., 2023a).

Several clustering surveys have highlighted how these techniques can be applied to hotspot detection (Appiah et al., 2022; Ezugwu et al., 2022; Zubaroğlu & Atalay, 2021; Pramanik et al., 2023a). In particular, these surveys emphasised the strengths of various models: DBSCAN, which detects arbitrary-shaped clusters; OPTICS, which handles clusters of varying densities; Hierarchical Density-Based Spatial Clustering of Applications with Noise (HDBSCAN), which extends DBSCAN to identify clusters with varying densities; and DENsity-based CLUstEring (DENCLUE), which effectively manages noise and outliers (Zhang et al., 2023; Hauchi et al., 2024; Oyewole & Thopil, 2023; Bhattacharjee & Mitra, 2021).

However, these surveys also stress the limitations of clustering methods, including parameter sensitivity, scalability issues, difficulties with dynamic or high-dimensional data, and challenges in interpretability (Zhang et al., 2023; Hauchi et al., 2024; Oyewole & Thopil, 2023; Bhattacharjee & Mitra, 2021). Despite these obstacles, DBSCAN remains one of the most influential models (Sahu, 2022). Further, research directions focus on improving efficiency, developing methods for streaming data, and exploring deep or hybrid clustering approaches, all of which show strong potential for enhancing crime hotspot detection (Oyewole & Thopil, 2023; Bhattacharjee & Mitra, 2021; Ezugwu et al., 2022).

Streaming Clustering

Real-time crime analysis requires models capable of processing continuous data streams while ensuring clustering quality and computational efficiency (Ahmed et al., 2020). Since data streams are continuous and evolving, many stream clustering models adopt a two-phase architecture consisting of an online phase and an offline phase (Ahmed et al., 2020; Tareq et al., 2021; Zubaroğlu & Atalay, 2021). The online phase generates micro-clusters, which are subsequently re-clustered in the offline phase to form macro-clusters. Models that follow this approach include CluStream, DenStream, Density-Based Clustering over Evolving Data Streams (DStream), Clustering Tree (ClusTree), and Density and Grid-Based Clustering Algorithm for Data Stream (DGStream) (Ahmed et al., 2020; Tareq et al., 2021; Zubaroğlu & Atalay, 2021; Ding et al., 2015). CluStream, developed by Aggarwal (2003), pioneered this dual-phase framework for dynamic data streams. DenStream, a density-based model extending DBSCAN, introduces time-weighted micro-clusters: potential micro-clusters (p-micro) for monitoring dense, evolving areas and outlier micro-clusters (o-micro) for capturing sparse or emerging patterns (Zubaroğlu & Atalay, 2021; Bhattacharjee & Mitra, 2021).

Ding et al. (2015) reviewed the evolution of stream clustering models such as Balanced Iterative Reducing and Clustering using Hierarchies (BIRCH), LocalSearch, Stream, and CluStream, whilst Tareq et al. (2021) conducted a systematic literature review of density grid-based clustering algorithms. Both studies identified persistent limitations, including low accuracy, difficulties with real-time extraction, challenges in handling arbitrarily shaped and uncertain data, and instability across models (Ding et al., 2015; Tareq et al., 2021). Ahmed et al. (2020) addressed these issues through an investigative experiment evaluating DGStream against DenStream, DStream, and ClusTree, finding that DGStream consistently outperformed the baselines with near-perfect purity, a higher F1-score, excellent recall, and faster runtimes. Zubaroğlu and Atalay (2021) subsequently examined newer models and emphasised trade-offs between computational complexity, clustering quality, and adaptability to dynamic data. Collectively, these studies highlight the need for standardised evaluation frameworks and suggest that advancements in self-adaptive and hybrid algorithms, deep learning, and edge computing could significantly enhance real-time stream clustering, with applications ranging from network intrusion detection to proactive crime prevention in prioritised hotspot areas (Ding et al., 2015; Tareq et al., 2021; Zubaroğlu & Atalay, 2021).

Hotspot Ranking Approaches

Beyond hotspot identification, effective crime hotspot analysis requires sophisticated ranking mechanisms to prioritise areas based on threat levels, enabling faster and more informed responses with efficient resource allocation (Mohler et al., 2020; Baek et al., 2021). The hotspot ranking approach enables risk score calculation within crime types, allowing law enforcement to assess risk levels appropriately (Baek et al., 2021).

Sherman et al. (2016) emphasised that not all crimes are equal: each crime type should be weighted according to its relative harm to victims, as defined by baseline sentencing guidelines. To align with this severity logic, the authors proposed the Crime Harm Index (CHI) for measuring total harm, which aggregates total harm rather than simply counting incidents (Sherman et al., 2016; Curtis-Ham, 2022). The CHI applies a weighted sum of the form 'harm score × number of incidents per crime type', summed across categories, producing a single index that reflects both severity and frequency (Sherman et al., 2016). However, one limitation is that sentencing guidelines differ across jurisdictions, which affects the generalisability of the approach. Furthermore, whilst the CHI has proved influential, recent scholarship has highlighted important challenges relating to its operational application. Ariel (2023) highlighted significant implementation challenges associated with hotspot policing, including officers' motivation, organisational resistance, and technological failures, raising questions about the extent to which evidence-based hotspot strategies are translated into routine police practice. Similarly, Alhafedhi (2025) developed and critically evaluated a Crime Harm Index for Rochester, New York, demonstrating that harm-based measurement offers valuable insights into crime patterns but also noting that sentencing-based harm weights can be influenced by political factors and may not always reflect the genuine social impact of offences.

Mohler et al. (2020) introduced CrimeRank, a learning-to-rank boosting algorithm that directly optimises the Predictive Accuracy Index (PAI) for top-k hotspot identification. Their method integrates gradient boosting with a floating-grid approach and greedy hotspot selection. CrimeRank achieved substantial improvements in PAI across different crime types compared to traditional methods (Mohler et al., 2020). Wu and Meghanathan (2023) proposed the Crime Hot Spot Score, a Principal Component Analysis (PCA)-based scoring mechanism designed to assess the severity of crime hotspots rather than treating hotspot identification as a binary classification problem. Their approach applies PCA to multi-year crime data to derive a linear scoring function, which computes weighted scores for each region and ranks areas by severity.

Whilst several studies have proposed scoring methods for crime variables that focus on single factors determining the score, very limited research explicitly combines all three components such as frequency, severity, and reporting consistency in a single weighted scoring model as proposed in this study (Sherman et al., 2016; Mohler et al., 2020; Wu & Meghanathan, 2023). These existing approaches face key limitations: they are often static and jurisdiction-dependent, with limited temporal decay modelling in dynamic environments, and rely on retrospective static datasets (Sherman et al., 2016; Mohler et al., 2020; Wu & Meghanathan, 2023). The existing work provides a foundation for pinpointing crime hotspots with greater accuracy, but the absence of key influential factors for understanding what is happening within detected hotspots limits more flexible utilisation of crime hotspot analysis results.

Hence, this research integrates streaming clustering with a multi-factor crime type weight-based ranking mechanism that accounts for frequency, severity, and reporting consistency, coupled with real-time spatio-temporal visualisation. The proposed approach integrates a severity logic approach to obtain crime type weights, which are then incorporated into the clustering models to detect ranked clusters (Baek et al., 2021). The experiment processes incoming crime data streams generated from Stats SA crime data, along with police station coordinates (Heiduk, 2017), and applies the weight-based ranking mechanism to streaming clustering models (DenStream and CluStream) to detect ranked hotspots. The comparative analysis is conducted using Silhouette Score, Calinski–Harabasz Index, Davies–Bouldin Index, Adjusted Rand Index, Normalised Mutual Information, along with execution time, memory usage, and cluster evolution metrics (Chaudhry et al., 2023). This unified framework enables adaptive, weighted-based hotspot prioritisation to support proactive crime prevention strategies.

MODELS AND METHODOLOGY

Figure 1 illustrates a three-layer crime hotspot detection framework consisting of the data layer, model layer, and decision layer. The data layer ingests Stats SA crime records and police station coordinates data, applies preprocessing and severity scoring, and streams the data for real-time analysis. The model layer runs two clustering algorithms in parallel: DenStream (a density-based approach with exponential decay) and CluStream (a two-phase framework with time-based snapshots). It incorporates a weight-based ranking mechanism and evaluates the models using established evaluation metrics. The decision layer transforms the analytical outputs into interactive crime hotspot maps and visualisation tools that support law enforcement in planning, resource allocation, and field operations.

Figure 1. Multi-layer crime weighted-ranked hotspot detection

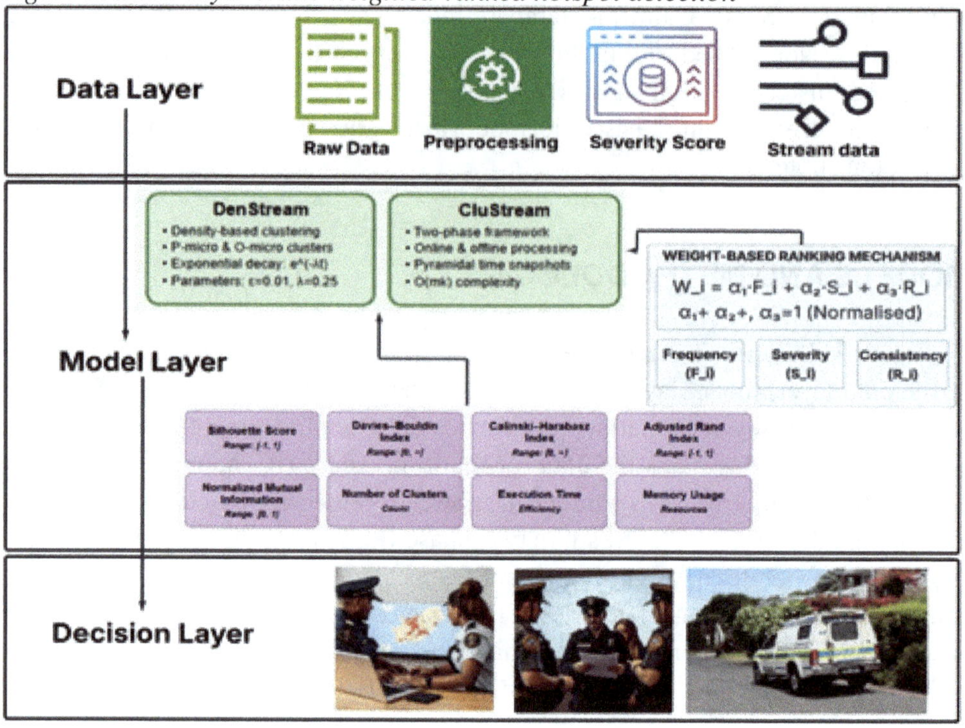

Selected Clustering Models

The DenStream Algorithm

DenStream is a density-based clustering algorithm for streaming data that extends DBSCAN by maintaining two types of time-decayed micro-clusters: potential (p-micro) clusters, which capture dense, evolving regions, and outlier (o-micro) clusters, which track sparse or emerging regions (Zubaroğlu & Atalay, 2021; Bhattacharjee & Mitra, 2021). The algorithm, outlined following this section, applies an exponential decay function, with base e, $f(t) = e^{-\lambda t}$, where t represents the time elapsed since a point was added to the cluster, thereby giving greater weight to recently added points and reducing the influence of older points over time (Ahmed et al., 2020). During the online phase, each incoming point p at time t is first merged into a nearby p-micro cluster if its distance is $\leq \varepsilon$ and density is preserved; if that fails, it is merged into the nearest o-micro cluster, which is promoted to a p-micro if its accumulated weight exceeds the threshold μ; otherwise, a new o-micro cluster is created (Tareq et al., 2021; Ding et al., 2015). Periodic pruning removes micro-clusters whose decayed weights fall below a predefined threshold. In the offline phase, a modified DBSCAN is applied to the surviving p-micro clusters to produce the final clusters, whilst o-micro clusters are treated as outliers or candidates for future clusters (Zubaroğlu & Atalay, 2021). This design enables DenStream to continuously and efficiently cluster high-velocity data streams, adapt to evolving patterns, detect arbitrarily shaped clusters, and explicitly track outliers (Ahmed et al., 2020). However, DenStream requires careful tuning of the neighbourhood radius (ε), minimum points threshold(μ), and temporal decay rate(λ), and it may incur high memory usage as micro-clusters accumulate (Ahmed et al., 2020; Tareq et al., 2021).

Algorithm 1: DenStream Algorithm

Require: Data stream, decay factor λ, neighbourhood radius ε, weight threshold μ, outlier factor β, pruning interval T

Ensure: Cluster assignment $\{C_1, ..., C_n\}$

Initialise p-micro-clusters (PMC) and o-micro-clusters (OMC)
for each new point p at time t **do**
Find closest $pc_i \in$ PMC
if dist(p, pc_i) $\leq \varepsilon$ **then**
Update pc_i with time decay $f(t) = e{-}\lambda t$
else
Find nearest $oc_j \in$ OMC
if dist(p, oc_j) $\leq \varepsilon$ **then**
Update oc_j with point p
if $w(oc_j) \geq \beta \cdot \mu$ **then**
Promote oc_j to PMC
end if
else
Create new o-micro-cluster with point p
end if
end if
if t **mod** $T = 0$ **then**
Prune weak OMC and PMC clusters
end if
end for
Offline phase:
Apply modified DBSCAN to PMC
return Cluster assignment $\{C_1, ..., C_n\}$

The CluStream Algorithm

CluStream is a two-phase framework for clustering evolving data streams, first introduced by Aggarwal (2003). In the online micro-clustering phase, each incoming point is either absorbed into its nearest micro-cluster—updating the cluster-feature vector, timestamp, and count—if it falls within a predefined distance threshold, or else a new micro-cluster is created (Aggarwal, 2003). When the system reaches its capacity, the oldest or weakest cluster is discarded to maintain efficiency (Ahmed et al., 2020; Tareq et al., 2021; Zubaroğlu & Atalay, 2021). To preserve temporal granularity, CluStream stores periodic snapshots of all micro-clusters using a pyramidal time frame, enabling efficient historical analysis (Ding et al., 2015; Tareq et al., 2021). In the offline macro-clustering phase, users can select a snapshot corresponding to a specific time window and apply a conventional clustering algorithm to the micro-cluster centres, producing final cluster assignments and facilitating retrospective, multi-horizon analysis (Tareq et al., 2021). By decoupling real-time summary maintenance from offline clustering, CluStream achieves both scalability and flexibility, allowing analysis at different time scales (Ding et al., 2015). Despite these strengths, CluStream's performance depends on the careful tuning of distance thresholds and time-horizon parameters (Ahmed et al., 2020; Tareq et al., 2021). Nonetheless, its low memory footprint and linear time complexity $O(mk)$, where m is the number of micro-clusters and k the data dimensionality, make CluStream particularly effective for real-time, large-scale applications (Tareq et al., 2021).

Algorithm 2: CluStream Algorithm

Require: Data stream DS, max micro-clusters q, history window h, snapshot interval Δt

Ensure: Cluster assignment $\{C_1, C_2, ..., C_k\}$

1: Initialise micro-cluster set MC ← $\{mc_1, ..., mc_q\}$ with first q points from DS

2: **for each** incoming point p in DS **do**

3: Find nearest micro-cluster mc_i in MC to p

4: **if** dist(p, mc_i) $\leq \varepsilon$ **then**

5: Update mc_i with point p and current timestamp t

6: **else**

7: Create new micro-cluster mc_{new} with point p

8: **if** |MC| $> q$ **then**

9: Remove oldest micro-clusters where $t - t_{last} > h$

10: **if** |MC| $> q$ **then**

11: // Still over capacity:

12: Merge closest pair of micro-clusters in MC

13: **end if**

end if
end if
if t **mod** $\Delta t = 0$ **then**
Store snapshot of MC at time t
end if
end for
Offline phase:
Select micro-clusters active in time window $[t_{start}, t_{end}]$
Apply weighted k-means on selected micro-clusters, $O(mk)$ complexity
return Cluster assignment $\{C_1, ..., C_k\}$

Table 1. Parameters used in hotspot detection models

Parameters	Description / Context
ε	Distance threshold for cluster merging (DenStream)
μ	Min. points to form a cluster (DenStream)
λ	Temporal decay in $f(t) = e{-}\lambda t$ (DenStream)
β	Outlier → core promotion factor (DenStream)
T	Pruning interval for weak clusters (DenStream)
C_1	Cluster formed (DenStream, CluStream)
q	Max. number of micro-clusters (CluStream)
h	History window length (CluStream)
Δt	Snapshot storage interval (CluStream)
m	Number of micro-clusters, $O(mk)$ (CluStream)
k	Data dimensionality, $O(mk)$ (CluStream)

Table 1 summarises the key parameters employed in both DenStream and CluStream models along with their respective descriptions.

Hotspot Ranking Mechanism: Weight-Based Ranking

This research proposes a three-factor crime-type weight-based ranking mechanism that incorporates frequency, severity, and reporting consistency of each crime type within a given dataset. The weight Wi for crime type i is defined as:

$$W = \alpha_1 \cdot F + \alpha_2 \cdot S + \alpha_3 \cdot R \qquad (1)$$

where Fi is the frequency weight, Si is the severity weight, Ri is the reporting consistency weight, and α_1, α_2, α_3 are weighting coefficients. To ensure that the weight remains within a predictable range, the weighting coefficients were normalised such that $\alpha_1 + \alpha_2 + \alpha_3 = 1$ (Dean, 2022). The frequency weight is obtained by calculating the total number of crimes of a given type across the temporal range and dividing by the maximum total count among all crime types.

$$F_i = \frac{\sum_{y=Y_{start}}^{Y_{end}} C_{i,y}}{\max_k\left(\sum_{y=Y_{start}}^{Y_{end}} C_{k,y}\right)} \tag{2}$$

where:

1. $C_{i,y}$ = number of crimes of type i in year y
2. Y_{start}, Y_{end} = start and end years of the temporal range
3. k = index over all crime types

The severity score for each crime type was assigned based on the classification logic presented in Table 2, adapted from the Cambridge Crime Harm Index sentencing guidelines (Sherman et al., 2016) and the South African Criminal Law Amendment Act (Act 105 of 1997) sentencing frameworks (Goliath, 2023).

Table 2. Crime severity classification logic

Score Range	Severity Logic & Crime Examples
10.0	**Loss of life** (Murder)
9.0	**Severe trauma + long-term impact** (Sexual Offences, Attempted Murder)
8.0–8.5	**Violence + property + death potential** (Carjacking, Bank Robbery)
7.0–7.5	**Serious violence** (Robberies with aggravation)
6.0–6.5	**Physical harm + property** (Assault with intent to inflict Grievous Bodily Harm, Burglary residential)
4.0–5.5	**Moderate harm** (Common assault, Drug crimes)
2.0–3.0	**Property/minor offenses** (Theft, Driving Under the Influence, Shoplifting)

Table 2 presents a crime severity classification framework that assigns numerical scores to crime types based on their relative severity and potential harm. Severity scores were adapted from the Cambridge Crime Harm Index (CHI) sentencing guidelines (Sherman et al., 2016) and the South African Criminal Law Amendment Act (Act 105 of 1997) sentencing frame- works (Goliath, 2023). The assigned range of 8.0–8.5 for carjacking and bank robbery reflects multiple compounded risk dimensions: the likelihood of violent confrontation (an aggravating factor), substantial property loss, and the potential for fatal outcomes. This positions these crimes between serious assault resulting in grievous bodily harm (severity 7.0) and attempted murder (severity 9.0).

$$S_i = \frac{Severity\ Index_i}{10.0} \tag{3}$$

The reporting consistency weight measures the reliability and stability of crime reporting patterns across the dataset. It is defined using the inverse of the coefficient of variation, such that a higher value indicates more consistent and stable reporting (low variability relative to the mean), whereas lower values reflect erratic, seasonal, or unreliable reporting patterns.

$$R_i = \frac{1}{1 + CV_i} \tag{4}$$

where the coefficient of variation is given by:

$$CV_i = \frac{\sigma_i}{\mu_i} \tag{5}$$

with σi and μi representing the standard deviation and mean of crime counts for crime type i, respectively. The mean number of crimes of type i per year is calculated as:

$$\mu_i = \frac{1}{Y_{end} - Y_{start} + 1} \sum_{y=Y_{start}}^{Y_{end}} C_{i,y} \tag{6}$$

The standard deviation of crime counts for type i across years is:

$$\sigma_i = \sqrt{\frac{1}{Y_{end} - Y_{start} + 1} \sum_{y=Y_{start}}^{Y_{end}} \left(C_{i,y} - \mu_i\right)^2} \tag{7}$$

Where:

- Ci,y = number of crimes of type i in year y
- $Ystart$, $Yend$ = start and end years of the temporal range
- μi = mean annual count for crime type i
- σi = standard deviation of annual counts for crime type i

A higher R_i indicates more consistent and stable reporting (low variability relative to the mean), whereas lower values reflect erratic, seasonal, or unreliable reporting patterns. .This weighting improves hotspot reliability by down-weighting crime types influenced by sporadic recording practices, data-entry delays, or seasonal enforcement campaigns that may artificially inflate particular periods.

$$Weight\ Score\left(C_j\right) = \sum_i W_i \times N_{i,j} \tag{8}$$

where $N_{i,j}$ denotes the number of crimes of type i in cluster j.

For a cluster Cj containing multiple crime types, the weighted score aggregates each crime type's weight multiplied by its count within that cluster, providing an operationally meaningful composite score that reflects the overall severity profile of each detected hotspot.

Evaluation Metrics

This study employs both internal and external evaluation metrics to provide a comprehensive assessment of clustering quality.

Internal Metrics

The Silhouette Score, Davies–Bouldin Index, and Calinski–Harabasz Index—evaluate cluster cohesion and separation without relying on ground-truth labels (Chaudhry et al., 2023; Ezugwu et al., 2021).

Silhouette Score

The Silhouette Score evaluates the balance between intra-cluster cohesion and inter-cluster separation, with values closer to 1 indicating well-defined clusters.

$$S(i) = \frac{b(i) - a(i)}{\max(a(i), b(i))}, S \in [-1,1] \tag{9}$$

where $a(i)$ is the mean intra-cluster distance and $b(i)$ is the mean nearest-cluster distance. Higher scores indicate well-defined clusters (Chaudhry et al., 2023, Ezugwu et al., 2021, Zhang et al., 2023,Hauchi et al., 2024).

Davies–Bouldin Index

The Davies–Bouldin Index quantifies cluster overlap, with lower values indicating better separation (Chaudhry et al., 2023, Zhang et al., 2023, Hauchi et al., 2024, Ezugwu et al., 2021).

$$DB = \frac{1}{k}\sum_{i=1}^{k} \frac{\max_{j \neq i}\left(\sigma_i + \sigma_j\right)}{d\left(C_i, C_j\right)}, DB \in [0, \infty) \quad (10)$$

Calinski–Harabasz Index

The Calinski–Harabasz Index measures the ratio of between-cluster to within-cluster variance, with higher values indicating compact and well-separated clusters (Chaudhry et al., 2023; Zhang et al., 2023; Ezugwu et al., 2021).

$$CH = \frac{SS_B}{SS_W} \bullet \frac{N-K}{K-1}, CH \in [0, \infty) \quad (11)$$

External Evaluation

External evaluation metrics require ground-truth labels and measure the agreement between predicted and actual cluster assignments.

Adjusted Rand Index (ARI)

The Adjusted Rand Index corrects for chance agreement, with values close to 1 indicating strong agreement with ground truth (Zhang et al., 2023; Ezugwu et al., 2021).

$$ARI = \frac{RI - E[RI]}{\max(RI) - E[RI]}, ARI \in [-1,1] \quad (12)$$

where $E[RI]$ is the expected value of the Rand Index under random clustering.

Normalized Mutual Information (NMI):

Normalised Mutual Information measures the shared information between predicted and ground-truth labels (Zhang et al., 2023; Ezugwu et al., 2021).

$$NMI = \frac{I(U,V)}{\sqrt{H(U)H(V)}}, NMI \in [0,1] \tag{13}$$

where I is mutual information and H denotes entropy (Zhang et al., 2023, Ezugwu et al., 2021, Ezugwu et al., 2022).

Practical performance was also evaluated by monitoring runtime and memory consumption, which are essential for real-time applications as they indicate both algorithmic efficiency and suitability for deployment in operational environments (Macingwane & Isafiade, 2025).

Data Used and Data Preprocessing

The study utilised the Stats SA crime and police station coordinates dataset, which contains over 21 million recorded incidents across 1,143 police station coordinates spanning nine provinces and 28 crime categories (Heiduk, 2017). The dataset includes no personal identifiers. For this study, the dataset was filtered to retain only Western Cape records for 2015–2016, using the province as a test case. Because the Stats SA dataset reports crime only as station-level aggregates, individual incident-level records were synthetically generated to enable spatial–temporal streaming analysis. For each aggregated count, an equivalent number of incident records was created and assigned sampled attributes, including month, day of week, hour, date, date-time, latitude, and longitude. Crime types with zero or missing values were removed. Coordinates were sampled within the official boundaries of each police station to ensure realistic spatial placement, resulting in a dataset of 490,383 incident-level records.

The resulting Western Cape dataset aligns well with existing research in crime data analysis, falling within the upper range of large-scale crime and streaming-based clustering research, making it well suited for evaluating real-time hotspot detection and incremental cluster optimisation. Each crime type was assigned a severity score based on the classification logic presented in Table 2. Data streaming was implemented by partitioning the dataset into batches of 50 data points, with processing continuing iteratively until all records were handled (Cesario et al., 2024). A sliding window buffer was employed to retain only the most recent data, automatically discarding older records when capacity was reached (Zubaroğlu & Atalay, 2021).

Figure 2 displays a colour-coded heatmap where red indicates high-risk hotspots and blue represents areas with minimal crime activity. This visualisation reveals that the Western Cape, Gauteng, and KwaZulu-Natal exhibit high crime concentration areas, and allows assessment of police station coverage and proximity to crime hotspots for strategic resource allocation.

Figure 2. Comparison of heatmaps from the Stats SA crime dataset

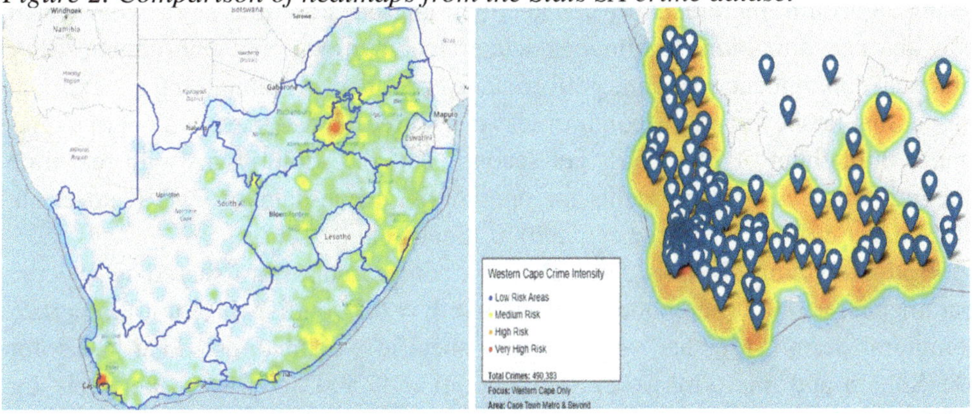

Experimental Setup

The experimental framework was implemented on a system equipped with an Intel Core i7-10700 CPU at 2.90 GHz and 64 GB of RAM. Python was used to perform the streaming analysis, clustering, and visualisation tasks. The weighting coefficients ($\alpha_1 = 0.40$, $\alpha_2 = 0.45$, $\alpha_3 = 0.15$) were selected through a principled framework that prioritises severity in accordance with Crime Harm Index principles, which demonstrate that high-harm offences exert disproportionate impact (Sherman et al., 2016; Curtis-Ham, 2022; Mohler et al., 2020; Baek et al., 2021; Dean, 2022). Frequency is weighted nearly equally, reflecting operational evidence that high-volume crime patterns drive sustained resource allocation (Mohler et al., 2020; Baek et al., 2021). Reporting consistency is assigned a smaller weight to serve as a data-quality safeguard against erratic recording patterns (Mohler et al., 2020). The coefficients are normalised to unity following multi-criteria decision analysis standards for public safety planning (Dean, 2022).

It should be acknowledged that the weighting coefficients, whilst grounded in established crime harm theory, involve inherent assumptions. The severity-first approach draws on the CHI logic, but as Ariel (2023) has noted, the implementation of hotspot policing faces persistent challenges relating to organisational adoption and operational fidelity. The present framework mitigates some of these concerns by integrating frequency and reporting consistency alongside severity, thereby reducing reliance on any single factor. Nevertheless, jurisdiction-specific calibration and sensitivity testing remain important considerations for operational deployment.

Real-time processing was simulated by streaming the dataset sequentially in batches of 50 records, with each batch processed immediately upon arrival rather than waiting for the full dataset to become available (Luo et al., 2023). The clustering algorithms incrementally updated their internal structures as each new batch was ingested, simulating continuous data arrival in operational environments. For practical deployment, real-time performance is defined as maintaining a maximum processing latency of two seconds or less per 50-record batch, equivalent to a minimum throughput of 25 records per second. This threshold aligns with real-time streaming analysis requirements for operational crime-data systems (Luo et al., 2023; Gorr & Lee, 2015; Lee et al., 2020; Baek et al., 2021).

Both streaming clustering models were configured with a shared set of core parameters: $\varepsilon = 0.1$ (neighbourhood radius), $\beta = 0.2$ (outlier threshold), $\lambda = 0.25$ (temporal decay), together with a model-specific weight threshold $\mu = 1.5$ for DenStream and micro/macro cluster capacities of 500 and 100 respectively for CluStream. These parameter selections align with established guidelines for density-based streaming clustering (Ahmed et al., 2020; Tareq et al., 2021; Zubaroğlu & Atalay, 2021), balancing clustering granularity with computational efficiency for real-time crime analysis applications.

RESULTS AND ANALYSIS

This section presents the outcomes of employing DenStream and CluStream on streaming crime data. The analysis highlights three key aspects: computational performance, clustering quality, and insights into the crime hotspots detected. Importantly, the results are discussed not only in terms of technical metrics but also with regard to their operational implications for spatial deployment and resource allocation decisions. Figure 3 presents the performance of the streaming clustering algorithms as they process 490,383 crime records in 9,808 sequential batches of 50 records each.

Figure 3. Assessing streaming clustering models on processing batches

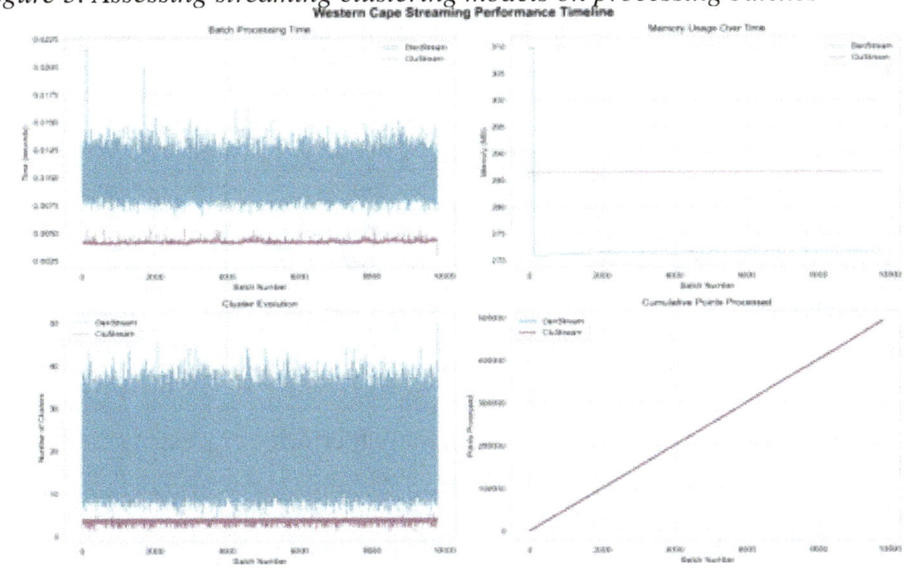

CluStream consistently processes each batch significantly faster than DenStream, maintaining processing times around 0.004 seconds per batch, whilst DenStream exhibits substantially higher per-batch processing times with occasional spikes. In terms of memory usage, DenStream shows an initial spike to approximately 310 MB before stabilising around 271 MB, whilst CluStream maintains stable usage at approximately 286 MB throughout. Regarding cluster evolution, DenStream generates a substantially larger and more fluctuating number of micro-clusters, typically ranging between 4 and 50, reflecting its adaptive density-based mechanism. CluStream maintains a far smaller and remarkably stable cluster count of approximately 2–4 macro-clusters. Both algorithms successfully processed all incoming data without loss or degradation. Table 3 compares the streaming performance of DenStream and CluStream on the same crime dataset.

Table 3. Comparison of streaming clustering algorithms

Metric	DenStream	CluStream
Batch Size	50	50
Total Batches	9,808	9,808
Processing Time (s)	455.11	160.54
Throughput (pts/s)	1,078	3,055

continued on following page

Table 3. Continued

Metric	DenStream	CluStream
Micro-clusters	50	4
Macro-clusters	4	2
Silhouette Score	0.1289	0.4914
Davies–Bouldin Index	0.81570	0.72959
Calinski–Harabasz Index	935,001.1	19,185.3
Adjusted Rand Index	0.0421	0.0025
Normalised Mutual Info	0.3175	0.0415
Fowlkes–Mallows Score	0.2410	0.1984

CluStream demonstrates clear computational superiority, processing the data 2.8 times faster than DenStream, completing processing in 160.54 seconds compared to DenStream's 455.11 seconds, and achieving a throughput of 3,055 records per second. For internal validation, CluStream delivers substantially better clustering quality: the Silhouette Score is 0.4914 compared to 0.1289 for DenStream, indicating far more cohesive and well-separated clusters. Similarly, CluStream achieves a lower Davies–Bouldin Index (0.7296 compared to 0.8157), indicating stronger intra-cluster similarity and greater inter-cluster dissimilarity. However, DenStream shows a substantially higher Calinski–Harabasz Index (935,001 compared to 19,185), suggesting tighter and more compact clusters.

The external validation metrics reveal a different perspective when evaluated against ground-truth station labels. DenStream achieves superior external validation scores across all three metrics: Adjusted Rand Index (0.0421 compared to 0.0025), Normalised Mutual Information (0.3175 compared to 0.0415), and Fowlkes–Mallows Score (0.2410 compared to 0.1984). This discrepancy between internal and external metrics reflects fundamental differences in the algorithms' clustering approaches: DenStream's density-based micro-clustering naturally captures finer spatial granularity that corresponds better to administrative boundaries, whilst CluStream's macro-clustering framework prioritises statistical summarisation and broader spatial aggregation. The low absolute values of all external metrics for both algorithms suggest that crime patterns do not strictly follow administrative police station boundaries—a finding consistent with criminological theory, which recognises that crime hotspots emerge from socio-economic and environmental factors rather than jurisdictional lines (Sherman et al., 2016; Mohler et al., 2020).

Figure 4 presents a comparative visualisation of crime type distributions across clusters detected by DenStream and CluStream. The visualisation reveals both the volume and composition of crimes within detected hotspots, enabling law enforcement to understand not only where crimes occur but what types of crimes dominate specific geographic areas. DenStream maintains four distinct clusters, with Cluster C0 showing the highest concentration across most crime categories, particularly drug-related crimes, theft, burglary at residential premises, and theft out of or from motor vehicles.

Figure 4. Weighted distribution of crime within a cluster

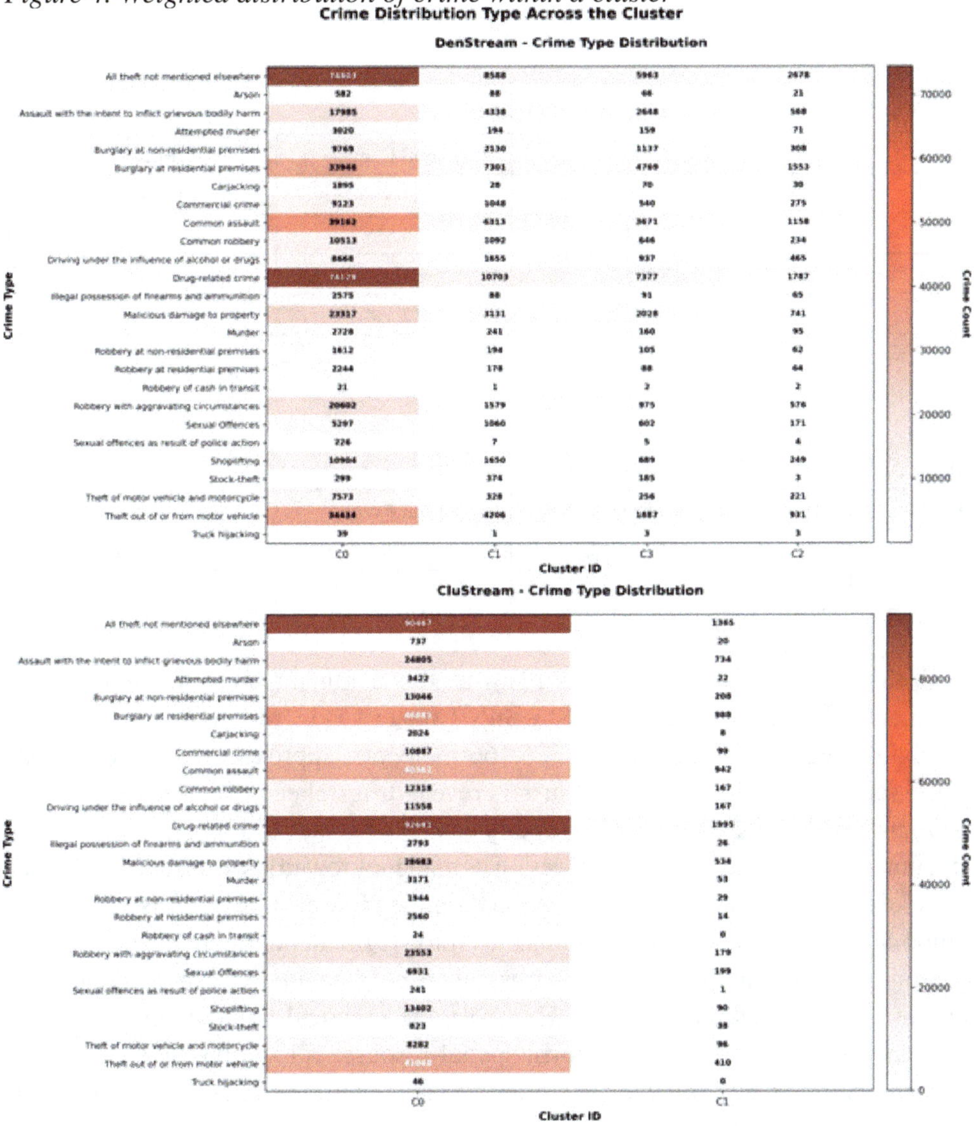

This granular cluster structure reflects DenStream's density-based evolution mechanism, which is advantageous for detecting emerging patterns and supporting short-term tactical strategies. CluStream produces two larger, aggregated macro-clusters, with its primary cluster demonstrating substantially higher crime volumes. This consolidation makes CluStream better suited for long-term strategic planning and high-level trend analysis.

Tables 4 and 5 present the top weighted clusters identified by the DenStream and CluStream algorithms. Each table reports the cluster rank, total weight, number of crimes within the cluster boundary, and the associated station area.

Table 4. Top 4 weighted clusters for DenStream

Rank	ID	Weight Score	Total Count	Station
1	C0	144,436.56	386,466	Mitchells Plain
2	C1	20,924.54	56,515	Oudtshoorn
3	C3	13,285.21	35,058	Kleinvlei
4	C2	4,851.81	12,344	Strand

Table 5. Top 2 weighted clusters for CluStream

Rank	ID	Weight Score	Total Count	Station
1	C0	180,338.68	481,909	Mitchells Plain
2	C1	3,159.46	8,474	Strandfontein

Both models identify Mitchells Plain as the dominant hotspot, though their dominant crime types differ. DenStream's Cluster C0 in Mitchells Plain carries a weight score of 144,436.56 and 386,466 incidents, approximately 78.8% of all processed crimes. The remaining clusters reveal drug-related offences dominating in Oudtshoorn and Kleinvlei, and property crime in Strand. CluStream's top cluster accounts for 98.3% of all crimes, reflecting its tendency towards spatial consolidation.

A key consideration for the operational application of these results is how the temporal analysis presented here translates into spatial deployment decisions. The streaming clustering framework processes crime data in real time, identifying temporal patterns as they emerge. However, the practical value of this temporal efficiency lies in its ability to inform spatial resource allocation—that is, where patrol units should be deployed, where surveillance should be intensified, and which areas require targeted interventions.

The results demonstrate that the proposed framework can function as a continuous analytical model: the temporal streaming analysis identifies emerging patterns and shifts in crime composition, which can then be translated into spatial deployment recommendations. For instance, the identification of drug-related crime dominance in specific clusters suggests the need for specialised narcotics enforcement in those geographic areas, whilst the prevalence of property crime in other clusters points towards enhanced theft-prevention initiatives and community-oriented security programmes. This linkage between temporal detection and spatial action represents a practical pathway from analytical output to operational decision-making.

Nevertheless, it is important to acknowledge the challenges inherent in translating hotspot analysis into effective policing practice. The implementation of hotspot policing has been subject to ongoing debate within criminological literature. Whilst evidence generally supports the effectiveness of focused deterrence at crime hotspots (Sherman et al., 2016), operational challenges remain, including the risk of crime displacement to adjacent areas, the need for community engagement to maintain legitimacy, and the resource constraints that may limit the duration and intensity of hotspot interventions. The harm indices used to weight crime types in this framework, whilst theoretically grounded, also face practical limitations: as Ariel (2023) has noted, implementing hotspot policing in practice faces challenges including officers' motivation, organisational resistance, and technological limitations, and as Alhafedhi (2025) has demonstrated, the construction of harm indices involves methodological choices that can influence the resulting crime picture. These considerations underscore the importance of interpreting the weighted clusters produced by this framework not as definitive prescriptions but as decision-support tools that should be contextualised within broader operational, community, and policy considerations.

The complementary nature of DenStream and CluStream is particularly relevant in this operational context. CluStream's broader spatial aggregation is well suited to strategic, citywide resource planning, whilst DenStream's finer granularity supports tactical, neighbourhood-level deployment decisions. Together, they provide a multi-resolution analytical capability that can serve different levels of policing decision-making, from high-level strategic allocation to localised tactical response

CONCLUSION

This study introduces a novel three-factor crime-type weighting mechanism that integrates crime frequency, severity, and reporting consistency to enhance hotspot prioritisation and operational interpretability. A comparative analysis was conducted using the Stats SA dataset for the Western Cape, with CluStream demonstrating superior performance for large-scale, real-time hotspot detection, balancing speed, accuracy, and scalability. DenStream's micro-clustering approach preserves neighbourhood-level variation and detects emerging hotspot patterns that are critical for tactical deployment and short-term operational decision-making.

Together, the models highlight dominant crime types, identify high-impact clusters, and generate actionable insights within a real-time streaming pipeline, representing a significant advancement over retrospective, static analyses. The weighted ranking mechanism proved essential for interpreting these clusters. Both models identified Mitchells Plain as the dominant hotspot, although their dominant crime types differed, enabling targeted interventions such as surveillance and theft-prevention initiatives in theft-heavy areas and specialised narcotics units in drug-dominated zones. By ranking clusters using multi-factor weights, the framework provides a more operationally meaningful prioritisation than traditional density-based hotspot methods, which typically rely solely on incident counts without considering crime severity or reporting reliability. Importantly, this study positions the temporal streaming analysis as a continuous analytical model that can inform spatial resource allocation. The efficiency of real-time temporal processing, as demonstrated by both clustering algorithms, provides the foundation for a system in which emerging crime patterns are detected and translated into spatial deployment recommendations. This bridging of temporal analysis and spatial operationalisation represents a key contribution of this work, offering law enforcement a pathway from data-driven pattern detection to practical, on-the-ground decision-making.

However, several limitations should be acknowledged. The models remain sensitive to parameter choices such as the density radius, outlier threshold, and temporal decay rate, all of which can significantly affect clustering outcomes. The weighting coefficients, although grounded in crime harm theory, may require jurisdiction-specific calibration, and the severity scores may not generalise across diverse legal contexts. The processed dataset, disaggregated from station-level counts, may lack the spatial precision of GPS-tagged incident data. Furthermore, whilst the harm indices employed in this framework are theoretically well-motivated, their operational application faces challenges including implementation difficulties in translating hotspot evidence into routine policing practice (Ariel, 2023) and the influence of methodological choices on resulting crime harm measurements (Alhafedhi, 2025). The implementation of hotspot policing itself involves practical considerations—including potential displacement effects, community engagement requirements, and resource constraints—that must be addressed in any operational deployment of this framework.

Future research should address these limitations by: conducting parameter sensitivity analysis using grid search or Bayesian optimisation; validating the models across multiple cities with varying population densities and crime profiles; incorporating temporal decay and area normalisation into the weighting model; augmenting the framework with additional contextual data such as socio-economic indicators, weather patterns, and special events; and deploying a real-time operational dashboard with live police data feeds, interactive mapping, and automated hotspot alerts. There is considerable potential to develop and embed both the technology and theory presented in this study into an efficient, continuous analytical model within policing that addresses criticisms of both hotspot policing implementation and harm indices, thereby strengthening the operational utility of data-driven crime prevention strategies.

REFERENCES

Aggarwal, C. C. (2003). A framework for diagnosing changes in evolving data streams. In *Proceedings of the 2003 ACM SIGMOD International Conference on Management of Data* (pp. 575–586). ACM. DOI: 10.1145/872757.872826

Ahmed, R., Dalkılıç, G., & Erten, Y. (2020). DGStream: High quality and efficiency stream clustering algorithm. *Expert Systems with Applications*, *141*, 112947. DOI: 10.1016/j.eswa.2019.112947

Alhafedhi, H. (2025). Understanding crime through harm: A multi-stage study of Rochester, NY [Master's project, Rochester Institute of Technology]. RIT Digital Institutional Repository. https://repository.rit.edu/theses/12455

Appiah, S. K., Wirekoh, K., Aidoo, E. N., Oduro, S. D., & Arthur, Y. D. (2022). A model-based clustering of expectation–maximization and k-means algorithms in crime hotspot analysis. *Research in Mathematics*, *9*(1), 1–12. DOI: 10.1080/27684830.2022.2073662

Ariel, B. (2023). Implementation issues with hot spot policing. *International Journal of Law, Crime and Justice*, *75*, 100629. DOI: 10.1016/j.ijlcj.2023.100629

Baek, M. S., Park, W., Park, J., Jang, K. H., & Lee, Y. T. (2021). Smart policing technique with crime type and risk score prediction based on machine learning for early awareness of risk situation. *IEEE Access : Practical Innovations, Open Solutions*, *9*, 131906–131915. DOI: 10.1109/ACCESS.2021.3112682

Bhattacharjee, P., & Mitra, P. (2021). A survey of density based clustering algorithms. *Frontiers of Computer Science*, *15*(1), 1–27. DOI: 10.1007/s11704-019-9059-3

Butt, U. M., Letchmunan, S., Hassan, F. H., Ali, M., Baqir, A., Koh, T. W., & Sherazi, H. H. R. (2021). Spatio-temporal crime predictions by leveraging artificial intelligence for citizens security in smart cities. *IEEE Access : Practical Innovations, Open Solutions*, *9*, 47516–47529. DOI: 10.1109/ACCESS.2021.3068306

Cesario, E., Lindia, P., & Vinci, A. (2023). Detecting multi-density urban hotspots in a smart city: Approaches, challenges and applications. *Big Data and Cognitive Computing*, *7*(1), 29. DOI: 10.3390/bdcc7010029

Cesario, E., Lindia, P., & Vinci, A. (2024). Multi-density crime predictor: An approach to forecast criminal activities in multi-density crime hotspots. *Journal of Big Data*, *11*(1), 75. DOI: 10.1186/s40537-024-00935-4

Chaudhry, M., Shafi, I., Mahnoor, M., Vargas, D. L. R., Thompson, E. B., & Ashraf, I. (2023). A systematic literature review on identifying patterns using unsupervised clustering algorithms: A data mining perspective. *Symmetry*, *15*(9), 1679. DOI: 10.3390/sym15091679

Curtis-Ham, S. (2022). Measuring harm with crime harm indices. In *The crime analyst's companion* (pp. 177–192). Springer. DOI: 10.1007/978-3-030-94364-6_13

Dean, M. (2022). A practical guide to multi-criteria analysis. University College London. https://www.ucl.ac.uk/bartlett/public-purpose/sites/bartlett_public_purpose/files/a_practical_guide_to_multi-criteria_analysis.pdf

Ding, S., Wu, F., Qian, J., Jia, H., & Jin, F. (2015). Research on data stream clustering algorithms. *Artificial Intelligence Review*, *43*(4), 593–600. DOI: 10.1007/s10462-013-9398-7

Dlamini, S. (2017). A criminological exploration of community policing forums in Durban, South Africa: A study based on Glenwood Suburb and Cato Manor Township [Doctoral dissertation, University of KwaZulu-Natal].

Ezugwu, A. E., Ikotun, A. M., Oyelade, O. O., Abualigah, L., Agushaka, J. O., Eke, C. I., & Akinyelu, A. A. (2022). A comprehensive survey of clustering algorithms: State-of-the-art machine learning applications, taxonomy, challenges, and future research prospects. *Engineering Applications of Artificial Intelligence*, *110*, 104743. DOI: 10.1016/j.engappai.2022.104743

Ezugwu, A. E., Shukla, A. K., Agbaje, M. B., Oyelade, O. N., José-García, A., & Agushaka, J. O. (2021). Automatic clustering algorithms: A systematic review and bibliometric analysis of relevant literature. *Neural Computing & Applications*, *33*(11), 6247–6306. DOI: 10.1007/s00521-020-05395-4

Goliath, A. (2023). A short critique of minimum sentences. *Obiter*, *43*(4), 779–796.

Gorr, W., & Lee, Y. (2015). Early warning system for temporary crime hot spots. *Journal of Quantitative Criminology*, *31*(1), 25–47. DOI: 10.1007/s10940-014-9223-8

Hauchi, W., Lisik, D., & Dinh, T. (2024). Data clustering: An essential technique in data science. arXiv preprint arXiv:2412.18760, 1–17.

Heiduk, J. (2017). Data visualisation with Python: Crime statistics for South Africa. Kaggle. Retrieved February 23, 2023, from https://www.kaggle.com/datasets/slweber/south-africa-crime-statistics

Hosseinzadeh, M., Hemmati, A., & Rahmani, A. M. (2022). Clustering for smart cities in the internet of things: A review. *Cluster Computing*, *25*(6), 4097–4127. DOI: 10.1007/s10586-022-03646-8

Isafiade, O. E., & Bagula, A. B. (2017). *Fostering smart city development in developing nations: A crime series data analytics approach. In 2017 ITU Kaleidoscope: Challenges for a Data-Driven Society*. IEEE.

Kaza, S., Wang, T., Gowda, H., & Chen, H. (2005). Target vehicle identification for border safety using mutual information. In *Proceedings of the 2005 IEEE Intelligent Transportation Systems* (pp. 1141–1146). IEEE. DOI: 10.1109/ITSC.2005.1520212

Lee, Y., SooHyun, O., & Eck, J. E. (2020). A theory-driven algorithm for real-time crime hot spot forecasting. *Police Quarterly*, *23*(2), 174–201. DOI: 10.1177/1098611119887809

Luo, L., Zhou, L., & Song, P. X.-K. (2023). Real-time regression analysis of streaming clustered data with possible abnormal data batches. *Journal of the American Statistical Association*, *118*(543), 2029–2044. DOI: 10.1080/01621459.2022.2026778 PMID: 37771510

Macingwane, A., & Isafiade, O. E. (2025). A novel HP-Growth model for enhancing community policing in South Africa. *Discover Computing*, *28*(1), 37. DOI: 10.1007/s10791-025-09529-x

Mohler, G., Porter, M., Carter, J., & LaFree, G. (2020). Learning to rank spatiotemporal event hotspots. *Crime Science*, *9*(1), 3. DOI: 10.1186/s40163-020-00112-x

Oyewole, G. J., & Thopil, G. A. (2023). Data clustering: Application and trends. *Artificial Intelligence Review*, *56*(7), 6439–6475. DOI: 10.1007/s10462-022-10325-y PMID: 36466764

Pramanik, A., Das, A. K., Pelusi, D., & Nayak, J. (2023a). An effective fuzzy clustering of crime reports embedded by a universal sentence encoder model. *Mathematics*, *11*(3), 611. DOI: 10.3390/math11030611

Pramanik, A., Das, A. K., Pelusi, D., & Nayak, J. (2023b). Crime pattern analysis using graph-based fuzzy clustering on heterogeneous crime data. *Expert Systems with Applications*, *213*, 119058. DOI: 10.1016/j.eswa.2022.119058

Safat, W., Asghar, S., & Gillani, S. A. (2021). Empirical analysis for crime prediction and forecasting using machine learning and deep learning techniques. *IEEE Access : Practical Innovations, Open Solutions*, *9*, 70080–70094. DOI: 10.1109/ACCESS.2021.3078117

Sahu, N. K. (2022). DBSCAN & hierarchical clustering algorithm: Analysis cyber crime data. *International Journal of Multidisciplinary Education and Research, 11*, 16–20.

Sherman, L., Neyroud, P. W., & Neyroud, E. (2016). The Cambridge Crime Harm Index: Measuring total harm from crime based on sentencing guidelines. Policing. *Journal of Policy Practice*, *10*(3), 171–183.

Tareq, M., Sundararajan, E. A., Harwood, A., & Bakar, A. A. (2021). A systematic review of density grid-based clustering for data streams. *IEEE Access : Practical Innovations, Open Solutions*, *10*, 579–596. DOI: 10.1109/ACCESS.2021.3134704

Tulumello, S., & Iapaolo, F. (2022). Policing the future, disrupting urban policy today: Predictive policing, smart city, and urban policy in Memphis (TN). *Urban Geography*, *43*(3), 448–469. DOI: 10.1080/02723638.2021.1887634

Wu, Y., & Meghanathan, N. (2023). A principal component analysis-based scoring mechanism to quantify crime hot spots in a city. In International Conference on Information Technology—New Generations (pp. 45–51). Springer. DOI: 10.1007/978-3-031-28332-1_6

Xie, Y., Shekhar, S., & Li, Y. (2022). Statistically-robust clustering techniques for mapping spatial hotspots: A survey. *ACM Computing Surveys*, *55*(2), 1–38. DOI: 10.1145/3487893

Zhang, C., Huang, W., Niu, T., Liu, Z., Li, G., & Cao, D. (2023). Review of clustering technology and its application in coordinating vehicle subsystems. *Automotive Innovation*, *6*(1), 89–115. DOI: 10.1007/s42154-022-00205-0

Zubaroğlu, A., & Atalay, V. (2021). Data stream clustering: A review. *Artificial Intelligence Review*, *54*(2), 1201–1236. DOI: 10.1007/s10462-020-09874-x

KEY TERMS AND DEFINITIONS

Crime Harm Index (CHI): A weighted scoring framework that quantifies the total harm associated with crime by multiplying the count of each crime type by a severity weight derived from sentencing guidelines, producing a single composite index that reflects both volume and seriousness of offences.

Crime Hotspot Detection: The process of identifying geographic areas with disproportionately high concentrations of criminal activity using data-driven clustering techniques, enabling law enforcement to prioritise resource deployment and targeted interventions.

Exponential Decay: A time-weighting function applied in streaming clustering models to reduce the influence of older data points on cluster formation, ensuring that the model remains responsive to recent patterns while gradually discounting historical observations.

Hotspot Prioritisation: The systematic ordering of detected crime hotspots by their relative threat level or harm score so that law enforcement can allocate limited resources to the areas of greatest need first.

Micro-Cluster: A compact, lightweight data structure maintained during the online phase of streaming clustering algorithms that summarises a localised group of data points using statistical descriptors such as weighted centroid, radius, and timestamp, enabling efficient incremental updates without retaining raw records.

Reporting Consistency: A data-quality measure that assesses the stability and reliability of crime recording patterns for a given crime type over time, calculated using the inverse coefficient of variation so that crime types with erratic or seasonally inflated reporting receive lower weight in the ranking model.

Spatio-Temporal Crime Analysis: The combined examination of where and when crimes occur by integrating geographic location data with temporal patterns, allowing analysts to detect how crime distributions shift across both space and time.

Streaming Clustering: A class of machine learning algorithms designed to group continuously arriving data points into clusters in real time, processing records incrementally rather than requiring the full dataset to be available in advance.

Weight-Based Ranking: A prioritisation mechanism that assigns composite numerical scores to detected clusters by combining multiple crime-type characteristics—such as frequency, severity, and reporting consistency—to rank hotspots according to their overall operational significance.

Chapter 9

Integrating LiDAR and Deep Learning for Semantic 3D Crime Scene Reconstruction: Background and Prospects

Mfundo Andrew Maneli
http://orcid.org/0000-0002-7080-5811
University of the Western Cape, South Africa

Omowunmi Elizabeth Isafiade
http://orcid.org/0000-0002-3028-6180
University of the Western Cape, South Africa

Oluwasola Mary Adedayo
http://orcid.org/0000-0003-1573-6232
University of Winnipeg, Canada

ABSTRACT

Accurate crime scene documentation is critical for investigations. Traditional methods are labor-intensive, error-prone, and fail to capture 3D data. LiDAR and Deep Learning (DL) offer solutions: LiDAR provides precise 3D point clouds, while DL automates analysis. Models like PointNet, PointNet++, and DGCNN enable object detection, segmentation, and classification. Challenges include high computational demands and sensitivity to sparse data. Integrating LiDAR and DL improves reconstruction, semantic understanding, and evidence documentation. Low-cost LiDAR

DOI: 10.4018/979-8-3373-5228-2.ch009

and efficient DL models offer practical opportunities for low-resource settings. This review (2015–2025) highlights gaps and potential in LiDAR–DL fusion for crime scene investigations.

INTRODUCTION

Crime scene investigations (CSIs) are crucial for the delivery of legal verdicts and achieving justice. These investigations necessitate meticulous documentation, comprehensive analysis, and careful interpretation of evidence to facilitate an accurate verdict in the courtroom (Maneli & Isafiade, 2025). Studies report that crime scene investigators in low-resource settings rely heavily on photography, hand sketching (Ren et al., 2017; Zubanska, 2018), manual measurements (Berezowski et al., 2020), and videography (Raneri, 2018), among other methods, to document crime scene data. While these methodologies are crucial to the investigative process, they have several limitations. These include being labour-intensive, prone to human error, cumbersome, and inadequate in accurately representing complex spatial crime scenes (Tredinnick et al., 2019; Wang et al., 2019). These limitations highlight the need for more advanced and automated techniques that can effectively capture both geometric structures and object interpretations and could contribute to more efficient documentation.

Rationale

Recent advances in machine learning (ML) and Light Detection and Ranging (LiDAR) technologies are transforming the landscape of CSI. ML algorithms can analyze large datasets, detect subtle patterns, and support investigative decisions, with applications ranging from predictive analysis and surveillance interpretation to fingerprint matching and anomaly detection (Glomb et al., 2018; Iacob et al., 2019; Jadhav et al., 2020; Liu et al., 2018; Wang et al., 2020). These enhance accuracy, speed, and objectivity in CSI workflows (Urschler et al., 2014). LiDAR technology offers outstanding geometric precision in point clouds by accurately capturing distances and spatial relationships in complex environments. This capability facilitates precise reconstructions and minimizes measurement errors (Galanakis et al., 2021; Kottner et al., 2023). LiDAR has already demonstrated its value in documenting building layouts (Galanakis et al., 2021), accident scenes (Dima & Covaciu, 2015), and detailed crime environments (Bahirat & Prabhakaran, 2017). Despite these strengths, LiDAR alone cannot interpret contextual meaning or visual details of a crime scene. Deep learning (DL) methodologies can fill this gap by autonomously identifying, classifying, and analyzing visual and spatial features (Boldt et al., 2018;

Naqa & Murphy, 2015). In CSI contexts, DL can facilitate suspect identification, event reconstruction, and evidence interpretation through tasks such as face recognition, video analysis, and image classification (Awais et al., 2018; Orozco et al., 2020).

Research Gap and Objectives

We hypothesize that the fusion of these two technologies may support improvements in crime scene reconstructions. LiDAR captures precise spatial coordinates, DL architectures such as PointNet, PointNet++, dynamic graph Convolutional Neural Networks (DGCNNs), voxel CNNs can extract semantic meaning from visual data (Bello et al., 2020; Mateen et al., 2019; Zhou & Qian, 2024). Combining these modalities potentially allows investigators to map semantic labels onto 3D point clouds, enabling accurate object recognition, spatial localization, and scene classification (Nelis et al., 2018). However, research that integrates LiDAR with DL for CSI workflows remains scarce. The limited CSI-specific literature identified in this chapter supports this claim. From 2015 to 2025, a minimal amount of research has focused on fusing LiDAR point cloud data with DL. Existing research has focused on semantic labelling and comprehension in areas such as autonomous driving (Li et al., 2021), robotics (Tsai et al., 2021), millimeter-wave beam selection (Klautau et al., 2019), and cultural heritage (Pierdicca et al., 2020), among others. Although these domains are not CSI, they share key tasks such as semantic labeling, dense 3D reconstruction, and uncertainty estimation, which are directly relevant to crime scene documentation. The key challenge is adapting these methods to forensic constraints. The majority of existing research has concentrated either on geometric reconstruction (Huang et al., 2024) or visual analysis (Cui et al., 2022), creating a considerable gap and opportunities in methodologies that effectively integrate both technologies for crime investigators. This chapter explores the potential of LiDAR-DL fusion and seeks to achieve the following objectives:

- Identify 3D spatial data acquisition methods used in CSI and evaluate their accuracy and limitations.
- Review LiDAR-DL fusion methods from adjacent domains and assess their potential applicability to CSI.
- Identify barriers and opportunities for integrating LiDAR-DL in CSI workflows.

This chapter addresses the following research questions (RQs) central to crime scene research through a structured narrative review that synthesizes interdisciplinary studies on 3D crime scene reconstruction, with a focus on the applicability and limitations of LiDAR-DL methods for CSI contexts. While this review does not claim exhaustive coverage, it synthesizes evidence from studies in CSI and related domains that are relevant to 3D reconstruction.

- RQ 1: What research developments and applications exist in employing 3D spatial data capture technologies to produce highly accurate and detailed reconstructions of crime scenes?
- RQ2: What fundamental characteristics of LiDAR technology make it theoretically superior to photogrammetry and other conventional 3D spatial documentation techniques for accurate and comprehensive 3D crime scene reconstruction?
- RQ 3: Which LiDAR-DL fusion methods from adjacent domains are potentially transferable to CSI, and what are the barriers (technical, legal, operational) to adoption?

The chapter is organized as follows:

- Section 2 provides the background and theoretical foundations
- Section 3 outlines the review methodology.
- Section 4 synthesizes the results and discussions on research questions.
- Section 5 concludes with recommendations for future research directions.

BACKGROUND AND THEORETICAL FOUNDATIONS

This section reviews previous research on the use of 3D spatial data acquisition techniques and DL in CSIs, both separately and in a hybridized form. It also examines studies from other domains that integrate 3D data acquisition with DL. The literature reveals a lack of comprehensive reviews that specifically fuse 3D acquisition methods, such as LiDAR, with DL for semantic 3D reconstruction in CSI. This gap highlights the need to evaluate and analyze each technology independently. The section summarizes prior scholarly contributions through concise narratives and culminates in an integrated synthesis of the findings. Studies were selected based on their relevance to CSI reconstruction, the availability of empirical validation, and their focus on LiDAR or DL methods applicable to 3D scene interpretation.

Review of Studies on 3D Spatial Documentation in CSI

These inaccuracies may be amplified when spatial reconstructions rely on data obtained through traditional methods. Recent literature indicates a growing interest in 3D spatial data acquisition techniques within CSI, including photogrammetry, terrestrial laser scanning, and structured light scanning (Maneli & Isafiade, 2022; Tredinnick et al., 2019). These techniques offer more accurate spatial data capture and improved visualization compared to conventional approaches, particularly in complex environments.

Berezowski et al. (2020) provided a foundational overview of geomatic techniques available to crime investigators, including total stations, photogrammetry, laser scanning, and structured light scanning. Their work highlights the distinct advantages and limitations of each approach, underscoring that the purpose of integrating new technologies is not to displace traditional methods, but to complement them. The authors also argue that while conventional documentation techniques remain valued for their reliability, LiDAR-based methods can achieve comparable or superior levels of accuracy while providing enhanced visual representation. The study concludes that crime investigators must understand the operational contexts in which these technologies are most effective.

The work of Balbudhe et al. (2025) situated CSIs as an intersection of science, law, and technology. Using the scoping review frameworks of Arksey and O'Malley and the Joanna Briggs Institute, the study examines the impact of 3D reconstruction tools such as LiDAR, photogrammetry, and virtual reality on CSI workflows. The review finds that these tools have significantly improved the precision and preservation of digital evidence, allowing investigators to revisit crime scenes virtually with high fidelity and reproducibility. However, this study did not address the integration of LiDAR in depth.

Building on this, Mohd Sabri et al. (2023) focused on the role of drones, or Unmanned Aerial Vehicles (UAVs), in criminal applications. Employing the same scoping review methodology as Balbudhe et al. (2025), the study reveals that UAVs have been effectively deployed in mapping outdoor crime and disaster scenes. Despite these advances, the authors noted that the integration of LiDAR-equipped drones remains underexplored, particularly in terms of their potential contribution to early disaster response. This gap underscores the need for further empirical research into UAV-LiDAR synergy in operational crime scene contexts.

Abbas and Abed (2024) examined the integration of low-cost LiDAR sensors into Apple devices to enable affordable 3D mapping. The review found that LiDAR-enabled Apple devices, though limited in range, were capable of capturing high-quality 3D point clouds of small to medium-sized objects efficiently. These devices are capable of capturing accurate point cloud data at a low cost. Its portability and affordability indicate strong potential for crime scene documentation, especially where traditional methods for crime scene documentation are impractical or unusable.

Overall, existing CSI reviews indicate increasing adoption of 3D spatial documentation tools. However, most work focuses on photogrammetry and high-end terrestrial scanners, with limited discussion of mobile LiDAR and its integration with

DL. This suggests a gap in research on scalable and affordable 3D capture methods that can be combined with automated semantic interpretation for CSI reconstruction.

Review of Studies on the Use of DL in CSI

Although many DL applications in CSI do not directly involve 3D reconstruction, they demonstrate the broader application of DL in extracting semantic information from crime scene evidence and integrating outputs into investigative processes. This is relevant to semantic 3D reconstruction because the same DL capabilities, such as object detection, pattern recognition, and inference from spatial data, can be transferred to 3D point clouds. In other words, these studies provide evidence that DL can generate reliable semantic labels, which is a critical step in converting geometric point clouds into meaningful crime scene reconstructions. Murugan et al. (2024) highlighted how DL based methods have enhanced the detection of key evidence types, such as weapons, footprints, and bloodstains. The authors emphasized that advanced algorithms not only improve the precision of detection but also streamline the documentation process. The authors argued that simplifying the documentation procedures leads to a more dependable and efficient investigative process that protects the integrity of the evidence.

Beyond evidence analysis, Mandalapu et al. (2023) utilized DL for predictive insights into criminal behavior. The authors provided a comprehensive review of over 150 studies to identify patterns and trends in criminal activity. Traditional ML models such as Decision Tree, Support Vector Machine, Logistic Regression, and Random Forest were analyzed. The study found that DL models, such as CNNs, are suitable for handling video, image, social media, and spatial crime data. The paper noted that algorithmic models trained on extensive datasets can predict potential crime hotspots, providing valuable tools for law enforcement agencies to prevent crime instead of merely responding to it.

Chokkadi (2019) proposed a study on advancing facial recognition systems. The authors noted how these systems had evolved significantly due to large data repositories and powerful hardware. They highlighted the importance of sketch recognition for law enforcement, stating that matching sketches to photos was challenging because sketches were based on eyewitness descriptions and often missed critical details. It was pointed out that traditional recognition systems relied on feature extraction and classification models. However, recent research has begun using DL to improve accuracy by automatically learning features from large datasets. The aim of (Chokkadi, 2019) was to review these DL approaches in face recognition and survey different techniques for matching composite sketches to photos. Although not directly related to 3D reconstruction, these DL applications demonstrate the broader potential of DL in CSI, which may support future integration with spatial documentation.

The aforementioned studies with emerging technologies collectively reflect a great transformation for CSIs. The narratives indicate that DL enables faster, more accurate, and objective analysis of physical evidence. Evidence such as weapons, footprints, and bloodstains simplifies documentation and can standardize certain analytical steps, subject to dataset and model limitations. Beyond evidence processing, DL can predict criminal behavior and identify crime hotspots, offering proactive tools for law enforcement. Additionally, DL has advanced facial recognition, sketch, and photo matching by automatically learning features from large datasets. Overall, DL is shifting CSIs toward more efficient, reliable, and technologically driven approaches.

Deep Learning Architectures for 3D Point Cloud Processing

DL methods for 3D point cloud analysis differ primarily in how they represent and process spatial data (K. Zhang et al., 2024). Unlike images, point clouds are irregular, unordered, and sparsely distributed in three-dimensional space, making them difficult to process using CNNs (Bello et al., 2020). To address these challenges, several architectural approaches have been utilized, each offering advantages and limitations depending on the application context.

One common strategy is projection-based methods, which convert 3D point clouds into 2D representations such as depth maps, range images, or multiple view projections (Inadomi & Chun, 2025). These representations allow the use of established 2D CNN architectures that are computationally efficient and well understood. However, projecting 3D data onto 2D planes can result in the loss of geometric information and spatial relationships that are important for accurate scene interpretation (Kellner et al., 2022).

Another approach involves voxel-based methods, where the 3D space is discretized into regular volumetric grids known as voxels (Shi et al., 2016). This representation allows 3D CNNs to be applied directly to spatial data, enabling the capture of volumetric context and spatial structure. Despite these advantages, voxelization can be computationally expensive and memory intensive, particularly when high-resolution grids are required.

More recent approaches process raw point clouds directly. Point-based architectures such as PointNet and its extension PointNet++ learn features directly from unordered point sets without converting them into intermediate representations (Qi et al., 2016). These models preserve fine geometric details and are efficient for irregular data, although early versions struggled to capture local structures within complex scenes. Hierarchical extensions address this limitation by learning features at multiple spatial scales.

DGCNNs represent another emerging category, where points are treated as nodes connected by edges based on spatial proximity (Wang et al., 2018). These methods can effectively model relationships between neighboring points and capture local geometric structures. However, they may introduce higher computational complexity depending on graph construction and neighborhood size.

The diversity of these architectural approaches reflects the ongoing effort to balance computational efficiency, geometric accuracy, and scalability when processing large and sparse 3D point clouds. Understanding these architectural differences is important when reviewing existing studies that apply DL to LiDAR data, as the choice of representation often determines the performance and suitability of a method for a specific task.

Reviewing DL Methods for LiDAR Data Fusion

Recent advances concerning fusion of point cloud data with DL have significantly enhanced perception-dependent systems in domains such as robotics and autonomous vehicles (Li et al., 2021; Tsai et al., 2021). The literature indicates that there is limited application of point cloud data fusion alongside DL for CSI. Accurate point cloud environmental understanding relies on multiple sensors, among which LiDAR stands out for its ability to capture precise spatial point cloud information (Maneli & Isafiade, 2022). As a result, DL with LiDAR point clouds has become increasingly vital for tasks such as object detection, segmentation, and tracking (W. Liu et al., 2019). However, LiDAR alone faces challenges in difficult conditions such as heavy rain or fog. This limitation motivates sensor fusion approaches that integrate LiDAR and DL to provide richer semantic meaning. These fusion techniques, while improving robustness, introduce new difficulties in balancing accuracy and computational efficiency (Wu et al., 2022).

Building on this, recent surveys emphasize the rapid progress of DL architectures designed for 3D LiDAR data, particularly in the context of autonomous driving. Processing large, sparse, and unstructured point clouds remains a core challenge. Li et al. (2021) presented a comprehensive review of over 140 studies on DL for LiDAR-based perception in autonomous driving, focusing on object detection, semantic segmentation, and classification. It covers voxel-based networks, point-based models such as PointNet and PointNet++, graph-based methods, and multi-view CNNs, noting their trade-offs in geometric accuracy, efficiency, and scalability. Common benchmarks include Karlsruhe Institute of Technology and Toyota Technological Institute (KITTI) and Semantic3D, with Intersection over Union (IoU) and Average Precision (AP) as key metrics. DL clearly outperforms traditional approaches, but no single 3D representation is best for all tasks. Findings in the literature highlight several key challenges. These include efficiency, scalable 3D representations, real-time performance on embedded platforms, unified multi-task systems, handling sparse and variable LiDAR data, achieving richer contextual understanding, and addressing the limited availability and high labeling cost of annotated 3D datasets.

Complementing these broader surveys, Alaba and Ball (2022) provided a structured overview of DL methods designed specifically for LiDAR-specific 3D object detection, focusing on how different data representation strategies address the challenges of sparse, irregular 3D point clouds. The survey categorizes existing approaches into three main groups. These are: (i) Projection-based methods, which convert point clouds into 2D views for efficient CNN processing; (ii) Voxel or pillar-based methods, which discretize space into regular 3D grids for volumetric or sparse convolution; and (iii) raw point cloud or graph-based methods, which operate directly on unstructured points using architectures derived from PointNet or Graph Neural Networks (GNNs). Standard datasets such as KITTI are highlighted as primary benchmarks for evaluating detection performance. Overall, the review concludes that the fusion of LiDAR and DL has advanced rapidly, producing highly accurate detectors across all representation families. However, it also emphasizes several remaining gaps. These include achieving real-time performance under compute constraints, improving robustness to sparsity, and occlusion.

In parallel, Diab et al. (2022) reviewed DL approaches for classifying LiDAR point clouds in remote-sensing applications. These include land mapping, terrain and urban scene analysis, and vegetation characterization. It organizes existing methods by their underlying data representations, covering projection-based, voxel, and point architectures. The authors note that point-based and graph-based models such as DGCNN and ConvPoint often achieve the strongest performance due to their ability to preserve fine-grained geometric structure. The survey highlights commonly used datasets, including Toronto3D, Paris-Lille 3D, International Society for Photogrammetry and Remote Sensing (ISPRS) datasets, and Stanford Large Scale 3D Indoor Spaces (S3DIS) as key benchmarks for training and evaluating classification performance. These findings suggest potential benefits for CSI applications if adapted appropriately, but direct evidence in CSI is lacking. However, the authors highlight several gaps, such as inconsistent dataset availability and benchmarking standards. Limited generalizations across diverse remote sensing contexts, challenges arising from noise, sparsity, and variability in real-world LiDAR data.

Rauch and Braml (2023) reviewed and critically analyzed the state of DL methods for semantic segmentation of 3D point clouds in construction applications. The authors categorize existing approaches into projection-based, voxel, and point-based methods. They noted that despite DL improving segmentation accuracy, no single approach dominates, and method choice depends on point-cloud type, scale, and resources.

Research findings highlight transformers for dense scans, projection methods for real-time use, and graph-based methods for large, sparse data. Limitations mentioned by the authors include a few publicly available construction-specific datasets, class imbalance, limited generalization from generic datasets, underdeveloped instance segmentation, and high computational demands. Highlighting the need for domain-specific data, better metrics, and hardware-efficient architectures for industry use.

Qi et al. (2017) noted that few studies had explored DL on point sets, with PointNet being a pioneering approach. However, PointNet does not capture local structures inherent in the metric space, limiting its ability to recognize fine patterns and generalize to complex scenes. To address this, they introduce PointNet++, a hierarchical neural network that recursively applies PointNet on a nested partitioning of the input point set. By leveraging metric space distances, the network learns local features across increasing contextual scales. They also propose novel set learning layers to handle varying point densities, improving robustness and performance. Experiments demonstrate that Point-Net++ efficiently learns deep point set features and significantly outperforms previous methods on challenging 3D point cloud benchmarks.

Synthesis of Findings on LiDAR Data Fusion

These reviewed studies demonstrate that DL models for point cloud processing, ranging from voxel, projection, point, and graph-based architectures to specialized frameworks such as PointNet++, DGCNN, and large-scale LiDAR perception networks, have achieved significant advances across domains such as autonomous driving, robotics, and remote sensing. These methods consistently show strong capabilities in object detection, segmentation, classification, and structural understanding. These methods have been validated on rich benchmark datasets and complex real-world environments. However, despite rapid progress and clear applicability to spatial tasks, these models have not been applied to CSI using point cloud data. Bridging this gap presents an opportunity to improve CSIs. This can potentially improve reconstruction accuracy, evidence interpretation, and scene understanding in a spatial crime scene.

REVIEW METHODOLOGY

This chapter adopts a scoping-style narrative literature review to map and critically synthesize research on LiDAR sensing and DL for semantic 3D reconstruction in CSI. Narrative reviews are particularly suitable for interdisciplinary and emerging domains where relevant literature is dispersed across multiple fields (Grant and

Booth, 2009). Unlike systematic reviews, which aim for exhaustive coverage and strict reproducibility, this approach provides a structured synthesis of influential studies selected for their relevance, methodological rigor, and applicability to crime scene investigation contexts. The approach is especially appropriate for areas such as LiDAR–DL fusion in crime scene reconstruction, where the literature spans multiple domains including autonomous driving, cultural heritage digitization, robotics, and forensic investigation.

Purpose and Scope

The objective of this narrative review is to:

- Summarize major advances in LiDAR sensing and DL relevant to 3D reconstruction and semantic annotation.
- Identify potential applications and limitations for CSI processes.
- Highlight research gaps and future directions specifically applicable to crime scene investigators.

The review focuses on LiDAR-based 3D capture, point-cloud processing, semantic segmentation, and CSIs. Studies exclusively addressing unrelated policing tasks such as crime prediction, facial recognition, and CCTV weapon detection are intentionally excluded unless they provide transferable insights directly relevant to 3D reconstruction or crime investigation interpretation.

Search Strategy and Selection Rationale

Literature was identified through targeted searches in established academic databases and repositories, including Web of Science, IEEE Xplore, and relevant conference proceedings. Given the interdisciplinary nature of the topic, a narrative approach was chosen to allow integration of insights from adjacent domains that are methodologically relevant to crime scene reconstruction. Considering the fact that this is a narrative review, a full reproducible search protocol is not provided. Studies were selected based on the following:

- Relevance to LiDAR and point-cloud processing, including acquisition, segmentation, and semantic labeling.
- Use of DL methods applied to LiDAR point clouds or 3D reconstruction.
- Potential applicability to crime scene reconstruction, such as accuracy requirements, scene complexity, and real-world deployment constraints.

- Contribution to understanding challenges such as noise, occlusion, low-cost sensors, and real-time processing.

Inclusion and Exclusion Criteria (Narrative Rationale)

To maintain coherence and CSI relevance, the review excludes studies that:

- Focus solely on non-3D AI policing tasks without any direct link to reconstruction.
- Address purely theoretical ML research without experimental evaluation or practical application.
- Present unrelated sensor modalities such as purely RGB-only approaches without depth.

The selection is not exhaustive; rather, it is intentionally selective to provide a coherent and meaningful synthesis for practitioners and policymakers. A full list of the reviewed studies is provided in the references.

Synthesis and Interpretation

The selected studies were analyzed using a thematic synthesis approach. Key themes were extracted and compared across studies, including:

- Accuracy and reliability of LiDAR sensors (TLS and low-cost)
- DL methods for point cloud segmentation and classification
- Integration for 3D crime scene reconstruction and CSI processes
- Practical constraints and ethical considerations

This narrative synthesis aims to identify patterns, strengths, limitations, and gaps in the literature without claiming statistical completeness or strict reproducibility.

RESULT AND ANALYSIS

Research Question 1

What research developments and applications exist in employing 3D spatial data capture technologies to produce highly accurate and detailed reconstructions of crime scenes?

Recent research increasingly employs advanced 3D spatial data acquisition technologies such as LiDAR, photogrammetry, and structured light to produce 3D reconstructions of crime scenes (Maneli & Isafiade, 2022). Prior approaches, however, achieved accuracy only through systems that were costly, cumbersome, and required advanced training, particularly when using terrestrial laser scanners (TLSs) (Costantino et al., 2016; Tredinnick et al., 2019). Contemporary studies, in contrast, explore more accessible and mobile alternatives, comparing various 3D acquisition methods for efficient crime scene documentation (H. Liu et al., 2016).

The following authors have commented on current advancements: Kottner et al. (2023) observed that while 3D documentation relied on costly TLSs and expert operators, the integration of Apple Incorporation's LiDAR technology into mobile devices made 3D scanning more accessible for crime scene use. Similarly, Sheshtar et al. (2025) evaluated two LiDAR-enabled mobile devices, the iPhone 15 Pro Max and the Leica BLK360, and photogrammetry under various lighting and scanning conditions. The research found that the iPhone scan conducted in daylight with a five-minute fast sweep achieved the highest accuracy, with an average error of 0.1084mand 90% of point clouds under 0.1224 m error. This demonstrates the potential of mobile LiDAR for rapid and efficient crime scene documentation. These findings underscore a broader trend toward handheld and portable sensors capable of capturing crime scenes efficiently in time sensitive contexts. While suitable for rapid scene capture and visualization, this level of error may be insufficient for tasks requiring sub-centimetre precision, such as ballistic trajectory analysis.

Similar advances have also emerged in photogrammetry-based 3D data acquisition. Edelman and Aalders (2018) explored photogrammetry enhanced with multispectral imaging, demonstrating how combining infrared, hyperspectral, and thermal data can improve the visualization and chemical analysis of latent evidence. These multispectral 3D tools allowed for the capturing of crime scenes in their original state, showcasing both the feasibility and challenges of applying such techniques in practice. This research highlights the practical value of photogrammetry not only for structural reconstruction but also for CSI evidence enhancement, particularly where surface composition or lighting is challenging.

Complementing the work of Edelman, Sieberth et al. (2018), investigated light field cameras, which record both light intensity and direction to enable post-capture refocusing and depth estimation. This technology allows novice users to gather 3D data quickly, even in uncertain or dynamic conditions, improving reconstruction quality and offering a flexible complement to LiDAR scanning. Although not as precise as LiDAR, light field imaging provides flexibility and ease of use, making it a practical supplementary tool for investigators.

Galanakis et al. (2021) emphasized the gradual shift from traditional photography and manual measurement toward 3D digital documentation, which offers enhanced accuracy and reproducibility. Despite its benefits, adoption has been slow due to the cost and complexity of existing tools. The study reviewed practical considerations such as scene type, size, and time constraints and introduced a publicly available multimodal dataset from a simulated indoor crime scene to support further research. This dataset provides a foundation for benchmarking and advancing future methods, reflecting the increasing push toward reproducible forensic research.

RQ1: Summary and key insights

Collectively, these contemporary developments reveal a clear trajectory concerning crime scene spatial data acquisition and reconstruction. 3D data acquisitions are moving away from costly and cumbersome implementations and moving toward more accessible, accurate 3D documentation methods. Cost-effective LiDAR devices such as the iPhone earlier mentioned, enhanced photogrammetry, and light field imaging are emerging as practical, scalable alternatives to traditional TLS-based workflows. These innovations not only reduce cost and expertise barriers but also expand on real-world applicability. This enables faster, more comprehensive, and more reproducible CSI across diverse criminal environments.

Research Question 2

What fundamental characteristics of LiDAR technology make it theoretically superior to photogrammetry and other conventional 3D spatial documentation techniques for accurate and comprehensive 3D crime scene reconstruction?

The acquisition of 3D spatial data refers to the process of capturing geometric information that defines the shape, position, and dimensions of objects within a measurable volume of space (Villa et al., 2023). This process forms the foundation for spatial reconstruction and analysis in various fields, such as architecture (Q. Wang et al., 2020), autonomous navigation (Reiser et al., 2017), and CSI (Galanakis et al., 2021). The goal is to collect reliable and quantifiable spatial information that can be used to recreate, interpret, and analyze real-world environments.

A range of technologies has been developed to achieve 3D spatial data acquisition, each relying on different sensing principles and computational approaches.

The most prominent include LiDAR (Lohani & Ghosh, 2017), photogrammetry (Georgopoulos & Stathopoulou, 2017; Sapirstein, 2016), structured-light scanning (Lilienblum & Al-Hamadi, 2015), Time of Flight (ToF) cameras (He & Chen, 2019), and stereo-vision systems (Islam et al., 2020). These technologies differ in terms of operating mechanisms, achievable resolution, data density, and computational complexity. Selecting the appropriate technique depends on factors such as the scale of the environment, the required level of accuracy, ambient lighting conditions, and the logistical constraints of the investigation (Galanakis et al., 2021).

LiDAR typically measures distance by emitting laser pulses and measuring ToF, although some systems use phase-shift or triangulation methods. (Behroozpour et al., 2017). The combination of thousands or even millions of these distance measurements yields a dense 3D point cloud that represents the geometry of a scene (Maneli & Isafiade, 2022). Photogrammetry, by contrast, reconstructs 3D structures from multiple overlapping two-dimensional (2D) photographs captured from different viewpoints (Berezowski et al., 2020). Through feature detection, camera pose estimation, and triangulation, photogrammetry produces textured 3D models (Buck et al., 2020). Structured light scanning involves projecting a predetermined light pattern, such as grids, stripes, or dots, onto the surface of an object and analyzing the pattern deformation to compute depth (Lilienblum & Al-Hamadi, 2015). ToF cameras determine depth by measuring the time required for emitted light to travel to a surface and back, thereby producing per-pixel depth maps of the entire scene in real time (He & Chen, 2019). Finally, stereovision systems employ two or more spatially separated cameras; depth is inferred by identifying corresponding image features in each view and calculating disparity through triangulation (Islam et al., 2020).

Table 1 summarizes and compares the capabilities of the main 3D spatial data acquisition methods. Key abbreviations include: LI - light independence; LRA – long-range accuracy; SRA - short-range accuracy; High Res - high resolution. This table summarizes general tendencies reported in the literature. Actual performance depends on device class, environment, and specific use case scenario; the table is illustrative rather than definitive.

Table 1. General tendencies of 3D spatial data acquisition methods (H = High, M = Medium, L = Low)

Technology	LI	LRA	SRA	High Res	Real Time	Surface Sensitivity	Cost Effective
LiDAR	H	H	H	H	M	M	L
Photogrammetry	L	H	H	H	L	H	H
Structured Light	L	L	H	H	M	M	M

Technology	LI	LRA	SRA	High Res	Real Time	Surface Sensitivity	Cost Effective
ToF	M	L	M	M	H	M	H
Stereo Vision	L	L	M	M	H	H	H

Among these technologies, LiDARis widely regarded as the most robust and versatile tool for high-fidelity 3D documentation (Buck et al., 2020). As shown in Table 1, its primary drawback is the high cost. Unlike photogrammetry and structured light, which are limited by lighting conditions and surface characteristics, LiDAR generates dense, accurate point clouds regardless of illumination or texture (Burdziakowski & Bobkowska, 2021). In the context of CSIs, the characteristics of LiDAR render it particularly effective for capturing intricate or cluttered environments (Galante et al., 2022).

According to Maneli et al. (Maneli & Isafiade, 2023), high-end TLS systems and some consumer-grade LiDAR can achieve below 5 mm accuracy under controlled conditions, error margins depending on range and surface properties. This allows investigators to maintain the geometric integrity and spatial relationships among evidence items. The accuracy achieved in these reconstruction captures facilitates a variety of data collection activities, such as trajectory analysis (Zhao et al., 2019), event reconstruction (Zancajo-Blazquez et al., 2015), and courtroom visualizations (EngstrÅNom, 2018). The capability of LiDAR to preserve accurate scale proportions and precise spatial relationships is essential for assessing variables such as the distances between items at a crime scene. This capability reduces the potential for subjective interpretations among crime scene investigators compared to employing traditional techniques, such as photography, for the reconstruction of crime scenes (Wang et al., 2019).

RQ2: Summary and key insights

Despite the aforementioned advantages of LiDAR, raw LiDAR point cloud data alone conveys only geometric and positional information. LiDAR point cloud data alone lacks semantic meaning; it does not inherently convey what objects are. LiDAR captures where objects are located but not what those objects represent (Dewan et al., 2017). Consequently, such data cannot distinguish a weapon from a bloodstain or a piece of furniture without further interpretation. This limitation underscores the need for integrating semantic understanding into 3D renders.

Research Question 3

Which LiDAR–DL fusion methods from adjacent domains are potentially transferable to CSI, and what are the barriers (technical, legal, operational) to adoption?

The fusion of 3D spatial data with DL methodologies has demonstrated transformative potential in domains such as cultural heritage and millimeter-wave beam selection (Klautau et al., 2019; Pierdicca et al., 2020). Although these approaches have not yet been applied to CSI workflows, their capabilities, such as automated point cloud segmentation and object recognition, may offer valuable insights. Empirical validation in CSI contexts remains a critical area for future research. The research gap, therefore, lies not in algorithmic development itself but in the translation, adaptation, and assessment of existing methods to meet CSI-specific requirements, building on lessons from domains such as autonomous driving, robotics, and cultural heritage.

LiDAR-DL fusion

Various DL models, including graph-based architectures, PointNet++, and multi-view approaches, have demonstrated strong performance in 3D point cloud segmentation tasks (Azmil et al., 2024; Melotti et al., 2020; Pierdicca et al., 2020). These models can effectively handle sparse, irregular, and noisy point clouds (Bello et al., 2020; Ding et al., 2023; R. Zhang et al., 2023), which parallels challenges encountered in crime scene reconstructions (Dima & Covaciu, 2015; Galanakis et al., 2021). While these techniques have not yet been rigorously validated in CSI contexts, they may provide valuable insights for improving object recognition, semantic segmentation, and scene interpretation in future CSI workflows.

The following section summarizes relevant research conducted by other scholars, alongside observations made in this research regarding the potential prospects for crime investigators during investigation processes. The authors draw parallels to crime investigation processes. Pierdicca et al. (2020) presented a study on a DL framework tailored for architectural heritage documentation. The authors proposed an enhanced DGCNN that incorporated both surface normals and color features to improve segmentation quality. A beneficial feature that could be applied to point cloud data obtained from cost-effective LiDAR-enabled devices, as mentioned in these studies (Kottner et al., 2023; Maneli & Isafiade, 2022; Sheshtar et al., 2025), could further enhance the analysis. Rauch and Braml (2023) reviewed DL-based methods for point cloud semantic segmentations in the construction industry. The authors noted that DL methods significantly improve object and component recognition in construction environments. Hybrid methods that combine multiple data representations show the most robust performance. These insights can be leveraged in CSIs that use cost-effective LiDAR point cloud devices. DL and hybrid representation methods can enhance the recognition and classification of scene elements. Elements such as weapons and structural features can be identified even when the captured point clouds are sparse or noisy, especially from low-cost LiDAR devices.

Bello et al. (2020) summarized the advances of 3D point cloud merged with DL, comparing point-based models such as PointNet++ with graph-based and voxel-based CNN approaches. The authors conducted benchmarks and results on datasets such as ModelNet and ShapeNet, which consistently indicated strong performance. Concerning hybrid models, combining multiple representations indicates growing promise. The authors highlighted that DL methodologies improved object recognition, and hybrid models, combining multiple representations, can help automatically identify objects, evidence, or structural features in complex crime scene point clouds. Another point where parallels can be drawn is with enhanced reconstruction accuracy. The authors mention in the literature that graph-based and point-based models can better handle irregular geometries; these techniques can improve the fidelity of 3D crime scene reconstructions from LiDAR scans. Ding et al. (2023) surveyed current DL frameworks for point cloud analysis. The authors covered and compared similar implementations mentioned above concerning point-based, voxel-based, graph-based, and multi-view representations. They evaluated their strengths and computational trade-offs. Widely known datasets were used, such as ModelNet, ShapeNet, KITTI, and ScanNet. The authors highlighted that point-based methods offer notable efficiency and flexibility, whereas voxel methods tend to yield more accurate spatial reasoning at greater computational cost. Building on this, ModelNet and ScanNet are great Computer-Aided Design (CAD)-based datasets that can easily aid in identifying point cloud data on indoor scans and object identification when utilised correctly. Building on this, ModelNet and ScanNet are valuable datasets, ModelNet being Computer-Aided Design (CAD)-based and ScanNet are derived from real indoor scans that can aid in point cloud analysis and object identification when used in crime scene scans. In summary, integrating DL with a low-cost LiDAR-enabled device could inform future CSI studies. These techniques have proven to have semantic understanding and adaptability to diverse 3D structures, suggesting strong potential for automating evidence identification and improving reconstructions.

Challenges and Limitations

Despite the positive attributes of fusing LiDARpoint clouds with DL techniques, several limitations have been noted. Domain-specific annotated datasets are scarce (Pierdicca et al., 2020). Moreover, Rauch and Braml (2023) stated that progress is limited by the lack of construction-specific datasets and the high computational demands of modern architectures. Models trained on general datasets such as

ModelNet, ShapeNet, an SemanticKITTI often struggle to generalize to sparse, noisy, or irregular real-world point clouds. High computational costs and scalability issues limit the processing of large or complex scenes. Bello et al. (2020) stated that challenges persist, such as sparse and irregular point clouds remaining difficult to process efficiently, and many architectures cannot scale to large scenes without heavy computational resources. While fine-grained classes and intricate geometries remain challenging. Moreover, Ding et al. (2023) identified two key issues: the lack of standardized evaluation across studies and the limited availability of large-scale, real-world datasets. Based on empirical research findings, DL models trained on general datasets lack crime scene specialization, reducing transferability. Another point that cannot be overlooked is that low-cost LiDAR sensors can compromise point cloud quality, resulting in noisy data.

RQ3: Summary and key insights

Existing DL methods for point cloud segmentation and object recognition demonstrate strong potential for improving crime scene reconstruction through semantic labeling and automated interpretation. However, the transferability of these approaches to CSI remains limited due to the scarcity of annotated crime scene datasets, the variability and noise of low-cost LiDAR data, and high computational requirements. Future work must focus on developing CSI-specific datasets, adapting architectures for noisy and sparse data, and balancing accuracy with operational feasibility in real-world investigations.

Ethical concerns in CSI

Beyond technical and operational challenges, implementing LiDAR–DL systems in CSIs raises significant ethical and legal concerns. A key issue is the transparency and explainability of DL outputs: models used for semantic segmentation and scene interpretation often produce results that are difficult for investigators, legal professionals, or juries to interpret (Hunter et al., 2020). Richmond and Primeau (2025) note the "hermeneutic risk," where AI outputs may be misunderstood, potentially affecting legal decisions.Without clear explanations, AI-derived analyses risk being misinterpreted or overvalued in court.

Closely linked is the reliability and admissibility of artificial intelligence (AI)-generated evidence. Legal standards require evidence to be verifiable, reproducible, and accurate (Richmond & Primeau, 2025). However, uncertainties from model predictions, sensor limitations, or dataset biases can compromise evidentiary credibility, raising doubts about whether algorithmic interpretations can meet the "beyond a reasonable doubt" standard, especially when expert testimony is needed to clarify findings.

While this chapter does not seek to resolve these complex ethical and legal questions, acknowledging them is essential for guiding the responsible deployment of LiDAR–DL technologies in CSI practices. By understanding the limitations and risks associated with algorithmic evidence, researchers can work toward solutions that balance technological innovation with legal integrity and ethical accountability.

CONCLUSION AND RECOMMENDATIONS

This review has synthesized research from 2015 to 2025 concerning the integration of 3D spatial data acquisition and DL for CSI. The evidence indicates a clear transition from high-cost, stationary terrestrial laser scanner toward mobile, accessible LiDAR and photogrammetric solutions. While these emerging tools lower the barrier to entry for digital documentation, their integration into forensic workflows requires addressing specific technical and evidentiary gaps.

Summary of Findings

LiDAR technology provides a robust foundation for 3D documentation due to its light independence and geometric precision. However, the raw point clouds generated lack inherent semantic context, necessitating manual interpretation that is time-consuming and subject to human error. This review identified that DL architectures, specifically point-based and graph-based models, offer a technically viable pathway for automating the classification of forensic evidence within these 3D environments. While adjacent fields like autonomous driving have achieved high performance in these tasks, the transferability to CSI is currently constrained by a lack of domain-specific annotated datasets and the noise profiles of low-cost mobile sensors.

Evidence-Based Recommendations

To advance the operational use of LiDAR-DL fusion in CSI, the following actions are recommended:

- **Standardization of Accuracy Metrics:** Forensic practitioners should adopt a dual-tier accuracy standard. Mobile LiDAR is suitable for rapid scene visualization and "walk-throughs," whereas high-precision tasks (e.g., bloodstain pattern or trajectory analysis) must continue to rely on TLS or calibrated photogrammetry offering sub-centimeter precision.

- **Development of Forensic Datasets:** Future research must focus on creating publicly available, annotated 3D point cloud datasets of crime-specific objects (e.g., firearms, biological evidence, forced entry markers) to reduce the "domain gap" when training DL models.
- **Hybrid Frameworks:** Developers should prioritize hybrid architectures that combine geometric data from LiDAR to improve the reliability of semantic segmentation in cluttered crime scenes.
- **Admissibility Protocols:** Given the "hermeneutic risk" of AI-derived evidence, the deployment of DL models must be accompanied by explainability frameworks that allow forensic experts to verify the reasoning behind an automated classification in a court of law.

In conclusion, the fusion of LiDAR and DL represents a significant potential shift toward objective and scalable CSI documentation. However, moving from "proof-of-concept" to "courtroom-ready" requires rigorous validation of error bounds and a commitment to transparent, reproducible AI methodologies.

REFERENCES

Abbas, S., & Abed, F. M. (2024). Revolutionizing depth sensing: A review study of apple lidarsensor for as-built scanning applications. *Journal of Engineering*, *30*(4), 175–199. DOI: 10.31026/j.eng.2024.04.11

Alaba, S. Y., & Ball, J. E. (2022). A survey on deep-learning-based lidar 3d object detection for autonomous driving. *Sensors (Basel)*, *22*(24), 9577. Advance online publication. DOI: 10.3390/s22249577 PMID: 36559950

Awais, M., Naeem, F., Rasool, N., & Mahmood, S. (2018). Identification of sex from footprint dimensions using machine learning: A study on population of punjab in pakistan. *Egyptian Journal of Forensic Sciences*, *8*(1), 72. DOI: 10.1186/s41935-018-0106-2

Azmil, R., Mohd Ariff, M. F., Razali, A. F., Azmy, S. N., Darwin, N., & Idris, K. M. (2024). Transforming physical crime scene into geospatial-based point cloud data. Engineering, Technology amp. *Applied Scientific Research*, *14*(3), 13974–13981. DOI: 10.48084/etasr.6888

Bahirat, K., & Prabhakaran, B. (2017, July). A study on lidar data forensics. DOI: 10.1109/ICME.2017.8019395

Balbudhe, M. S., Shetty, B. S. K., Arun Kumar, N., Singh, D., & Sherekar, A. I. (2025). Crime scene reconstruction: A scoping review. *Egyptian Journal of Forensic Sciences*, *15*(1), 79. DOI: 10.1186/s41935-025-00495-5

Behroozpour, B., Sandborn, P. A. M., Wu, M. C., & Boser, B. E. (2017). Lidar system architectures and circuits. *IEEE Communications Magazine*, *55*(10), 135–142. DOI: 10.1109/MCOM.2017.1700030

Bello, S. A., Yu, S., Wang, C., Adam, J. M., & Li, J. (2020). Review: Deep learning on 3d point clouds. *Remote Sensing (Basel)*, *12*(11), 1729. Advance online publication. DOI: 10.3390/rs12111729

Berezowski, V., Mallett, X., & Moffat, I. (2020, March). Geomatic techniques in forensic science. *RE:view*, *60*(2), 99–107. Advance online publication. DOI: 10.1016/j.scijus.2019.10.006 PMID: 32111294

Boldt, M., Borg, A., Svensson, M., & Hildeby, J. (2018). Predicting burglars' risk exposure and level of pre-crime preparation using crime scene data. *Intelligent Data Analysis*, *22*(1), 167–190. DOI: 10.3233/IDA-163220

Buck, U., Buße, K., Campana, L., Gummel, F., Schyma, C., & Jackowski, C. (2020). What happened before the run over? morphometric 3d reconstruction. *Forensic Science International*, *306*, 110059. Advance online publication. DOI: 10.1016/j.forsciint.2019.110059 PMID: 31780351

Burdziakowski, P., & Bobkowska, K. (2021). Uav photogrammetry under poor lighting conditions—Accuracy considerations. *Sensors (Basel)*, *21*(10), 3531. Advance online publication. DOI: 10.3390/s21103531 PMID: 34069500

Chokkadi, S. (2019). Astudy on various state of the art of the art face recognition system using deep learning techniques. *International Journal of Advanced Trends in Computer Science and Engineering*, **•••**, 1590–1600. DOI: 10.30534/ijatcse/2019/84842019

Costantino, D., Angelini, M. G., & Mazzone, F. (2016). Integrated survey methodology for the crime reconstruction. *Imaging Science Journal*, *64*(6), 341–351. DOI: 10.1080/13682199.2016.1219528

Cui, Y., Chen, R., Chu, W., Chen, L., Tian, D., Li, Y., & Cao, D. (2022). Deep learning for image and point cloud fusion in autonomous driving: A review. *IEEE Transactions on Intelligent Transportation Systems*, *23*(2), 722–739. DOI: 10.1109/TITS.2020.3023541

Dewan, A., Oliveira, G. L., & Burgard, W. (2017). Deep semantic classification for 3d lidar data. *2017 IEEE/RSJ International Conference on Intelligent Robots and Systems (IROS)*, 3544-3549. DOI: 10.1109/IROS.2017.8206198

Diab, A., Kashef, R., & Shaker, A. (2022). Deep learning for lidar point cloud classification in remote sensing. *Sensors (Basel)*, *22*(20), 7868. Advance online publication. DOI: 10.3390/s22207868 PMID: 36298220

Dima, D., & Covaciu, D. (2015). Simulation method in pc crash using point cloud files. ANNALS OF THE ORADEA UNIVERSITY. Fascicle of Management and Technological Engineering. [XIV]. *XXIV*, *2015*(1). Advance online publication. DOI: 10.15660/AUOFMTE.2015-1.13105

Ding, Z., Sun, Y., Xu, S., Pan, Y., Peng, Y., & Mao, Z. (2023). Recent advances and perspectives in deep learning techniques for 3d point cloud data processing. *Robotics (Basel, Switzerland)*, *12*(4), 100. Advance online publication. DOI: 10.3390/robotics12040100

Edelman, G. J., & Aalders, M. C. (2018). Photogrammetry using visible, infrared, hyperspectral and thermal imaging of crime scenes. *Forensic Science International*, *292*, 181–189. DOI: 10.1016/j.forsciint.2018.09.025 PMID: 30321744

Galanakis, G., Zabulis, X., Evdaimon, T., Fikenscher, S.-E., Allertseder, S., Tsikrika, T., & Vrochidis, S. (2021). A study of 3d digitisation modalities for crime scene investigation. *Forensic Science, 1*(2), 56–85. DOI: 10.3390/forensicsci1020008

Galante, N., Cotroneo, R., Furci, D., Lodetti, G., & Casali, M. B. (2022). Applications of artificial intelligence in forensic sciences: C urrent potential benefits, limitations and perspectives. *International Journal of Legal Medicine, 137*(2), 445–458. DOI: 10.1007/s00414-022-02928-5 PMID: 36507961

Georgopoulos, A., & Stathopoulou, E. K. (2017). Data acquisition for 3d geometric recording: State of the art and recent innovations. In Vincent, M. L., Lopez-Menchero Bendicho, V. M., Ioannides, M., & Levy, T. E. (Eds.), *Heritage and archaeology in the digital age: Acquisition, curation, and dissemination ofspatial cultural heritage data* (pp. 1–26). Springer International Publishing., DOI: 10.1007/978-3-319-65370-9_1

Glomb, P., Romaszewski, M., Cholewa, M., & Domino, K. (2018). Application of hyperspectral imaging and machine learning methods for the detection of gunshot residue patterns. *Forensic Science International, 290*, 227–237. 10.1016/j.forsciint.2018.06.040. DOI: 10.1016/j.forsciint.2018.06.040 PMID: 30077814

Grant, M. J., & Booth, A. (2009). A typology of reviews: An analysis of 14 review types and associated methodologies. *Health Information and Libraries Journal, 26*(2), 91–108. 10.1111/j.1471-1842.2009.00848.x. DOI: 10.1111/j.1471-1842.2009.00848.x PMID: 19490148

He, Y., & Chen, S. (2019). Recent advances in 3d data acquisition and processing by time-of flight camera. *IEEE Access : Practical Innovations, Open Solutions, 7*, 12495–12510. DOI: 10.1109/ACCESS.2019.2891693

Huang, Z., Wen, Y., Wang, Z., Ren, J., & Jia, K. (2024). Surface reconstruction from point clouds: A survey and a benchmark. *IEEE Transactions on Pattern Analysis and Machine Intelligence, 46*(12), 9727–9748. DOI: 10.1109/TPAMI.2024.3429209 PMID: 39012756

Hunter, D., Bagaric, M., & Stobbs, N. (2020). A framework for the efficient and ethical use of artificial intelligence in the criminal justice system'(2020). *Fla St UL Rev, 47*, 749.

Iacob, D., Furst, A., & Hadrys, T. (2019). Amachine learning model to predict the origin of forensically relevant body fluids. *Forensic Science International. Genetics Supplement Series, 7*(1), 392–394. 10.1016/j.fsigss.2019.10.025. DOI: 10.1016/j.fsigss.2019.10.025

Inadomi, S., & Chun, P. (2025). A comparative study of projection-based vs. point-based point clouds segmentation for 3d bridge modeling. *Structure and Infrastructure Engineering*, *0*(0), 1–13. DOI: 10.1080/15732479.2025.2494257

Islam, A., Asikuzzaman, M., Khyam, M. O., Noor-A-Rahim, M., & Pickering, M. R. (2020). Stereo vision-based 3d positioning and tracking. *IEEE Access : Practical Innovations, Open Solutions*, *8*, 138771–138787. DOI: 10.1109/ACCESS.2020.3011360

Jadhav, E., Sankhla, M. S., & Kumar, R. (2020). Artificial intelligence: Advancing automation in forensic science criminal investigation. *Seybold Report*, *15*, 2064–2075.

Kellner, M., Stahl, B., & Reiterer, A. (2022). Fused projection-based point cloud segmentation. *Sensors (Basel)*, *22*(3), 1139. Advance online publication. DOI: 10.3390/s22031139 PMID: 35161890

Klautau, A., Gonzalez-Prelcic, N., & Heath, R. W. (2019). Lidar data for deep learningbased mmwave beam-selection. *IEEE Wireless Communications Letters*, *8*(3), 909–912. DOI: 10.1109/LWC.2019.2899571

Kottner, S., Thali, M. J., & Gascho, D. (2023). Using the iphone's lidar technology to capture 3d forensic data at crime and crash scenes. *Forensic Imaging*, *32*, 200535. 10.1016/j.fri.2023.200535. DOI: 10.1016/j.fri.2023.200535

Li, Y., Ma, L., Zhong, Z., Liu, F., Chapman, M. A., Cao, D., & Li, J. (2021). Deep learning for lidar point clouds in autonomous driving: A review. *IEEE Transactions on Neural Networks and Learning Systems*, *32*(8), 3412–3432. DOI: 10.1109/TNNLS.2020.3015992 PMID: 32822311

Lilienblum, E., & Al-Hamadi, A. (2015). A structured light approach for 3-d surface reconstruction with a stereo line-scan system. *IEEE Transactions on Instrumentation and Measurement*, *64*(5), 1258–1266. DOI: 10.1109/TIM.2014.2364105

Liu, H., Yan, Y., Zhang, X., & Wu, Z. (2016). 3d scene reconstruction based on 3d laser point cloud combining uav images. 2nd ISPRS International Conference on Computer Vision in Remote Sensing (CVRS 2015), 9901, 99011C. DOI: 10.1117/12.2234802

Liu, W., Sun, J., Li, W., Hu, T., & Wang, P. (2019). Deep learning on point clouds and its application: A survey. *Sensors (Basel)*, *19*(19), 4188. DOI: 10.3390/s19194188 PMID: 31561639

Liu, Y., Hu, D., & Fan, J.-l. (2018). A survey of crime scene investigation image retrieval. *ACTA ELECTONICA SINICA*, *46*, 761.

Lohani, B., & Ghosh, S. (2017). Airborne lidar technology: A review of data collection and processing systems. *Proceedings of the National Academy of Sciences. India. Section A, Physical Sciences*, *87*(4), 567–579. DOI: 10.1007/s40010-017-0435-9

Mandalapu, V., Elluri, L., Vyas, P., & Roy, N. (2023, March). Crime prediction using machine learning and deep learning: A systematic review and future directions. Institute of Electrical; Electronics Engineers (IEEE).

Maneli, M. A., & Isafiade, O. E. (2022). *3d forensic crime scene reconstruction involving immersive technology: A systematic literature review*. IEEE., DOI: 10.1109/ACCESS.2022.3199437

Maneli, M. A., & Isafiade, O. E. (2023). Exploration of 3d augmented reality solution for crime scene investigators in low-resource settings. Southern Africa Telecommunication Networks and Applications Conference (SATNAC) 2023, 20–25. https://www.satnac.org.za/proceedings

Maneli, M. A., & Isafiade, O. E. (2025). Towards reliable 3d crime scene investigation in low-resource regions using lidar. 2025 IST-Africa Conference (IST-Africa), 1–13. DOI: 10.23919/IST-Africa67297.2025.11060517

Mateen, M., Wen, J., Nasrullah, , Song, S., & Huang, Z. (2019). Fundus image classification using vgg-19 architecture with pca and svd. *Symmetry*, *11*(1), 1. Advance online publication. DOI: 10.3390/sym11010001

Melotti, G., & Premebida, C., & Gonc.alves, N. (2020). Multimodal deep-learning for object recognition combining camera and lidar data. 2020 IEEE International Conference on Autonomous Robot Systems and Competitions (ICARSC), 177-182. DOI: 10.1109/ICARSC49921.2020.9096138

Mohd Sabri, N. E., Chainchel Singh, M. K., Mahmood, M. S., Khoo, L. S., Mohd Yusof, M. Y. P., Heo, C. C., Muhammad Nasir, M. D., & Nawawi, H. (2023). A scoping review on drone technology applications in forensic science. *SN Applied Sciences*, *5*(9), 233. Advance online publication. DOI: 10.1007/s42452-023-05450-4

Murugan, T., Aldahmani, F. K. A. M., Almehrzi, G. S. M. A., Alsereidi, E. M. S. M., Aldahmani, A. A. K. A., & Alahbabi, E. M. M. (2024). Recent research study on ai-based crime scene evidence detection. 2024 7th International Conference on Advanced Communication Technologies and Networking (CommNet), 1–8. DOI: 10.1109/CommNet63022.2024.10793266

Naqa, I. E., & Murphy, M. J. (2015). What is machine learning? (I. E. Naqa, R. Li, & M. J. Murphy, Eds.). Machine Learning in Radiation Oncology: Theory and Applications, 3–11. DOI: 10.1007/978-3-319-18305-3 1

Nelis, J., Desmet, S., Wauters, J., Haelterman, R., Borgers, E., & Kun, D. (2018). Virtual crime scene. *2018 IEEE International Conference on Artificial Intelligence and Virtual Reality (AIVR)*, 165–168. DOI: 10.1109/AIVR.2018.00035

Orozco, A. L. S. HuamaÅLn, C. Q., AÅL lvarez, D. P., & Villalba, L. J. G. (2020). A machine learning forensics technique to detect post-processing in digital videos. Future Generation Computer Systems, 111, 199–212. 10.1016/j.future.2020.04.041

Pierdicca, R., Paolanti, M., Matrone, F., Martini, M., Morbidoni, C., Malinverni, E. S., Frontoni, E., & Lingua, A. M. (2020). Point cloud semantic segmentation using a deep learning framework for cultural heritage. *Remote Sensing (Basel)*, *12*(6), 1005. Advance online publication. DOI: 10.3390/rs12061005

Qi, C. R., Su, H., Mo, K., & Guibas, L. J. (2016). Pointnet: Deep learning on point sets for 3d classification and segmentation. CoRR, abs/1612.00593. https://arxiv.org/abs/1612.00593

Qi, C. R., Yi, L., Su, H., & Guibas, L. J. (2017). Pointnet++: Deep hierarchical feature learning on point sets in a metric space. https://arxiv.org/abs/1706.02413

Raneri, D. (2018). Enhancing forensic investigation through the use of modern threed-imensional (3d) imaging technologies for crime scene reconstruction. *The Australian Journal of Forensic Sciences*, *50*, 697–707. DOI: 10.1080/00450618.2018.1424245

Rauch, L., & Braml, T. (2023). Semantic point cloud segmentation with deep-learningbased approaches for the construction industry: A survey. *Applied Sciences (Basel, Switzerland)*, *13*(16), 9146. Advance online publication. DOI: 10.3390/app13169146

Reiser, D., Paraforos, D. S., Khan, M. T., Griepentrog, H. W., & Vazquez-Arellano, M. (2017). Autonomous field navigation, data acquisition and node location in wireless sensor networks. *Precision Agriculture*, *18*(3), 279–292. DOI: 10.1007/s11119-016-9477-2

Ren, P., Zhou, M., Liu, J., Fan, Y., Zhao, W., & Shui, W. (2017). Sketch-based modeling and immersive display techniques for indoor crime scene presentation. Lecture Notes of the Institute for Computer Sciences. *Social-Informatics and Telecommunications Engineering, LNICST*, *216*, 181–194. DOI: 10.1007/978-3-319-73697-6 14

Richmond, K. M., & Primeau, C. (2025). Ai in the criminal justice system: From 'ai ethics' to 'hermeneutic risk' [PMID: 41428648]. *Medicine, Science, and the Law*, *0*(0), 00258024251407531. DOI: 10.1177/00258024251407531

Sapirstein, P. (2016). Accurate measurement with photogrammetry at large sites. *Journal of Archaeological Science*, *66*, 137–145. 10.1016/j.jas.2016.01.002. DOI: 10.1016/j.jas.2016.01.002

Sheshtar, F. M., Alhatlani, W. M., Moulden, M., & Kim, J. H. (2025). Comparative analysis of lidar and photogrammetry for 3d crime scene reconstruction. *Applied Sciences (Basel, Switzerland)*, *15*(3), 1085. Advance online publication. DOI: 10.3390/app15031085

Shi, X., Xing, F., Cai, J., Zhang, Z., Xie, Y., & Yang, L. (2016). Kernel-based supervised discrete hashing for image retrieval. In Leibe, B., Matas, J., Sebe, N., & Welling, M. (Eds.), *Computer vision – eccv 2016* (pp. 419–433). Springer International Publishing. DOI: 10.1007/978-3-319-46478-7_26

Sieberth, T., Wackrow, R., Hofer, V., & Barrera, V. (2018). Light field camera as tool for forensic photogrammetry. International Archives of the Photogrammetry, Remote Sensing and Spatial Information Sciences - ISPRS Archives, 42, 393–399. DOI: 10.5194/isprs-archives-XLII-1-393-2018

Tredinnick, R., Smith, S., & Ponto, K. (2019). A cost-benefit analysis of 3d scanning technology for crime scene investigation. *Forensic Science International. Reports*, *1*, 100025. DOI: 10.1016/j.fsir.2019.100025

Tsai, C.-Y., Nisar, H., & Hu, Y.-C. (2021). Mapless lidar navigation control of wheeled mobile robots based on deep imitation learning. *IEEE Access : Practical Innovations, Open Solutions*, *9*, 117527–117541. DOI: 10.1109/ACCESS.2021.3107041

Urschler, M., Holler, J., Bornik, A., Paul, T., Giretzlehner, M., Bischof, H., Yen, K., & Scheurer, E. (2014). Intuitive presentation of clinical forensic data using anonymous and person-specific 3d reference manikins. *Forensic Science International*, *241*, 155–166. DOI: 10.1016/j.forsciint.2014.05.017 PMID: 24952238

Villa, C., Lynnerup, N., & Jacobsen, C. (2023). A virtual, 3d multimodal approach to victim and crime scene reconstruction. *Diagnostics (Basel)*, *13*(17), 2764. Advance online publication. DOI: 10.3390/diagnostics13172764 PMID: 37685302

Wang, J., Li, Z., Hu, W., Shao, Y., Wang, L., Wu, R., Ma, K., Zou, D., & Chen, Y. (2019). Virtual reality and integrated crime scene scanning for immersive and heterogeneous crime scene reconstruction. *Forensic Science International*, *303*, 109943. Advance online publication. DOI: 10.1016/j.forsciint.2019.109943 PMID: 31546165

Wang, J., Wang, C., Fu, L., Wang, Q., Fu, G., Lu, C., Feng, J., Cong, B., & Li, S. (2020). Circular rna as a potential biomarker for forensic age prediction using multiple machine learning models: A preliminary study. *bioRxiv*, 2020.11.DOI: 10.376418. 10.1101/2020.11.10.376418

Wang, Q., Tan, Y., & Mei, Z. (2020). Computational methods of acquisition and processing of 3d point cloud data for construction applications. *Archives of Computational Methods in Engineering*, *27*(2), 479–499. DOI: 10.1007/s11831-019-09320-4

Wang, Y., Sun, Y., Liu, Z., Sarma, S., Bronstein, M., & Solomon, J. (2018). Dynamic graph CNN for learning on point clouds. CoRR, abs/1801.07829. https://arxiv.org/abs/1801.07829

Wu, D., Liang, Z., & Chen, G. (2022). Deep learning for lidar-only and lidar-fusion 3d perception: A survey. *Intelligence Robotics*, *2*(2), 105–129. Advance online publication. DOI: 10.20517/ir.2021.20

Zancajo-Blazquez, S., Gonzalez-Aguilera, D., Gonzalez-Jorge, H., & Hernandez-Lopez, D. (2015). An automatic image-based modelling method applied to forensic infography. *PLoS One*, *10*(3), e0118719. Advance online publication. DOI: 10.1371/journal.pone.0118719 PMID: 25793628

Zhang, K., Zhang, A., Wang, X., & Li, W. (2024). Deep-learning-based point cloud completion methods: A review. *Graphical Models*, *136*, 101233. 10.1016/j.gmod.2024.101233. DOI: 10.1016/j.gmod.2024.101233

Zhang, R., Wu, Y., Jin, W., & Meng, X. (2023). Deep-learning-based point cloud semantic segmentation: A survey. *Electronics (Basel)*, *12*(17), 3642. Advance online publication. DOI: 10.3390/electronics12173642

Zhao, J., Xu, H., Wu, J., Zheng, Y., & Liu, H. (2019). Trajectory tracking and prediction of pedestrian's crossing intention using roadside lidar. IET Intelligent Transport Systems, 13(5), 789–795. 10.1049/ietits. 2018.5258

Zhou, Y., & Qian, H. (2024). Real-time object detection method with single-domain generalization based on yolov8. *Journal of Real-Time Image Processing*, *21*(6), 191. DOI: 10.1007/s11554-024-01572-z

Zubanska, M. (2018). Improvement of crime scene examination and reduction of cognitive deficit – the need to implement a newimaging and dimensioning technique. Issues of Forensic Science, 302, 54–62. DOI: 10.34836/pk.2018.302.3

Chapter 10
Detection of Deepfake Videos: A Deep Learning Approach Using Res-Next and LSTM

K. Ganesh Kumar
http://orcid.org/0000-0002-5719-6193
Velalar College of Engineering and Technology, India

K. Balamurugan
http://orcid.org/0000-0003-4560-3801
K.S.R. College of Engineering, India

S. Rajalakshmi
http://orcid.org/0000-0003-4768-1029
Dr. N.G.P. Institute of Technology, India

N. V. Keerthana
http://orcid.org/0000-0001-8878-2083
Velalar College of Engineering and Technology, India

ABSTRACT

The machines gain increasing computational capacity in deep learning algorithms results in generation of highly realistic videos, termed as deepfake videos. These videos are especially face-swapped deepfakes and are very risky because they may be employed for some malevolent intentions. This proposal concerns the differentiation between a real and a deepfake using a novel hybrid approach in deep learning through a Res-Next Convolutional Neural Network that followed the architecture of

DOI: 10.4018/979-8-3373-5228-2.ch010

Long Short-Term Memory based Recurrent Neural Network. Its frame-level feature extraction was performed through a Res-Next Convolutional Neural Network that performs both replacement and recreation of deepfakes videos.

INTRODUCTION

The Growing Threat of Deepfake Technology

Deepfake technology is transforming the digital landscape by enabling the creation of highly realistic synthetic media, particularly manipulated videos and images. Although this technology has legitimate applications in entertainment, education, and creative industries, it also presents significant risks when used maliciously. Deepfakes are now an increasing threat because they can be exploited to spread fake news, disseminate political propaganda, commit identity theft, and circulate non-consensual sexual content. Manipulated media can cause substantial harm to individuals, organisations, and governments by violating privacy, damaging reputations, and undermining trust in digital platforms.

Due to recent advances in generative AI, convincing deepfakes can now be created by almost anyone. Previously, producing such content required specialist technical knowledge and powerful computing resources. Today, however, freely available online tools allow users to generate realistic fake media with minimal effort. The volume of deepfake content online has increased sharply, extending beyond political disinformation and financial fraud to include the non-consensual sharing of intimate images, which can be especially harmful to victims (Verdoliva, 2020) (Dang & Nguyen, 2023). Law enforcement agencies such as Europol have identified synthetic media as one of the most serious emerging threats facing digital investigators. Beyond its immediate harms, deepfake technology also weakens confidence in truth itself. If video evidence can be convincingly fabricated, its value for journalism, legal proceedings, and democratic accountability is significantly diminished.

Against this backdrop, it is unsurprising that automated deepfake detection has become a major area of research. Human reviewers cannot realistically cope with the vast volume of synthetic content being produced, while conventional forensic techniques are increasingly challenged by sophisticated GAN-based generation methods. Deep learning offers a more robust basis for detection, as models trained on large datasets of authentic and manipulated videos can learn to identify the features that distinguish real content from synthetic content at the pixel, frame, and temporal levels (Afchar, Nozick, Yamagishi, & Echizen, 2018; Shiohara & Yamasaki, 2022). This chapter examines an approach that combines a ResNeXt convolutional neural network (CNN) for spatial feature extraction with a Long Short-Term Memory

(LSTM) network for temporal sequence analysis. The following sections review the relevant literature, outline the proposed method, present the findings, and identify directions for future research.

ROLE OF AI IN DEEPFAKE DETECTION

Artificial Intelligence forms the foundation of modern deepfake detection systems. Unlike traditional methods that rely on handcrafted features, AI models can learn to identify manipulations by analysing complex patterns in video data. These systems are commonly built using Convolutional Neural Networks (CNNs) and Recurrent Neural Networks (RNNs), allowing them to detect both spatial anomalies, such as unnatural textures and lighting inconsistencies, and temporal anomalies, such as irregularities across successive frames.

CNN-based systems have shown strong performance in detecting pixel-level artefacts, including unusual lighting conditions and distorted facial features (Verdoliva, 2020) (Afchar et al., 2018). RNNs, particularly Long Short-Term Memory (LSTM) networks, are well suited to analysing temporal changes across frames. By combining multiple model types, AI systems can achieve high levels of accuracy in distinguishing authentic from manipulated content, particularly when analysing complex and highly realistic deepfakes.

Convolutional Neural Networks for Spatial Feature Analysis

Convolutional Neural Networks form the backbone of many deepfake detection systems. CNNs extract spatial features from images or video frames, enabling the detection of subtle visual irregularities such as unnatural lighting, blurred edges, texture inconsistencies, and pixel-level distortions. Even the most advanced deepfake generation methods often struggle to reproduce fine-grained visual details accurately, including skin texture, eye reflections, and the continuity of micro-expressions

When trained on sufficiently large datasets of genuine and manipulated media, CNN-based models can learn to recognise these subtle visual discrepancies. Convolutional layers detect local features such as facial landmarks, colour gradients, and geometric patterns, which are then abstracted through deeper layers, pooling operations, and activation functions. This process enables the model to distinguish between authentic and fabricated content.

Several CNN architectures, including XceptionNet, VGGFace, and ResNet, have demonstrated promising results in detecting subtle manipulations. In particular, XceptionNet has shown strong performance when fine-tuned on deepfake datasets, as it can identify spatial artefacts introduced during face-swapping and blending processes. Because of their effectiveness in pixel-level and frame-level analysis, CNNs have become essential components of video-based deepfake detection systems (L. Li et al., 2020) (Zhou, Chen, & Ruan, 2025).

Recurrent Neural Networks for Temporal Analysis

While CNNs are effective at detecting spatial anomalies, RNNs, particularly their Long Short-Term Memory (LSTM) variant, are designed to identify temporal inconsistencies across consecutive frames. Many deepfakes contain unnatural motion patterns, such as abrupt facial movements, irregular blinking, or poor lip synchronisation. These issues may be difficult for a human observer to detect but can be identified through temporal modelling.

RNNs process frame sequences as time-series data, allowing the system to retain information over time and detect distortions in motion and continuity. LSTMs are especially useful because they address the vanishing gradient problem and can therefore model long-term dependencies between frames. For example, sudden changes in facial lighting between adjacent frames or lip movements that do not correspond with speech can be detected as temporal irregularities, indicating possible manipulation (Kumar, Sowndharya, Pradeep, Suriya, & Kumar, 2024)

By combining CNN and RNN architectures in a hybrid model, detection systems can analyse both visual and temporal dimensions simultaneously, improving performance even when assessing highly realistic deepfakes.

Generative Adversarial Networks in Detection and Counter-Detection

Interestingly, the same underlying technology used to create deepfakes can also be used to detect them. Generative Adversarial Networks (GANs) consist of two competing neural networks: one generates synthetic content, while the other attempts to distinguish fake data from real data. Through this adversarial process, both networks improve over time, often producing highly realistic outputs.

Researchers have adapted this principle by training discriminators specifically to detect synthetic artefacts (Müller et al., 2025). In deepfake detection, adversarially trained models can identify subtle indicators of manipulation, including compression artefacts and distortions in the frequency domain. GAN-based detection methods may also adapt more quickly to emerging manipulation techniques, helping them remain effective as deepfake generation methods evolve.

However, GAN-based detection also faces ongoing challenges. As generation models improve, detection methods must advance at a similar pace. This creates a continuing arms race between the production of synthetic content and the development of reliable AI-based detection systems (Zhang, Pang, Huang, Wang, & Zhou, 2025).

Multimodal AI Models for Audio-Visual Cross-Verification

Many deepfakes manipulate not only visual content but also audio, including speech patterns, tone, rhythm, and even vocal identity. To address this, multimodal AI models analyse both video and audio signals to assess cross-modal consistency. These systems evaluate whether facial movements, lip synchronisation, and vocal characteristics align naturally.

For instance, if the phonemes implied by mouth movements do not match the accompanying speech, the model may flag the recording as a potential deepfake. More recent deep learning models, such as AVFakeNet and SyncNet, use synchronised embeddings from audio and video streams to evaluate coherence. This approach improves reliability, particularly when analysing realistic talking-head videos and political deepfakes. By integrating multiple data modalities, these systems reflect the way humans judge authenticity through consistency between what is seen and heard. As a result, multimodal approaches can improve both accuracy and robustness in deepfake detection.

Ensemble and Hybrid Learning Approaches

Deepfake detection models often perform better when combined within an ensemble learning framework. These systems integrate outputs from different models, such as CNNs for spatial analysis, RNNs for temporal modelling, and GAN-based discriminators for adversarial pattern recognition, to produce a more balanced and accurate detection outcome. Ensemble methods reduce the limitations of any one model and improve adaptability across different datasets and manipulation techniques.

Hybrid architectures may also incorporate traditional machine learning classifiers, such as Support Vector Machines or Random Forests, using extracted deep features as inputs for authenticity classification (Zhang et al., 2025) (Jain, Quadri, & Khattar, 2024). These combined approaches have achieved strong performance on benchmark datasets such as Face Forensics++, DFDC, and Celeb-DF, with reported detection accuracies exceeding 95%. The integration of multiple AI components therefore provides a more comprehensive and resilient method for identifying even highly sophisticated and realistic deepfakes.

DOMAIN OVERVIEW

Deepfake detection systems are designed to address the challenges created by artificial intelligence techniques that manipulate digital video content. Advances in neural network methods, particularly Generative Adversarial Networks (GANs), have contributed to the dual nature of deepfakes: on the one hand, they support creative and legitimate uses in entertainment and media production; on the other, they can be used maliciously to spread misinformation, damage reputations, and facilitate identity theft, with serious consequences for individuals, organisations, and institutions worldwide. Deepfake detection therefore seeks to distinguish authentic content from manipulated content by identifying inconsistencies within video data. Manual inspection and traditional rule-based approaches are now largely insufficient for identifying sophisticated modern deepfakes (Verdoliva, 2020) (Dang & Nguyen, 2023). In response, machine learning and deep learning techniques have been introduced to automate pattern recognition and anomaly detection.

A major challenge in this field is the issue of imbalanced data, as genuine videos often far outnumber manipulated examples, which can lead detection models to develop biased decision patterns. At the same time, increasingly sophisticated deepfake generation methods require detection systems that can identify highly subtle, high-definition manipulations. Effective real-time detection is also essential, as the rapid spread of fake content demands systems capable of processing large volumes of data continuously and efficiently. The present study addresses these challenges through a dual detection framework that combines spatial analysis using a CNN with temporal analysis using an LSTM. Research in this area continues to expand as scholars work to develop more scalable, adaptive, and accurate systems capable of responding to evolving deepfake threats (Dang & Nguyen, 2023) (Tiwari, Dave, & Vanamala, 2023) (M. Singh, Jain, & Khan, 2025). The two-part system proposed in this study, combining spatial analysis through ResNeXt CNN and temporal modelling through LSTM, directly responds to this operational gap by offering a scalable, real-time solution that does not depend on metadata availability (T. M. Singh, Kumar, Munawar, Lippert, & Doss) (Zeba & Amjad, 2025).

PROBLEM DESCRIPTION

It is becoming increasingly difficult for people to distinguish authentic video content from deepfake material. Using Generative Adversarial Networks (GANs), deepfakes can produce highly convincing synthetic videos that may appear genuine to human observers. These videos are often used for harmful purposes, including the spread of misinformation, political manipulation, blackmail, and the non-consensual creation of explicit content, causing serious harm to both individuals and organisations (Y. Li & Lyu, 2018).

Detecting deepfakes is especially challenging because advances in generation techniques have produced highly realistic synthetic content that can be difficult to identify. Many current detection systems analyse video frames individually, focusing on visible artefacts such as lighting inconsistencies or textural distortions, but often fail to account for temporal patterns across successive frames. As a result, some existing systems struggle to identify high-quality deepfake videos and may incorrectly classify them as authentic.

Real-time detection presents an additional challenge, particularly when processing large-scale data or analysing live-streamed content. This project addresses these limitations by proposing a deep learning framework that combines ResNeXt CNN for detailed frame-level feature extraction with LSTM for identifying temporal inconsistencies across video sequences. By integrating both spatial and temporal analysis, the system aims to improve the accuracy and robustness of deepfake detection across different types of manipulated video while also supporting real-time performance (Sun & Li, 2025). Approaches that rely on only one modality, whether spatial or temporal, face a fundamental limitation in their ability to generalise across the full range of deepfake generation techniques currently in use (P. Li et al., 2026).

DISCUSSION ON EXISTING WORKS

A substantial body of research has examined methods for detecting deepfake videos in response to the increasing quality and sophistication of manipulated media (Shiohara & Yamasaki, 2022). One example is MesoNet, which focuses on identifying irregularities in facial textures and illumination patterns. However, such methods may be less effective when applied to high-resolution or particularly well-generated deepfakes. Temporal analysis approaches, such as eye-blink detection, examine sequential behaviour by identifying unnatural human motion patterns, including abnormal blinking behaviour. Although these approaches can be effective in some contexts, they are often limited in scope and may fail to detect more sophisticated manipulations. Hybrid models, including Capsule Networks and ensemble approaches, have improved detection performance, but they can also be computationally intensive and may be too slow for real-time applications (Afchar et al., 2018).

More recent advances in deep learning, particularly those combining CNNs and RNNs, have improved reliability in deepfake detection. CNNs are effective at identifying spatial irregularities, such as unnatural lighting or texture distortion, while RNNs, especially LSTMs, are better suited to detecting inconsistencies across consecutive video frames. Despite their effectiveness, CNN- and RNN-based detection systems still face challenges relating to dataset imbalance, computational efficiency, and scalability. Performance can degrade when datasets contain far more authentic videos than manipulated ones, particularly when models become biased towards classifying content as genuine and therefore fail to detect fake videos.

In addition, many existing studies do not fully integrate spatial and temporal features in a balanced way, which limits their ability to detect the wide range of manipulations used in deepfake generation, including face swaps and facial reenactments. These limitations highlight the need for adaptive systems that can support real-time detection with high levels of accuracy and efficiency, particularly as deepfake technologies continue to evolve. Newer hybrid architectures, especially those combining CNN-based spatial analysis with recurrent temporal modelling, have shown important progress in addressing this generalisation problem by enabling systems to identify both the pixel-level traces left by synthesis algorithms and the temporal irregularities that reveal manipulated video sequences (Wang, Zhang, Yang, Guo, & Chen, 2024).

MOTIVATION OF THE CHAPTER

Advances in mobile phone cameras, combined with the widespread use of social media platforms, have made the creation and sharing of digital video easier than ever. At the same time, generative models, among the most influential developments in deep learning, have made it possible to produce highly realistic images, speech, music, and video. These technologies also have legitimate and beneficial uses, such as improving accessibility through text-to-speech applications and supporting data generation in areas such as medical imaging. However, these advances have also introduced new risks. Among the most serious is the rise of deepfakes, namely AI-generated manipulated videos produced using generative models. Since their emergence in 2017, deepfakes have increased rapidly in both availability and sophistication (Tiwari et al., 2023).

Although deepfakes may be used harmlessly in some entertainment contexts, they are inherently dual-use and can pose a serious threat to both individuals and wider society. Distributed through social media, deepfakes can fuel disinformation, create confusion, and generate public alarm. For example, a fabricated video showing a political leader or public figure appearing to say inflammatory or false statements could have serious social, political, or security consequences.

Addressing this problem requires reliable systems capable of detecting deepfake videos before they spread further. This chapter is motivated by the need to develop an effective deep learning-based approach for distinguishing authentic from manipulated video content. The development of robust deepfake detection systems is essential if the harmful effects of AI-generated manipulation are to be reduced. Automated detection tools that can be deployed at scale, whether through social media moderation systems, digital forensic investigations, or real-time broadcast monitoring, offer a practical response to a threat that is already growing in both scale and severity.

PURPOSE OF THIS STUDY

This study aims to develop an effective and reliable system for detecting deepfake videos by combining ResNeXt CNN and LSTM networks. The proposed method is designed to address three major challenges in deepfake detection: identifying high-quality manipulations, learning from imbalanced datasets, and maintaining the speed required for real-time applications. By integrating ResNeXt CNN for spatial feature extraction with LSTM for temporal sequence analysis, the system seeks to improve the detection of face-swapped and reenacted videos while remaining efficient enough for practical deployment.

The main objective of this research is therefore to enhance deepfake detection performance by combining spatial and temporal modelling within a single framework. By unifying these approaches, the system can identify both pixel-level inconsistencies and temporal irregularities across video sequences while maintaining strong overall performance. The model is trained and evaluated using multiple benchmark datasets, including FaceForensics++, the Deepfake Detection Challenge dataset, and Celeb-DF, in order to improve generalisability across different video formats and manipulation types. The findings of this study are intended to support the development of scalable, efficient, and adaptive deepfake detection systems capable of responding to misinformation and synthetic media abuse. As such, the contribution of this chapter is relevant not only to researchers working in deepfake detection, but also to practitioners concerned with the integrity and authenticity of digital media (Sun & Li, 2025).

LITERATURE REVIEW

One early line of research focused on the detection of face warping artefacts. This approach uses a CNN-based model to compare warped facial regions with their surrounding areas in order to identify manipulation artefacts. The method is based on the observation that many earlier deepfake algorithms generated images at fixed resolutions, which then had to be blended back into the original frame. As a result, visual inconsistencies could emerge between the manipulated facial area and the surrounding image. However, this method is limited because it does not incorporate temporal analysis across video frames, which is increasingly important for detecting more sophisticated deepfakes (Shiohara & Yamasaki, 2022).

Another approach is eye-blink detection, which treats blinking behaviour as an important cue for classifying videos as real or fake. In this method, eye-blink sequences are extracted from cropped facial images and analysed temporally using a Long-term Recurrent Convolutional Network (LRCN). However, more recent deepfake generation methods have advanced to the point where manipulated videos may include realistic blinking patterns, meaning that eye-blink detection alone is no longer a sufficiently reliable indicator. Other visual cues, such as cheek movement, eyebrow placement, and dental inconsistencies, may also need to be considered when detecting deepfakes.

(Dang & Nguyen, 2023), in *Capsule-Forensics: Using Capsule Networks to Detect Forged Images and Videos*, applied Capsule Networks (CapsNets) to the problem of facial forgery detection in both images and videos. CapsNets are particularly effective at capturing spatial hierarchies within data, which makes them useful for identifying subtle inconsistencies in facial alignment and texture. The authors showed that CapsNets could outperform traditional CNNs on some datasets, particularly where fake media contained fewer obvious artefacts. This suggests that CapsNets may offer a more nuanced approach to deepfake detection, especially in cases involving high-quality manipulations where visual irregularities are more subtle.

(Dang & Nguyen, 2023), in their work on the detection of digital face manipulation, proposed new deep learning approaches based on multi-task learning. Their framework is designed not only to identify manipulated video segments but also to detect compression-related patterns that assist with recognising both high- and low-resolution fake videos. By analysing video data in this way, the model is able to extract features that reveal temporal inconsistencies, such as unnatural facial motion and irregular frame construction. Their findings suggest that multi-task learning improves model robustness, especially when dealing with compressed media, and reinforces the importance of temporal information in video-based face manipulation detection.

(Tolosana, Vera-Rodriguez, Fierrez, Morales, & Ortega-Garcia, 2020) examined a wide range of facial manipulation techniques, including face swapping and facial reenactment, as well as the detection methods used to identify them. The authors grouped current detection approaches into broad categories, including CNN-based methods, GAN-based methods, and more traditional handcrafted approaches such as facial landmark analysis and texture-based detection. Their review highlighted several important challenges, particularly limited generalisability across datasets and the vulnerability of detection systems to adversarial attacks. As deepfake generation techniques become increasingly sophisticated, the authors argue that more advanced and adaptable detection methods are required.

(Rossler et al., 2019) introduced Face Forensics++ as a major benchmark dataset for manipulated video detection. The dataset includes four categories of manipulation: Face Swap, Neural Textures, Face2Face, and Deep Fakes. This work provided an important resource for both training and evaluating detection models. The study also compared several deep learning approaches, including CNNs and RNNs, to establish baseline levels of performance in face manipulation detection. The results showed that models performed well on uncompressed video but struggled more with highly compressed content, highlighting a major challenge for real-world deployment. This study therefore laid an important foundation for subsequent research while also underscoring the need for models that can cope more effectively with the compression artefacts common in practical media environments.

(Afchar et al., 2018) proposed MesoNet as a lightweight deep learning model for detecting facial manipulation in video. The model focuses on identifying mesoscopic features such as texture distortions and unusual lighting patterns that often emerge in manipulated facial imagery. Because MesoNet uses fewer layers than more complex architectures, it offers faster prediction speeds and is therefore more suitable for real-time applications. Although it is less complex than larger models such as XceptionNet, MesoNet still achieved strong performance in detecting synthetic facial content. The study suggests that compact models can provide a useful balance between speed and accuracy where rapid detection is required.

METHODOLOGY

This study outlines the method used to develop a deepfake detection system designed to operate efficiently and accurately. To address the challenges posed by deepfake videos, the proposed approach is based on the observation that manipulated media generated through neural network techniques, particularly GAN-based methods, often contain subtle spatial artefacts and temporal inconsistencies that may not be readily detectable by human observers. The system was therefore designed as a hybrid model capable of identifying anomalies through both spatial and temporal analysis.

Figure 1. System Architecture

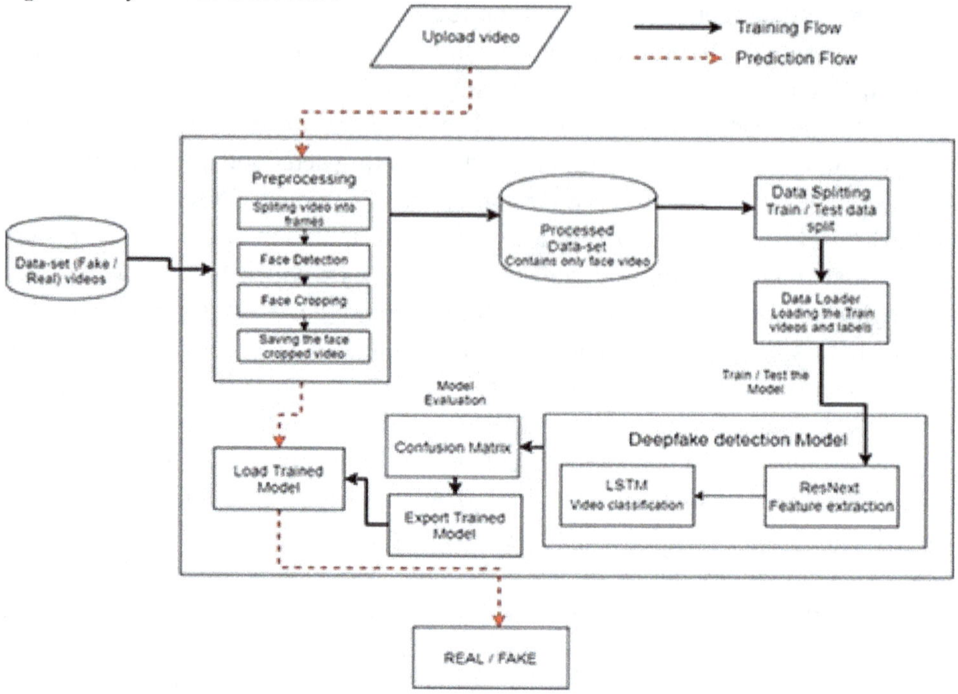

The proposed framework combines a ResNeXt CNN with an LSTM network. The CNN is used to extract spatial features from individual video frames, while the LSTM models sequential dependencies across frames. This two-level architecture enables the system to detect frame-level inconsistencies, such as lighting mismatches and unnatural textures, as well as temporal anomalies, including irregular blinking and inconsistent facial expressions. Figure 1 illustrates the overall system design, showing the workflow from video input through to final deepfake classification.

The diagram presents the full pipeline of the proposed deepfake detection model. First, the video is preprocessed through temporal frame sampling, face detection, facial alignment, and image resizing. Next, a ResNeXt CNN extracts spatial features from each frame in order to capture texture, lighting, and facial irregularities. These features are then passed to an LSTM network, which analyses their temporal progression across consecutive frames to identify unnatural motion patterns or inconsistencies over time. Finally, a classifier uses the extracted features to determine whether the input video should be labelled as **REAL** or **FAKE**. This combined approach enables the system to detect deepfakes more effectively across a range of sample videos.

Data Collection and Preparation

To build a reliable model for real-time deepfake detection, data were collected from three publicly available benchmark datasets: FaceForensics++, Celeb-DF, and the Deepfake Detection Challenge (DFDC) dataset. These datasets were selected because they contain a broad range of video qualities, lighting conditions, and facial motion patterns, thereby providing variation that is useful for robust model training. The dataset used in this study comprised 6,000 video files in total, balanced equally between 3,000 authentic videos and 3,000 manipulated videos in order to reduce potential training bias. Of these, DFDC contributed 3,000 real and 3,000 fake videos, while FaceForensics++ and Celeb-DF contributed 2,000 real and 2,000 fake videos, and 1,000 real and 1,000 fake videos respectively. The preprocessing script excluded audio-manipulated videos from DFDC because audio-based deepfake detection fell outside the scope of this study.

During data preparation, video frames were extracted in order to capture both spatial and temporal characteristics from the input material. Frames were labelled according to the metadata provided in the original datasets to ensure consistency throughout processing. A variety of face-swap and facial reenactment manipulations were included so that the model could be trained on multiple forms of deepfake content while retaining a focused approach to detection. This preparation phase was intended to improve generalisability and provide a stronger foundation for real-world detection performance.

Data Preprocessing

Preprocessing of the raw video data was a critical step in preparing the dataset for training. Each video was first divided into individual frames, after which face detection was applied and the detected facial region was cropped. Only facial regions were retained for analysis, while the rest of each frame was discarded. Because processing every frame in a full video sequence would exceed the available GPU capacity, the frame rate was standardised, and each clip was limited to 150 frames. Specifically, the first 150 sequential frames from each video were extracted and resized to a standard resolution of 112×112 pixels at 30 frames per second. This ensured data consistency and created a manageable input structure for temporal modelling using the LSTM network.

To improve model robustness, data augmentation techniques were also applied, including horizontal flipping, brightness adjustment, and random cropping. In addition, pixel values were normalised to place all inputs on a consistent numerical scale before being passed to the model. To address class imbalance, oversampling was applied to underrepresented manipulated samples, while excess authentic video frames were reduced where necessary in order to maintain balance across the dataset.

Figure 2. Pre-processing of video

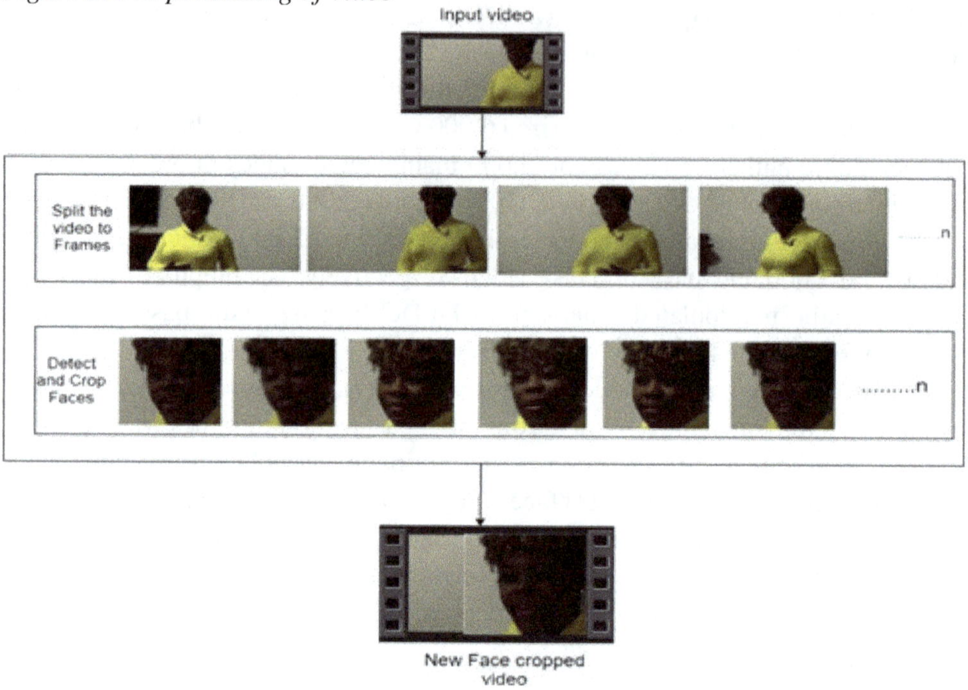

This figure illustrates the preprocessing steps applied before each video is passed into the deep learning detection framework. Each video is first converted into individual frames, and only the facial region is retained so that the analysis focuses on the most relevant area. The extracted frames are then resized, normalised, and standardised to ensure that the model receives consistent input across all videos. Data augmentation techniques, including horizontal flipping and brightness adjustment, are also applied to improve model accuracy and reduce the risk of overfitting. Overall, the preprocessing stage prepares the dataset for reliable feature extraction and stable model training, ensuring that the deepfake detection system receives consistent and well-balanced inputs throughout the learning process.

Feature Extraction

Feature extraction is a fundamental stage in deepfake detection because it enables the model to identify important patterns within video frames that may indicate manipulation. In this study, ResNeXt CNN is used to perform spatial feature extraction from each video frame. This section explains the importance of feature extraction, outlines the architecture of ResNeXt, and describes its relevance to the detection of manipulated media.

Importance of Feature Extraction

In the context of deepfake detection, feature extraction serves two main purposes.

Spatial Analysis

First, it enables the detection of pixel-level artefacts, such as inconsistent lighting, texture mismatches, and unnatural blending between facial regions.

Input Representation

Second, it converts raw image frames into compact and meaningful feature vectors that can be processed more effectively by the model. Traditional hand-crafted approaches, such as manually identifying edges or texture inconsistencies, are often insufficient for detecting sophisticated, high-definition deepfakes. By contrast, ResNeXt CNN performs feature extraction automatically, making the process both more efficient and more accurate.

ResNeXt CNN Architecture

To improve feature extraction, the ResNeXt CNN architecture extends ResNet by introducing grouped convolutions, which address several limitations of standard convolutional networks. Grouped convolutions improve computational efficiency while also increasing the model's ability to learn diverse patterns from visual data. This design makes ResNeXt particularly effective for high-dimensional image analysis tasks such as deepfake detection.

Key Features of ResNeXt

Residual Connections

Residual connections are a core component of ResNeXt because they allow gradients to flow more effectively through the network during backpropagation. This helps to address the vanishing gradient problem commonly found in deep architectures and allows the model to become deeper without suffering major performance loss. As a result, ResNeXt can improve representational capacity while reducing the risk of degraded learning performance (M. Singh et al., 2025).

Grouped Convolutions

Grouped convolutions operate by dividing channels into separate groups, which are processed in parallel. This increases pattern diversity while reducing computational cost compared with standard convolutional layers. In the context of deepfake detection, grouped convolutions are particularly useful for identifying subtle spatial inconsistencies, such as unnatural textures and lighting artefacts.

Scalability Through Cardinality

A distinctive feature of ResNeXt is cardinality, which refers to the number of groups used within a convolutional layer. Increasing cardinality allows the model to learn a wider variety of features without a disproportionate increase in computational cost. This improves the balance between efficiency and performance, making ResNeXt well suited to real-time applications.

Hierarchical Processing

ResNeXt processes video frames hierarchically, extracting progressively more complex features at deeper layers of the network.

- **Early layers:** These detect basic visual patterns, such as edges, corners, and simple textures.
- **Intermediate layers:** These learn more advanced spatial details, including facial structures, boundaries, and relationships between regions.
- **Final layers:** These generate a 2048-dimensional feature vector that acts as the main spatial representation of each frame.

Figure 3. Res-Next architecture

stage	output	ResNeXt-50 (32×4d)
conv1	112×112	7×7, 64, stride 2
conv2	56×56	3×3 max pool, stride 2 $\begin{bmatrix} 1\times1, 128 \\ 3\times3, 128, C=32 \\ 1\times1, 256 \end{bmatrix} \times 3$
conv3	28×28	$\begin{bmatrix} 1\times1, 256 \\ 3\times3, 256, C=32 \\ 1\times1, 512 \end{bmatrix} \times 4$
conv4	14×14	$\begin{bmatrix} 1\times1, 512 \\ 3\times3, 512, C=32 \\ 1\times1, 1024 \end{bmatrix} \times 6$
conv5	7×7	$\begin{bmatrix} 1\times1, 1024 \\ 3\times3, 1024, C=32 \\ 1\times1, 2048 \end{bmatrix} \times 3$
	1×1	global average pool 1000-d fc, softmax
# params.		**25.0**$\times 10^6$

Figure 3 illustrates the ResNeXt architecture used to extract spatial features from video frames. ResNeXt combines residual connections with grouped convolutions to learn fine-grained patterns from facial images efficiently. This architecture is well suited to detecting subtle artefacts commonly associated with deepfake media, including unnatural blending, irregular skin texture, and lighting inconsistencies. Unlike earlier approaches that rely more heavily on traditional image-processing techniques, ResNeXt analyses images hierarchically, beginning with simple low-level features such as edges and progressing to higher-level facial representations. The output of this network is then passed to the LSTM layer for temporal analysis.

Workflow for Feature Extraction

Feature extraction using ResNeXt CNN involves the following stages:

Framing of Input Features

Each video frame is resized to 112 × 112 pixels to match the input requirements of the model.

Convolutional Layers

The convolutional layers apply multiple filters to the image in order to detect different visual features, including edges, textures, and facial structures. Grouped convolutions improve the model's ability to identify subtle spatial irregularities associated with deepfake manipulation.

Pooling Layers

Pooling layers reduce the dimensionality of the feature maps, removing less important information while retaining the most relevant spatial patterns. This improves computational efficiency without losing essential information.

Residual Blocks

Residual connections preserve information learned in earlier layers and allow deeper layers to refine that information more effectively. This helps improve training stability and overall model performance.

Feature Vector Generation

At the final stage, the extracted spatial information from each frame is compressed into a 2048-dimensional feature vector. This vector serves as a compact representation of the main discriminative spatial features required for manipulation detection.

Role of LSTM in Deepfake Detection

Temporal Feature Analysis

The LSTM component is used to analyse temporal relationships between video frames, allowing the system to detect inconsistencies that cannot be identified through static spatial analysis alone. While the ResNeXt CNN produces a 2048-dimensional spatial feature vector for each frame, the LSTM processes these vectors sequentially so that information from earlier frames can be retained and compared with later ones. This enables the system to detect unusual temporal patterns, such as unnatural facial movement, inconsistent expressions, or abrupt motion transitions across frames.

Enhanced Detection Capabilities

LSTM networks use three gates, namely the forget gate, input gate, and output gate, to regulate the flow of information through the sequence. This allows the network to retain important temporal information while discarding irrelevant details. As a result, LSTM-based analysis can detect behavioural and sequential anomalies that may be missed by models relying only on frame-by-frame analysis. In this study, the LSTM layer uses 2048 latent dimensions and a dropout rate of 0.4 to help reduce overfitting during training. The resulting temporal representation is then passed through classification layers, after which a Softmax function produces the final output, classifying the video as real or fake together with a confidence score.

By combining LSTM for temporal modelling with ResNeXt CNN for spatial feature extraction, the proposed framework achieves a more complete representation of manipulated video content. This integrated design improves detection performance across different types of deepfake manipulation. Training and evaluation across multiple datasets also strengthens the reliability and generalisability of the approach.

Web Interface for Deepfake Detection

A web interface was developed using Flask to allow users to interact with the deepfake detection system (Sun & Li, 2025). The main detection processes operate on the backend, while the frontend provides users with a simple interface through which they can upload videos and view classification results. Flask enables communication between the frontend and backend, allowing uploaded videos to be processed and classified as either **REAL** or **FAKE**.

Users can upload a video directly through the homepage using the upload button. Once submitted, the system processes the video and returns a classification result together with the associated probability score. Following the upload, the backend initiates the detection pipeline automatically. During this process, secure handling of uploaded data, validation checks, and privacy protections are important considerations. The interface was designed to support efficient operation and accessible use, enabling practical testing of the model in a controlled environment. Such systems may help strengthen efforts to detect and limit the spread of deepfake media.

Mathematical Representation of Models

The architecture proposed in this study is based on a hybrid design in which a Convolutional Neural Network is used for spatial feature extraction and a Long Short-Term Memory network is used for temporal analysis. These two components can be expressed mathematically as follows.

Convolutional Neural Network

During the CNN stage, spatial features are extracted from individual video frames. Each frame, denoted by *X*, is processed through a series of convolutional layers, where filters are applied to detect local spatial patterns. In general form, the output of convolutional layer *l*can be expressed as follows:

Long Short-Term Memory (LSTM)

The Long Short-Term Memory network analyses sequential dependencies between frames by maintaining both a hidden state and a cell state, enabling it to capture temporal features across a video sequence. For a sequence of spatial feature vectors $\{h_1, h_2, \ldots, h_T\}$extracted by the CNN, the LSTM computes its states as follows:

Model Training

Training–Test Split

The datasets were divided into training and testing subsets using a 70:30 ratio. A total of 4,200 videos were allocated to training, while the remaining 1,800 videos were reserved for testing. This split was balanced so that both subsets contained an equal proportion of real and fake videos, with each dataset comprising 50% authentic and 50% manipulated examples.

Data Loader

A dedicated data loader was used to process video files and their corresponding labels in batches of four during training.

Training

The model was trained for 20 epochs using the Adam optimiser (Yuan & Gao, 2020). The learning rate was set to 0.00001 (1e-5), and the weight decay was set to 0.001 (1e-3). The Adam optimiser was selected because its adaptive learning rate mechanism helps improve convergence during training. Cross-entropy loss was used to measure prediction error and guide model optimisation (Kaur, Noori Hoshyar, Saikrishna, Firmin, & Xia, 2024).

Softmax Layer

The final stage of the network used a softmax layer to generate probabilistic outputs between 0 and 1. Because the model was designed for binary classification, it produced two output classes: **REAL** and **FAKE**. The softmax layer therefore converted the final logits into class probabilities, allowing the system not only to generate a prediction but also to indicate the confidence associated with that prediction (Zhou et al., 2025).

Figure 4 presents the binary classification structure of the neural network. The model passes extracted features through fully connected layers, where relevant patterns are learned. The final logits are then normalised by the softmax function to produce probabilities corresponding to the two classes, **REAL** and **FAKE**. The final classification is determined by the class with the highest probability score.

Figure 4. Softmax layer

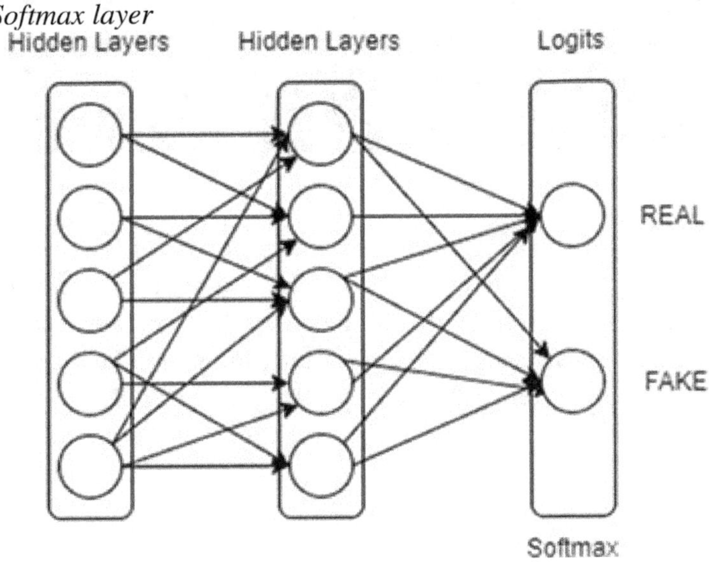

This figure illustrates the final classification stage of the model. After the spatial and temporal features have been extracted, the softmax function converts the output values into class probabilities. Two probability scores are produced, one for the "REAL" class and one for the "FAKE" class. The final decision is based on whichever class receives the higher probability. This stage also provides a transparent indication of model confidence for the user.

RESULTS AND FINDINGS

Output:

Figure 5. Real video output

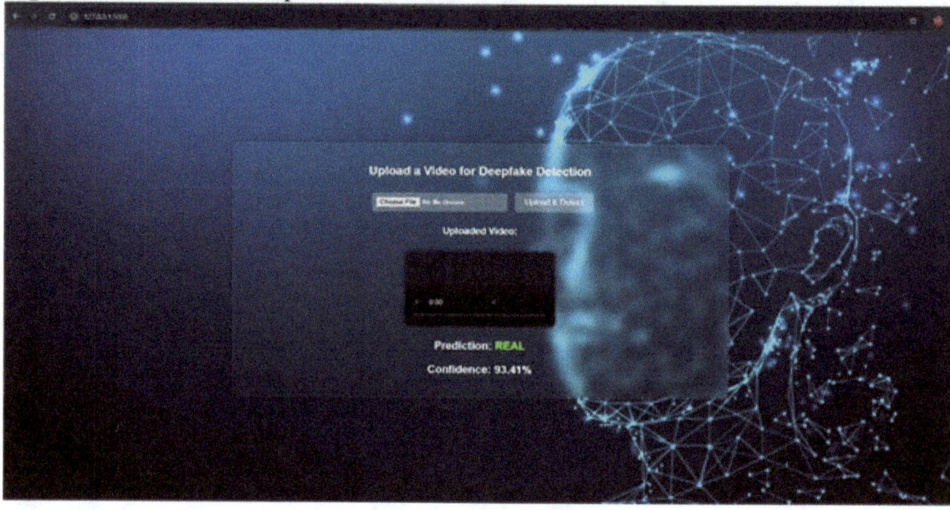

The figure shows the system classifying the uploaded video as real. The output displays the label "REAL" together with a confidence score indicating the model's level of certainty in its prediction. This suggests that the facial movements, textures, and frame-to-frame consistency were consistent with natural human patterns. The result demonstrates the system's ability to identify authentic video content and helps provide users with greater confidence in the reliability of the verification process.

Figure 6. Fake video output

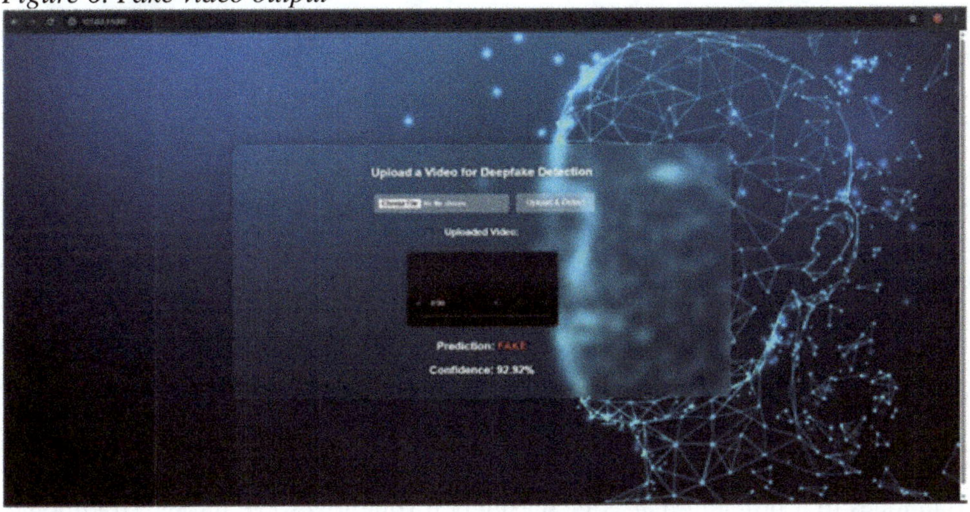

This figure shows the system classifying the uploaded video as fake. The prediction is based on detected irregularities such as texture inconsistencies, unnatural transitions between facial expressions, or unconvincing motion patterns. The output also includes a confidence score indicating the model's level of certainty in its decision. This demonstrates the system's ability to identify manipulated content, even where the video appears visually convincing to a human observer. In practical terms, such detection can help reduce the risk of individuals being misled by harmful deepfake media.

Trained model & results:

Table 1. Model along with Dataset and Attributes

Name of model	All Datasets	Total videos	Noof frames	Accuracy
80_frames_model	Face-Forensic++	2000	80	97.743
60_frames_model	Face-Forensic++	2000	60	97.481
40_frames_model	Face-Forensic++	2000	40	95.222
20_frames_model	Face-Forensic++	2000	20	90.951
100_frames_model	Celeb_DF+andFace- Forensic++	2000	100	96.975
40_frames_model	Otherdatasets	1000	40	89.342
20_frames_model	Otherdatasets	1000	20	87.794

Table 1 compares the model's performance across different datasets and varying numbers of input frames. In general, accuracy improves as the number of frames increases, as this provides the model with more temporal information for analysis. Overall, the results support the strong performance of the hybrid ResNeXt + LSTM model across multiple deepfake datasets, with accuracy exceeding 90% in all but two cases. This consistency suggests that the model is both robust and generalisable. Taken together, the findings indicate that the proposed approach offers a viable solution for real-time deepfake detection across different video qualities and manipulation types.

CONCLUSION

The proposed system detects deepfakes by applying advanced deep learning techniques to a problem that is increasingly difficult to solve through traditional methods alone. By combining a ResNeXt CNN with a temporally aware LSTM network, the model achieves high detection accuracy while maintaining computational efficiency. An additional strength of the system is its confidence scoring mechanism, which provides users with an indication of the model's certainty and supports more reliable interpretation of results across diverse datasets. Designed to operate on large-scale video data, the system not only improves the accuracy of deepfake detection but also provides a strong foundation for future development. One possible extension would be to convert the web-based application into a browser extension, making deepfake detection more accessible and convenient for everyday users. Such developments could strengthen efforts to counter the misuse of deepfake technology and support the detection of increasingly sophisticated manipulations, including those involving full-body synthesis rather than facial manipulation alone. More broadly, the system provides a useful basis for further academic research and technical innovation in this important area.

The wider implications of this work are especially important for law enforcement and investigative practice. As synthetic media is increasingly weaponised for purposes such as fraud, blackmail, political interference, and the creation of non-consensual intimate imagery, the need for detection tools that are reliable, accessible, and computationally efficient has become increasingly urgent. The system developed in this research responds to that need by offering strong detection performance, including accuracy above 97% on the FaceForensics++ benchmark, processing speeds compatible with real-time use, and a user-facing web interface that does not require specialist knowledge. These features make the system valuable not only as an academic contribution, but also as a practical tool for digital forensic investigators, trust and safety teams, and policymakers seeking technical responses to the deepfake problem (Yang et al., 2023). The model's strong performance across multiple datasets also suggests that the hybrid ResNeXt and LSTM architecture is effective in combining spatial and temporal information in ways that single-model approaches may not achieve as well.

Future Scope

Future development of this approach could extend detection beyond facial deepfakes to include full-body manipulations, incorporating gesture and motion analysis as part of the detection process. The framework could also be enhanced through improved image stabilisation and greater sensitivity to subtle manipulations under a wider range of video conditions. In addition, the system could be expanded to detect audio deepfakes alongside visual manipulations, creating a more comprehensive multimodal detection capability. Further deployment options, including mobile applications, desktop software, and cloud-based services, could also support wider adoption. In particular, converting the current web interface into a browser plug-in could allow users to assess video content more easily in near real-time environments.

From a strategic and policy perspective, investment in deepfake detection tools should be understood as an essential part of digital infrastructure. As states, international organisations such as the European Union and the United Nations, and platform providers continue to confront the regulatory and technical challenges posed by synthetic media, studies such as this provide useful evidence for the development of practical responses. There is also considerable value in closer collaboration between academic researchers and operational practitioners, including digital forensic units, intelligence agencies, and content moderation teams, so that detection systems are designed around real investigative needs rather than benchmark performance alone. Future versions of this system should be tested on videos collected from live social media environments, evaluated against adversarially optimised deepfakes designed to evade detection, and assessed for bias across demographic groups in order to ensure equitable performance. Together, these directions point to a research agenda of considerable social importance, one that extends beyond the technical contribution of a single model and addresses the broader challenge of preserving trust in visual evidence in an era of rapidly advancing synthetic media generation.

REFERENCES

Afchar, D., Nozick, V., Yamagishi, J., & Echizen, I. (2018). *Mesonet: a compact facial video forgery detection network.* Paper presented at the 2018 IEEE international workshop on information forensics and security (WIFS). DOI: 10.1109/WIFS.2018.8630761

Dang, M., & Nguyen, T. N. (2023). Digital face manipulation creation and detection: A systematic review. *Electronics (Basel), 12*(16), 3407. DOI: 10.3390/electronics12163407

Jain, P. R., Quadri, S., & Khattar, A. (2024). EM-UDA: Emotion detection using unsupervised domain adaptation for classification of facial images. *IEEE Access : Practical Innovations, Open Solutions, 12*, 140262–140276. DOI: 10.1109/ACCESS.2024.3467990

Kaur, A., Noori Hoshyar, A., Saikrishna, V., Firmin, S., & Xia, F. (2024). Deepfake video detection: Challenges and opportunities. *Artificial Intelligence Review, 57*(6), 159. DOI: 10.1007/s10462-024-10810-6

Kumar, K. G., Sowndharya, A., Pradeep, D. M., Suriya, S., & Kumar, K. D. (2024). *Detection of Deepfake Videos Using a Deep Learning Approach with ResNext and LSTM.* Paper presented at the 2024 13th International Conference on System Modeling & Advancement in Research Trends (SMART). DOI: 10.1109/SMART63812.2024.10882518

Li, L., Bao, J., Zhang, T., Yang, H., Chen, D., Wen, F., & Guo, B. (2020). *Face x-ray for more general face forgery detection.* Paper presented at the Proceedings of the IEEE/CVF conference on computer vision and pattern recognition. DOI: 10.1109/CVPR42600.2020.00505

Li, P., Huang, Q., Shuang, F., Cai, Y., Cheng, H., & Li, Q. (2026). Anchor-based Multimodal Verification: A Dynamic Query Framework for Fake News Forensics in Short Videos. *IEEE Transactions on Information Forensics and Security, 21*, 2047–2060. Advance online publication. DOI: 10.1109/TIFS.2026.3658995

Li, Y., & Lyu, S. (2018). Exposing deepfake videos by detecting face warping artifacts. *arXiv preprint arXiv:1811.00656.* DOI: 10.3897/bdj.11.e100784.figure2c

Müller, N., Kawa, P., Choong, W.-H., Stan, A., Bukkapatnam, A. T., Pizzi, K., . . . Sperl, P. (2025). Replay attacks against audio deepfake detection. *arXiv preprint arXiv:2505.14862.* /arXiv.2505.14862.DOI: 10.21437/Interspeech.2025-20

Rossler, A., Cozzolino, D., Verdoliva, L., Riess, C., Thies, J., & Nießner, M. (2019). *Faceforensics++: Learning to detect manipulated facial images.* Paper presented at the Proceedings of the IEEE/CVF international conference on computer vision. DOI: 10.1109/ICCV.2019.00009

Shiohara, K., & Yamasaki, T. (2022). *Detecting deepfakes with self-blended images.* Paper presented at the Proceedings of the IEEE/CVF conference on computer vision and pattern recognition. DOI: 10.1109/CVPR52688.2022.01816

Singh, M., Jain, S., & Khan, L. (2025). *Fake video detection Emerging Trends in Computer Science and Its Application*. CRC Press., DOI: 10.33009/FSU_caf24cdb-69d0-4b9e-a08c-118aca59b212

Singh, T. M., Kumar, R. C. K., Munawar, M., Lippert, K., & Doss, S. Securing the Metaverse: AI and machine learning approaches to threat detection and prevention *Defending the Metaverse* (pp. 144-170): CRC Press. .DOI: 10.33009/FSU_2a4dc970-2d4b-4b41-8611-80c464fb6462

Sun, W., & Li, Y. (2025). Emotion Recognition in Consumer Electronics Using Multimodal Deep Learning. *IEEE Transactions on Consumer Electronics*, *71*(3), 7636–7650. Advance online publication. DOI: 10.1109/TCE.2025.3568882

Tiwari, A., Dave, R., & Vanamala, M. (2023). *Leveraging deep learning approaches for deepfake detection: A review.* Paper presented at the Proceedings of the 2023 7th international conference on intelligent systems, metaheuristics & swarm intelligence. DOI: 10.1145/3596947.3596959

Tolosana, R., Vera-Rodriguez, R., Fierrez, J., Morales, A., & Ortega-Garcia, J. (2020). Deepfakes and beyond: A survey of face manipulation and fake detection. *Information Fusion*, *64*, 131–148. DOI: 10.1016/j.inffus.2020.06.014

Verdoliva, L. (2020). Media forensics and deepfakes: An overview. *IEEE Journal of Selected Topics in Signal Processing*, *14*(5), 910–932. DOI: 10.1109/JSTSP.2020.3002101

Wang, S., Zhang, H., Yang, G., Guo, Z., & Chen, J. (2024). A two-stage fake face image detection algorithm with expanded attention. *Multimedia Tools and Applications*, *83*(18), 55709–55730. DOI: 10.1007/s11042-023-17672-0

Yang, J., Sun, Y., Mao, M., Bai, L., Zhang, S., & Wang, F. (2023). Model-agnostic method: Exposing deepfake using pixel-wise spatial and temporal fingerprints. *IEEE Transactions on Big Data*, *9*(6), 1496–1509. DOI: 10.1109/TBDATA.2023.3284272

Yuan, W., & Gao, K.-X. (2020). EAdam optimizer: How $\epsilon $ impact adam. *arXiv preprint arXiv:2011.02150.* /arXiv.2011.02150.DOI: 10.48550

Zeba, S., & Amjad, M. (2025). Identification and location monitoring through Live video Streaming by using blockchain. *Multimedia Tools and Applications*, *84*(24), 27549–27576. DOI: 10.1007/s11042-024-20197-9

Zhang, Y., Pang, Z., Huang, S., Wang, C., & Zhou, X. (2025). Unmasking AI-created visual content: A review of generated images and deepfake detection technologies. *Journal of King Saud University. Computer and Information Sciences*, *37*(6), 148. DOI: 10.1007/s44443-025-00154-8

Zhou, L., Chen, M., & Ruan, H. (2025). Structural Consistency for Face Forgery Detection via Frequency Domain Enhancement and Self-Predictive Learning. *IEEE Transactions on Biometrics, Behavior, and Identity Science*. Advance online publication. DOI: 10.1109/WIFS.2018.8630761

Chapter 11
Emerging Frontiers in Cybercrime and Law Enforcement Challenges

Nikhil Kumar Goyal
http://orcid.org/0009-0007-4532-8033
Poornima University, Jaipur, India

ABSTRACT

The chapter cross-refers the evolution of artificial intelligence and ransomware/advanced persistent threats (APTs) as they have evolved to become new frontiers in the evolving sphere of cybercrimes. It studies how AI is used to supplement the classical models of attack through automation, real-time evasion, and deepfake-powered deceit, upending speed and sophistication in an attack. The discussion is also relevant to APTs, whose actors are nation-state, organized groups who are increasingly using AI as a means of continuing their hold undetected and over time with precision. The dual-purpose of AI is highlighted, where AI proves to be useful in helping with defensive cybersecurity preventions, but also at the same time open to malicious use. The causes of law enforcement challenges are critically evaluated citing jurisdiction issues, attribution problem, and inadequacy of the existing legal frameworks.

INTRODUCTION

Artificial Intelligence in Cybercrime

One of the most significant paradigm shifts in the evolution of cyber threats has been the integration of Artificial Intelligence (AI) into the cybercrime ecosystem.

DOI: 10.4018/979-8-3373-5228-2.ch011

Traditionally, cyberattacks were manual or only partially automated, and their success often depended on the attacker's prior knowledge, skill, and persistence. Although such attacks could still cause considerable harm, they were constrained by practical limitations, including time, technical capability, and the expertise required to execute them effectively. With the emergence of machine learning and AI-driven systems, attackers now have access to tools that can automate reconnaissance, tailor lures to victims with unprecedented precision, and evade defensive systems more effectively than before (Rishad et al., 2025).

AI-enabled cybercrime has developed in part as a response to advances in cyber defence. As cybersecurity tools increasingly incorporated intrusion detection systems (IDS), next-generation firewalls, and behavioural analytics, malicious actors began using AI to bypass these protections. Machine learning algorithms can analyse defensive systems and adapt attack vectors dynamically, reducing the likelihood that ransomware or intrusion attempts will be detected. Similarly, generative AI can produce highly convincing phishing messages, deepfake voices, and manipulated videos, enabling attackers to exploit human trust and circumvent conventional authentication safeguards.

Importantly, the use of AI in cybercrime is no longer limited to highly sophisticated or state-sponsored actors. As AI tools have become more widely available, the barrier to entry has fallen substantially. Open-source frameworks, combined with malicious AI-as-a-service offerings on the dark web, have enabled less experienced offenders to launch more advanced attacks. This democratisation not only increases the frequency and scale of attacks, but also makes attribution more difficult, as methods once associated primarily with elite threat actors are now increasingly common. The development of AI in cybercrime can therefore be understood not only as part of an ongoing technological arms race, but also as a consequence of the growing accessibility of powerful computational tools (Svet et al., 2025).

Ransomware and APTs

Ransomware and Advanced Persistent Threats (APTs) are not new phenomena, but their development has been significantly shaped by technological innovation, including AI. Ransomware first emerged in the late 1980s with the so-called AIDS Trojan, which encrypted file names and instructed victims to send payment by post. Since then, ransomware has evolved into a global threat, with major variants such as WannaCry and Ryuk causing billions of dollars in losses. Earlier forms of ransomware typically relied on relatively simple encryption methods and were distributed at scale through exploited vulnerabilities, often using polymorphic code to reduce the likelihood of signature-based detection (Pekepok et al., 2025).

Figure 1. Types of ransomware attacks

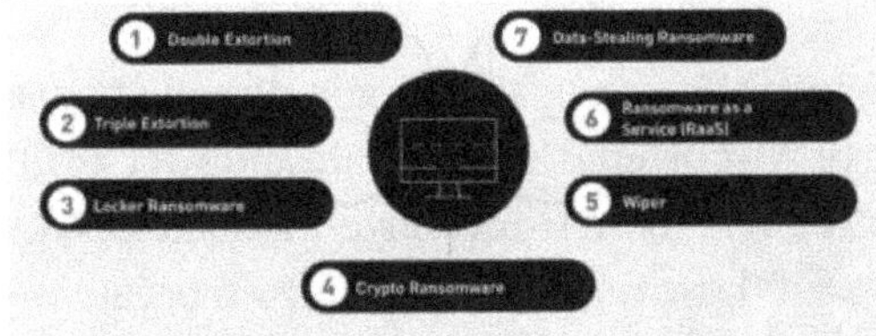

Figure 1 illustrates the major categories of ransomware attacks, showing how attack types differ in terms of propagation methods, encryption strategies, and overall impact.

APTs, by contrast, represent a more covert and persistent form of cybercrime. Unlike ransomware, which is usually designed for rapid financial gain, APTs involve long-term intrusion and are typically associated with espionage, sabotage, or strategic disruption. State-linked operations such as *Stuxnet* and *Operation Aurora* demonstrated the technical sophistication of well-resourced actors capable of infiltrating critical infrastructure and enterprise networks. AI is now extending the capabilities of APTs still further. For example, automated anomaly detection can help attackers imitate normal user behaviour in order to conceal malicious activity, while reinforcement learning can enable them to adapt their tactics in response to defensive measures. This not only makes AI-enhanced APTs harder to detect, but also allows them to become more resilient over time (Deleon et al., 2024).

The evolution of ransomware and APTs demonstrates a convergence not only of methods, but also of motives. As ransomware increasingly adopts persistence and stealth capabilities, some APT actors have also incorporated ransomware as a final disruptive stage within broader campaigns. AI is accelerating this convergence and further blurring the boundary between financially motivated cybercrime and geopolitically motivated cyber conflict. The result is a threat landscape in which both individuals and states face adaptive and increasingly dangerous forms of AI-driven attack.

Objectives and Scope of the Chapter

The primary aim of this chapter is to examine how AI is reshaping the landscape of ransomware and Advanced Persistent Threats, and to explore the implications for cybersecurity, law enforcement, and public policy. Rather than offering a purely technical discussion, the chapter highlights the dual role of AI as both a defensive tool and an offensive weapon. Through the use of case studies, emerging attack methods, and evolving defence strategies, it provides a detailed assessment of AI-related threats in this area.

The discussion is organised across three main dimensions. First, it examines the technical development of AI-powered ransomware and APTs, with particular attention to the features that distinguish them from conventional attacks. Second, it considers the wider consequences of these threats, ranging from organisational disruption and financial loss to the geopolitical implications of state-sponsored campaigns. Third, it critically assesses the challenges these threats pose to law enforcement, including issues of jurisdiction, attribution, and the limitations of existing legal frameworks (Denis et al., 2024).

A further objective of the chapter is to help bridge the gap between academia, industry, and policymaking. For researchers, it offers insight into an emerging frontier in cybercrime. For practitioners, it identifies strategies and technologies that may help mitigate AI-related threats. For policymakers, it emphasises the need to revise legal frameworks, strengthen international cooperation, and invest in AI-based defence systems. Overall, the chapter argues strongly for a multi-stakeholder response to AI-enabled ransomware and APTs, recognising that the future of cybersecurity will depend on the integration of technology, psychology, and governance (Goyal et al., 2025).

AI-POWERED RANSOMWARE

Traditional Ransomware vs. AI-Enhanced Ransomware

Ransomware has long been one of the most disruptive forms of cybercrime, involving the use of malicious software to encrypt a victim's files and demand payment, often in cryptocurrency, in exchange for restoration. Traditional ransomware was comparatively simple. It was typically distributed through phishing emails or malicious attachments and relied on basic encryption routines. Although detection was not always straightforward, such attacks could often be mitigated through signature-based antivirus systems and user awareness training. The effectiveness of early ransomware campaigns depended largely on scale: attackers infected as many systems as possible in the hope that some victims would pay (Abadjiev et al., 2024).

AI-enhanced ransomware changes this model significantly. Rather than relying on a broad and indiscriminate approach, AI allows ransomware to become more adaptive, targeted, and efficient. Machine learning can be used to analyse large volumes of data in order to identify vulnerable systems or high-value targets. Instead of generic phishing emails, AI can generate tailored lures based on a victim's workflow, interests, or recent online behaviour. It may also enable ransomware to adjust its behaviour in real time according to the characteristics of the target environment.

The contrast between conventional ransomware and AI-enhanced ransomware reflects a broader shift from quantity-driven attacks to quality-driven attacks. Where earlier ransomware relied on mass distribution, AI enables greater efficiency, adaptability, and precision. The result is a new generation of ransomware campaigns that are harder to detect, more profitable for offenders, and significantly more dangerous to both individuals and organisations (Hossain & Islam, 2024).

Techniques of AI-Powered Ransomware

The integration of AI into ransomware introduces a range of capabilities that go well beyond basic encryption. These include:

- **Evasion through polymorphism and obfuscation:** Traditional ransomware could often be detected through signature-based analysis. AI-enabled ransomware can continuously alter its code, making it polymorphic and more difficult to detect. Neural networks may also be used to analyse antivirus heuristics and adjust malware behaviour in order to avoid detection (Mata-Torres et al., 2023).
- **Automated exploitation:** Rather than relying entirely on human operators, AI can scan networks in real time to identify vulnerabilities, misconfigurations, and outdated software. Once such weaknesses are found, the ransomware can exploit them automatically, increasing the speed and efficiency of infection (Bakır & Bakır, 2024).
- **Target prioritisation:** AI-based reconnaissance can help attackers identify the victims most likely to pay. For example, algorithms may prioritise organisations that hold valuable intellectual property or operate in sectors such as healthcare, where downtime is especially costly. This enables attackers to maximise profit by ranking targets strategically.
- **Adaptive timing:** Timing is a critical element in ransomware deployment. AI can monitor user behaviour, system logs, and network traffic in order to determine the most effective moment to activate. For example, ransomware may wait until backup systems are offline, during holiday periods, or when IT staffing levels are low.
- **Deceptive communication:** Large language models and other generative AI systems can produce ransom notes that appear more credible, detailed, and persuasive. Attackers may also use AI-powered chatbots to negotiate with victims, adjusting ransom demands according to the responses they receive (Kaggle, n.d.).

Together, these techniques show that AI not only makes ransomware more technically sophisticated, but also enhances its ability to exploit victims psychologically, thereby increasing the likelihood of successful extortion.

Case Studies of Emerging AI-Driven Ransomware Campaigns

Although AI-enabled ransomware remains a relatively new development, several real-world examples and proof-of-concept cases demonstrate how such capabilities may operate in practice.

One example involves AI-assisted spear-phishing. In a 2020 case, a European energy company reportedly experienced a ransomware attack initiated through emails that appeared to have been written by senior executives. Analysis suggested that natural language processing (NLP) had been used to imitate the communication style of those executives, thereby increasing the likelihood of employee engagement (Maddireddy, 2020).

Another important example is *DeepLocker*, a proof-of-concept malware developed by cybersecurity researchers. This system used a neural network to conceal a malicious payload within legitimate software and to activate only under specific conditions, such as recognising a target's face or voice. Although *DeepLocker* has not been reported as active in the wild, it provides a clear illustration of how AI could support stealth, personalisation, and selective execution in future ransomware campaigns.

In addition, security analysts have observed that criminal groups are beginning to incorporate AI into ransomware-as-a-service (RaaS) platforms. On dark web markets, such services make sophisticated ransomware tools available to less experienced offenders. If integrated with AI, these platforms could automate parts of target selection, infection, and adaptation, thereby making more advanced attacks accessible to a wider range of actors (Goyal, 2025).

These examples suggest that AI-driven ransomware is no longer merely theoretical. Whether through imitation, adaptive payloads, or automated reconnaissance, the intersection of AI and ransomware is already reshaping the threat landscape.

Potential Impact on Individuals, Organizations, and Critical Infrastructure

The consequences of AI-powered ransomware extend far beyond conventional financial extortion.

For individuals, AI-driven personalisation makes attacks much harder to recognise. Instead of generic phishing messages or standard ransom demands, victims may receive highly convincing and individually tailored communications based on their online behaviour. The psychological harm can also be substantial, as victims may feel violated not only financially but also personally. This effect is intensified when AI exploits cognitive biases such as urgency, authority, or fear.

For organisations, the risks are even greater. AI-enhanced ransomware may enter a network, remain dormant, and disable backup systems before initiating encryption. The result may include prolonged operational disruption, severe financial loss, and reputational damage. Sectors such as healthcare, finance, and energy are particularly vulnerable, because even short periods of downtime can have serious consequences. For instance, a hospital disabled by ransomware may face not only financial costs but also direct risks to patient safety (Jimmy, 2021a).

The threat to critical infrastructure is perhaps the most serious of all. AI-driven ransomware could be directed at transport networks, energy grids, or water systems. Its adaptive capabilities may enable it to circumvent conventional security controls and trigger large-scale disruption. Many critical infrastructure systems still rely on older technologies that are poorly equipped to resist AI-enabled threats. In geopolitical terms, AI-assisted ransomware could also function as a tool of cyber warfare, used by state-sponsored actors not primarily for profit, but for coercion or destabilisation.

Overall, the impact of AI-powered ransomware reaches well beyond conventional cybercrime. It poses serious risks to economic stability, public safety, and trust in digital infrastructure. Addressing this threat will require not only technical defences, but also interdisciplinary responses drawing on psychology, law, and public policy (Jimmy, 2021b).

ADVANCED PERSISTENT THREATS (APTs) IN THE AI ERA

Characteristics and Life Cycle of APTs

Advanced Persistent Threats (APTs) are among the most sophisticated and enduring forms of cyberattack. Unlike ransomware, which is often rapid and disruptive, APTs are typically designed to remain covert and maintain access over extended periods. Their defining characteristics include targeted intrusion, long-term presence within a network, and strategic objectives such as espionage, information theft, or sabotage. The actors behind APT campaigns are usually well-resourced organisations, often linked to state interests, that possess the time, funding, and expertise required to sustain covert operations over months or even years (Jimmy, 2022).

Figure 2. Advanced persistent threats lifecycle and characteristics

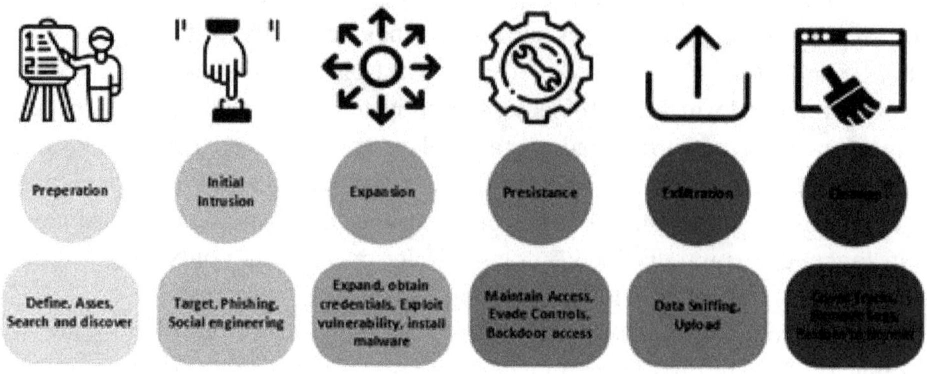

Figure 2 presents the lifecycle of Advanced Persistent Threats, illustrating the sequential stages from reconnaissance through to persistence.

The typical lifecycle of an APT consists of five stages. First, attackers conduct reconnaissance, gathering information about the target's network, personnel, and vulnerabilities. This is followed by initial intrusion, which often occurs through spear-phishing, supply chain compromise, or the exploitation of a zero-day vulnerability. Once inside the organisation, the attacker establishes access by deploying malware or backdoors that can be used to maintain future access. The third stage involves lateral movement, during which the attacker moves across the network, escalates privileges, and identifies valuable assets. The fourth stage consists of either data exfiltration or sabotage, depending on the attacker's objectives. Finally, the attacker ensures persistence so that access can be regained even if part of the operation is detected and removed (Jimmy, 2024).

Traditionally, APTs have been difficult to detect because their activities often resemble those of legitimate users. With the addition of AI, these campaigns are becoming even harder to identify, as attackers can use machine learning to enhance each stage of the attack lifecycle.

AI-Enabled Tools for Stealth and Persistence

The incorporation of AI into APT operations increases both stealth and adaptability. Machine learning algorithms can be used to analyse network traffic and user behaviour so that malicious activity more closely resembles normal activity within the organisation. Reinforcement learning, for example, can help attackers determine the most effective times to move laterally or escalate privileges while minimising the risk of detection. Similarly, anomaly detection methods may be used in reverse by attackers to understand how defensive systems operate and how they can be avoided.

AI can also strengthen persistence. By analysing patching cycles and security policies, an APT can anticipate how an organisation is likely to respond to threats and adapt its behaviour accordingly. In addition, AI may support the development of polymorphic malware, allowing malicious code to change over time and remain difficult to detect. Natural language processing (NLP) tools can also be used to generate convincing internal emails or messages, enabling attackers to manipulate insiders without raising suspicion (Goyal et al., 2025).

Perhaps the most concerning development is the growing ability of AI to support large-scale autonomous operations. Unlike human operators, AI systems can make rapid tactical decisions in real time, such as whether to escalate privileges, exfiltrate data, or remain dormant in order to avoid detection. This level of autonomy allows APT campaigns to scale more effectively without requiring constant manual intervention.

Nation-State Actors and AI-Supported Cyber Espionage

APTs are most commonly associated with nation-state actors whose objectives extend beyond financial gain. Their aims often include intelligence collection, disruption of critical infrastructure, and the exercise of geopolitical influence. AI is increasingly acting as a force multiplier in such operations, enabling cyber espionage campaigns to be conducted at greater scale and speed.

For example, stolen diplomatic communications, intellectual property, or military data can be processed rapidly using AI in order to identify patterns, extract useful information, and generate actionable intelligence. Deepfake technologies also create opportunities for sophisticated psychological operations, including the use of fabricated audio or video to discredit political figures or manipulate public opinion. In addition, AI-assisted reconnaissance tools can map relationships between organisations and identify weaker third-party suppliers or service providers that may provide indirect access to high-value targets (Vegesna & Adepu, 2024).

The use of AI in nation-state APTs is especially concerning because of the resources available to these actors. With access to substantial computing power, advanced algorithms, and large datasets, state-sponsored groups can conduct operations that move faster than many organisations are able to defend against. The result is a widening gap between offensive and defensive cyber capability, raising serious concerns for both national and international security.

Real-World Examples of AI-Enhanced APT Campaigns

Although fully autonomous AI-powered APTs remain largely conceptual, several real-world developments point in this direction. For example, some malware strains have reportedly used machine learning techniques to detect sandbox environments and delay execution until they are outside those controlled settings. Likewise, AI-assisted spear-phishing campaigns have been observed in which attackers used natural language models trained on publicly available social media data to generate highly personalised messages.

A well-known example is IBM's DeepLocker proof of concept. Although it was not developed as malicious software for use in the wild, DeepLocker demonstrated how AI could conceal malware within apparently benign applications and activate only when specific conditions were met, such as recognising a particular face or voice. This type of selective activation would make APT attacks both more precise and more difficult to detect (Islam et al., 2024).

There have also been reports that some APT groups, including those associated with state actors, are experimenting with AI to manage large botnets, automate reconnaissance, and improve persistence within compromised environments. Although the full details are not yet public, the available evidence suggests that AI-enhanced APTs should be understood not as a distant possibility, but as an emerging operational reality.

AI AS A DUAL-USE TECHNOLOGY

Offensive Use of AI in Cybercrime

The use of AI in cybercrime illustrates the inherently dual-use nature of technological innovation: the same technology can be applied for beneficial or harmful purposes. On the offensive side, AI provides cybercriminals with powerful tools for automation, personalised social engineering, and evasion. Neural networks, for example, can be used to generate polymorphic malware that continually changes its structure in order to avoid traditional antivirus detection. Reinforcement learning can also optimise attack strategies in real time by determining the most effective moments to enter a network, move laterally, or exfiltrate data.

Machine learning methods extend these capabilities even further by enabling the creation of synthetic identities and deepfakes that can be used for fraud, blackmail, or political disinformation. Generative adversarial networks (GANs), for instance, allow attackers to produce highly convincing images, audio, and video, undermining trust in digital communication. AI can also be used to model and exploit human behaviour, such as identifying the time of day when employees are most likely to click on phishing links or comply with fraudulent requests (Ofoegbu et al., 2024).

The offensive use of AI therefore represents a major escalation in cybercrime capability, introducing levels of precision, sophistication, and psychological manipulation that are difficult to achieve through traditional malware or manual hacking alone.

Defensive Applications of AI in Cybersecurity

On the defensive side, AI has become an important component of modern cybersecurity. Machine learning algorithms allow security systems to monitor network traffic in real time, identify suspicious behavioural patterns, and respond quickly to potential threats. For example, intrusion detection systems (IDS) can analyse very large volumes of data across networks and identify abnormal behaviour that may not be immediately visible to human analysts.

Figure 3. Role of AI in cyber security

Figure 3 depicts the dual role of AI in cybersecurity, emphasizing both its defensive capabilities and its exploitation by malicious actors.

Behavioural analytics tools use AI to establish a baseline of normal user activity and can then identify deviations that may indicate compromise. Similarly, predictive models can anticipate likely attack pathways by analysing historical data, allowing organisations to take preventive action. AI can also reduce incident response times by automating containment measures, such as blocking malicious IP addresses or isolating infected devices.

Digital forensics also benefits from AI, as it can accelerate the analysis of large volumes of data and help investigators identify root causes and attacker footprints more efficiently. As cyberattacks continue to increase in both scale and complexity, the use of AI on the defensive side has become essential in helping defenders keep pace with evolving threats (Baskerville & Siponen, 2020).

Ethical and Legal Concerns of Dual-Use AI

The dual-use nature of AI raises significant ethical and legal concerns. One of the most important questions is that of responsibility: when AI is used offensively, who should be held accountable—the developer of the system, the actor who deploys it maliciously, or both? Similar concerns arise on the defensive side, where autonomous or semi-autonomous AI systems may inadvertently cause harm, for example by wrongly classifying legitimate behaviour as malicious or by infringing privacy through excessive data collection.

Existing legal frameworks are struggling to keep pace with these developments. Although some international mechanisms exist to regulate other dual-use technologies, such as nuclear materials or biotechnology, there is currently no comparable global regime governing the use of AI in cyberspace. The transnational nature of cybercrime makes this even more difficult, as AI tools developed in one jurisdiction can be deployed almost instantly across the world (Bilge et al., 2020).

From an ethical perspective, escalation is also a major concern. As states and organisations increase their use of AI for defence, adversaries are likely to respond by enhancing their own offensive capabilities. This creates an arms-race dynamic that increases the risk of unintended consequences, including collateral harm, excessive reliance on automation, and the erosion of human judgement in security-related decision-making.

LAW ENFORCEMENT CHALLENGES IN THE AGE OF AI-DRIVEN CYBERCRIME

Jurisdictional and Cross-Border Issues

One of the most significant challenges in addressing AI-driven cybercrime is that such offences rarely fall neatly within a single legal jurisdiction. Unlike conventional crime, which usually takes place within a defined territorial boundary, cyberattacks may originate in one country, pass through servers in several others, and target victims across multiple continents. This creates major legal and operational difficulties for law enforcement agencies.

AI further complicates these jurisdictional problems by enabling the automation and concealment of attacks. For example, an AI-enabled ransomware campaign may dynamically redirect traffic through global botnets, obscuring its true origin and making tracing far more difficult. Similarly, AI-supported APT operations linked to nation-state actors may be routed through infrastructure located in neutral jurisdictions, further masking the real source of the attack (Buczak & Guven, 2016).

These difficulties are compounded by uneven national legal frameworks. Some jurisdictions have robust cybercrime laws and strong investigative capacity, while others lack both the legal clarity and technical resources needed to pursue offenders effectively. International agreements such as the Budapest Convention on Cybercrime represent important efforts toward harmonisation, but participation remains incomplete and several major states remain outside its framework. As a result, law enforcement agencies often operate within fragmented legal environments that attackers are well positioned to exploit.

Technical Complexity of AI-Driven Threats

The challenge of responding to AI-enabled cybercrime is not only legal, but also deeply technical. Unlike traditional malware, which often leaves recognisable signatures, AI-driven cyber threats are adaptive and dynamic. Advanced AI-enhanced ransomware may continuously modify its code to avoid detection, while AI-supported APTs may adapt their behaviour to resemble legitimate user activity. For investigators, this creates a classic needle-in-a-haystack problem, as malicious behaviour may appear indistinguishable from ordinary network activity.

The adaptive nature of these threats also complicates digital forensics. Traditional investigations often rely on static artefacts such as log files, IP addresses, or file hashes. AI-powered malware, however, may leave minimal traces, delete itself after execution, or generate misleading evidence intended to confuse investigators. In some cases, adversarial AI may feed false data into defensive systems, diverting attention toward decoy activity while the real intrusion remains hidden (Dilek et al., 2015).

A further layer of complexity arises from the use of advanced encryption in AI-driven ransomware attacks. Contemporary variants may employ AI-optimised encryption routines that adapt to the characteristics of the victim's system. Decrypting such systems may require substantial resources that many law enforcement agencies do not possess, leaving victims under pressure to pay ransom even while investigations are ongoing.

Attribution Difficulties in AI-Enabled Attacks

Attribution has always been one of the most difficult aspects of cybercrime investigation, and AI makes it even more challenging. Attribution involves both identifying who carried out an attack and generating evidence sufficient to support prosecution. AI-enabled tools, however, can introduce multiple layers of obfuscation that make both tasks substantially harder.

For example, attackers may use AI to automate false-flag operations by imitating the tactics, techniques, and procedures (TTPs) of other known threat groups. This can mislead investigators into attributing attacks to the wrong actors and may even contribute to geopolitical tension. Similarly, AI can generate convincing digital personas capable of interacting, negotiating, or communicating on behalf of attackers, further complicating attribution (Goyal et al., 2025).

Nation-state actors in particular may benefit from these ambiguities. By using AI to automate deception and misdirection, they can strengthen plausible deniability and make it extremely difficult for law enforcement or intelligence agencies to establish responsibility with confidence. This uncertainty undermines not only criminal prosecutions but also international policymaking, as states may hesitate to respond to suspected attacks where attribution remains probabilistic rather than certain (Eling, 2019).

Resource and Skill Gaps in Law Enforcement Agencies

Another major issue is the imbalance in resources between attackers and defenders. Many law enforcement agencies, particularly in developing contexts, do not possess the technical infrastructure, specialist personnel, or financial capacity needed to investigate AI-enabled threats effectively. By contrast, cybercriminal organisations and state-sponsored groups often have access to substantial resources, advanced tools, and highly specialised expertise.

Recruitment and retention are especially difficult. Skilled cybersecurity professionals are often drawn to the private sector, where salaries and working conditions are more competitive. As a result, many agencies face staff shortages and limited technical training, leaving them poorly equipped to investigate sophisticated AI-driven attacks (goodfellow et al., 2018).

In addition, bureaucratic processes and the slow adoption of innovation in law enforcement can hinder effective response. While adversaries may adopt AI-based methods rapidly, public agencies often take years to introduce comparable capabilities. This delay widens the gap between offence and defence, weakens investigative effectiveness, and leaves victims with limited confidence that meaningful enforcement action will follow (Goodfellow et al., 2016).

Cooperation Between Law Enforcement, Industry, and Academia

Addressing AI-enabled cybercrime requires coordinated action across multiple sectors. The private sector controls much of the world's digital infrastructure and therefore plays a central role in threat detection, mitigation, and reporting. Academic researchers also contribute by developing new methods for threat detection, attribution, and digital forensic analysis.

Public–private partnerships have become especially important in closing these gaps. For example, information-sharing arrangements between governments and industry can improve the early detection of emerging threats. Joint task forces, such as those supported by Europol or Interpol, also demonstrate the value of combining expertise across sectors in order to dismantle cybercriminal networks (Gupta et al., 2021).

However, cooperation is not without obstacles. Companies may be reluctant to share sensitive data because of privacy obligations or fears of reputational damage. Academia, while rich in expertise, may not always produce outputs that align closely with operational law enforcement needs. Overcoming these barriers will require trust, clearer legal frameworks for data sharing, and incentives that encourage collaboration. Only through sustained and coordinated effort is the wider community likely to remain ahead of AI-enabled cybercriminals.

Case Studies of Investigative Challenges

Several high-profile cases illustrate the difficulties law enforcement faces in the AI era. One example is the emergence of ransomware-as-a-service (RaaS) platforms that incorporate AI-related capabilities. Agencies attempting to investigate such platforms have often found that they operate through decentralised structures spanning multiple jurisdictions, while offenders use AI-enabled anonymisation techniques, including synthetic identities and encrypted communication channels.

Another example concerns APT campaigns in which AI-assisted false flags diverted investigators for extended periods. In one case, forensic evidence initially pointed to a well-known threat group in Eastern Europe. Later investigation suggested that the attackers had deliberately imitated that group's methods while operating from another region entirely. Such cases illustrate how AI can complicate attribution, prolong investigations, and allow attackers to continue operating while enforcement efforts are delayed (Goyal et al., 2025).

Even where attackers are identified, prosecution may remain difficult. The Snowden case in 2013, although not AI-related, demonstrated how psychological and technical vulnerabilities can be exploited by insiders to evade security controls.

In an AI-enabled environment, similar insider threats may become even harder to detect, as machine learning tools could be used to exfiltrate data in ways that blend into trusted system activity. This raises important questions about how law enforcement will gather evidence and build cases against actors operating from within legitimate environments.

FUTURE DIRECTIONS AND POLICY RECOMMENDATIONS

Strengthening AI-Driven Defensive Systems

A central priority in addressing the risks posed by AI-enabled ransomware and APTs is the strengthening of defensive systems that also make use of AI. Traditional cybersecurity tools are increasingly inadequate against attacks that are adaptive, data-driven, and capable of modifying their behaviour in real time. As a result, defensive AI systems must move beyond signature-based detection and place greater emphasis on behavioural analysis, anomaly detection, and predictive threat modelling.

One promising direction is the use of adversarial AI for defensive purposes. Just as attackers may use techniques such as generative adversarial networks (GANs) to create polymorphic malware, defenders can use comparable methods to simulate realistic attack scenarios and train systems to recognise novel threats before they emerge in the wild. This approach supports a more proactive form of defence by enabling systems to anticipate attacker innovation. Reinforcement learning may also be useful in defensive settings, as it allows systems to adapt dynamically to new attack vectors as they arise (Gupta et al., 2020).

Defensive AI must also be explainable. One of the main criticisms of AI in cybersecurity is the so-called black-box problem, whereby operators cannot clearly understand why an AI system has flagged certain behaviour as suspicious. Explainable AI (XAI) can improve transparency by enabling human decision-makers to understand, validate, and challenge automated outputs. This is particularly important in law enforcement settings, where evidence generated through opaque systems may be difficult to justify or rely upon in court.

Finally, defensive AI must be both scalable and collaborative. Cyber threats do not respect organisational or national boundaries, and effective defence increasingly depends on the real-time sharing of information among companies, government agencies, and international partners. A distributed and cooperative defensive infrastructure would enable lessons learned from one incident to strengthen prevention elsewhere.

Enhancing International Cooperation and Legal Frameworks

Because AI-driven cybercrime is inherently transnational, effective responses require strong international coordination and greater convergence in legal frameworks. Current approaches remain fragmented. For example, although the Budapest Convention on Cybercrime has been adopted by many countries, several major cyber powers, including Russia and China, are not parties to it, which limits its overall reach and effectiveness.

A key future priority is the development of shared definitions, procedures, and penalties for AI-related cybercrime across jurisdictions. Without common legal terminology and aligned investigative standards, cross-border inquiries are often slowed or obstructed by conflicting legal rules. Greater consensus through forums such as the United Nations, the G20, or specialised cyber alliances could help reduce these gaps (Khan et al., 2021).

Mutual legal assistance arrangements also need to be modernised. Traditional mutual legal assistance treaty (MLAT) procedures are often too slow and procedurally burdensome to match the speed of AI-enabled attacks. Faster data-sharing mechanisms and more agile forms of coordinated investigation are needed. This could include the creation of international rapid-response cybercrime frameworks supported by shared databases of AI-related indicators of compromise.

At the policy level, states should also consider agreements aimed at limiting the weaponisation of AI in cyberspace, particularly in the context of state-sponsored cyber operations. Just as treaties have been developed to regulate the use of nuclear, chemical, and biological weapons, future agreements may be necessary to establish acceptable boundaries for the use of AI in cyber conflict.

Building Human Expertise and Training

AI-driven cybercrime cannot be addressed through technology alone. Human expertise remains essential, particularly in digital forensics, behavioural analysis, intelligence, and international law. Yet many law enforcement agencies currently lack the specialist skills required to investigate complex AI-enabled incidents effectively.

Future policy should therefore prioritise targeted training. This must include not only technical skills, such as reverse engineering AI-enabled malware, but also a deeper understanding of AI ethics, legal frameworks, and wider policy implications. Interdisciplinary training is especially important: investigators need to understand both the technical foundations of AI systems and the broader social and geopolitical contexts in which AI-related attacks occur.

Universities and industry also have a role to play. Higher education institutions can develop integrated programmes that combine cybersecurity, machine learning, and legal studies, while private-sector partners can contribute applied case studies and operational insight. Law enforcement academies may also benefit from simulation-based learning, allowing investigators to respond to realistic AI-enabled attack scenarios in controlled environments.

Governments should also invest in talent retention. Skilled cybersecurity professionals are often drawn to the private sector by higher salaries and better career opportunities. Competitive pay, ongoing professional development, and recognition of the strategic importance of cyber expertise in law enforcement may help reduce attrition and preserve institutional capability over time (Kumar & Goyal, 2021).

Public Awareness and Education

Although AI-enabled ransomware and APTs are technically sophisticated threats, many attacks still depend on human vulnerability. Phishing, social engineering, and insider activity remain important attack vectors, even where AI is used to enhance the effectiveness of those methods. Public awareness and cyber hygiene must therefore form part of any long-term response.

Educational efforts should be tailored to different audiences. At the individual level, people should be taught how to identify suspicious communications, verify digital identities, and maintain secure systems through timely updates. Within organisations, training should reinforce the idea that employees are part of the security posture and not merely passive users of technology. At the policy level, there should be greater awareness that AI-enabled cybercrime is not simply a technical issue, but a broader economic and societal threat requiring proactive investment and governance.

AI can itself be used to support awareness and training. For example, AI-powered chatbots can simulate phishing attempts in order to train employees how to respond, while adaptive and gamified learning systems can tailor educational content to user performance. By making cybersecurity training engaging, continuous, and responsive, organisations and societies may be better positioned to reduce the success of AI-enhanced social engineering attacks (Goyal, 2025).

Policy Recommendations for Balancing Security and Privacy

As AI-based defences against cybercrime become more widespread, important questions arise concerning privacy and civil liberties. If poorly governed, AI-enabled monitoring systems may intrude on individual rights by analysing network traffic, user behaviour, or biometric data in overly invasive ways. Policymakers must therefore strike an appropriate balance between improving security and protecting privacy.

One important recommendation is the adoption of privacy-by-design principles in all AI-based defence systems. This means embedding privacy protections at the design stage, including data minimisation, anonymisation, and clear limits on retention. Organisations should also be transparent about what data they collect, how it is used, and how long it is stored.

A second recommendation is the establishment of independent oversight mechanisms. Just as financial institutions are subject to external auditing, AI-enabled cyber defence systems should be reviewed regularly by independent bodies. These reviews should assess not only technical effectiveness but also ethical compliance, ensuring that the pursuit of security does not come at the expense of fundamental rights (LeCun et al., 2015).

Finally, governments should establish clear accountability frameworks for AI-enabled defence. Where an AI system causes harm, for example by blocking legitimate activity or failing to prevent an attack, there should be well-defined procedures for redress and responsibility. Accountability should be shared appropriately among technology providers, operators, and law enforcement bodies according to their respective roles.

Future Research Directions

The academic community has an important role to play in responding to AI-enabled cybercrime. Future research should focus on several key areas.

- **Adversarial AI:** Developing methods to defend against attacks that exploit weaknesses in machine learning systems, such as poisoned training data or adversarial inputs.
- **Explainable AI:** Designing transparent models capable of producing human-readable explanations, especially in forensic and legal contexts.
- **Human–AI collaboration:** Exploring how human analysts and AI systems can work together effectively, combining human judgement and creativity with the scalability of automated systems.
- **Global cyber norms:** Examining how international agreements and governance frameworks might regulate the use of AI in cyberspace.
- **Sociotechnical impacts:** Investigating how AI-driven cybercrime interacts with wider social processes, including disinformation, political polarisation, and economic disruption.

By advancing knowledge in these areas, academic research can help narrow the gap between the offensive use of AI by cybercriminals and the defensive capacities available to society more broadly.

CONCLUSION

Artificial intelligence has transformed both the opportunities, and the threats present in cyberspace. AI-enabled ransomware and Advanced Persistent Threats (APTs) illustrate how threat actors are increasingly using automation, adaptability, and data-driven intelligence to conduct more sophisticated and harmful operations. Unlike earlier forms of cybercrime, these threats can adapt in real time, personalise their attacks, and exploit both technological weaknesses and human behaviour.

This chapter has shown that AI-enabled cybercrime presents major challenges for law enforcement. Jurisdictional problems, attribution difficulties, and growing technical complexity combine to make investigations slower, more uncertain, and more resource-intensive. At the same time, many agencies continue to face substantial shortages in expertise, funding, and infrastructure. The increasing use of AI-enhanced social engineering also demonstrates that cybersecurity is not purely a technical matter, but also a deeply human one.

At the same time, AI is not only a tool for attackers; it is also an important source of defensive capability. Through predictive modelling, anomaly detection, deep learning, and adversarial training, AI can help organisations identify and respond to threats more effectively. However, closing the gap between offence and defence will also require international cooperation, legal reform, and sustained investment in human expertise. These efforts must be pursued in ways that preserve privacy and civil liberties, so that measures intended to improve safety do not undermine public trust.

Ultimately, the threat posed by AI-enabled ransomware and APTs does not lie in the technology alone, but in how societies choose to respond to it. Through stronger technical defences, international collaboration, legal reform, education, and ethical safeguards, the risks can be managed and more resilient forms of protection can be built. The future of cybersecurity may depend on whether AI is allowed to become primarily a tool of exploitation or is instead shaped into a powerful ally in the defence of the digital world.

REFERENCES

Abadjiev, D., Adams, T., Adzic, P., Ahmad, M., Amendola, C., Andrews, M. B., Arcidiacono, R., Argiro, S., Askew, A., Auffray, E., Azzolini, V., Bailleux, D., Band, R., Barney, D., Barria, P., Bartosik, N., Basile, C., Bastos, D., Bell, K. W., & Zygal, L. (2024). Autoencoder-Based Anomaly Detection System for Online Data Quality Monitoring of the CMS Electromagnetic Calorimeter. *Computing and Software for Big Science*, *8*(1), 11. Advance online publication. DOI: 10.1007/s41781-024-00118-z

Bakır, R., & Bakır, H. (2024). Swift detection of XSS attacks: Enhancing XSS attack detection by leveraging hybrid semantic embeddings and AI techniques. *Arabian Journal for Science and Engineering*, *50*(2), 1191–1207. DOI: 10.1007/s13369-024-09140-0

Baskerville, R., & Siponen, M. (2020). Integrating AI into cybersecurity: Real-time network traffic analysis for anomaly detection. *Journal of Cybersecurity*, *16*(2), 115–129.

Bilge, L., Balzarotti, D., & Kaafar, M. A. (2020). Data-driven cybersecurity: Approaches and challenges. *ACM Computing Surveys*, *52*(5), 1–35.

Buczak, A. L., & Guven, E. (2016). A survey of data mining and machine learning methods for cybersecurity intrusion detection. *IEEE Access : Practical Innovations, Open Solutions*, *4*, 14040–14057.

Deleon, J., Hatherleigh, C., Cumberbatch, A., Ashworth, J., & Heathcote, L. (2024, December). Predictive profiling framework for ransomware detection using contextual signature extraction. DOI: 10.31219/osf.io/fwkqd

Denis, J., Featherstone, J., Beaufort, O., & Edelstein, H. (2024, December). A novel algorithmic framework for autonomous ransomware detection using multi-layer temporal anomaly patterns. DOI: 10.31219/osf.io/g7yku

Dilek, S., Çakır, H., & Aydın, M. (2015). Applications of artificial intelligence techniques to combating cybersecurity challenges: A survey. *Journal of Information Security*, *6*(3), 113–122. DOI: 10.4236/jis.2015.63012

Eling, S. (2019). IBM's QRadar: AI-enhanced security intelligence for the modern enterprise. *Journal of Cybersecurity*, *5*(3), 72–84.

Goodfellow, I., Bengio, Y., & Courville, A. (2016). *Deep learning*. MIT Press.

Goodfellow, I., Shlens, J., & Szegedy, C. (2018). Explaining and harnessing adversarial examples. *arXiv*. https://arxiv.org/abs/1412.6572

Goyal, N. K. (2025). Weaponizing misinformation and cyberattacks on supply chains. In Bukhari, S., & Zafar, I. (Eds.), *Mass media and impact of fake news on supply chains* (pp. 177–210). IGI Global Scientific Publishing., DOI: 10.4018/979-8-3373-2175-2.ch007

Goyal, N. K. (2025). Security and privacy in IoT, fog, and blockchain networks. In Sathio, A. (Eds.), *Energy-efficient deep learning approaches in IoT, fog, and green blockchain revolution* (pp. 371–398). IGI Global Scientific Publishing., DOI: 10.4018/979-8-3373-0300-0.ch015

Goyal, N. K., Dandotiya, M., Qurashi, J. A., Kumari, M., & Sharma, S. (2025). AI-driven predictive analytics for disease management. In Ouaissa, M. (Eds.), *Utilizing AI of medical things for healthcare security and sustainability* (pp. 231–276). IGI Global Scientific Publishing., DOI: 10.4018/979-8-3373-0690-2.ch008

Gupta, P., Singh, A., & Kaur, R. (2021). AI-based threat hunting and incident response in cybersecurity. *International Journal of Information Security*, *29*(4), 345–359.

Gupta, S., Kumar, R., & Sharma, A. (2020). AI-driven cybersecurity solutions: The case of Cylance. *Journal of Computer Security*, *28*(4), 231–247.

Hossain, M. A., & Islam, M. S. (2024). Enhanced detection of obfuscated malware in memory dumps: A machine learning approach for advanced cybersecurity. *Cybersecurity*, *7*(1), 1–23. DOI: 10.1186/s42400-024-00205-z

Islam, S. M., Bari, M. S., Sarkar, A., Khan, A. O. R., & Paul, R. (2024). AI-powered threat intelligence: Revolutionizing cybersecurity with proactive risk management for critical sectors. *JAIGS*, *7*(1), 1–8. DOI: 10.60087/jaigs.v7i01.291

Jimmy, F. (2021a). Emerging threats: The latest cybersecurity risks and the role of artificial intelligence in enhancing cybersecurity defenses. *Valley International Journal Digital Library*, *1*(2), 564–574. DOI: 10.18535/ijsrm/v9i2.ec01

Jimmy, F. N. U. (2021b). Understanding ransomware attacks: Trends and prevention strategies. DOI: 10.60087/jklst.vol2.n1.p214

Jimmy, F. N. U. (2022). Zero trust security: Reimagining cyber defense for modern organizations. *Valley International Journal Digital Library*, 887–905.

Jimmy, F. N. U. (2024). Cybersecurity threats and vulnerabilities in online banking systems. *Valley International Journal Digital Library*, 1631–1646.

Kaggle. (n.d.). Microsoft malware classification challenge (BIG 2015). https://www.kaggle.com/c/malware-classification

Khan, F., Zubair, A., & Umer, T. (2021). AI-driven cloud security: Protecting the cloud infrastructure. *Cloud Computing Research*, *12*(3), 233–249.

Kumar, R., & Goyal, D. (2021). Artificial intelligence in cybersecurity: Applications and challenges. *Computer Science Review*, *41*, 100413. DOI: 10.1016/j.cosrev.2021.100413

LeCun, Y., Bengio, Y., & Hinton, G. (2015). Deep learning. *Nature*, *521*(7553), 436–444. DOI: 10.1038/nature14539 PMID: 26017442

Maddireddy, B. R. (2020). Proactive cyber defense: Utilizing AI for early threat detection and risk assessment. *International Journal of Advanced Engineering Technology & Innovations*, *1*(2), 64–83.

Mata-Torres, J. A., Tello-Leal, E., Hernandez-Resendiz, J. D., & Ramirez-Alcocer, U. M. (2023). Evaluation of machine learning techniques for malware detection. In *Intelligent Systems Reference Library* (Vol. 226, pp. 121–140). DOI: 10.1007/978-3-031-08246-7_6

Ofoegbu, K. D. O., Osundare, O. S., Ike, C. S., Fakeyede, O. G., & Ige, A. B. (2024). Data-driven cyber threat intelligence: Leveraging behavioral analytics for proactive defense mechanisms.

Pekepok, K., Kirkwood, P., Christopolous, E., Braithwaite, F., & Nightingale, O. (2025). Hierarchical pattern decryption methodology for ransomware detection using probabilistic cryptographic footprints.

Rishad, S. S. I., Shakil, F., Tisha, S. A., Afrin, S., Hassan, M. M., Choudhury, M. Z. M. E., & Rahman, N. (2025). Leveraging AI and machine learning for predicting, detecting, and mitigating cybersecurity threats: a comparative study of advanced models. *Academic Reseach Library for International Journal of Computer Science & Information System, 10*(01), 06-25.

Svet, L., Brightwell, A., Wildflower, A., & Marshwood, C. (2025). Unveiling zero-space detection: A novel framework for autonomous ransomware identification in high-velocity environments. *arXiv preprint arXiv:2501.12811.*

Vegesna, V. V., & Adepu, A. (2024). Leveraging artificial intelligence for predictive cyber threat intelligence. *International Journal of Creative Research in Computer Technology and Design*, *6*(6), 1–19.

Compilation of References

Abadjiev, D., Adams, T., Adzic, P., Ahmad, M., Amendola, C., Andrews, M. B., Arcidiacono, R., Argiro, S., Askew, A., Auffray, E., Azzolini, V., Bailleux, D., Band, R., Barney, D., Barria, P., Bartosik, N., Basile, C., Bastos, D., Bell, K. W., & Zygal, L. (2024). Autoencoder-Based Anomaly Detection System for Online Data Quality Monitoring of the CMS Electromagnetic Calorimeter. *Computing and Software for Big Science*, *8*(1), 11. Advance online publication. DOI: 10.1007/s41781-024-00118-z

Abbas, S., & Abed, F. M. (2024). Revolutionizing depth sensing: A review study of apple lidarsensor for as-built scanning applications. *Journal of Engineering*, *30*(4), 175–199. DOI: 10.31026/j.eng.2024.04.11

Ada Lovelace Institute & The Alan Turing Institute. (2022). How do people feel about AI? A nationally representative survey of public attitudes to artificial intelligence in Britain. In Executive Summary. https://www.adalovelaceinstitute.org/wp-content/uploads/2023/06/Ada-Lovelace-Institute-The-Alan-Turing-Institute-How-do-people-feel-about-AI.pdf

Adams, I. T. (2024). Large language models and artificial intelligence for police report writing. *CrimRxiv*. DOI: 10.21428/cb6ab371.779603ee

Adams, I. T. (2025). Automation and artificial intelligence in police body-worn cameras: Experimental evidence of impact on perceptions of fairness among officers. *Journal of Criminal Justice*, *97*, 102373. DOI: 10.1016/j.jcrimjus.2025.102373

Adams, I. T., Barter, M., McLean, K., Boehme, H. M., & Geary, I. A.Jr. (2024). No man's hand: Artificial intelligence does not improve police report writing speed. *Journal of Experimental Criminology*, •••, 1–18. DOI: 10.21428/cb6ab371.4a6d42e9

Adams, I. T., McCrain, J. M., Schiff, D. S., Schiff, K. J., & Mourtgos, S. M. (2025). Police reform from the top down: Experimental evidence on police executive support for civilian oversight. *Journal of Policy Analysis and Management*, *44*(2), 403–427. DOI: 10.1002/pam.22620

Adams, P. A. (2021). Terrorism as the quest for justice in contemporary Nigeria. *UJAH: Unizik Journal of Arts and Humanities*, *22*(2), 85–102.

Afchar, D., Nozick, V., Yamagishi, J., & Echizen, I. (2018). *Mesonet: a compact facial video forgery detection network.* Paper presented at the 2018 IEEE international workshop on information forensics and security (WIFS). DOI: 10.1109/WIFS.2018.8630761

Afzal, M., & Panagiotopoulos, P. (2025). Data in policing: An integrative review. *International Journal of Public Administration*, *48*(7), 411–430. DOI: 10.1080/01900692.2024.2360586

Aggarwal, C. C. (2003). A framework for diagnosing changes in evolving data streams. In *Proceedings of the 2003 ACM SIGMOD International Conference on Management of Data* (pp. 575–586). ACM. DOI: 10.1145/872757.872826

Aguilar-Ortiz, J., Zamudio-García, V. M., & Simancas-Acevedo, E. (2025). Sustainable Development Goal 16 Peace and Justice Criminal Justice and Artificial Intelligence Applications for a More Efficient and Fair System. In *Machine and Deep Learning Solutions for Achieving the Sustainable Development Goals* (pp. 435-460). IGI Global Scientific Publishing. DOI: 10.4018/979-8-3693-8161-8.ch022

Ahmad, R., & Thurasamy, R. (2022, July 17). Routine activity theory and cybercrime: A systematic literature review. *Journal of Cyber Security and Mobility*, *11*(1).

Ahmed, S., Khan, M. F., Singh, B., Singh, N., & Sharma, B. (2025). Enhancing Crime Scene Analysis: The Impact of AI Technologies on Evidence Processing. In *Forensic Intelligence and Deep Learning Solutions in Crime Investigation* (pp. 63-84). IGI Global Scientific Publishing. DOI: 10.4018/979-8-3693-9405-2.ch004

Ahmed, R., Dalkılıç, G., & Erten, Y. (2020). DGStream: High quality and efficiency stream clustering algorithm. *Expert Systems with Applications*, *141*, 112947. DOI: 10.1016/j.eswa.2019.112947

Al Shamsi, H. R. S., & Safei, S. A. (2023). Artificial intelligence adoption in predictive policing to predict crime mitigation performance. *International Journal of Sustainable Construction Engineering and Technology*, *14*(3), 289–298. DOI: 10.30880/ijscet.2023.14.03.025

Alaba, S. Y., & Ball, J. E. (2022). A survey on deep-learning-based lidar 3d object detection for autonomous driving. *Sensors (Basel)*, *22*(24), 9577. Advance online publication. DOI: 10.3390/s22249577 PMID: 36559950

Alakayleh, O. (2025). The Use of Artificial Intelligence Systems in Crime Detection and Prevention: Applications and Challenges. Available at *SSRN* 5132225. DOI: 10.2139/ssrn.5132225

Alam, A. (2023a). Media multitasking with M-learning technology in real-time classroom learning: Analysing the dynamics in formal educational settings for the future of E-learning in India. In *2023 2nd International Conference on Smart Technologies and Systems for Next Generation Computing (ICSTSN)* (pp. 1-6). IEEE. DOI: 10.1109/ICSTSN57873.2023.10151509

Alam, A. (2023b). The secret sauce of student success: Cracking the code by navigating the path to personalized learning with educational data mining. In *2023 2nd International Conference on Smart Technologies and Systems for Next Generation Computing (ICSTSN)* (pp. 1-8). IEEE. DOI: 10.1109/ICSTSN57873.2023.10151558

Alam, A., & Mohanty, A. (2023b). Design, development, and implementation of software engineering virtual laboratory: A boon to computer science and engineering (CSE) education during Covid-19 pandemic. In *Proceedings of third international conference on sustainable expert systems: ICSES 2022* (pp. 1-20). Singapore: Springer Nature Singapore. DOI: 10.1007/978-981-19-7874-6_1

Alam, A., & Mohanty, A. (2023c). From bricks to clicks: The potential of big data analytics for revolutionizing the information landscape in higher education sector. In *International Conference on Data Management, Analytics & Innovation* (pp. 721-732). Singapore: Springer Nature Singapore. DOI: 10.1007/978-981-99-1414-2_51

Alam, A., & Mohanty, A. (2023d). Learning on the move: a pedagogical framework for state-of-the-art mobile learning. In *International Conference on Data Management, Analytics & Innovation* (pp. 735-748). Singapore: Springer Nature Singapore. DOI: 10.1007/978-981-99-1414-2_52

Alam, A. (2023c). Leveraging the power of 'modeling and computer simulation' for education: An exploration of its potential for improved learning outcomes and enhanced student engagement. In *2023 International Conference on Device Intelligence, Computing and Communication Technologies, (DICCT)* (pp. 445-450). IEEE. DOI: 10.1109/DICCT56244.2023.10110159

Alam, A., & Mohanty, A. (2023a). Implications of virtual reality (VR) for school teachers and instructional designers: An empirical investigation. *Cogent Education, 10*(2), 2260676. DOI: 10.1080/2331186X.2023.2260676

Alam, A., & Mohanty, A. (2024). Framework of Self-Regulated cognitive engagement (FSRCE) for sustainable pedagogy: A model that integrates SRL and cognitive engagement for holistic development of students. *Cogent Education*, *11*(1), 2363157. DOI: 10.1080/2331186X.2024.2363157

Albrecht, J. F., & Den Heyer, G. (Eds.). (2025). *Special Topics in Policing: Critical Issues and Global Perspectives* (Vol. 3). Springer Nature., DOI: 10.1007/978-3-032-06680-0

Alda, E. (2025). Productivity on patrol: Measuring efficiency gains from AI-assisted police reports with a global malmquist index. *CrimRxiv*. DOI: 10.21428/cb6ab371.d923f490

Alhafedhi, H. (2025). Understanding crime through harm: A multi-stage study of Rochester, NY [Master's project, Rochester Institute of Technology]. RIT Digital Institutional Repository. https://repository.rit.edu/theses/12455

Alikhademi, K., Drobina, E., Prioleau, D., Richardson, B., Purves, D., & Gilbert, J. E. (2022). A review of predictive policing from the perspective of fairness. *Artificial Intelligence and Law*, *30*(1), 1–17. DOI: 10.1007/s10506-021-09286-4

Alimardani, A., & Istiqomah, M. (2025). Beyond black boxes and biases: Advancing artificial intelligence in sentencing. *Current Issues in Criminal Justice*, 1–21. DOI: 10.1080/10345329.2025.2527994

Aljanaahi, A., Hakeem, M. K., Aljanaahi, A., & Shah, I. (2025). A review of analytical and chemometric strategies for forensic classification of homemade explosives. *Analytical Science Advances*, *6*(1), e70010. DOI: 10.1002/ansa.70010 PMID: 40242023

Allen, A. L., & Muhawe, C. (2025). Is Privacy Really a Civil Right? *Berkeley Technology Law Journal*, *40*, 1.

Allertseder, S., Okon, G., & Schweer, T. (2022). Chances and challenges of predictive policing for law enforcement agencies. In Markarian, G., Karlović, R., Nitsch, H., & Chandramouli, K. (Eds.), *Security technologies and social implications*. DOI: 10.1002/9781119834175.ch12

Al-Shamsi, A., & Ahmad, N. B. (2024). Opportunities and Challenges of AI Adoption by the Abu Dhabi Police: A Review Study. *International Journal of Academic Reserach in Economics and Management Sciences*, *13*(3). Advance online publication. DOI: 10.6007/IJAREMS/v13-i3/22719

Amazon Web Services Inc. (2024). What is Artificial Intelligence (AI)? https://aws.amazon.com/what-is/artificial-intelligence/#:~:text=Artificial%20intelligence%20(AI)%20is%20a,and%20make%20data%2Dbased%20predictions

Amnesty International. (2022). Ban the scan - Amnesty International. https://www.amnesty.org/en/petition/ban-the-scan-petition

Anderson, R. (2006). The economics of information security', 314(5799), pp. 610–613. *Science, 314*(5799), 610–613. DOI: 10.1126/science.1130992 PMID: 17068253

Andresen, M. A., & Hodgkinson, T. (2025). Il Y a Quelque Chose sur la Carte: A Modern Spatial Analysis of Crime in Early 19th Century France. *American Journal of Criminal Justice, 50*(4), 565–584. DOI: 10.1007/s12103-025-09798-8

Apene, O. Z., Blamah, N. V., & Aimufua, G. I. O. (2024). Advancements in crime prevention and detection: From traditional approaches to artificial intelligence solutions. *European Journal of Applied Science. Engineering and Technology, 2*(2), 285–297. DOI: 10.59324/ejaset.2024.2(2).20

Apolinar, C. (2023). *Examining the Secondary Effects of the Los Angeles Police Department's Operation LASER on Los Angeles Neighborhoods* (Master's thesis, University of California, Irvine).

Apostolakis, K. C., Dimitriou, N., Margetis, G., Ntoa, S., Tzovaras, D., & Stephanidis, C. (2022). DARLENE–Improving situational awareness of European law enforcement agents through a combination of augmented reality and artificial intelligence solutions. *Open Research Europe, 1*, 87. DOI: 10.12688/openreseurope.13715.2 PMID: 37645167

Appiah, S. K., Wirekoh, K., Aidoo, E. N., Oduro, S. D., & Arthur, Y. D. (2022). A model-based clustering of expectation–maximization and k-means algorithms in crime hotspot analysis. *Research in Mathematics, 9*(1), 1–12. DOI: 10.1080/27684830.2022.2073662

Archbold, C. A. (2025). Special issue on police reform. Policing. *Policing (Oxford, England), 19*, paaf013. Advance online publication. DOI: 10.1093/police/paaf013

Ariel, B. (2023). Implementation issues with hot spot policing. *International Journal of Law, Crime and Justice, 75*, 100629. DOI: 10.1016/j.ijlcj.2023.100629

Aslam, M. M. (2025, July 6). High-tech terrorism: The use of AI in terrorism industry. Retrieved from Islamic Military Counter Terrorism Coalition (IMCTC) eLibrary.: https://www.imctc.org/en/eLibrary/Articles/Pages/article1762025.aspx

Atkin, R. (1974). *Mathematical Structure in Human Affairs*. Heinemann Educational Books.

Atkin, R. (1981). *Multidimensional Man: Can Man Live in 3-Dimensional Space?* Penguin Books.

Awais, M., Naeem, F., Rasool, N., & Mahmood, S. (2018). Identification of sex from footprint dimensions using machine learning: A study on population of punjab in pakistan. *Egyptian Journal of Forensic Sciences*, *8*(1), 72. DOI: 10.1186/s41935-018-0106-2

Awoyemi, O., Attah, R. U., Basiru, J. O., & Leghemo, I. M. (2025). A community-policing innovation model to build sustainable trust and effectively reduce crime in urban areas. DOI: 10.54660/.IJMRGE.2025.6.1.848-853

Azmil, R., Mohd Ariff, M. F., Razali, A. F., Azmy, S. N., Darwin, N., & Idris, K. M. (2024). Transforming physical crime scene into geospatial-based point cloud data. Engineering, Technology amp. *Applied Scientific Research*, *14*(3), 13974–13981. DOI: 10.48084/etasr.6888

Ba, B., Ge, H., Kaplan, J., Knox, D., Komisarchik, M., Lanzalotto, G., Mariman, R., Mummolo, J., Rivera, R., & Torres, M. (2025). Political diversity in U.S. police agencies. *American Journal of Political Science*, *69*(4), 1–19. DOI: 10.1111/ajps.12945 PMID: 40881318

Babuta, A., & Oswald, M. (2020). *Data analytics and algorithms in policing in England and Wales: Towards a new policy framework*. Royal United Services Institute. rusi_pub_165_2020_01_algorithmic_policing_babuta_final_web_copy.pdf.

Bacalu, F. (2021). Digital policing tools as social control technologies: Data-driven predictive algorithms, automated facial recognition surveillance, and law enforcement biometrics. *Analysis and Metaphysics*, *20*(0), 74–88. DOI: 10.22381/AM2020215

Baek, M. S., Park, W., Park, J., Jang, K. H., & Lee, Y. T. (2021). Smart policing technique with crime type and risk score prediction based on machine learning for early awareness of risk situation. *IEEE Access : Practical Innovations, Open Solutions*, *9*, 131906–131915. DOI: 10.1109/ACCESS.2021.3112682

Bag, A., Roy, S., & Pandey, A. (2024). Harnessing the Power of Artificial Intelligence in Law Enforcement: A Comprehensive Review of Opportunities and Ethical Challenges. *Exploring the Ethical Implications of Generative AI*, 121-145. DOI: 10.4018/979-8-3693-1565-1.ch008

Bag, A., Shashikant, S., Mishra, P., & Pradhan, A. (2024, March). Using artificial intelligence in US law enforcement-a review. In. AIP Conference Proceedings: Vol. 2816. *No. 1* (p. 050002). AIP Publishing LLC., DOI: 10.1063/5.0179536

Bahirat, K., & Prabhakaran, B. (2017, July). A study on lidar data forensics. DOI: 10.1109/ICME.2017.8019395

Bakır, R., & Bakır, H. (2024). Swift detection of XSS attacks: Enhancing XSS attack detection by leveraging hybrid semantic embeddings and AI techniques. *Arabian Journal for Science and Engineering*, *50*(2), 1191–1207. DOI: 10.1007/s13369-024-09140-0

Balbudhe, M. S., Shetty, B. S. K., Arun Kumar, N., Singh, D., & Sherekar, A. I. (2025). Crime scene reconstruction: A scoping review. *Egyptian Journal of Forensic Sciences*, *15*(1), 79. DOI: 10.1186/s41935-025-00495-5

Barabasi, A.-L. (2014). *Linked*. Basic Books.

Barnum, T. C., & Logan, M. K. (2023). Radicalized environmental extremism and situational decision-making. *Journal of Research in Crime and Delinquency*, *61*(3), 406–444. DOI: 10.1177/00224278231152439

Barocas, S., & Selbst, A. D. (2016). Big data's disparate impact. *California Law Review*, *104*(3), 671–732.

Basharat, M. F., Sajid, N., Fattah Shah, S. A., & Kazmi, S. G. A. (2025). National Policy and Legislative Framework for AI Governance in Law Enforcement Agencies and Criminal Justice System of Pakistan. *Available at SSRN* 5248649. DOI: 10.2139/ssrn.5248649

Baskerville, R., & Siponen, M. (2020). Integrating AI into cybersecurity: Real-time network traffic analysis for anomaly detection. *Journal of Cybersecurity*, *16*(2), 115–129.

Bathaee, Y. (2018). The artificial intelligence black box and the failure of intent and causation. *Harvard Journal of Law & Technology*, *31*(2), 905. https://www.questia.com/library/journal/1G1-547758123/the-artificial-intelligence-black-box-and-the-failure

Batool, A., Kalhoro, H. B., & Bano, M. (2023). Responsible AI governance: A systematic literature review. *arXiv*. https://arxiv.org/abs/2401.10896

Becker, G. S. (1968, March-April). Crime and Punishment: An Economic Approach. *Journal of Political Economy*, *76*(2), 169–217. DOI: 10.1086/259394

Bécue, A., Praça, I., & Gama, J. (2021, June). Artificial intelligence, cyber-threats and Industry 4.0: Challenges and opportunities. *Artificial Intelligence*, *54*(5), 3849–3886.

Behaviour, A.-S. Crime and Policing Act (2014), c. 11 (UK). https://www.legislation.gov.uk/ukpga/2014/12/contents

Behroozpour, B., Sandborn, P. A. M., Wu, M. C., & Boser, B. E. (2017). Lidar system architectures and circuits. *IEEE Communications Magazine*, *55*(10), 135–142. DOI: 10.1109/MCOM.2017.1700030

Bello, S. A., Yu, S., Wang, C., Adam, J. M., & Li, J. (2020). Review: Deep learning on 3d point clouds. *Remote Sensing (Basel)*, *12*(11), 1729. Advance online publication. DOI: 10.3390/rs12111729

Benedict, T. J. (2022). The computer got it wrong: Facial recognition technology and establishing probable cause to arrest. *Washington and Lee Law Review*, *79*, 849.

Bennett Moses, L., & Chan, J. (2018). Algorithmic prediction in policing: Assumptions, evaluation, and accountability. *Policing and Society*, *28*(7), 806–822. DOI: 10.1080/10439463.2016.1253695

Berezowski, V., Mallett, X., & Moffat, I. (2020, March). Geomatic techniques in forensic science. *RE:view*, *60*(2), 99–107. Advance online publication. DOI: 10.1016/j.scijus.2019.10.006 PMID: 32111294

Berk, R. A. (2021). Artificial intelligence, predictive policing, and risk assessment for law enforcement. *Annual Review of Criminology*, *4*(1), 209–237. DOI: 10.1146/annurev-criminol-051520-012342

Bhattacharjee, P., & Mitra, P. (2021). A survey of density based clustering algorithms. *Frontiers of Computer Science*, *15*(1), 1–27. DOI: 10.1007/s11704-019-9059-3

Big Brother Watch. (n.d). Landmark legal challenges launched against facial recognition after police and retailer misidentifications. https://bigbrotherwatch.org.uk/press-releases/landmark-legal-challenges-launched-against-facial-recognition-after-police-and-retailer-misidentifications/

Big Brother Watch. (n.d). Stop Facial Recognition - Big Brother Watch. https://bigbrotherwatch.org.uk/campaigns/stop-facial-recognition

Bilge, L., Balzarotti, D., & Kaafar, M. A. (2020). Data-driven cybersecurity: Approaches and challenges. *ACM Computing Surveys*, *52*(5), 1–35.

Blount, K. (2024). Using artificial intelligence to prevent crime: Implications for due process and criminal justice. *AI & Society*, *39*(1), 359–368. DOI: 10.1007/s00146-022-01513-z

Boehme, H. M., & Mourtgos, S. M. (2024). The effect of formal de-policing on police traffic stop behavior and crime: Early evidence from the LAPD's policy to restrict discretionary traffic stops. *Criminology & Public Policy*, *23*(3), 517–542. DOI: 10.1111/1745-9133.12673

Bois, R. D., & Reyes, A. T. (2023). *Dual-use and cyber-surveillance: EU policies and current practices. European Parliament Briefing No. 754439*. European Parliament.

Boldt, M., Borg, A., Svensson, M., & Hildeby, J. (2018). Predicting burglars' risk exposure and level of pre-crime preparation using crime scene data. *Intelligent Data Analysis*, *22*(1), 167–190. DOI: 10.3233/IDA-163220

Bossler, A. M., & Holt, T. J. (2010). Bossler, A.M. and Holt, T.J. (2010) 'The effect of self-control on victimization in the cyberworld', Crime & Delinquency, 56(4), pp. 539–568. *Crime and Delinquency*, *56*(4), 539–568.

Bowen, S. A., & Pashentsev, E. N. (2025). AI, biases and cultures. In Cheng, Y., & Verčič, D. (Eds.), *AI and strategic communication*. DOI: 10.1002/9781394275434.ch12

Bowers, K., & Johnson, S. (2024). Facing the future of crime: A framework for police use of technology. *The Political Quarterly*, *95*(3), 480–488. DOI: 10.1111/1467-923X.13426

Boyle, M. J. (2023). The choice for terrorism: Possession and milieu goals among terrorist groups. *Perspectives on Terrorism*, *17*(3), 1–22.

Brayne, S. (2020). *Predict and surveil: Data, discretion, and the future of policing*. Oxford University Press. DOI: 10.1093/oso/9780190684099.001.0001

Brems, R. (2025). Transforming police reporting with generative AI: Insights from the Oklahoma City Police Department. *The Police Journal*, 0032258X251346365.

Broeders, D., Cristiano, F., & Kaminska, M. (2023). In search of digital sovereignty and strategic autonomy: Normative power Europe to the test of its geopolitical ambitions. *Journal of Common Market Studies*, *61*(5), 1261–1280. DOI: 10.1111/jcms.13462

Brożek, B., Furman, M., Jakubiec, M., & Kucharzyk, B. (2023). The black box problem revisited. Real and imaginary challenges for automated legal decision making. *Artificial Intelligence and Law*, *32*(2), 427–440. DOI: 10.1007/s10506-023-09356-9

Buades-Rotger, M., Martínez Catena, A., Recio, G., Cano Gallent, M., Niñerola i Maymí, J., Figueras Masip, A., & Gallardo-Pujol, D. (2025). Personality predicts internalizing symptoms and quality of life in police cadets: A comparison of artificial intelligence and parametric approaches. *Health & Justice*, *13*(1), 43. DOI: 10.1186/s40352-025-00351-7 PMID: 40613989

Buck, U., Buße, K., Campana, L., Gummel, F., Schyma, C., & Jackowski, C. (2020). What happened before the run over? morphometric 3d reconstruction. *Forensic Science International*, *306*, 110059. Advance online publication. DOI: 10.1016/j.forsciint.2019.110059 PMID: 31780351

Buczak, A. L., & Guven, E. (2016). A survey of data mining and machine learning methods for cybersecurity intrusion detection. *IEEE Access : Practical Innovations, Open Solutions*, *4*, 14040–14057.

Buolamwini, J., & Gebru, T. (2018). Gender Shades: Intersectional accuracy Disparities in commercial gender classification. Proceedings of Machine Learning Research, 81, 1–15. https://proceedings.mlr.press/v81/buolamwini18a/buolamwini18a.pdf

Buolamwini, J., & Gebru, T. (2018, January). Gender shades: Intersectional accuracy disparities in commercial gender classification. In *Conference on fairness, accountability and transparency* (pp. 77-91). PMLR.

Burdziakowski, P., & Bobkowska, K. (2021). Uav photogrammetry under poor lighting conditions—Accuracy considerations. *Sensors (Basel)*, *21*(10), 3531. Advance online publication. DOI: 10.3390/s21103531 PMID: 34069500

Butt, U. M., Letchmunan, S., Hassan, F. H., Ali, M., Baqir, A., Koh, T. W., & Sherazi, H. H. R. (2021). Spatio-temporal crime predictions by leveraging artificial intelligence for citizens security in smart cities. *IEEE Access : Practical Innovations, Open Solutions*, *9*, 47516–47529. DOI: 10.1109/ACCESS.2021.3068306

Carruthers & Jackson. (2023). *Data Model*. https://carruthersandjackson.com/data-maturity/

Casti, J. L. (1997b). *Would-be Worlds: How Simulation is Changing the Frontiers of Science*. John Wiley & Sons, Inc.

Cesario, E., Lindia, P., & Vinci, A. (2023). Detecting multi-density urban hotspots in a smart city: Approaches, challenges and applications. *Big Data and Cognitive Computing*, *7*(1), 29. DOI: 10.3390/bdcc7010029

Cesario, E., Lindia, P., & Vinci, A. (2024). Multi-density crime predictor: An approach to forecast criminal activities in multi-density crime hotspots. *Journal of Big Data*, *11*(1), 75. DOI: 10.1186/s40537-024-00935-4

Chaudhry, M., Shafi, I., Mahnoor, M., Vargas, D. L. R., Thompson, E. B., & Ashraf, I. (2023). A systematic literature review on identifying patterns using unsupervised clustering algorithms: A data mining perspective. *Symmetry*, *15*(9), 1679. DOI: 10.3390/sym15091679

Chen, Y., & Meng, J. (2024, November). Agility and Resilience: The Governance of Ethical Alienation in Police Artificial Intelligence. In 2024 8th Asian Conference on Artificial Intelligence Technology (ACAIT) (pp. 274-276). IEEE. DOI: 10.1109/ACAIT63902.2024.11021763

Cheng, S. (2025). Predictive Policing in Practice: A Case Study of Chicago's Strategic Subject List.

Choi, S., Dearden, T., & Parti, K. (2024). Understanding the Use of Artificial Intelligence in Cybercrime. *International Journal of Cybersecurity Intelligence and Cybercrime*, *7*(2), 1–3. DOI: 10.52306/2578-3289.1185

Chokkadi, S. (2019). Astudy on various state of the art of the art face recognition system using deep learning techniques. *International Journal of Advanced Trends in Computer Science and Engineering*, •••, 1590–1600. DOI: 10.30534/ijatcse/2019/84842019

Chowdhury, M. (2023). Going cyberpunk: Conceptualizing the smart (er) artificially intelligent firearm for policing's Utopian future. *International Journal of Police Science & Management*, *25*(3), 324–337. DOI: 10.1177/14613557231184689

Chukaieva, A., & Matulienė, S. (2023). Possibilities of applying artificial intelligence in the work of law enforcement agencies. *Scientific Journal of the National Academy of Internal Affairs*, *3*(28), 28–37. DOI: 10.56215/naia-herald/3.2023.28

Clarke, R. V., & Eck, J. E. (2005). *Crime Analysis for Problem-Solvers in 60 Small Steps*. U.S. Department of Justice, Office of Community Oriented Policing Services.

Clarke, R., & Cornish, D. (1985). Modeling offenders' decisions: A framework for research and policy. In Andresen, M. A., Brantingham, P. J., & Kinney, J. B. (Eds.), *Crime Opportunity Theories: Routine Activity, Rational Choice and their Variants* (pp. 157–195). Taylor and Francis.

Coe, J., & Atay, M. (2021). Evaluating impact of race in facial recognition across machine learning and deep learning algorithms. *Computers*, *10*(9), 113. DOI: 10.3390/computers10090113

Cohen, L., & Felson, M. (1979). Social change and crime rate trends: A routine activity approach. *American Sociological Review*, *44*(4), 588–608. DOI: 10.2307/2094589

College of Policing. (2014). *Authorised Professional Practice for Management of Police Information (MOPI).* https://www.college.police.uk/app/information-management/management-police-information

College of Policing. (2022). Watchlist. https://www.college.police.uk/app/live-facial-recognition/watchlist

College of Policing. (2024). *Code of Ethics.* https://www.college.police.uk/ethics/code-of-ethics

College of Policing. (2025). *Data Ethics Principles.* https://www.college.police.uk/app/data-ethics/data-ethics-principles

College of Policing. (2025). *Executive Leadership Programme* https://www.college.police.uk/career-learning/courses/executive-leaders-programme-elp

College of Policing. (n.d.). Code of Ethics. https://www.college.police.uk/ethics/code-of-ethics

Conway, M. (2017). Determining the Role of the Internet in Violent Extremism and Terrorism: Six Suggestions for Progressing Research. *Studies in Conflict and Terrorism, 40*(1), 77–98. DOI: 10.1080/1057610X.2016.1157408

Cornish, D. (1994). The procedural analysis of offending and its relevance for situational prevention. In R. V. Clarke (Ed.), Crime prevention studies (Vol. 3, pp. 151–196). Criminal Justice Press. Crime prevention studies, 3, 151-196.

Cosenz, F., & Noto, G. (2016). Applying system dynamics modelling to strategic management: A literature review. *Systems Research and Behavioral Science, 33*(6), 703–741. DOI: 10.1002/sres.2386

Costantino, D., Angelini, M. G., & Mazzone, F. (2016). Integrated survey methodology for the crime reconstruction. *Imaging Science Journal, 64*(6), 341–351. DOI: 10.1080/13682199.2016.1219528

Crenshaw, K. (1991). Mapping the Margins: Intersectionality, Identity Politics, and Violence against Women of Color. *Stanford Law Review, 43*(6), 1241. DOI: 10.2307/1229039

Crenshaw, M. (1981). The causes of terrorism. *Comparative Politics, 13*(4), 379–399. DOI: 10.2307/421717

Cucoreanu, C. (2024). Public Order and the Technological Revolution: Implications for Police and Citizen Safety. *European Journal of Law and Public Administration, 11*(1), 39–52. DOI: 10.18662/eljpa/11.1/219

Cui, M., Li, W., & Kamoche, K. (2025). Building trust in decision-support artificial intelligence: A boundary spanning perspective. *Information Systems Journal*, •••, 1–22. DOI: 10.1111/isj.70015

Cui, Y., Chen, R., Chu, W., Chen, L., Tian, D., Li, Y., & Cao, D. (2022). Deep learning for image and point cloud fusion in autonomous driving: A review. *IEEE Transactions on Intelligent Transportation Systems*, *23*(2), 722–739. DOI: 10.1109/TITS.2020.3023541

Curtis-Ham, S. (2022). Measuring harm with crime harm indices. In *The crime analyst's companion* (pp. 177–192). Springer. DOI: 10.1007/978-3-030-94364-6_13

Dahal, A., McNevin, D., Chikhani, M., & Ward, J. (2023). An interdisciplinary forensic approach for human remains identification and missing persons investigations. *WIREs Forensic Science*, *5*(4), e1484. DOI: 10.1002/wfs2.1484

Dang, M., & Nguyen, T. N. (2023). Digital face manipulation creation and detection: A systematic review. *Electronics (Basel)*, *12*(16), 3407. DOI: 10.3390/electronics12163407

Darehbidi, Z. N. (2025). The Use of Artificial Intelligence Technology in Preventing Female Delinquency: A Novel Approach to Situational Crime Prevention. *Legal Studies in Digital Age*, *4*(1), 1–10. DOI: 10.61838/kman.lsda.131

Das, S., Malik, P. K., & Pandey, A. (2025). Challenges and advances in underwater sonar systems and AI-driven signal processing for modern naval operations: A systematic review. *Journal of Field Robotics*, •••, 1–33. DOI: 10.1002/rob.70077

Data Protection Act. (2018).

Davies, P. (2024) *Applications of Complexity Theory in an English Metropolitan Police Force*. [Doctoral dissertation, Open University]. Centre of Policing Research & Learning.

Davies, A., & Krame, G. (2023). AI-Driven Innovation in Law Enforcement: The Synergistic Potential of Police Body Cameras and Drones as a Complementary Policing Tool for Tactical and Operational Enhancement. *Policing (Oxford, England)*, *17*(1), 1–13. DOI: 10.1093/police/paad083

Davtyan, T. (2025). The us approach to ai regulation: federal laws, policies, and strategies explained. *Journal of Law, Technology, & the Internet*, *16*(2), 223.

DCAF. (2025, February 17). The double-edged sword of artificial intelligence in security sector governance. Geneva Centre for Security Sector Governance. Retrieved from DCAF: https://www.dcaf.ch/double-edged-sword-artificial-intelligence-security-sector-governance#

Dean, M. (2022). A practical guide to multi-criteria analysis. University College London. https://www.ucl.ac.uk/bartlett/public-purpose/sites/bartlett_public_purpose/files/a_practical_guide_to_multi-criteria_analysis.pdf

Dehghanniri, H., & Borrion, H. (2019). Crime scripting: A systematic review. *European Journal of Criminology*, *18*(4).

Deleon, J., Hatherleigh, C., Cumberbatch, A., Ashworth, J., & Heathcote, L. (2024, December). Predictive profiling framework for ransomware detection using contextual signature extraction. DOI: 10.31219/osf.io/fwkqd

Dempsey, R. P., Brunet, J. R., & Dubljević, V. (2023). Exploring and understanding law enforcement's relationship with technology: A qualitative interview study of police officers in North Carolina. *Applied Sciences (Basel, Switzerland)*, *13*(6), 3887. DOI: 10.3390/app13063887

Denis, J., Featherstone, J., Beaufort, O., & Edelstein, H. (2024, December). A novel algorithmic framework for autonomous ransomware detection using multi-layer temporal anomaly patterns. DOI: 10.31219/osf.io/g7yku

Devlin, K. (2023). Power in AI. In Gallagher, M., & Montiel, A. V. (Eds.), *The handbook of gender, communication, and women's human rights*. DOI: 10.1002/9781119800729.ch8

Dewan, A., Oliveira, G. L., & Burgard, W. (2017). Deep semantic classification for 3d lidar data. *2017 IEEE/RSJ International Conference on Intelligent Robots and Systems (IROS)*, 3544-3549. DOI: 10.1109/IROS.2017.8206198

Diab, A., Kashef, R., & Shaker, A. (2022). Deep learning for lidar point cloud classification in remote sensing. *Sensors (Basel)*, *22*(20), 7868. Advance online publication. DOI: 10.3390/s22207868 PMID: 36298220

Diamond, L. (2008). *Twelve Simple Rules of Systems Thinking for Complex Systems*. https://icasc.ca/twelve-simple-rules-of-systems-thinking-for-complex-global-issues/

Dilek, S., Çakır, H., & Aydın, M. (2015). Applications of artificial intelligence techniques to combating cybersecurity challenges: A survey. *Journal of Information Security*, *6*(3), 113–122. DOI: 10.4236/jis.2015.63012

Dima, D., & Covaciu, D. (2015). Simulation method in pc crash using point cloud files. ANNALS OF THE ORADEA UNIVERSITY. Fascicle of Management and Technological Engineering. [XIV]. *XXIV*, *2015*(1). Advance online publication. DOI: 10.15660/AUOFMTE.2015-1.13105

Ding, S., Wu, F., Qian, J., Jia, H., & Jin, F. (2015). Research on data stream clustering algorithms. *Artificial Intelligence Review*, *43*(4), 593–600. DOI: 10.1007/s10462-013-9398-7

Ding, Z., Sun, Y., Xu, S., Pan, Y., Peng, Y., & Mao, Z. (2023). Recent advances and perspectives in deep learning techniques for 3d point cloud data processing. *Robotics (Basel, Switzerland)*, *12*(4), 100. Advance online publication. DOI: 10.3390/robotics12040100

Dlamini, S. (2017). A criminological exploration of community policing forums in Durban, South Africa: A study based on Glenwood Suburb and Cato Manor Township [Doctoral dissertation, University of KwaZulu-Natal].

Drawve, G., Thomas, S. A., & Walker, J. T. (2014). The Likelihood of Arrest: A Routine Activity Theory Approach. *American Journal of Criminal Justice*, *39*(3), 450–470. DOI: 10.1007/s12103-013-9226-2

Dubravova, H., Cap, J., Holubova, K., & Hribnak, L. (2024). Artificial intelligence as an innovative element of support in policing. *Procedia Computer Science*, *237*, 237–244. DOI: 10.1016/j.procs.2024.05.101

Dworzecki, J., & Nowicka, I. (2021). Artificial intelligence (AI) and ICT-enhanced solutions in the activities of police formations in Poland. In *Artificial Intelligence and Its Contexts: Security, Business and Governance* (pp. 161–181). Springer International Publishing., DOI: 10.1007/978-3-030-88972-2_11

Dzuba, C. (2025). Artificial intelligence in social engineering: A literature review through the lens of routine activity theory. *Issues in Information Systems*, *26*(2), 452–465.

Edco, H., Simbolon, W., Nita, S., & Koto, Z. (2025). Optimization of Predictive Policing Technology for Prevention of Brawling Crimes at Bekasi City Metro Police Station. *Journal of Law. Politic and Humanities*, *5*(3), 1447–1457. DOI: 10.38035/jlph.v5i3.1313

Edelman, G. J., & Aalders, M. C. (2018). Photogrammetry using visible, infrared, hyperspectral and thermal imaging of crime scenes. *Forensic Science International*, *292*, 181–189. DOI: 10.1016/j.forsciint.2018.09.025 PMID: 30321744

Egbert, S., & Esposito, E. (2024). Algorithmic crime prevention. From abstract police to precision policing. *Policing and Society*, *34*(6), 521–534. DOI: 10.1080/10439463.2024.2326516 PMID: 38974932

EHRC. (2022). Artificial intelligence in public services. https://www.equalityhumanrights.com/guidance/artificial-intelligence-public-services?returnurl=https%3A%2F%2Fwww.equalityhumanrights.com%2Fsearch%3Fkeys%3DARTIFICIAL%2BINTELLIGENCE%2BIN%2BPUBLIC%2BPLACES

Eke, R. N. (2025). Adopting Artificial Intelligence-Based Predictive Policing in Nigeria: Prospects and Difficulties. *African Journal of Advances in Science and Technology Research*, *18*(1), 142–164. DOI: 10.62154/ajastr.2025.018.010680

El Fadel, N. (2025). Facial Recognition Algorithms: A Systematic Literature Review. *Journal of Imaging*, *11*(2), 58. DOI: 10.3390/jimaging11020058 PMID: 39997560

Eling, S. (2019). IBM's QRadar: AI-enhanced security intelligence for the modern enterprise. *Journal of Cybersecurity*, *5*(3), 72–84.

Enders, W., & Sandler, T. (2012). Enders, W. and Sandler, T. (2012) The Political Economy of Terrorism. 2nd edn. Cambridge: Cambridge University Press. Cambridge: Cambridge University Press.

Epstein, J. M. (1999). Agent-Based Computational Models and Generative Social Science. *Complexity*, *4*(5), 41–60. DOI: 10.1002/(SICI)1099-0526(199905/06)4:5<41::AID-CPLX9>3.0.CO;2-F

Ersöz, F., Ersöz, T., Marcelloni, F., & Ruffini, F. (2025). *Artificial Intelligence in Crime Prediction: A Survey With a Focus on Explainability*. IEEE., DOI: 10.1109/ACCESS.2025.3553934

European Commission. (2021). *Proposal for a regulation laying down harmonised rules on artificial intelligence (Artificial Intelligence Act)*. https://eur-lex.europa.eu

Europol. (2022). *Artificial intelligence and policing*. Publications Office of the European Union.

Europol. (2025). Steal, Deal and Repeat. The Hague: Europol. Retrieved from Internet Organised Crime Threat Assessment (IOCTA: https://www.europol.europa.eu/publication-events/main-reports/steal-deal-and-repeat-how-cybercriminals-trade-and-exploit-your-data

Ezugwu, A. E., Ikotun, A. M., Oyelade, O. O., Abualigah, L., Agushaka, J. O., Eke, C. I., & Akinyelu, A. A. (2022). A comprehensive survey of clustering algorithms: State-of-the-art machine learning applications, taxonomy, challenges, and future research prospects. *Engineering Applications of Artificial Intelligence, 110*, 104743. DOI: 10.1016/j.engappai.2022.104743

Ezugwu, A. E., Shukla, A. K., Agbaje, M. B., Oyelade, O. N., José-García, A., & Agushaka, J. O. (2021). Automatic clustering algorithms: A systematic review and bibliometric analysis of relevant literature. *Neural Computing & Applications, 33*(11), 6247–6306. DOI: 10.1007/s00521-020-05395-4

Fan, X., Salehzadeh, R., Korivand, S., Bordbar, F., Cousin, C., Griffin, D. J., & Jalili, N. (2024). Exploring law enforcement officers' expectations and attitudes about communication robots in police work. *Human Technology, 20*(1), 25–44. DOI: 10.14254/1795-6889.2024.20-1.2

Faqir, R. S. (2023). Digital criminal investigations in the era of artificial intelligence: A comprehensive overview. *International Journal of Cyber Criminology, 17*(2), 77–94.

FBI IC3. (2024). Federal Bureau of Investigation - Internet Crime Report 2024. Washington, DC: Internet Crime Complaint Center. Retrieved from https://www.google.com/search?q=FBI+IC3+(2024b)+2024+IC3+Annual+Report.+Washington%2C+DC%3A+Internet+Crime+Complaint+Center%2C+Federal+Bureau+of+Investigation.&rlz=1C5CHFA_enAE1042AE1042&oq=FBI+IC3+(2024b)+2024+IC3+Annual+Report.+Washington%2C+DC%3A+Inter

FBI IC3. (2024, December 3). Criminals Use Generative Artificial Intelligence to Facilitate Financial Fraud. Retrieved from FBI Public Service Announcement: https://www.ic3.gov/PSA/2024/PSA241203

Ferguson, A. G. (2017). *The rise of big data policing: Surveillance, race, and the future of law enforcement*. New York University Press. DOI: 10.18574/nyu/9781479854608.001.0001

Ferguson, A. G. (2021). Surveillance and the tyrant test. *Geological Journal, 110*, 205.

Ferguson, A. G. (2025). Generative Suspicion and the Risks of AI-Assisted Police Reports. *Nw. UL Rev., 120*, 299.

Ferrag, M. A., Alwahedi, F., Battah, A. A., Cherif, B., Mechri, A., Tihanyi, N., . . . Debbah, M. (2024). Generative AI in Cybersecurity: A Comprehensive Review of LLM Applications and Vulnerabilities. arXiv:2405.12750, 1-52.

Fitzgerald, E. (2024). AI in predictive policing and its ethical challenges. *International Journal of Artificial Intelligence and Machine Learning*. https://itaimle.com/index.php/ijaiml/article/view/245

Foucault, M. (1977). *Discipline and punish: the birth of the prison*. Penguin Group.

Fraerman, A. (2024). Relying on Unreliable Tech: Unchecked Police Use of Algorithmic Technologies. *Santa Clara High-Technology Law Journal, 40*, 115.

Friedman, B., Heydari, F., Isaacs, M., & Kinsey, K. (2022). Policing police tech: A soft law solution. *Berkeley Technology Law Journal, 37*, 701.

Fussey, P., & Murray, D. (2019). Independent report on the London Metropolitan Police Service's trial of live facial recognition technology. In University of Essex Human Rights Centre. https://repository.essex.ac.uk/24946/1/London-Met-Police-Trial-of-Facial-Recognition-Tech-Report-2.pdf

Future of Life Institute. (2025). *High-level summary of the AI Act.* https://artificialintelligenceact.eu/high-level-summary/

Galanakis, G., Zabulis, X., Evdaimon, T., Fikenscher, S.-E., Allertseder, S., Tsikrika, T., & Vrochidis, S. (2021). A study of 3d digitisation modalities for crime scene investigation. *Forensic Science, 1*(2), 56–85. DOI: 10.3390/forensicsci1020008

Galante, N., Cotroneo, R., Furci, D., Lodetti, G., & Casali, M. B. (2022). Applications of artificial intelligence in forensic sciences: C urrent potential benefits, limitations and perspectives. *International Journal of Legal Medicine, 137*(2), 445–458. DOI: 10.1007/s00414-022-02928-5 PMID: 36507961

Gambín, Á. F., Yazidi, A., Vasilakos, A., Haugerud, H., & Djenouri, Y. (2024). Gambín, Á.F., del Ser, J., Etxaniz, J. and Muguerza, J. (2024) 'Deepfakes: Current and future trends', Artificial Intelligence Review, 57, article 64. *Artificial Intelligence Review, 57*(64), 1–32.

Ganaie, N. A. (2026, January 6). The role of artificial intelligence in radicalisation, recruitment and terrorist propaganda: Deconstructing violent extremism and reimagining counterterrorism in contemporary digital ecosystems. *Frontiers in Political Science, 7*, 7. DOI: 10.3389/fpos.2025.1718396

Ganguli, P. (2025). Digital policing: Using social media surveillance to tackle cybercrime. *Available at SSRN* 5124657. DOI: 10.2139/ssrn.5124657

Gargan, N. (2025). *Learning from the inside out.* [Conference Presentation] Staffordshire Police Leadership Team (08/07/25).

Gavrilovic, N. (2016). The All-Seeing Eye in the Sky: Drone Surveillance and the Fourth Amendment. *U. Det. Mercy L. Rev.*, *93*, 529.

Gentile, G. (2024). Does big brother exist?: facial recognition technology in the United Kingdom.

Georgopoulos, A., & Stathopoulou, E. K. (2017). Data acquisition for 3d geometric recording: State of the art and recent innovations. In Vincent, M. L., Lopez-Menchero Bendicho, V. M., Ioannides, M., & Levy, T. E. (Eds.), *Heritage and archaeology in the digital age: Acquisition, curation, and dissemination ofspatial cultural heritage data* (pp. 1–26). Springer International Publishing., DOI: 10.1007/978-3-319-65370-9_1

Gershenson, C. (2024) *Complexity, Artificial Life, and Artificial Intelligence*. Artificial Life 1-15. Massachusetts Institute of Technology.

Gershenson, C. (2025). Complexity, artificial life, and artificial intelligence. *Artificial Life*, *31*(3), 289–303. DOI: 10.1162/artl_a_00462 PMID: 39576152

Gerstner, D. (2018). Predictive policing in the context of residential burglary: An empirical illustration on the basis of a pilot project in Baden-Württemberg, Germany. *European Journal for Security Research*, *3*(2), 115–138. DOI: 10.1007/s41125-018-0033-0

Ghorbani, A., Dechesne, F., Dignum, V., & Jonker, C. (2014). Enhancing ABM into an Inevitable Tool for Policy Analysis. *Policy and Complex Systems*, *1*(1), 61–76. DOI: 10.18278/jpcs.1.1.3

Gikay, A. A. (2024). Risks, innovation, and adaptability in the UK's incrementalism versus the European Union's comprehensive artificial intelligence regulation. *International Journal of Law and Information Technology*, *32*, eaae013. Advance online publication. DOI: 10.1093/ijlit/eaae013

Gilbert, N., & Troitzsch, K. (2011). *Simulation for the Social Scientist* (2nd ed.). Open University Press.

Gill, P. H., & Deckert, P. (2014). Bombing alone: Tracing the motivations and antecedent behaviors of lone-actor terrorists. *Journal of Forensic Sciences*, *59*(2), 425–435. DOI: 10.1111/1556-4029.12312 PMID: 24313297

Gkougkoudis, G., Pissanidis, D., & Demertzis, K. (2022). Intelligence-led policing and the new technologies adopted by the Hellenic Police. *Digital*, *2*(2), 143–163. DOI: 10.3390/digital2020009

Glomb, P., Romaszewski, M., Cholewa, M., & Domino, K. (2018). Application of hyperspectral imaging and machine learning methods for the detection of gunshot residue patterns. *Forensic Science International, 290*, 227–237. 10.1016/j.forsciint.2018.06.040. DOI: 10.1016/j.forsciint.2018.06.040 PMID: 30077814

Goliath, A. (2023). A short critique of minimum sentences. *Obiter, 43*(4), 779–796.

Golose, P. R. (2022). Cyber Terrorism- A Perspective of Policy Analysis. *International Journal of Cyber Criminology, 16*(2), 149–161.

González, R. J. (2024). Algorithmic policing: Part 1. Tech startups, venture capital and law enforcement in America. *Anthropology Today, 40*(5), 23–27. DOI: 10.1111/1467-8322.12916

Goodfellow, I., Bengio, Y., & Courville, A. (2016). *Deep learning*. MIT Press.

Goodfellow, I., Shlens, J., & Szegedy, C. (2018). Explaining and harnessing adversarial examples. *arXiv*. https://arxiv.org/abs/1412.6572

Gorr, W., & Lee, Y. (2015). Early warning system for temporary crime hot spots. *Journal of Quantitative Criminology, 31*(1), 25–47. DOI: 10.1007/s10940-014-9223-8

GOV.UK. (1984). Police and Criminal Evidence Act 1984, s. 64A https://www.legislation.gov.uk/ukpga/1984/60/section/64A

GOV.UK. (1998). Human Rights Act 1998, s. 6. Available at: Legislation.gov.uk. https://www.legislation.gov.uk/ukpga/1998/42/contents

GOV.UK. (2024). The model for responsible innovation. https://www.gov.uk/government/publications/the-model-for-responsible-innovation/the-model-for-responsible-innovation and Live facial recognition.

Government of India. (2000). *The Information Technology Act, 2000*. Ministry of Law and Justice. https://www.indiacode.nic.in

Goyal, N. K. (2025). Security and privacy in IoT, fog, and blockchain networks. In Sathio, A. (Eds.), *Energy-efficient deep learning approaches in IoT, fog, and green blockchain revolution* (pp. 371–398). IGI Global Scientific Publishing., DOI: 10.4018/979-8-3373-0300-0.ch015

Goyal, N. K. (2025). Weaponizing misinformation and cyberattacks on supply chains. In Bukhari, S., & Zafar, I. (Eds.), *Mass media and impact of fake news on supply chains* (pp. 177–210). IGI Global Scientific Publishing., DOI: 10.4018/979-8-3373-2175-2.ch007

Goyal, N. K., Dandotiya, M., Qurashi, J. A., Kumari, M., & Sharma, S. (2025). AI-driven predictive analytics for disease management. In Ouaissa, M. (Eds.), *Utilizing AI of medical things for healthcare security and sustainability* (pp. 231–276). IGI Global Scientific Publishing., DOI: 10.4018/979-8-3373-0690-2.ch008

Grant, M. J., & Booth, A. (2009). A typology of reviews: An analysis of 14 review types and associated methodologies. *Health Information and Libraries Journal, 26*(2), 91–108. 10.1111/j.1471-1842.2009.00848.x. DOI: 10.1111/j.1471-1842.2009.00848.x PMID: 19490148

Greco, M., & Stenner, P. (Eds.). (2008). *Emotions: A social science reader*. Routledge.

Greene, D., & Patterson, G. (2018). Can we trust computer with body-cam vidio? Police departments are being led to believe AI will help, but they should be wary. *IEEE Spectrum, 55*(12), 36–48. DOI: 10.1109/MSPEC.2018.8544982

Grinbaum, A., & Adomaitis, L. (2024). Dual use concerns of generative AI and large language models. *Journal of Responsible Innovation, 11*(1), 2304381. DOI: 10.1080/23299460.2024.2304381

Grother, P. (2022). Face recognition vendor test (FRVT) part 8: Summarizing demographic differentials. [NIST]. *National Institute of Standards and Technology, 8429*, 8. DOI: 10.6028/NIST.IR.8429.ipd

Guariglia, M. (2025). *Anchorage police department: AI-generated police reports don't save time*. Electronic Frontier Foundation.

Gültekin-Várkonyi, D. G. (2022). Predictive Policing and Bias in a Nutshell: Technical and Practical Aspects of Personal Data Processing for Law Enforcement Purposes. *Digital Criminal Justice: A Studybook Selected Topics for Learners and Researchers. Krisztina Karsai, Adem Sözüer, Liane Wörner (eds.). Istanbul.* DOI: 10.2139/ssrn.4238774

Gupta, M., Sood, R. P., & Singh, R. (2025). Artificial Intelligence in Criminal Investigation: Transforming Law Enforcement and Forensic Analysis. In *Rethinking the Police for a Better Future: Navigating Policing Challenges with Accountability and Trust* (pp. 311-323). Cham: Springer Nature Switzerland. DOI: 10.1007/978-3-031-83173-7_21

Gupta, M., Akiri, C., Aryal, K., Parker, E., & Praharaj, L. (2023). From ChatGPT to ThreatGPT: Impact of Generative AI in Cybersecurity and Privacy. *IEEE Access : Practical Innovations, Open Solutions, 11*, 80218–80245. DOI: 10.1109/ACCESS.2023.3300381

Gupta, P., Singh, A., & Kaur, R. (2021). AI-based threat hunting and incident response in cybersecurity. *International Journal of Information Security*, *29*(4), 345–359.

Gupta, S., Kumar, R., & Sharma, A. (2020). AI-driven cybersecurity solutions: The case of Cylance. *Journal of Computer Security*, *28*(4), 231–247.

Hahn, J. (2025). Predictive policing and the implications of AI across global frameworks. *Cornell International Law Journal*, *57*(3). https://publications.lawschool.cornell.edu/cilj/2025/08/28/predictive-policing-and-the-implications-of-ai-across-global-frameworks

Haley, P., & Burrell, D. N. (2025). Integrating Artificial Intelligence into Law Enforcement: Socioeconomic and Ethical Challenges. *SocioEconomic Challenges (SEC), 9*(2).

Haley, P. (2025). The Impact of Biometric Surveillance on Reducing Violent Crime: Strategies for Apprehending Criminals While Protecting the Innocent. *Sensors (Basel)*, *25*(10), 3160. DOI: 10.3390/s25103160 PMID: 40431950

Haley, P., & Burrell, D. N. (2025). Integrating Artificial Intelligence into Law Enforcement: Socioeconomic and Ethical Challenges. [SEC]. *SocioEconomic Challenges*, *9*(2), 60–77. Advance online publication. DOI: 10.61093/sec.9(2).60-77.2025

Halcy, P., & Burrell, D. N. (2025). Using Artificial Intelligence in Law Enforcement and Policing to Improve Public Health and Safety. *Law. Economics and Society*, *1*(1), 46–p46. DOI: 10.30560/les.v1n1p46

Hall, S. W., Sakzad, A., & Choo, K.-K. R. (2022). Explainable artificial intelligence for digital forensics. *WIREs Forensic Science*, *4*(2), e1434. DOI: 10.1002/wfs2.1434

Harris, H. (2022). Artificial intelligence and policing of financial crime: a legal analysis of the state of the field. *Financial technology and the law: Combating financial crime*, 281-299. DOI: 10.1007/978-3-030-88036-1_12

Harris, H., & Burke, A. (2021, October). Artificial Intelligence, Policing and Ethics–a best practice model for AI enabled policing in Australia. In *2021 IEEE 25th International Enterprise Distributed Object Computing Workshop (EDOCW)* (pp. 53-58). IEEE. DOI: 10.1109/EDOCW52865.2021.00032

Hauchi, W., Lisik, D., & Dinh, T. (2024). Data clustering: An essential technique in data science. arXiv preprint arXiv:2412.18760, 1–17.

Hawdon, J., Costello, M., Barrett-Fox, R., & Bernatzky, C. (2019). Hawdon, J., Costello, M., Barrett-Fox, R., & Bernatzky, C. (2018). The perpetuation of online hate: A criminological analysis of factors associated with participating in an online attack., 15(1), 157–181. *Journal of Hate Studies*, *15*(1). Advance online publication. DOI: 10.33972/jhs.166

Heath, B., Hill, R., & Ciarallo, F. (2009). *A survey of agent-based modeling practices* (January 1998 to July 2008). *Journal of Artificial Societies and Social Simulation*, *12*, 9.

He, D. S., & Wang, T. S. (2025). An exploration of the service and crime prevention performance of the municipal police departments of Taiwan's counties: The perspective of broken windows theory. *Policing*, *48*(1), 136–156. DOI: 10.1108/PIJPSM-05-2024-0088

Heiduk, J. (2017). Data visualisation with Python: Crime statistics for South Africa. Kaggle. Retrieved February 23, 2023, from https://www.kaggle.com/datasets/slweber/south-africa-crime-statistics

He, Q.-C., Nie, T., Yang, Y., & Shen, Z.-J. (2021). Beyond repositioning: Crowdsourcing and geo-fencing for shared-mobility systems. *Production and Operations Management*, *30*(10), 3448–3466. DOI: 10.1111/poms.13442

Herke, C. (2026). Automated Fingerprint Identification: The Role of Artificial Intelligence in Crime Scene Investigation. *Forensic Science*, *6*(1), 6. DOI: 10.3390/forensicsci6010006

Hernandez, P. (2013). Is Crime Contagious? A Near-Repeat Pattern Analysis of Burglary Incidents in Winston-Salem, 2012. *Journal of Justice Studies, 3.*

He, Y., & Chen, S. (2019). Recent advances in 3d data acquisition and processing by time-of flight camera. *IEEE Access : Practical Innovations, Open Solutions*, *7*, 12495–12510. DOI: 10.1109/ACCESS.2019.2891693

Himachal Pradesh Police. (2024). *Annual report and digital modernization overview.* Government of Himachal Pradesh. https://hppolice.gov.in

Hobart, L. N. (2025). AI, Bias, and National Security Profiling. *Berkeley Technology Law Journal*, *40*, 165.

Hoffman, A., & Schweitzer, Y. (2015). Cyber Jihad in the Service of the Islamic State (ISIS). Strategic Assessment, 18(2).

Hojda, M. H., Mieila, M., Mieila, C., & Dafina, L. C. (2024). Rational Choice And Cybersecurity. [Constantin Brancoveanu University]. *Contemporary Economy Journal*, *9*(4), 60–67.

Holt, T. J., Turner, N. D., Freilich, J. D., & Chermak, S. M. (2021). Examining the Characteristics That Differentiate Jihadi-Associated Cyberattacks Using Routine Activities Theory. *Social Science Computer Review*, *40*(6), 1614–1630. DOI: 10.1177/08944393211023324

Holt, T., & Bossler, A. (2009). Examining the applicability of lifestyle-routine activities theory for cybercrime victimization. *Deviant Behavior*, *30*(1), 1–25. DOI: 10.1080/01639620701876577

Home Office. (2024). *Home Secretary announces major policing reforms*. https://www.gov.uk/government/news/home-secretary-announces-major-policing-reforms

Home Office. (2024). *Police Grant Report: 2025 to 2026*. https://www.gov.uk/government/publications/provisional-police-grant-report-2025-to-2026

Home Office. (2026). *From Local to National: A New Model for Policing*. https://www.gov.uk/government/publications/from-local-to-national-a-new-model-for-policing

Horgan, J. (2005). *The Psychology of Terrorism*. Routledge.

Hossain, M. A., & Islam, M. S. (2024). Enhanced detection of obfuscated malware in memory dumps: A machine learning approach for advanced cybersecurity. *Cybersecurity*, *7*(1), 1–23. DOI: 10.1186/s42400-024-00205-z

Hosseinzadeh, M., Hemmati, A., & Rahmani, A. M. (2022). Clustering for smart cities in the internet of things: A review. *Cluster Computing*, *25*(6), 4097–4127. DOI: 10.1007/s10586-022-03646-8

Huang, Z., Wen, Y., Wang, Z., Ren, J., & Jia, K. (2024). Surface reconstruction from point clouds: A survey and a benchmark. *IEEE Transactions on Pattern Analysis and Machine Intelligence*, *46*(12), 9727–9748. DOI: 10.1109/TPAMI.2024.3429209 PMID: 39012756

Huber, E., Pospisil, B., Sauter, T., & Treytl, A. (2025). Cybercrime Victimisation and Categorization – A View from the Perspective of Routine-Activity-Theory (RAT). Kriminologie - Das Online-Journal | Criminology - The Online Journal, 7, 100-123.

Hung, T., & Yen, C. (2021). On the person-based predictive policing of AI. *Ethics and Information Technology*, *23*(3), 165–176. DOI: 10.1007/s10676-020-09539-x

Hunter, D., Bagaric, M., & Stobbs, N. (2020). A framework for the efficient and ethical use of artificial intelligence in the criminal justice system'(2020). *Fla St UL Rev*, *47*, 749.

Hynek, N., Gavurová, B., & Kubák, M. (2025). Risks and benefits of artificial intelligence deepfakes: Systematic review and comparison of public attitudes in seven European Countries. *Journal of Innovation & Knowledge*, *10*(100782), 1–19. DOI: 10.1016/j.jik.2025.100782

Iacob, D., Furst, A., & Hadrys, T. (2019). Amachine learning model to predict the origin of forensically relevant body fluids. *Forensic Science International. Genetics Supplement Series*, *7*(1), 392–394. 10.1016/j.fsigss.2019.10.025. DOI: 10.1016/j.fsigss.2019.10.025

ICO. (2019). Information Commissioner's Opinion: The use of live facial recognition technology by law enforcement in public places. https://ico.org.uk/media/about-the-ico/documents/2616184/live-frt-law-enforcement-opinion-20191031.pdf

Ilcic, A., Fuentes, M., & Lawler, D. (2025). Artificial intelligence, complexity, and systemic resilience in global governance. *Frontiers in Artificial Intelligence*, *8*, 1562095. DOI: 10.3389/frai.2025.1562095 PMID: 40529642

Inadomi, S., & Chun, P. (2025). A comparative study of projection-based vs. point-based point clouds segmentation for 3d bridge modeling. *Structure and Infrastructure Engineering*, *0*(0), 1–13. DOI: 10.1080/15732479.2025.2494257

Independent, The. *Spending review a 'huge blow' for police and 'will hamper efforts to recruit 13,000 neighbourhood police officers' (*https://www.independent.co.uk/news/uk/crime/police-spending-review-npcc-reeves-b2768233.html

Insight, P. (2025). *UK Police Digital Experience Survey 2025: Headline Findings*. Policing Insight. https://policinginsight.com

Internet Freedom Foundation. (2021). *Panoptic surveillance in India: A study of facial recognition deployments*. https://internetfreedom.in

INTERPOL. (2024). *Beyond Illusions: Unmasking the Threat of Synthetic Media for Law Enforcement*. INTERPOL.

INTERPOL. (2024). *Global Financial Fraud Assessment*. INTERPOL.

Investigatory Powers Act. (2016).

Isaac, W. S. (2017). Hope, hype, and fear: The promise and potential pitfalls of artificial intelligence in criminal justice. *Ohio St. J. Crim. L.*, *15*, 543.

Isafiade, O. E., & Bagula, A. B. (2017). *Fostering smart city development in developing nations: A crime series data analytics approach. In 2017 ITU Kaleidoscope: Challenges for a Data-Driven Society*. IEEE.

Ishchenko, T., Nikitina, I., & Das, B. (2024). Innovations in Law Enforcement Education: the Impact of Artificial Intelligence Tools. DOI: 10.32782/2078-3566-2024-4-27

Islam, A., Asikuzzaman, M., Khyam, M. O., Noor-A-Rahim, M., & Pickering, M. R. (2020). Stereo vision-based 3d positioning and tracking. *IEEE Access : Practical Innovations, Open Solutions*, *8*, 138771–138787. DOI: 10.1109/ACCESS.2020.3011360

Islam, S. M., Bari, M. S., Sarkar, A., Khan, A. O. R., & Paul, R. (2024). AI-powered threat intelligence: Revolutionizing cybersecurity with proactive risk management for critical sectors. *JAIGS*, *7*(1), 1–8. DOI: 10.60087/jaigs.v7i01.291

Jadhav, E., Sankhla, M. S., & Kumar, R. (2020). Artificial intelligence: Advancing automation in forensic science criminal investigation. *Seybold Report*, *15*, 2064–2075.

Jaffal, N. O., Alkhanafseh, M., & Mohaisen, D. (2025). Large Language Models in Cybersecurity: Applications, Vulnerabilities, and Defense Techniques. arXiv:2507.13629, 1-21.

Jain, P. R., Quadri, S., & Khattar, A. (2024). EM-UDA: Emotion detection using unsupervised domain adaptation for classification of facial images. *IEEE Access : Practical Innovations, Open Solutions*, *12*, 140262–140276. DOI: 10.1109/ACCESS.2024.3467990

Jarrett, A., & Choo, K. K. R. (2021). The impact of automation and artificial intelligence on digital forensics. *WIREs Forensic Science*, *3*(6), e1418. DOI: 10.1002/wfs2.1418

Jimmy, F. N. U. (2021b). Understanding ransomware attacks: Trends and prevention strategies. DOI: 10.60087/jklst.vol2.n1.p214

Jimmy, F. N. U. (2022). Zero trust security: Reimagining cyber defense for modern organizations. *Valley International Journal Digital Library*, 887–905.

Jimmy, F. N. U. (2024). Cybersecurity threats and vulnerabilities in online banking systems. *Valley International Journal Digital Library*, 1631–1646.

Jimmy, F. (2021a). Emerging threats: The latest cybersecurity risks and the role of artificial intelligence in enhancing cybersecurity defenses. *Valley International Journal Digital Library*, *1*(2), 564–574. DOI: 10.18535/ijsrm/v9i2.ec01

Joh, E. E. (2016). Policing police robots. *UCLA L. Rev. Discourse*, *64*, 516.

Joh, E. E. (2017). The undue influence of surveillance technology companies in policing. *SSRN*, *92*, 19. DOI: 10.2139/ssrn.2924620

Joh, E. E. (2022). Ethical AI in American Policing. *Notre Dame J. on Emerging Tech.*, *3*, 261.

Johnson, J. (2006, October). Can Complexity Help Us Better Understand Risk? *Risk Management*, *8*(4), 227–267. DOI: 10.1057/palgrave.rm.8250023

Johnson, J. (2013). *Hypernetworks in the Science of Complex Systems*. World Scientific.

Johnson, J., & Cook, M. (2014). Policy Design: A New Area of Design Research and Practice. In Aiguier, M., Boulanger, F., Krob, D., & Marchal, C. (Eds.), *Complex Systems Design & Management* (pp. 51–62). Springer International Publishing. DOI: 10.1007/978-3-319-02812-5_4

Johnson, J., Denning, P., Odlysko, A., Walker, M., Delic, K., Yaffe, P., & Picton, P. (2025) *Foundational Technologies of Artificial Intelligence. Ubiquity Symposium, an Association for Computing Machinery publication*.

Johnson, J., Nowak, A., Ormerod, P., Rosewell, B., & Zhang, Y.-C. (2017). *Non-Equilibrium Social Science and Policy*. Springer Open. DOI: 10.1007/978-3-319-42424-8

Johnson, T. L., Johnson, N. N., McCurdy, D., & Olajide, M. S. (2022). Facial recognition systems in policing and racial disparities in arrests. *Government Information Quarterly*, *39*(4), 101753. DOI: 10.1016/j.giq.2022.101753

Jones, C. (2020). Law enforcement use of facial recognition: Bias, disparate impacts on people of color, and the need for federal legislation. *NCJL & Tech.*, *22*, 777.

Jones, M. (2008). A Complexity Science View of Modern Police Administration. *Public Administration Quarterly*, *32*, 433–457.

Kaggle. (n.d.). Microsoft malware classification challenge (BIG 2015). https://www.kaggle.com/c/malware-classification

Kanwel, S., Khan, M. I., & Usman, M. (2023). From bytes to bars: The transformative influence of artificial intelligence on criminal justice. *Qlantic Journal of Social Sciences*, *4*(4), 84–89. DOI: 10.55737/qjss.059046443

Kapsokoli, E. (2023). Cyberterrorism A New Wave of Terrorism or Not? In Ferrag, M. A., Kantzavelou, I., Maglaras, L., & Janicke, H. (Eds.), *Hybrid Threats, Cyberterrorism and Cyberwarfare*. Routledge.

Kasri, W., Himeur, Y., Alkhazaleh, H. A., Tarapiah, S., Atalla, S., Mansoor, W., & Al-Ahmad, H. (2025). From Vulnerability to Defense: The Role of Large Language Models in Enhancing Cybersecurity. *Computation (Basel, Switzerland), 13*(30), 1–59. DOI: 10.3390/computation13020030

Kaufmann, M. (2024). AI in policing and law enforcement. In *Handbook on Public Policy and Artificial Intelligence* (pp. 295–306). Edward Elgar Publishing., DOI: 10.4337/9781803922171.00031

Kaur, R., Gabrijelčič, D., & Klobučar, T. (2023). Artificial intelligence for cybersecurity: Literature review and future research directions. Information Fusion, 97(article 101804), 1-29.

Kaur, A., Hoshyar, A. N., Saikrishna, V., Firmin, S., & Xia, F. (2024, May 29). Deepfake video detection: Challenges and opportunities. *Artificial Intelligence Review*, *57*(159), 1–47.

Kavidharani, R. (2025). Predictive policing and constitutional morality: An evaluation of AI-based crime forecasting technologies in India. *LIJDLR, 3*(2), 903–913. https://lijdlr.com/2025/07/31/predictive-policing-and-constitutional-morality-an-evaluation-of-ai-based-crime-forecasting-technologies-in-india

Kayalvili, S., Rajulu, G. G., Changala, R., & Kumbhkar, M. (2023, October). Integration of Machine Learning and Computer Vision to Detect and Prevent the Crime. In *2023 International Conference on New Frontiers in Communication, Automation, Management and Security (ICCAMS)* (Vol. 1, pp. 1-5). IEEE. DOI: 10.1109/ICCAMS60113.2023.10526105

Kaza, S., Wang, T., Gowda, H., & Chen, H. (2005). Target vehicle identification for border safety using mutual information. In *Proceedings of the 2005 IEEE Intelligent Transportation Systems* (pp. 1141–1146). IEEE. DOI: 10.1109/ITSC.2005.1520212

Kellner, M., Stahl, B., & Reiterer, A. (2022). Fused projection-based point cloud segmentation. *Sensors (Basel), 22*(3), 1139. Advance online publication. DOI: 10.3390/s22031139 PMID: 35161890

Khan, F., Zubair, A., & Umer, T. (2021). AI-driven cloud security: Protecting the cloud infrastructure. *Cloud Computing Research, 12*(3), 233–249.

Khan, I. A., & Ullah, A. (2024). The Role of Artificial Intelligence in Enhancing Social Governance: A Framework for Ethical Implementation and Policy Development in Pakistan. *Journal of Management & Social Science, 1*(4), 274–289. DOI: 10.63075/9fzpbn74

Khoei, T. T., & Singh, A. (2024). A survey of Emotional Artificial Intelligence and crimes: Detection, prediction, challenges and future direction. *Journal of Computational Social Science*, *7*(3), 2359–2402. DOI: 10.1007/s42001-024-00313-3

Kigerl, A. (2011). Kigerl, A. (2012) 'Routine activity theory and the determinants of high cybercrime countries', 30(4), pp. 470–486. *Social Science Computer Review*, *30*(4), 470–486. DOI: 10.1177/0894439311422689

Kim, S., Khoreva, V., & Vaiman, V. (2025). Strategic human resource management in the era of algorithmic technologies: Key insights and future research agenda. *Human Resource Management*, *64*(2), 447–464. DOI: 10.1002/hrm.22268

Klautau, A., Gonzalez-Prelcic, N., & Heath, R. W. (2019). Lidar data for deep learningbased mmwave beam-selection. *IEEE Wireless Communications Letters*, *8*(3), 909–912. DOI: 10.1109/LWC.2019.2899571

Kolt, N., Shur-Ofry, M., & Cohen, R. (2025). *Lessons from complexity theory for AI governance*. arXiv. .DOI: 10.1016/j.patter.2025.101341

Kotter, J. P. (1995). Leading change: Why transformational efforts fail. *Harvard Business Review*, *73*(2), 59–67.

Kottner, S., Thali, M. J., & Gascho, D. (2023). Using the iphone's lidar technology to capture 3d forensic data at crime and crash scenes. *Forensic Imaging*, *32*, 200535. 10.1016/j.fri.2023.200535. DOI: 10.1016/j.fri.2023.200535

Krishna, S., Aljohani, N., Mishra, D., Garg, N., Verma, V., & Malathy, V. (2023). Applications of Artificial Intelligence in Public Sector and its Challenges. *4th International Conference on Computation, Automation and Knowledge Management*. DOI: 10.1109/ICCAKM58659.2023.10449594

Kumar, K. G., Sowndharya, A., Pradeep, D. M., Suriya, S., & Kumar, K. D. (2024). *Detection of Deepfake Videos Using a Deep Learning Approach with ResNext and LSTM*. Paper presented at the 2024 13th International Conference on System Modeling & Advancement in Research Trends (SMART). DOI: 10.1109/SMART63812.2024.10882518

Kumar, M., Kumar, M., Dabur, S., Yadav, R., Kumar, K., & Tyagi, M. (2025, April). Exploring the Implementation of Artificial Intelligence in the Indian Legal System. In *2025 3rd International Conference on Communication, Security, and Artificial Intelligence (ICCSAI)* (Vol. 3, pp. 1545-1551). IEEE. DOI: 10.1109/ICCSAI64074.2025.11064188

Kumar, J. S., Amiruzzaman, M., Bhuiyan, A. A., & Bhati, D. (2024). Predictive Analytics in Law Enforcement: Unveiling Patterns in NYPD Crime through Machine Learning and Data Mining. *Research Briefs on Information and Communication Technology Evolution*, *10*, 36–59. DOI: 10.64799/rebicte.v10.3

Kumar, N. (2025). From surveillance to sentencing: Evaluating AI's role in Indian criminal justice. *Science Bulletin*, *30*(1), 68–78. https://sciendo.com/article/10.2478/bsaft-2025-0008

Kumar, R., & Goyal, D. (2021). Artificial intelligence in cybersecurity: Applications and challenges. *Computer Science Review*, *41*, 100413. DOI: 10.1016/j.cosrev.2021.100413

Kydd, A., & Walter, B. (2006). The strategies of terrorism'. *International Security*, *31*(1), 49–80. DOI: 10.1162/isec.2006.31.1.49

Lakomy, M. (2023, December 15). Artificial intelligence as a terrorism enabler? Understanding the potential impact of chatbots and image generators on online terrorist activities. Retrieved from Global Network on Extremism & Technology: https://gnet-research.org/2023/12/15/artificial-intelligence-as-a-terrorism-enabler-understanding-the-potential-impact-of-chatbots-and-image-generators-on-online-terrorist-activities/

LeCun, Y., Bengio, Y., & Hinton, G. (2015). Deep learning. *Nature*, *521*(7553), 436–444. DOI: 10.1038/nature14539 PMID: 26017442

Lee, N. T., & Chin, C. (2022). Police surveillance and facial recognition: Why data privacy is imperative for communities of color. *The Brookings Institution. Erişim adresi:* https://www. brookings. edu/research/police-surveillance-and-facial-recognition-why-data-privacy-is-an-imperative-for-communities-of-color

Lee, Y., SooHyun, O., & Eck, J. E. (2020). A theory-driven algorithm for real-time crime hot spot forecasting. *Police Quarterly*, *23*(2), 174–201. DOI: 10.1177/1098611119887809

Leslie, D., Burr, C., Aitken, M., Cowls, J., Katell, M., & Briggs, M. (2021). Artificial intelligence, Human Rights, Democracy, and the Rule of Law: A primer. SSRN Electronic Journal. DOI: 10.2139/ssrn.3817999

Leukfeldt, E., & Yar, M. (2016). Applying routine activity theory to cybercrime: A theoretical and empirical analysis'. *Deviant Behavior*, *37*(3), 263–280. DOI: 10.1080/01639625.2015.1012409

Li, L., Bao, J., Zhang, T., Yang, H., Chen, D., Wen, F., & Guo, B. (2020). *Face x-ray for more general face forgery detection.* Paper presented at the Proceedings of the IEEE/CVF conference on computer vision and pattern recognition. DOI: 10.1109/CVPR42600.2020.00505

Li, Y., & Lyu, S. (2018). Exposing deepfake videos by detecting face warping artifacts. *arXiv preprint arXiv:1811.00656*. DOI: 10.3897/bdj.11.e100784.figure2c

Liang, C. S. (2023). Terrorist digitalis: Preventing terrorists from using emerging technologies. In Institute for Economics and Peace (Ed.), Global Terrorism Index 2023 (pp. 72-74).

Liaropoulos, A. (2014). On cyber-terrorism: Redefining terror in cyberspace. Politika, Annual Journal, 41-88.

Lilienblum, E., & Al-Hamadi, A. (2015). A structured light approach for 3-d surface reconstruction with a stereo line-scan system. *IEEE Transactions on Instrumentation and Measurement*, *64*(5), 1258–1266. DOI: 10.1109/TIM.2014.2364105

Lin, L. S. (2025). Integrating Artificial Intelligence in Police Education: An Analysis of the Top-Down Approach at Taiwan's Central Police University. In *Transforming Vocational Education and Training Using AI* (pp. 131-164). IGI Global Scientific Publishing. DOI: 10.4018/979-8-3693-8252-3.ch006

Li, P., Huang, Q., Shuang, F., Cai, Y., Cheng, H., & Li, Q. (2026). Anchor-based Multimodal Verification: A Dynamic Query Framework for Fake News Forensics in Short Videos. *IEEE Transactions on Information Forensics and Security*, *21*, 2047–2060. Advance online publication. DOI: 10.1109/TIFS.2026.3658995

Liu, H., Yan, Y., Zhang, X., & Wu, Z. (2016). 3d scene reconstruction based on 3d laser point cloud combining uav images. 2nd ISPRS International Conference on Computer Vision in Remote Sensing (CVRS 2015), 9901, 99011C. DOI: 10.1117/12.2234802

Liu, W., Sun, J., Li, W., Hu, T., & Wang, P. (2019). Deep learning on point clouds and its application: A survey. *Sensors (Basel)*, *19*(19), 4188. DOI: 10.3390/s19194188 PMID: 31561639

Liu, Y., Hu, D., & Fan, J.-l. (2018). A survey of crime scene investigation image retrieval. *ACTA ELECTONICA SINICA*, *46*, 761.

Li, Y., Ma, L., Zhong, Z., Liu, F., Chapman, M. A., Cao, D., & Li, J. (2021). Deep learning for lidar point clouds in autonomous driving: A review. *IEEE Transactions on Neural Networks and Learning Systems*, *32*(8), 3412–3432. DOI: 10.1109/TNNLS.2020.3015992 PMID: 32822311

Lohani, B., & Ghosh, S. (2017). Airborne lidar technology: A review of data collection and processing systems. *Proceedings of the National Academy of Sciences. India. Section A, Physical Sciences, 87*(4), 567–579. DOI: 10.1007/s40010-017-0435-9

López-Ruiz, R. (2025). *AI and Statistical Complexity*. Complex Systems with Artificial Intelligence – IntechOpen.

Lum, K., & Isaac, W. (2016). To predict and serve? *Significance, 13*(5), 14–19. DOI: 10.1111/j.1740-9713.2016.00960.x

Luo, L., Zhou, L., & Song, P. X.-K. (2023). Real-time regression analysis of streaming clustered data with possible abnormal data batches. *Journal of the American Statistical Association, 118*(543), 2029–2044. DOI: 10.1080/01621459.2022.2026778 PMID: 37771510

Lupovici, A. (2021). Lupovici, A. (2021). The dual-use security dilemma and the social construction of insecurity. Contemporary Security Policy, 42(3), 257–285. *Contemporary Security Policy, 42*(3), 257–285. DOI: 10.1080/13523260.2020.1866845

Lyytinen, K., Weber, B., Becker, M., & Pentland, B. (2024). Digital Twins of Organization: Implications for Organization Design. *Journal of Organization Design, 13*(3), 77–93. DOI: 10.1007/s41469-023-00151-z

Maathuis, C. (2024, November). Insights into Building VR Solutions in the Police Domain. In *Proceedings of the International Conference on Education Research*. Academic Conferences and publishing limited. DOI: 10.34190/icer.1.1.2800

Macingwane, A., & Isafiade, O. E. (2025). A novel HP-Growth model for enhancing community policing in South Africa. *Discover Computing, 28*(1), 37. DOI: 10.1007/s10791-025-09529-x

Maddireddy, B. R. (2020). Proactive cyber defense: Utilizing AI for early threat detection and risk assessment. *International Journal of Advanced Engineering Technology & Innovations, 1*(2), 64–83.

Mainzer, K. (2025). Complex systems and the evolution of artificial intelligence. In *Thinking in Complexity* (pp. 171–252). Springer.

Makuch, B. (2025, December 21). Extremists are using AI voice cloning to supercharge propaganda. Experts say it's helping them grow. Retrieved from The Guardian: https://www.theguardian.com/technology/2025/dec/21/ai-voice-cloning-nazis-islamic-state-extremism

Mandalapu, V., Elluri, L., Vyas, P., & Roy, N. (2023, March). Crime prediction using machine learning and deep learning: A systematic review and future directions. Institute of Electrical; Electronics Engineers (IEEE).

Mandavilli, V. K. C.VENKATA KALYAN CHAKRAVARTHY MANDAVILLI. (2025). SAP AI Applications Across Diverse Sectors: Education, Law Enforcement, and Art. *World Journal of Advanced Research and Reviews*, *26*(2), 2012–2019. DOI: 10.30574/wjarr.2025.26.2.1887

Maneli, M. A., & Isafiade, O. E. (2023). Exploration of 3d augmented reality solution for crime scene investigators in low-resource settings. Southern Africa Telecommunication Networks and Applications Conference (SATNAC) 2023, 20–25. https://www.satnac.org.za/proceedings

Maneli, M. A., & Isafiade, O. E. (2025). Towards reliable 3d crime scene investigation in low-resource regions using lidar. 2025 IST-Africa Conference (IST-Africa), 1–13. DOI: 10.23919/IST-Africa67297.2025.11060517

Maneli, M. A., & Isafiade, O. E. (2022). *3d forensic crime scene reconstruction involving immersive technology: A systematic literature review*. IEEE., DOI: 10.1109/ACCESS.2022.3199437

Mangkhalasiri, P., & Poothakool, K. (2025). Data Science in Policing in Thailand: Challenges and Future Directions–A Review From International Perspectives. *Journal of Contemporary Social Sciences and Humanities*, *12*(2), 18–34. DOI: 10.59796/jcsh.v12i2.18-34

Mansoor, S. I. U. (2026). AI and the Rule of Law in Urban Security: Upholding Police Accountability in Smart Cities. In AI-Driven Policing and Urban Security in Smart Cities (pp. 55-80). IGI Global Scientific Publishing. DOI: 10.4018/979-8-3373-0245-4.ch003

Mata-Torres, J. A., Tello-Leal, E., Hernandez-Resendiz, J. D., & Ramirez-Alcocer, U. M. (2023). Evaluation of machine learning techniques for malware detection. In *Intelligent Systems Reference Library* (Vol. 226, pp. 121–140). DOI: 10.1007/978-3-031-08246-7_6

Mateen, M., Wen, J., Nasrullah, , Song, S., & Huang, Z. (2019). Fundus image classification using vgg-19 architecture with pca and svd. *Symmetry*, *11*(1), 1. Advance online publication. DOI: 10.3390/sym11010001

Mathews, K. M., White, M., & Long, R. (1999). Why Study the Complexity Sciences in the Social Sciences? *Human Relations*, *52*(4), 439–462. DOI: 10.1177/001872679905200402

Matulionyte, R., & Zalnieriute, M. (2024). *The Cambridge Handbook of Facial Recognition in the Modern State*. Cambridge University Press. DOI: 10.1017/9781009321211

McCauley, C., & Moskalenko, S. (2008). Mechanisms of political radicalization: Pathways toward terrorism'. *Terrorism and Political Violence*, *20*(3), 415–433. DOI: 10.1080/09546550802073367

McDaniel, J. L., & Pease, K. (Eds.). (2021). *Predictive policing and artificial intelligence*. Routledge, Taylor & Francis Group. DOI: 10.4324/9780429265365

McDaniel, J. L. M., & Malik, N. (2023). Managing allegations concerning Black and Asian police officers, cultural competence and reflective practice under the Police (Conduct) Regulations 2020. *The Modern Law Review*, *86*(2), 498–517. DOI: 10.1111/1468-2230.12785

Meijer, A., & Wessels, M. (2019). Predictive policing: Review of benefits and drawbacks. *International Journal of Public Administration*, *42*(12), 1031–1039. DOI: 10.1080/01900692.2019.1575664

Melotti, G., & Premebida, C., & Gonc.alves, N. (2020). Multimodal deep-learning for object recognition combining camera and lidar data. 2020 IEEE International Conference on Autonomous Robot Systems and Competitions (ICARSC), 177-182. DOI: 10.1109/ICARSC49921.2020.9096138

Memon, M., Talpur, S., Narejo, S., Channa, A., & Pandey, J. K. (2026). Fundamentals of image processing for surveillance. In *Computational Intelligence in Surveillance Systems Using Image Processing* (pp. 13–24). Elsevier. DOI: 10.1016/B978-0-443-36408-2.00010-2

Miller, S., & Selgelid, M. J. (2007). Ethical and philosophical consideration of the dual-use dilemma in the biological sciences. *Science and Engineering Ethics*, *13*(4), 523–580. DOI: 10.1007/s11948-007-9043-4 PMID: 18060518

Ministry of Electronics and Information Technology (MeitY). (2025). *iCAST-25 cyber security workshop proceedings.*

Mirishli, S. (2025). Ethical implications of AI in data collection: Balancing innovation with privacy. *arXiv*. https://arxiv.org/abs/2503.14539

Mitcham, J. (2023). Agent-Based Simulation of Policy Funding Tradeoffs Through the Lens of Legitimacy and Hardship. *Journal of Artificial Societies and Social Simulation*, *26*(3), 12. DOI: 10.18564/jasss.5169

Mohd Sabri, N. E., Chainchel Singh, M. K., Mahmood, M. S., Khoo, L. S., Mohd Yusof, M. Y. P., Heo, C. C., Muhammad Nasir, M. D., & Nawawi, H. (2023). A scoping review on drone technology applications in forensic science. *SN Applied Sciences, 5*(9), 233. Advance online publication. DOI: 10.1007/s42452-023-05450-4

Mohler, G. O., Short, M. B., Malinowski, S., Johnson, M., Tita, G. E., Bertozzi, A. L., & Brantingham, P. J. (2015). Randomized controlled field trials of predictive policing. *Journal of the American Statistical Association, 110*(512), 1399–1411. DOI: 10.1080/01621459.2015.1077710

Mohler, G., Porter, M., Carter, J., & LaFree, G. (2020). Learning to rank spatio-temporal event hotspots. *Crime Science, 9*(1), 3. DOI: 10.1186/s40163-020-00112-x

Mourtgos, S. M., Adams, I. T., & Nix, J. (2022). Elevated police turnover following the summer of George Floyd protests: A synthetic control study. *Criminology & Public Policy, 21*(1), 9–33. DOI: 10.1111/1745-9133.12556

Mugari, I., & Obioha, E. E. (2021). Predictive policing and crime control in the United States of America and Europe: Trends in a decade of research and the future of predictive policing. *Social Sciences (Basel, Switzerland), 10*(6), 234. DOI: 10.3390/socsci10060234

Muir, R., & O'Connell, F. (2025). *Policing and Artificial Intelligence*. The Police Foundation.

Müller, N., Kawa, P., Choong, W.-H., Stan, A., Bukkapatnam, A. T., Pizzi, K., . . . Sperl, P. (2025). Replay attacks against audio deepfake detection. *arXiv preprint arXiv:2505.14862*. /arXiv.2505.14862.DOI: 10.21437/Interspeech.2025-20

Mundlamuri, R., Gunnam, G. R., Mysari, N. K., & Pujuri, J. (2025). The Evolution of AI: From Classical Machine Learning to Modern Large Language Models. *IEEE Access : Practical Innovations, Open Solutions, 13*, 178302–178341. DOI: 10.1109/ACCESS.2025.3621344

Murugan, T., Aldahmani, F. K. A. M., Almehrzi, G. S. M. A., Alsereidi, E. M. S. M., Aldahmani, A. A. K. A., & Alahbabi, E. M. M. (2024). Recent research study on ai-based crime scene evidence detection. 2024 7th International Conference on Advanced Communication Technologies and Networking (CommNet), 1–8. DOI: 10.1109/CommNet63022.2024.10793266

Naqa, I. E., & Murphy, M. J. (2015). What is machine learning? (I. E. Naqa, R. Li, & M. J. Murphy, Eds.). Machine Learning in Radiation Oncology: Theory and Applications, 3–11. DOI: 10.1007/978-3-319-18305-3 1

National Academies of Sciences, Engineering, and Medicine. (2024). *Facial recognition technology: Current capabilities, future prospects, and governance.*

National Audit Office. (2015). *Financial Sustainability of Police Forces in England and Wales.* https://www.nao.org.uk/reports/financial-sustainability-of-police-forces-in-england-and-wales/

National e-Governance Division. (2025, April 8). *Cyber Security Workshop iCAST-25.*

National e-Governance Division. (2025, May 20). *AI for Good Governance: Driving transparency, efficiency, and impact (Press Release).*

National Police Chiefs Council (NPCC) (2025). *National Policing Digital Strategy 2025-2030.*

National Police Chiefs Council (NPCC). (2025). *About Us.* https://www.npcc.police.uk/About-Us/about-us/

National Police Chiefs Council (NPCC). (2025). *Artificial Intelligence (AI) Playbook for Policing.* https://library.college.police.uk/docs/NPCC/Artificial-intelligence-playbook-policing-2025.pdf

National Police Chiefs' Council (NPCC). (2024). NPCC welcomes first ever lead for Artificial Intelligence (AI). https://news.npcc.police.uk/releases/npcc-welcomes-first-ever-lead-for-artificial-intelligence-ai

National Police Chiefs' Council. (2023). *Covenant for using artificial intelligence (AI) in policing.* https://science.police.uk/delivery/resources/covenant-for-using-artificial-intelligence-ai-in-policing/

National Research Council. (2004). *Biotechnology Research in an Age of Terrorism. Washington (DC).* National Academies Press.

NCSC. (2024). *NCSC Annual Review 2024.* National Cyber Security Centre.

NCSC. (2025). Impact of AI on Cyber Threat from Now to 2027. Retrieved from National Cyber Security Centre.: https://www.ncsc.gov.uk/report/impact-ai-cyber-threat-now-2027

NEC Software Solutions. (2024). Facial Recognition Software. https://www.necsws.com/solutions/evidence-insights/facial-recognition-software/

Nelis, J., Desmet, S., Wauters, J., Haelterman, R., Borgers, E., & Kun, D. (2018). Virtual crime scene. *2018 IEEE International Conference on Artificial Intelligence and Virtual Reality (AIVR)*, 165–168. DOI: 10.1109/AIVR.2018.00035

Nelu, C. (2024, June 10). International Centre for Counter-Terrorism. Retrieved from Exploitation of generative AI by terrorist groups.: https://icct.nl/publication/exploitation-generative-ai-terrorist-groups

Nespeca, V., Comes, T., & Brazier, F. (2023). A Methodology to Develop Agent-Based Models for Policy Support Via Qualitative Inquiry. *Journal of Artificial Societies and Social Simulation*, *26*(1), 10. DOI: 10.18564/jasss.5014

Nicolella, E. (2023). Evolving Privacy Protections for Emerging Machine Learning Data under Carpenter v. United States. *FIU L. Rev., 17*, 453.

Nussbaum, M. C. (2011). Creating capabilities: The human development approach. *Choice (Chicago, Ill.)*, *49*(02), 49–0784. DOI: 10.5860/CHOICE.49-0784

Ofoegbu, K. D. O., Osundare, O. S., Ike, C. S., Fakeyede, O. G., & Ige, A. B. (2024). Data-driven cyber threat intelligence: Leveraging behavioral analytics for proactive defense mechanisms.

Orozco, A. L. S. HuamaÅLn, C. Q., AÅL lvarez, D. P., & Villalba, L. J. G. (2020). A machine learning forensics technique to detect post-processing in digital videos. Future Generation Computer Systems, 111, 199–212. 10.1016/j.future.2020.04.041

Oswald, M., & Paul, A. (2024). Bias. Handbook of Digital Criminology (De Gruyter, 2024, Forthcoming). https://papers.ssrn.com/sol3/papers.cfm?abstract_id=4738337

Oswald, M., Paterson-Young, C., McBride, P., Maher, M., Calder, M., Gill, G., Tiarks, E., & Noble, W. (2024). Ethical review to support Responsible Artificial Intelligence (AI) in policing: A preliminary study of West Midlands Police's specialist data ethics review committee. Northumbria University Research Portal. https://researchportal.northumbria.ac.uk/en/publications/ethical-review-to-support-responsible-artificial-intelligence-ai-

Oyewole, G. J., & Thopil, G. A. (2023). Data clustering: Application and trends. *Artificial Intelligence Review*, *56*(7), 6439–6475. DOI: 10.1007/s10462-022-10325-y PMID: 36466764

P E Manjang v Uber Eats UK Ltd and others (2022). Employment Tribunal, 3206212/2021. https://assets.publishing.service.gov.uk/media/62dab66b8fa8f5649dbef494/Mr_P_E_Manjang_-v-_Uber_Eats_UK_Ltd___Others_-_3206212_2021_-_Preliminary_Judgment.pdf

Parliament, U. K. (2021). Police Powers: An Introduction. House of Commons Library. https://commonslibrary.parliament.uk/research-briefings/cbp-8637/

Partridge, J., & Zaghloul, F. (2025). Policing the data: Can data analytics help law enforcement? *Journal of Information Technology Teaching Cases*, *15*(1), 90–94. DOI: 10.1177/20438869231212214

Patrick, G., Mei, N., & Kayee, H. (2019). Face recognition vendor test (frvt) part 3: Demographic effects. *National Institute of Standards and Technology, Report NISTIR, 8280.*

Pech, R. J., & Slade, B. W. (2005). Imitative terrorism: A diagnostic framework for identifying catalysts and designing interventions. *Foresight*, *7*(1), 47–60. DOI: 10.1108/14636680510581312

Pei, Y. (2025). The Integration of Artificial Intelligence into Smart Policing Systems: Applications and Risk Governance. *Advances in Management and Intelligent Technologies*, *1*(4). Advance online publication. DOI: 10.62177/amit.v1i4.486

Pekepok, K., Kirkwood, P., Christopolous, E., Braithwaite, F., & Nightingale, O. (2025). Hierarchical pattern decryption methodology for ransomware detection using probabilistic cryptographic footprints.

Perry, W. L., McInnis, B., Price, C. C., Smith, S., & Hollywood, J. S. (2013). *Predictive policing: Forecasting crime for law enforcement*. RAND Corporation.

Pierdicca, R., Paolanti, M., Matrone, F., Martini, M., Morbidoni, C., Malinverni, E. S., Frontoni, E., & Lingua, A. M. (2020). Point cloud semantic segmentation using a deep learning framework for cultural heritage. *Remote Sensing (Basel)*, *12*(6), 1005. Advance online publication. DOI: 10.3390/rs12061005

Prakash, L. N. C. K., Ravva, S. K., Rathnamma, M. V., & Suryanarayana, G. (2023). AI applications of drones. In S. N. Mohanty, J. V. R. Ravindra, G. Surya Narayana, C. R. Pattnaik, & Y. Mohamed Sirajudeen (Eds.), *Drone technology*. DOI: 10.1002/9781394168002.ch7

Pramanik, A., Das, A. K., Pelusi, D., & Nayak, J. (2023a). An effective fuzzy clustering of crime reports embedded by a universal sentence encoder model. *Mathematics*, *11*(3), 611. DOI: 10.3390/math11030611

Pramanik, A., Das, A. K., Pelusi, D., & Nayak, J. (2023b). Crime pattern analysis using graph-based fuzzy clustering on heterogeneous crime data. *Expert Systems with Applications*, *213*, 119058. DOI: 10.1016/j.eswa.2022.119058

Pratt, T., Holtfreter, K., & Reisig, M. (2010). Routine online activity and Internet fraud targeting: Extending the generality of routine activity theory. *Journal of Research in Crime and Delinquency*, *47*(3), 267–296. DOI: 10.1177/0022427810365903

Press Trust of India. (2024). *HP: Ways to integrate AI in policing deliberated upon at northern regional police meeting*. The Print.

Pretty v United Kingdom (2002) 35 EHRR 1, 61

Pyrooz, D. C., Decker, S., & Moule, R. K. (2013). Criminal and routine activities in online settings: Gangs, offenders, and the Internet. *Justice Quarterly*, *30*(4), 1–30.

Qi, C. R., Su, H., Mo, K., & Guibas, L. J. (2016). Pointnet: Deep learning on point sets for 3d classification and segmentation. CoRR, abs/1612.00593. https://arxiv.org/abs/1612.00593

Qi, C. R., Yi, L., Su, H., & Guibas, L. J. (2017). Pointnet++: Deep hierarchical feature learning on point sets in a metric space. https://arxiv.org/abs/1706.02413

Qiu, Y. (2025). Policing AI-generated crimes: An ethnographic study on anti-cybercrime police in China. *Security Journal*, *38*(1), 34. DOI: 10.1057/s41284-025-00491-3

Qudrat-Ullah, H. (2025). *Navigating Complexity: AI and Systems Thinking for Smarter Decisions*. Springer. DOI: 10.1007/978-3-031-82742-6

R (on the application of Edward Bridges) v The Chief Constable of South Wales Police & Ors [2020] EWCA Civ 1058

R (Razgar) v Secretary of State for the Home Department [2004] 2 AC 368, 383, 9

R v Gough (1993). 2 WLR 883

Radiya-Dixit, E., & Neff, G. (2023). A sociotechnical audit: Assessing police use of facial recognition. *ACM Conference on Fairness, Accountability, and Transparency*, 1334–1346. https://doi.org/DOI: 10.1145/3593013.3594084

Raffaelli, R., Zuzul, T., Gulati, R., & Rivkin, J. (2025). Outcome and process frames: Strategic renewal and capability reprioritisation at the Federal Bureau of Investigation. *Strategic Management Journal*, *46*(6), 1325–1362. DOI: 10.1002/smj.3697

Raji, I., & Sholademi, D. (2024). Predictive Policing: The Role of AI in Crime Prevention. *International Journal of Computer Applications Technology and Research*, *13*(10), 66–78.

Ramesh Babu, B., Usha Rani, T., & Naga Kumari, Y. V. (2024). AI's Watchful Eye: Protecting Children from Sexual Abuse with Artificial Intelligence. In *Child Sexual Abuse: A Public Health Problem in India* (pp. 441–455). Springer Nature Singapore. DOI: 10.1007/978-981-99-8745-0_37

Raneri, D. (2018). Enhancing forensic investigation through the use of modern threed-imensional (3d) imaging technologies for crime scene reconstruction. *The Australian Journal of Forensic Sciences, 50*, 697–707. DOI: 10.1080/00450618.2018.1424245

Rani, S. (2025). Digital surveillance and predictive justice: Constitutional boundaries in AI-enabled law enforcement. *Civil Law Journal, 5*(2), 166. https://www.civillawjournal.com/archives/2025.v5.i2.C.166

Rani, M. (2024). Impacts and ethics of using Artificial Intelligence (AI) by the Indian Police. *Public Administration and Policy, 27*(2), 182–192. DOI: 10.1108/PAP-06-2023-0081

Rauch, L., & Braml, T. (2023). Semantic point cloud segmentation with deep-learningbased approaches for the construction industry: A survey. *Applied Sciences (Basel, Switzerland), 13*(16), 9146. Advance online publication. DOI: 10.3390/app13169146

Rautenberg, N., & Murray, D. (2024). Making tangible the Long-Term harm linked to the chilling effects of AI-enabled surveillance: Can human flourishing inform human rights? *Human Rights Review (Piscataway, N.J.), 25*(3), 293–315. DOI: 10.1007/s12142-024-00727-6

Rawat, R., & Kaushal, N. (2026, January 6). AI in terrorism: Emerging threats for state security. Retrieved from Observer Research Foundation (ORF): https://www.orfonline.org/expert-speak/ai-in-terrorism-emerging-threats-for-state-security

Regulation (EU) 2016/679 (2016) *General Data Protection Regulations (GDPR).*

Reiner, R. (2010). *The Politics of the Police* (4th ed.). Oxford University Press. DOI: 10.1093/he/9780199283392.001.0001

Reiser, D., Paraforos, D. S., Khan, M. T., Griepentrog, H. W., & Vazquez-Arellano, M. (2017). Autonomous field navigation, data acquisition and node location in wireless sensor networks. *Precision Agriculture, 18*(3), 279–292. DOI: 10.1007/s11119-016-9477-2

Ren, P., Zhou, M., Liu, J., Fan, Y., Zhao, W., & Shui, W. (2017). Sketch-based modeling and immersive display techniques for indoor crime scene presentation. Lecture Notes of the Institute for Computer Sciences. *Social-Informatics and Telecommunications Engineering, LNICST, 216*, 181–194. DOI: 10.1007/978-3-319-73697-6 14

Riccio, V., Jia, D., & Das, D. K. (Eds.). (2024). *Challenges of Contemporary Policing: Higher Education, Technology, and Officers' Well-Being*. Taylor & Francis., DOI: 10.4324/9781003452379

Richardson, R., Schultz, J., & Crawford, K. (2019). Dirty data, Bad predictions: How civil rights violations impact police data, predictive policing systems, and justice. New York University Law Review Online, 192

Richardson, R., Schultz, J. M., & Crawford, K. (2019). Dirty data, bad predictions: How civil rights violations impact police data, predictive policing systems, and justice. *NYUL Rev. Online*, *94*, 15.

Richmond, K. M., & Primeau, C. (2025). Ai in the criminal justice system: From 'ai ethics' to 'hermeneutic risk' [PMID: 41428648]. *Medicine, Science, and the Law*, *0*(0), 00258024251407531. DOI: 10.1177/00258024251407531

Rigano, C. (2019). Using artificial intelligence to address criminal justice needs. *National Institute of Justice Journal, 280*(1-10), 17.

Riley, B. K., & Dixon, A. (2024). Emotional and cognitive trust in artificial intelligence: A framework for identifying research opportunities. *Current Opinion in Psychology*, *58*, 101833. DOI: 10.1016/j.copsyc.2024.101833 PMID: 38991423

Rishad, S. S. I., Shakil, F., Tisha, S. A., Afrin, S., Hassan, M. M., Choudhury, M. Z. M. E., & Rahman, N. (2025). Leveraging AI and machine learning for predicting, detecting, and mitigating cybersecurity threats: a comparative study of advanced models. *Academic Reseach Library for International Journal of Computer Science & Information System, 10*(01), 06-25.

Roksandić, S., Protrka, N., & Engelhart, M. (2022, May). Trustworthy Artificial Intelligence and its use by Law Enforcement Authorities: where do we stand? In *2022 45th jubilee international convention on information, communication and electronic technology (MIPRO)* (pp. 1225-1232). IEEE. DOI: 10.23919/MIPRO55190.2022.9803606

Rossler, A., Cozzolino, D., Verdoliva, L., Riess, C., Thies, J., & Nießner, M. (2019). *Faceforensics++: Learning to detect manipulated facial images.* Paper presented at the Proceedings of the IEEE/CVF international conference on computer vision. DOI: 10.1109/ICCV.2019.00009

Ruhrmann, H. (2019). Facing the future: protecting human rights in policy strategies for facial recognition technology in law enforcement.

Ruijer, E., Dingelstad, J., & Meijer, A. (2021). Studying complex systems through design interventions Probing open government data ecosystems in the Netherlands. *Public Management Review*, •••, 1–21.

Safat, W., Asghar, S., & Gillani, S. A. (2021). Empirical analysis for crime prediction and forecasting using machine learning and deep learning techniques. *IEEE Access : Practical Innovations, Open Solutions*, *9*, 70080–70094. DOI: 10.1109/ACCESS.2021.3078117

Sagana, A., Zhang, M., & Sauerland, M. (2025). Public attitudes towards police use of AI-driven face recognition technology. *Computers in Human Behavior*, 108821.

Sager, M. A., Arshad, M., Ahmed, T., Abbas, S. S., & Khan, M. S. (2025). Enhancing Police Effectiveness in Punjab: Integrating Training and Capacity Building Initiatives for Sustainable Impact. *Journal of Social Sciences Review*, *5*(1), 526–537. DOI: 10.62843/jssr.v5i1.517

Sahu, N. K. (2022). DBSCAN & hierarchical clustering algorithm: Analysis cyber crime data. *International Journal of Multidisciplinary Education and Research*, *11*, 16–20.

Saini, I. S., & Kaur, N. (2023, July). The power of predictive analytics: forecasting crime trends in high-risk areas for crime prevention using machine learning. In *2023 14th International Conference on Computing Communication and Networking Technologies (ICCCNT)* (pp. 1-10). IEEE. DOI: 10.1109/ICCCNT56998.2023.10306731

Salem, A. H., Azzam, S. M., Emam, O. E., & Abohany, A. A. (2024). Advancing cybersecurity: A comprehensive review of AI-driven detection techniques. *Journal of Big Data*, *11*(105), 1–38. DOI: 10.1186/s40537-024-00957-y

Sandler, T., & Enders, W. (2004, June). An economic perspective on transnational terrorism. *European Journal of Political Economy*, *20*(2), 301–316. DOI: 10.1016/j.ejpoleco.2003.12.007

Sankin, A. (2024). *Senators Demand Justice Department Halt Funding to Predictive Policing Programs*. The Markup.

Sapirstein, P. (2016). Accurate measurement with photogrammetry at large sites. *Journal of Archaeological Science*, *66*, 137–145. 10.1016/j.jas.2016.01.002. DOI: 10.1016/j.jas.2016.01.002

Sarzaeim, P., Mahmoud, Q. H., Azim, A., Bauer, G., & Bowles, I. (2023). A systematic review of using machine learning and natural language processing in smart policing. *Computers*, *12*(12), 255. DOI: 10.3390/computers12120255

Saunders, J., Hunt, P., & Hollywood, J. S. (2016). Predictions put into practice: A quasi-experimental evaluation of Chicago's predictive policing pilot. *Journal of Experimental Criminology*, *12*(3), 347–371. DOI: 10.1007/s11292-016-9272-0

Schaefer, L., & Mazerolle, L. (2017). Putting process into routine activity theory. *Security Journal, 30*(1), 266–289. DOI: 10.1057/sj.2015.39

Schein, E. H. (2010). *Organizational culture and leadership* (4th ed.). Jossey-Bass.

Schiff, K. J., Schiff, D. S., Adams, I. T., McCrain, J., & Mourtgos, S. M. (2025). Institutional factors driving citizen perceptions of AI in government: Evidence from a survey experiment on policing. *Public Administration Review, 85*(2), 451–467. DOI: 10.1111/puar.13754

Schildkraut, P. J., Kim, J. W., Marotta, M., Courtney Jr, J. V., & Waters, P. J. (2023). The Blueprint for an" AI Bill of Rights". *The Journal of Robotics, Artificial Intelligence & Law, 6*.

Schmitt, M., & Flechais, I. (2024). Digital deception: Generative artificial intelligence in social engineering and phishing. *Artificial Intelligence Review, 57*(12), 1–18. DOI: 10.1007/s10462-024-10973-2

Schuckers, M. E. (2010). False Non-Match Rate. In *Computational Methods in Biometric Authentication: Statistical Methods for Performance Evaluation* (pp. 47–96). Springer London. DOI: 10.1007/978-1-84996-202-5_3

Shah, N., Bhagat, N., & Shah, M. (2021). Crime forecasting: A machine learning and computer vision approach to crime prediction and prevention. *Visual Computing for Industry, Biomedicine, and Art, 4*(1), 9. DOI: 10.1186/s42492-021-00075-z PMID: 33913057

Shapiro, A. (2023). Optimizing the immeasurable: On the techno-ethical limits of predictive policing. In *Artificial intelligence and the city* (pp. 240–257). Routledge., DOI: 10.4324/9781003365877-18

Shaw, M. S., Toliver, S. R., & Tanksley, T. (2024). The internet does not exist in the sky: Literacy, AI, and the digital middle passage. *Reading Research Quarterly, 59*(4), 690–705. DOI: 10.1002/rrq.537

Sherman, L., Neyroud, P. W., & Neyroud, E. (2016). The Cambridge Crime Harm Index: Measuring total harm from crime based on sentencing guidelines. Policing. *Journal of Policy Practice, 10*(3), 171–183.

Sheshtar, F. M., Alhatlani, W. M., Moulden, M., & Kim, J. H. (2025). Comparative analysis of lidar and photogrammetry for 3d crime scene reconstruction. *Applied Sciences (Basel, Switzerland), 15*(3), 1085. Advance online publication. DOI: 10.3390/app15031085

Shiohara, K., & Yamasaki, T. (2022). *Detecting deepfakes with self-blended images.* Paper presented at the Proceedings of the IEEE/CVF conference on computer vision and pattern recognition. DOI: 10.1109/CVPR52688.2022.01816

Shi, X., Xing, F., Cai, J., Zhang, Z., Xie, Y., & Yang, L. (2016). Kernel-based supervised discrete hashing for image retrieval. In Leibe, B., Matas, J., Sebe, N., & Welling, M. (Eds.), *Computer vision – eccv 2016* (pp. 419–433). Springer International Publishing. DOI: 10.1007/978-3-319-46478-7_26

Sieberth, T., Wackrow, R., Hofer, V., & Barrera, V. (2018). Light field camera as tool for forensic photogrammetry. International Archives of the Photogrammetry, Remote Sensing and Spatial Information Sciences - ISPRS Archives, 42, 393–399. DOI: 10.5194/isprs-archives-XLII-1-393-2018

Simon, H. (1996). *The Sciences of the Artificial.* MIT Press.

Singh, S., & Mohapatra, H. (2025). AI ethics, governance and privacy in a rapidly advancing digital world. *Systemic Analytics, 3*(2), 135–151. https://www.sa-journal.org/index.php/systemic/article/view/49

Singh, T. M., Kumar, R. C. K., Munawar, M., Lippert, K., & Doss, S. Securing the Metaverse: AI and machine learning approaches to threat detection and prevention *Defending the Metaverse* (pp. 144-170): CRC Press. .DOI: 10.33009/FSU_2a4dc970-2d4b-4b41-8611-80c464fb6462

Singh, M., Jain, S., & Khan, L. (2025). *Fake video detection Emerging Trends in Computer Science and Its Application.* CRC Press., DOI: 10.33009/FSU_caf24cdb-69d0-4b9e-a08c-118aca59b212

Singh, P. (2025). Mass surveillance in the age of AI: The Indian dilemma of security versus privacy. *International Journal of Civil Law and Legal Research, 5*(2), 74–78. https://www.civillawjournal.com/archives/2025.v5.i2.A.146. DOI: 10.22271/civillaw.2025.v5.i2a.146

Sir William Macpherson of Cluny. (1999). The Stephen Lawrence Inquiry Report of an Inquiry https://assets.publishing.service.gov.uk/media/5a7c2af540f0b645ba3c7202/4262.pdf

Snowden, D. J., & Boone, M. E. (2007). A leader's framework for decision making. *Harvard Business Review, 85*, 68. PMID: 18159787

Sohail, A., & Zhang, L. (2025). Using large language models to facilitate academic work in the psychological sciences. *Current Psychology (New Brunswick, N.J.), 44*(9), 7910–7918. DOI: 10.1007/s12144-025-07438-2 PMID: 40438548

Solove, D. J. (2007). The First Amendment as criminal procedure. SSRN Electronic Journal. https://scholarship.law.gwu.edu/faculty_publications/946

Southerland, V. M. (2023). The Master's Tool and a Mission: Using Community Control and Oversight Laws to Resist and Abolish Police Surveillance Technologies. *UCLA Law Review. University of California, Los Angeles. School of Law*, *70*, 2.

Springs, D. (2024). Smart city planning focused on the US cities in need of policing innovations and public health safety technologies and strategies. *Health Economics and Management Review*, *5*(1), 117–128. DOI: 10.61093/hem.2024.1-09

Steventon, M. (2025). Policing in Practice. In *Understanding Policing and Professional Practice* (pp. 123–140). Routledge., DOI: 10.4324/9781041057758-10

Sun, W., & Li, Y. (2025). Emotion Recognition in Consumer Electronics Using Multimodal Deep Learning. *IEEE Transactions on Consumer Electronics*, *71*(3), 7636–7650. Advance online publication. DOI: 10.1109/TCE.2025.3568882

Supreme Court of India. (2017). *K.S. Puttaswamy (Retd.) v. Union of India,* (2017) 10 SCC 1, AIR 2017 SC 4161.

Svet, L., Brightwell, A., Wildflower, A., & Marshwood, C. (2025). Unveiling zero-space detection: A novel framework for autonomous ransomware identification in high-velocity environments. *arXiv preprint arXiv:2501.12811.*

Swaminathan, N., & Danks, D. (2024). Application of the NIST AI risk management framework to surveillance technology. *arXiv preprint arXiv:2403.15646.*

Syed, S., & Albalawi, E. M. (2024). Transforming Law Enforcement: Exploiting Big Data Science and Data Analytics for Precision Decision-Making and Crime Pattern Anticipation in Police Operations. DOI: 10.21203/rs.3.rs-4677394/v1

Tabi, C., Hewage, C., Bakhsh, S. T., & Ukwandu, E. (2023). Contemporary issues in child protection: police use of artificial intelligence for online child protection in the UK. In *Digital Transformation in Policing: The Promise, Perils and Solutions* (pp. 85–107). Springer International Publishing., DOI: 10.1007/978-3-031-09691-4_5

Taddeo, M., McCutcheon, T., & Floridi, L. (2021, April 30). Trusting Artificial Intelligence in Cybersecurity, a Double-Edged Sword. *SSRN*, 1-12. DOI: 10.1007/978-3-030-81907-1_15

Tang, X. (2024). Innovative Paradigms in Policing: A Quantitative Study of Technology, Training, and Community Engagement in China. *European Journal on Criminal Policy and Research*, •••, 1–29. DOI: 10.1007/s10610-024-09608-7

Tareq, M., Sundararajan, E. A., Harwood, A., & Bakar, A. A. (2021). A systematic review of density grid-based clustering for data streams. *IEEE Access : Practical Innovations, Open Solutions*, *10*, 579–596. DOI: 10.1109/ACCESS.2021.3134704

Tariq, M. U. (2025). The role of AI-powered learning analytics in enhancing student engagement and performance. In J. Moore, S. Gupta, M. Sharma, A. Garg, & H. Josephine V. L. (Eds.), *Transforming education with data science in the AI era* (pp. 123–148). IGI Global Scientific Publishing. DOI: 10.4018/979-8-3373-2185-1.ch005

Tariq, M. U. (2025). Innovation and agility: Adapting business strategies for sustainable growth in dynamic markets. In Ananthan, S., Kohli, A., Manickam, T., & Dhanabalan, T. (Eds.), *New business development strategies for achieving sustainable growth* (pp. 113–140). IGI Global Scientific Publishing. DOI: 10.4018/979-8-3373-2048-9.ch005

Tariq, M. U. (2025). Integration of artificial intelligence and machine learning in business intelligence: Enhancing decision making and operational efficiency. In Ishtaiwi, A., Al-Qerem, A., Al Khaldy, M., & Alauthman, M. (Eds.), *Driving modern business intelligence architecture for operational efficiency* (pp. 279–306). IGI Global Scientific Publishing. DOI: 10.4018/979-8-3373-2125-7.ch009

Taylor, R. B. (2015). *Community criminology: Fundamentals of spatial and temporal scaling, ecological indicators, and selectivity bias*. NYU Press. DOI: 10.18574/nyu/9780814724187.001.0001

Teece, D. J. (2022). A wider-aperture lens for global strategic management: The multinational enterprise in a bifurcated global economy. *Global Strategy Journal*, *12*(3), 488–519. DOI: 10.1002/gsj.1462

The Office of the Police Chief Scientific Adviser (OPCSA). (n.d.). Science and Technology in Policing. Covenant for using Artificial intelligence (AI) in policing. https://science.police.uk/delivery/resources/covenant-for-using-artificial-intelligence-ai-in-policing/#:~:text=This%20Covenant%20outlines%20a%20set,Council%20on%2028%20September%202023

The white mask. (2024). The Guardian. https://www.theguardian.com/technology/audio/2024/mar/18/episode-5-the-white-mask

Tiwari, A., Dave, R., & Vanamala, M. (2023). *Leveraging deep learning approaches for deepfake detection: A review.* Paper presented at the Proceedings of the 2023 7th international conference on intelligent systems, metaheuristics & swarm intelligence. DOI: 10.1145/3596947.3596959

Togelius, J. (2024). *Artificial General Intelligence*. MIT Press. DOI: 10.7551/mitpress/15378.001.0001

Tolosana, R., Vera-Rodriguez, R., Fierrez, J., Morales, A., & Ortega-Garcia, J. (2020). Deepfakes and beyond: A survey of face manipulation and fake detection. *Information Fusion*, *64*, 131–148. DOI: 10.1016/j.inffus.2020.06.014

Toros, H., & Gunning, J. (2009). Exploring a critical theory approach to terrorism studies. In Jackson, R., Smyth, M. B., & Gunning, J. (Eds.), *Critical Terrorism Studies: A New Research Agenda* (pp. 87–108). Routledge.

Torrible, C. N. (2022). Trust in the police and policing by consent in turbulent times. *Safer Communities*, *21-3*(3), 171–183. DOI: 10.1108/SC-08-2021-0036

Torsu, L. A. (2024). Crime prevention in the digital age: Challenges and technologies for policing in Aflao border township in Ghana. *The Police Journal*, 0032258X241309190. DOI: 10.1177/0032258X241309190

Tracol, X. (2025). The Use of Facial Recognition Technologies by Law Enforcement Authorities in the US and the EU: Towards a Convergence on Regulation? *Technology and Regulation*, *2025*, 289–315.

Treasury Board of Canada Secretariat. (2019). *Directive on automated decision-making*. Government of Canada.

Tredinnick, R., Smith, S., & Ponto, K. (2019). A cost-benefit analysis of 3d scanning technology for crime scene investigation. *Forensic Science International. Reports*, *1*, 100025. DOI: 10.1016/j.fsir.2019.100025

Treleaven, P., Barnett, J., Brown, D., Bud, A., Fenoglio, E., Kerrigan, C., & Schoernig, M. (2023). The future of Cybercrime AI and Emerging Technologies are creating a Cybercrime tsunami. *SSRN*, 1-34. DOI: 10.2139/ssrn.4507244

Tsabedze, L. T., Akinnuwesi, B. A., Dlamini, B., Mbunge, E., Fashoto, S. G., Olabanjo, O., Mashwama, P., Metfula, A. S., Nxumalo, M., Badeji-Ajisafe, B., & Egenti, G. (2025). Enhancing public safety in Eswatini: A machine learning–driven predictive policing model. *Human Behavior and Emerging Technologies*, *9939274*(1), 9939274. Advance online publication. DOI: 10.1155/hbe2/9939274

Tsai, C.-Y., Nisar, H., & Hu, Y.-C. (2021). Mapless lidar navigation control of wheeled mobile robots based on deep imitation learning. *IEEE Access : Practical Innovations, Open Solutions*, *9*, 117527–117541. DOI: 10.1109/ACCESS.2021.3107041

Tulinov, V. S., Bilykh, I. V., Merdova, O. M., Volobuieva, O. O., & Veselov, M. Y. (2022). Activities of Law Enforcement Agencies in the Context of the Introduction of Innovative Technologies (Comparative Legal Aspect). *Cuestiones Políticas*, *40*(72), 145–163. Advance online publication. DOI: 10.46398/cuestpol.4072.08

Tulumello, S., & Iapaolo, F. (2022). Policing the future, disrupting urban policy today: Predictive policing, smart city, and urban policy in Memphis (TN). *Urban Geography*, *43*(3), 448–469. DOI: 10.1080/02723638.2021.1887634

Turing, A. (2004). Computing Machinery and Intelligence (1950). In B. Jack Copeland (Ed.), The Essential Turing Seminal Writings in Computing, Logic, Philosophy, Artificial Intelligence United Nations. (2024). Practical toolkit for law enforcement officials to promote and protect human rights in the context of peaceful protests. https://www.ohchr.org/en/documents/tools-and-resources/practical-toolkit-law-enforcement-officials-promote-and-protect-human

Ugwudike, P. (2023). Algorithms, policing, and race. *The Routledge International Handbook on Decolonizing Justice*, 146.

UK Court of Appeal. (2020). *R (Bridges) v. Chief Constable of South Wales Police & Others,* EWCA Civ 1058.

UKAuthority News. (2025). *New Data Act for UK receives Royal assent.* https://www.ukauthority.com/articles/new-data-act-for-uk-receives-royal-assent

Umanah, E. A., Willie, C. E., & Daniel, U. S. (2024). Implications of Emerging Technologies on Social Behaviour and Crime Control in the 21st Century. *Journal of Advanced Research and Multidisciplinary Studies*, *4*(3), 152–162. DOI: 10.52589/JARMS-JL2NFQ57

UNICRI, & UNCCT. (2021). UNICRI, & UNCCT. (2021). Algorithms and terrorism: The malicious use of artificial intelligence for terrorist purposes. United Nations Interregional Crime and Justice Research Institute & United Nations Office of Counter-Terrorism. Retrieved from UNICRI: https://unicri.org/News/Algorithms-Terrorism-UNICRI-UNOCCT

UNISON. (2025). *Police Force Shortfalls 2025/26.* https://www.unison.org.uk/at-work/police-and-justice-staff/key-issues/police-force-shortfalls-2025-26/

United Nations General Assembly. (1948). Universal declaration of human rights, Article 19. (General Assembly Resolution 217A). https://www.un.org/en/about-us/universal-declaration-of-human-rights

Urschler, M., Holler, J., Bornik, A., Paul, T., Giretzlehner, M., Bischof, H., Yen, K., & Scheurer, E. (2014). Intuitive presentation of clinical forensic data using anonymous and person-specific 3d reference manikins. *Forensic Science International, 241*, 155–166. DOI: 10.1016/j.forsciint.2014.05.017 PMID: 24952238

Vakhitova, Z. I. (2025, January 22). Cyber-Routine Activity Theory. Oxford Research Encyclopedia of Criminology.

Van Brakel, R. (2025). Pre-emptive big data surveillance and its (dis) empowering consequences: The case of predictive policing. In *Exploring the boundaries of big data* (pp. 117–142). Routledge. DOI: 10.4324/9781003695202-7

Van Den Anker, R. K. S. C. (2005). The essentials of human rights. CiNii Books. https://ci.nii.ac.jp/ncid/BA75808387

Vegesna, V. V., & Adepu, A. (2024). Leveraging artificial intelligence for predictive cyber threat intelligence. *International Journal of Creative Research in Computer Technology and Design, 6*(6), 1–19.

Verdoliva, L. (2020). Media forensics and deepfakes: An overview. *IEEE Journal of Selected Topics in Signal Processing, 14*(5), 910–932. DOI: 10.1109/JSTSP.2020.3002101

Victoroff, J., & Kruglanski, A. (Eds.). (2009). *Psychology of Terrorism: Classic and Contemporary Insights*. Psychology Press.

Villa, C., Lynnerup, N., & Jacobsen, C. (2023). A virtual, 3d multimodal approach to victim and crime scene reconstruction. *Diagnostics (Basel), 13*(17), 2764. Advance online publication. DOI: 10.3390/diagnostics13172764 PMID: 37685302

Vohra, M. (2023). *Digital Twin Technology: Fundamentals and Applications*. Wiley-Scrivener publishers.

Von Hannover v Germany (2004) 40 EHRR 23

Wachter, S., & Mittelstadt, B. (2018). A Right to Reasonable Inferences: Re-Thinking Data Protection Law in the Age of Big Data and AI. Columbia Business Law Review, 2019(2). https://papers.ssrn.com/sol3/papers.cfm?abstract_id=3248829

Wachter, S., Mittelstadt, S., & Russell, C. (2017). Counterfactual explanations without opening the black box: automated decisions and the GDPR. SSRN Electronic Journal, 844. https://doi.org/DOI: 10.2139/ssrn.3063289

Wall, D. (2007). *Cybercrime: The Transformation of Crime in the Information Age*. Polity Press.

Walley, P., & Glasspoole-Bird, H. (2025). *An Evaluation of the Pilot Application of Artificial Intelligence to Witness Statement and Report Generation at Hertfordshire Constabulary*. Open University Centre for Policing Research & Learning Publication.

Wang, J., Li, Z., Hu, W., Shao, Y., Wang, L., Wu, R., Ma, K., Zou, D., & Chen, Y. (2019). Virtual reality and integrated crime scene scanning for immersive and heterogeneous crime scene reconstruction. *Forensic Science International*, *303*, 109943. Advance online publication. DOI: 10.1016/j.forsciint.2019.109943 PMID: 31546165

Wang, J., Wang, C., Fu, L., Wang, Q., Fu, G., Lu, C., Feng, J., Cong, B., & Li, S. (2020). Circular rna as a potential biomarker for forensic age prediction using multiple machine learning models: A preliminary study. *bioRxiv*, 2020.11.DOI: 10.376418. 10.1101/2020.11.10.376418

Wang, Q., Tan, Y., & Mei, Z. (2020). Computational methods of acquisition and processing of 3d point cloud data for construction applications. *Archives of Computational Methods in Engineering*, *27*(2), 479–499. DOI: 10.1007/s11831-019-09320-4

Wang, S., Zhang, H., Yang, G., Guo, Z., & Chen, J. (2024). A two-stage fake face image detection algorithm with expanded attention. *Multimedia Tools and Applications*, *83*(18), 55709–55730. DOI: 10.1007/s11042-023-17672-0

Wang, Y., Sun, Y., Liu, Z., Sarma, S., Bronstein, M., & Solomon, J. (2018). Dynamic graph CNN for learning on point clouds. CoRR, abs/1801.07829. https://arxiv.org/abs/1801.07829

Warren, S. D., & Brandeis, L. D. (1890). The right to privacy. *Harvard Law Review*, *4*(5), 193. DOI: 10.2307/1321160

Wasil, A. R., Grinbaum, A., & Adomaitis, L. (2024, October 7). Governing dual-use technologies: Case studies of international security agreements and lessons for AI governance (SSRN Working Paper). Retrieved from SSRN: https://papers.ssrn.com/sol3/papers.cfm?abstract_id=4946527&mirid=1 DOI: 10.2139/ssrn.4946527

Weimann, G., Winter, C., Köhler, D., & Brzuszkiewicz, S. (2024). Generating terror: The risks of generative AI exploitation. *CTC Sentinel*, *17*(1), 17–24.

Weisburd, D. L., Groff, E. R., & Yang, S.-M. (2013). *The Criminology of Place: Street Segments and Our Understanding of the Crime Problem*. Oxford University Press.

Wenger, A., & Cavelty, M. D. (2022). The ambiguity of cyber security politics in the context of multidimensional uncertainty. In Wenger, A., & Cavelty, M. D. (Eds.), *Cyber Security Politics*. Routledge.

Wheeler, A. P. (2020). Allocating police resources while limiting racial inequality. *Justice Quarterly*, *37*(5), 842–868. DOI: 10.1080/07418825.2019.1630471

William, P., Shrivastava, A., Shunmuga Karpagam, N., Mohanaprakash, T. A., Tongkachok, K., & Kumar, K. (2023). Crime analysis using computer vision approach with machine learning. In *Mobile Radio Communications and 5G Networks: Proceedings of Third MRCN 2022* (pp. 297-315). Singapore: Springer Nature Singapore. DOI: 10.1007/978-981-19-7982-8_25

Williams, M. L. (2016). Guardians Upon High: An Application of Routine Activities Theory to Online Identity Theft in Europe at the Country and Individual Level. *British Journal of Criminology*, *56*(1), 21–48. DOI: 10.1093/bjc/azv011

Wilson, C., Dalins, J., & Rolan, G. (2020) *Effective, Explainable and Ethical: AI for Law Enforcement and Community Safety.* 2020 IEEE / ITU International Conference on Artificial Intelligence for Good (AI4G), 2020, p.186-191 DOI: 10.1109/AI4G50087.2020.9311021

Winston, A. (2018). Palantir has secretly been using New Orleans to test its predictive policing technology. *The Verge, 27.*

Wirtz, B., Wyerer, J., & Geyer, C. (2019). Artificial Intelligence and the Public Sector – Applications and Challenges. *International Journal of Public Administration*, *42*(7), 595–615. DOI: 10.1080/01900692.2018.1498103

Wu, Y., & Meghanathan, N. (2023). A principal component analysis-based scoring mechanism to quantify crime hot spots in a city. In International Conference on Information Technology—New Generations (pp. 45–51). Springer. DOI: 10.1007/978-3-031-28332-1_6

Wu, D., Liang, Z., & Chen, G. (2022). Deep learning for lidar-only and lidar-fusion 3d perception: A survey. *Intelligence Robotics*, *2*(2), 105–129. Advance online publication. DOI: 10.20517/ir.2021.20

Xie, Y., Shekhar, S., & Li, Y. (2022). Statistically-robust clustering techniques for mapping spatial hotspots: A survey. *ACM Computing Surveys*, *55*(2), 1–38. DOI: 10.1145/3487893

Yamin, M. M., Ullah, M., Ullah, H., & Katt, B. (2021). Weaponized AI for cyber attacks. *Journal of Information Security and Applications*, *57*, 1–35. DOI: 10.1016/j.jisa.2020.102722

Yang, J., Sun, Y., Mao, M., Bai, L., Zhang, S., & Wang, F. (2023). Model-agnostic method: Exposing deepfake using pixel-wise spatial and temporal fingerprints. *IEEE Transactions on Big Data*, *9*(6), 1496–1509. DOI: 10.1109/TBDATA.2023.3284272

Yar, M. (2005). The novelty of "cybercrime": An assessment in light of routine activity theory. *European Journal of Criminology, 2*(4), 407–427. DOI: 10.1177/147737080556056

Yavorsky, M. A., & Mikheeva, S. V. (2022, April). The Use of Artificial Intelligence Technologies and Big Data in Law Enforcement. In *Proceedings of the International Conference Engineering Innovations and Sustainable Development* (pp. 669-675). Cham: Springer International Publishing. DOI: 10.1007/978-3-030-90843-0_76

Yen, C. P., & Hung, T. W. (2021). Achieving equity with predictive policing algorithms: A social safety net perspective. *Science and Engineering Ethics, 27*(3), 36. DOI: 10.1007/s11948-021-00312-x PMID: 34075448

Yeung, K. (2018). A study of the implications of advanced digital Technologies (Including AI Systems) for the concept of responsibility within a human rights framework. SSRN Electronic Journal. https://papers.ssrn.com/sol3/Delivery.cfm/SSRN_ID3286027_code830937.pdf?abstractid=3286027&mirid=1

Yeung, K., Howes, A., & Pogrebna, G. (2019). AI Governance by Human Rights-Centred Design, Deliberation and Oversight: An end to ethics washing. SSRN Electronic Journal. DOI: 10.2139/ssrn.3435011

Yuan, W., & Gao, K.-X. (2020). EAdam optimizer: How $\epsilon $ impact adam. *arXiv preprint arXiv:2011.02150.* /arXiv.2011.02150.DOI: 10.48550

Yu, S., & Carroll, F. (2022). Insights into the next generation of policing: understanding the impact of technology on the police force in the digital age. In *Artificial Intelligence and National Security* (pp. 169–191). Springer International Publishing., DOI: 10.1007/978-3-031-06709-9_9

Zagaynov, M. R. (2025). Interpol Activities and Artificial Intelligence Issues. *Sociopolitical Sciences, 15*(3), 93–99. DOI: 10.33693/2223-0092-2025-15-3-93-99

Zancajo-Blazquez, S., Gonzalez-Aguilera, D., Gonzalez-Jorge, H., & Hernandez-Lopez, D. (2015). An automatic image-based modelling method applied to forensic infography. *PLoS One, 10*(3), e0118719. Advance online publication. DOI: 10.1371/journal.pone.0118719 PMID: 25793628

Zeba, S., & Amjad, M. (2025). Identification and location monitoring through Live video Streaming by using blockchain. *Multimedia Tools and Applications, 84*(24), 27549–27576. DOI: 10.1007/s11042-024-20197-9

Zhang, C., Huang, W., Niu, T., Liu, Z., Li, G., & Cao, D. (2023). Review of clustering technology and its application in coordinating vehicle subsystems. *Automotive Innovation, 6*(1), 89–115. DOI: 10.1007/s42154-022-00205-0

Zhang, K., Zhang, A., Wang, X., & Li, W. (2024). Deep-learning-based point cloud completion methods: A review. *Graphical Models*, *136*, 101233. 10.1016/j.gmod.2024.101233. DOI: 10.1016/j.gmod.2024.101233

Zhang, R., Wu, Y., Jin, W., & Meng, X. (2023). Deep-learning-based point cloud semantic segmentation: A survey. *Electronics (Basel)*, *12*(17), 3642. Advance online publication. DOI: 10.3390/electronics12173642

Zhang, Y., Pang, Z., Huang, S., Wang, C., & Zhou, X. (2025). Unmasking AI-created visual content: A review of generated images and deepfake detection technologies. *Journal of King Saud University. Computer and Information Sciences*, *37*(6), 148. DOI: 10.1007/s44443-025-00154-8

Zhao, J., Xu, H., Wu, J., Zheng, Y., & Liu, H. (2019). Trajectory tracking and prediction of pedestrian's crossing intention using roadside lidar. IET Intelligent Transport Systems, 13(5), 789–795. 10.1049/ietits. 2018.5258

Zhou, Y., & Qian, H. (2024). Real-time object detection method with single-domain generalization based on yolov8. *Journal of Real-Time Image Processing*, *21*(6), 191. DOI: 10.1007/s11554-024-01572-z

Zocholl, M., Stampouli, D., Wittfoth, M., & Mounier, G. (2025). Fundamental considerations for the use of explainable AI in law enforcement. *Frontiers in Political Science*, *7*, 1605619. DOI: 10.3389/fpos.2025.1605619

Zubanska, M. (2018). Improvement of crime scene examination and reduction of cognitive deficit – the need to implement a newimaging and dimensioning technique. Issues of Forensic Science, 302, 54–62. DOI: 10.34836/pk.2018.302.3

Zubaroğlu, A., & Atalay, V. (2021). Data stream clustering: A review. *Artificial Intelligence Review*, *54*(2), 1201–1236. DOI: 10.1007/s10462-020-09874-x

Zuwanda, Z. S., Lubis, A. F., Solapari, N., Sakmaf, M. S., & Triyantoro, A. (2024). Ethical and Legal Analysis of Artificial Intelligence Systems in Law Enforcement with a Study of Potential Human Rights Violations in Indonesia. *The Easta Journal Law and Human Rights*, *2*(03), 176–185. DOI: 10.58812/eslhr.v2i03.283

About the Contributors

Eric Halford brings over 20 years of experience in UK policing, having served as a senior detective leading investigations into organised crime, terrorism, and major crime. Across his policing career, he received multiple commendations for leadership and investigative success. He is currently an Associate Researcher at Rabdan Academy in the United Arab Emirates, where he also serves as Lead Researcher for Policing and Security. In this role, he oversees research and programme evaluation across a broad range of policing, crime, and security themes. Since entering academia, he has developed a substantial international research profile, authoring nearly 50 Q1 Scopus-indexed publications and receiving multiple commendations for research excellence. He also holds several senior editorial roles in academic journals relating to forensic practice, criminology, and criminal justice. He holds degrees in Terrorism and Security Studies and in Forensics and Applied Science, and is regularly invited to advise government bodies in both the United Kingdom and the Middle East on matters relating to policing and security. His research spans a diverse portfolio of contemporary policing and security issues. He is internationally recognised for his work on the impact of pandemics on policing and has published extensively in this field. In 2023, he secured funding to evaluate the Abu Dhabi Police Virtual Reality Training Centre, leading an international research team that produced a series of studies on the use of virtual reality in policing. He has also developed a significant body of work in criminal investigation, crime prevention, and missing persons research. More recently, Dr Halford published Building an Outstanding Police Service: Understanding the Police Effectiveness, Efficiency, and Legitimacy (PEEL) Inspection Framework, a book that supports practitioners and scholars in understanding what is required to build a contemporary police service. He is also highly active in the field of artificial intelligence in policing and security. His work in this area includes publications on AI in police intelligence analysis and the detection of money laundering. In 2023, he introduced the Transformer-Led Policing (TLP) Model, the first strategic framework designed to support the practical adoption of AI in law enforcement. Underpinned by the TLP Matrix, the model provides agencies with a structured approach to implementing and evaluating AI technologies in practice. He also maintains a strong research interest in geographical and criminological profiling, contributing to a greater understanding of serial offender behaviour and crime prevention strategies.

***

Oluwasola Mary Adedayo received her Ph.D. degree in computer science from the University of Pretoria, South Africa, in 2015. She is currently an Assistant Professor at The University of Winnipeg, Manitoba, Canada. Her research interests include databases, database forensics, digital forensics, cybersecurity, privacy, and technology in society. She is a member of the Canadian Society of Forensic Science and the American Academy of Forensic Sciences.

Ashraf Alam currently holds the position of Research Faculty at the Centre of Excellence in Public Policy, Sustainability and ESG Research, housed within the Faculty of Law and Policy Studies at Alliance University, Bangalore. Renowned for his transdisciplinary acumen spanning education, technology, and policy studies, Dr. Ashraf has been distinguished as one of the World's Top 2% Scientists by Stanford University and Elsevier, an accolade that highlights the breadth and depth of his scholarly impact. His prolific academic output includes over fifty SCOPUS-indexed publications and more than one hundred conference presentations at esteemed national and international academic forums. His educational trajectory reflects both depth and versatility: a Ph.D. in Education from the Indian Institute of Technology (IIT) Kharagpur, an M.Ed. with a concentration in Mathematics Education, and a B.S. in Computer Science from the University of Delhi. He also holds postgraduate degrees in Public Administration (M.A.) and Mathematics (M.Sc.), supplemented by a suite of postgraduate diplomas in Higher Education, Guidance and Counselling, Educational Technology, Criminology and Police Administration, and Value Education. Dr. Ashraf is an active participant in global scholarly discourse. As Associate Editor of Frontiers in Education, he plays a pivotal role in curating and guiding intellectual contributions across the Educational, Pedagogical, and Learning Sciences. Concurrently, he serves as Founder and Director of Academic Chronicles Private Limited, where he orchestrates editorial board formation and develops strategic frameworks for peer-reviewed publishing in the Social, Behavioural, and Humanistic Sciences. His research has been disseminated through elite academic platforms, including Elsevier, Springer, Taylor & Francis, Wiley, Routledge, Sage, Emerald, and IEEE, and addresses a remarkably diverse array of topics such as pedagogical theories, educational administration, educational psychology, educational sociology, educational policy, technology-integrated learning, mathematics education, educational philosophy, educational technology, teacher education, and AI/ML in learning environments. Dr. Ashraf's scholarly rigor is further demonstrated by his success in qualifying multiple prestigious examinations including UGC-NET-JRF in both Education and Adult and Continuing Education, UGC- NET in Public Administration, and GATE in Humanities and Social Sciences. At the heart of Dr. Ashraf's intellectual ethos lies a steadfast belief in education as a catalytic and emancipatory force capable of engendering social justice, human flourishing, societal progress, and sustainable transformation. His recent explorations into 'Happiness Engineering' and holistic well- being in school ecosystems articulate a vision of education that transcends instrumentalist paradigms, prioritizing emotional intelligence, global consciousness, empathy, and psychosocial resilience among learners. His research agenda seeks to conceive educational praxis through the affordances of inclusive digital learning, gamified instructional design, and artificial intelligence (AIEd), thereby constructing robust, ethically grounded frameworks for 21st century education. At Alliance University, Dr. Ashraf remains committed to architecting pedagogical models that not only cultivate intellectual dexterity and cognitive excellence but also prepare learners for morally responsive leadership, intellectual nimbleness, and responsible global citizenship in an increasingly volatile, uncertain, complex, and ambiguous (VUCA) world.

Angelo Brown received his master's at Arizona State University and his Ph.D. Criminal Justice and Criminology at Washington State University. His research and teaching in criminal justice and criminology are primarily on policy and policing from a comparative and intersectional perspective.

Phil Davies is a senior UK police officer and the current police lead for the National Data Integration & Exploitation Service. He is the Vice-Chair of the Open University Centre for Policing Research & Learning, and a Visiting Fellow. His doctorate explored the application of complexity theory in UK policing operating model design. Phil has significant experience in police leadership, specialist operations, firearms and public order command, and change management. As programme director he has delivered several high-profile digital transformations for Greater Manchester Police, and he volunteers as the Data Foundations lead for the UK National Data & Analytics Office on behalf of the National Police Chief's Council.

Omowunmi Isafiade is an associate professor and NRF-Y-rated researcher in Computer Science at the University of the Western Cape (UWC), South Africa.

She received both MSc and PhD degrees in Computer Science from the University of Cape Town (UCT), South Africa, and another master's level (PGDip) degree in Mathematical Sciences from the African Institute for Mathematical Sciences (AIMS), South Africa (Cum Laude. She is a research leader and well-published scientist in her research field with many years of collaborative research and supervision experience. Her excellent work has garnered her considerable local and international recognition, obtaining numerous notable recognitions and awards such as the National Research Foundation and the Department of Science and Technology (NRF-DST) innovation fellowship, NRF Research Excellence Award for Early Career/Emerging Researchers, AfricaNoFilter and Meta grant, UWC Research and Recognition Awards, L'Oreal-UNESCO for Women in Science, UWC Science Faculty Best Early Career Researcher and Excellent Lecturer, an AIMS-DAAD fellowship, Paul G.Allen Family Price, Golden Key International award, Google Women Techmakers, HLF-GSO, among others

K. Balamurugan is a highly regarded academic and researcher with over 29 years of expertise in Information Technology and Computer Science. Currently, he is an Associate Professor in the Department of Information Technology at K.S.R. College of Engineering (Autonomous) in Tiruchengode, Namakkal Dt, Tamil Nadu. He completed his B.E. in Electronics and Communication Engineering from Kumaraguru College of Technology in 1995, M.E. in Multimedia Technology from the College of Engineering, Guindy, Anna University, in 2003, and earned his Ph.D. in Information and Communication Engineering from Anna University in 2018.

Ganesh Kumar K working as a Professor in the department of Information Technology, Velalar College of Engineering and Technology, Thindal, Erode, Tamilnadu, India with 16 years of teaching experience. He has published 15 articles in various national and international level journals. He is an active review member in various reputed journal. He has guided more than 25 undergraduate and 15 post graduate level students projects.

S. Rajalakshmi working as a Professor in the Department of Artificial Intelligence and Data Science at Dr. N.G.P. Institute of Technology, Coimbatore, Tamilnadu, India with 16 years of Academic and 10 Years of Research experience. She has published 14 research articles SCI/Scopus and 23 papers in refereed Journals. Her main research areas are Data mining, Artificial Intelligence, Cloud Computing and Wireless Networks.

Mfundo Andrew Maneli is a Lecturer and Doctoral Researcher in the Department of Computer Science at the University of the Western Cape (UWC), South Africa. A pioneer in the South African technological landscape, he holds the distinction of being the first student to graduate from UWC with an MSc in Computer Science specializing in Augmented and Virtual Reality (AR/VR), a degree he earned Magna Cum Laude. His academic trajectory—moving from early challenges to global recognition—informs his dedication to student mentorship and the democratization of high-tech education in Africa. His research sits at the cutting-edge intersection of Machine Learning, Computer Vision, and Blockchain Technology. Mfundo's work is driven by the mission to develop low-cost, high-integrity technological solutions for emerging economies. Specifically, he explores the synergy between handheld LiDAR-enabled 3D reconstruction and decentralized frameworks. By integrating Blockchain into forensic and immersive workflows, he addresses critical issues of data integrity and immutability in digital evidence, ensuring that 3D-captured crime scenes are both accurate and tamper-proof. This multidisciplinary approach to public safety and digital forensics earned him a Best Paper nomination and Young Author Recognition at the 14th ITU-Kaleidoscope conference. In 2023, Mfundo was selected as one of the 200 most qualified young researchers globally to attend the 10th Heidelberg Laureate Forum in Germany, where he engaged with Abel, Fields, and Turing Award winners. A member of the Golden Key International Honour Society and a frequent reviewer for IEEE Access, he is currently conducting doctoral research on the fusion of deep learning and distributed ledgers to create secure, immersive computing environments. His work serves as a bridge between high-level algorithmic intelligence and the practical, secure deployment of these tools in low-resource settings.

Keerthana N V is an Assistant Professor with 8 Years of experience in teaching and 1-year experience in research (IUCAA LIGO Data Centre, Pune). Her area of interest is Network Security, Blockchain, and Machine Learning Algorithms. She is pursuing PhD at Anna University in Blockchain Security. She has work experience in high-performance computing (HTCondor) for the LIGO INDIA Project.

Kundesh Sharma is an Assistant Professor in the Department of Government and Public Administration at Lovely Professional University, Punjab, India. His research interests include public administration, digital governance, public policy, and the ethical implications of artificial intelligence in governance and policing. He teaches graduate and postgraduate courses and actively contributes to academic discussions on governance reforms, rights-based governance, and technology-driven public administration.

Muhammad Usman Tariq is a strategic higher education leader and scholar with more than 17 years of international experience across academia, research, and industry. He holds dual doctorates, a PhD in Artificial Intelligence and a Doctorate in Business Administration and has published extensively as the author of research articles, case studies, book chapters, and academic texts. His contributions also include several patents, reflecting his applied research in technology, business, and education. He is the Founder and CEO of TheCaseHQ.com, a global hub for professional certification programmes, narrative and video case studies, and digital learning innovation. In addition, he serves as President of the Gulf Higher Education Network (Gulf HE), an initiative dedicated to advancing academic practice, faculty development, and institutional collaboration across the region. He is a Principal Fellow of Advance HE (UK), Chartered Fellow of the CIPD (UK), Senior Fellow of SEDA (UK), and a Senior Member of IEEE, reflecting his standing as both an academic innovator and a global professional leader.

Petros Violakis is an Assistant Professor of Homeland Security at Rabdan Academy in UAE, partner of the Strategic Communication and News Media Laboratory of Piraeus University and partner of the Laboratory of Intelligence and Cyber-security of Piraeus University . He holds a PhD degree in Politics from Exeter University, an MA in International Relations from University of Indianapolis, an MBA (focus in Marketing) and a BSc in Computer Science from University of Hertfordshire. His latest research is being situated within Cyber Security Policy, Politics, Communication, Policy Making and European Studies. More specifically, he investigates the Europeanisation of EU Defence and Security Policy through different perspectives and contributing factors, such as: domestic politics, political economy, establishment of a new security identity and culture, research and development (R&D), globalization and other institutional influence (NATO). The result of this research is published (2018) as an academic book (monograph), entitled "Europeanisation and the Transformation of EU Security Policy: Post-Cold War Developments in the Common Security and Defence Policy" by Routledge. In his book, Violakis incorporates all of his past knowledge and acquired skills related to academic research, technology, innovation (R&D), marketing research, economics, social impact, international relations and politics.

Index

A

B

C

D

E

F

G

V

W

X

www.ingramcontent.com/pod-product-compliance
Lightning Source LLC
LaVergne TN
LVHW081540300926
849161LV00006B/1498